EDITED BY
HOLLY M. KARIBO
AND
GEORGE T. DÍAZ

Border Policing

A History of Enforcement and Evasion in North America

University of Texas Press

Austin

Requests for permission to reproduce material from this work should be
sent to:

> Permissions
> University of Texas Press
> P.O. Box 7819
> Austin, TX 78713-7819
> utpress.utexas.edu/rp-form

♾ The paper used in this book meets the minimum requirements of
ANSI/NISO Z39.48-1992 (R1997) (Permanence of Paper).

Library of Congress Cataloging-in-Publication Data

Names: Karibo, Holly M., editor. | Díaz, George T., editor.
Title: Border policing : a history of enforcement and evasion in
North America / [edited by] Holly M. Karibo, George T. Díaz.
Description: First. | Austin : University of Texas Press, 2020. |
Includes bibliographical references and index.
Identifiers: LCCN 2019024365 (print) | LCCN 2019024366 (ebook)
   ISBN 978-1-4773-2067-9 (cloth)
   ISBN 978-1-4773-2128-7 (pbk.)
   ISBN 978-1-4773-2068-6 (library ebook)
   ISBN 978-1-4773-2069-3 (non-library ebook)
Subjects: LCSH: Border patrols—North America—History. | Law
enforcement—Mexican-American Border Region—History. | Law
enforcement—Canadian-American Border Region—History. |
Borderlands—United States—History. | Immigration enforcement—
United States—History. | Smuggling—United States—History. |
Border security—United States—History.
Classification: LCC HV8138 .B585 2020 (print) | LCC HV8138 (ebook) |
DDC 363.28/5097—dc23
LC record available at https://lccn.loc.gov/2019024365
LC ebook record available at https://lccn.loc.gov/2019024366
doi:10.7560/320679

Contents

Abbreviations

ACLU	American Civil Liberties Union
CBP	Customs and Border Protection [United States]
CBSA	Canadian Border Services Agency
DIA	Department of Indian Affairs [Canada]
DPS	Department of Public Safety [Texas]
FBN	Federal Bureau of Narcotics [United States]
HIDTA	High Intensity Drug Trafficking Areas [program]
INS	Immigration and Naturalization Service [United States]
LRGV	lower Rio Grande Valley
NCACT	National Coalition Against Contraband Tobacco
NWMP	North-West Mounted Police [Canada]
OIA	Office of Indian Affairs [United States]
RCMP	Royal Canadian Mounted Police
SQ	Sûreté du Québec
USCCR	US Commission on Civil Rights

Foreword

ELAINE CAREY AND ANDRAE MARAK

In front of you is *Border Policing: A History of Enforcement and Evasion in North America*, a collection of cutting-edge scholarship edited by two incredibly talented borderlands scholars: Holly M. Karibo and George T. Díaz. The introduction, afterword, and chapters present a historical arc of increased state and nonstate capacities to police borders over two hundred years. The chapters consider the uniqueness of place, and few places are as unique or as important as borders. It is precisely along borders that leaders of nation-states advocate for sharply demarcated and solidified national cultures and legal regimes.

Borderlands, especially those of the modern United States — which imposed arbitrary borders through the lands of already existing peoples — are places of immense cultural and legal overlap. For this reason, it is important that the chapters in this volume adopt a transnational approach that moves beyond localized studies of police and policing to contemplate an array of agencies and agents who engage in customs, immigration, and drug interdiction across different borders, both land and water. In examining these areas, the contributors embrace intersectionality to consider people, the colonial state, Native sovereignty, and boundary creation and border enforcement. This volume ignites a series of questions for consideration about the roles of policing in North American borderlands that are changing immigration controls, trade wars, and the decades-long drug wars (which we would argue began more than a century ago). At the same time, there has been alternating hardening and softening of borders as more items and people cross, even as some categories of people and goods are increasingly prevented from passing through borders and forced to adopt more dangerous and expensive means of crossing.

As borderlands historians have demonstrated, there is quite a bit of continuity along national divides, and we have much to learn by studying them through a historical lens. Take the most recent pressing borderlands issues as an example. Changes in technology combined with the rise of the opioid epidemic in the United States and Canada (along with ongoing drug violence and growing levels of addiction in Mexico) have altered policing and the role of police. Not only have policing objectives and practices changed; community responses have changed as well. Canadian and US health agencies have sounded the alarm regarding opioid addiction and its social and economic costs for two decades.[1] Sheriffs and police departments in the Midwest have found that the opioid epidemic has changed their roles as jails expand to incarcerate people and to serve as early drug intervention centers. Further, first responders and police now administer naloxone, a medication that reverses an opioid overdose by blocking its effects. At the same time, police and sheriff's departments, both large and small, must purchase Narcan, the nasal spray of naloxone. With a two-dose kit costing between $130 and $140 dollars, the expense that police departments incur can be substantial.

As a sign of how the state security apparatus has extended beyond the borderlands to closer inspection internally, some police departments ask recipients of Narcan or naloxone after an overdose to sign a waiver allowing access to their cell phones. In turn, the police hand over the data to a technician to analyze social media and phone contacts. The analyst scrutinizes the social networks of the addict to uncover the supplier of the drugs. As a result, police departments have been able to create a vast database that captures local and transnational social networks of drug distribution. By understanding the hierarchy, distribution patterns, and overlapping networks, policing agents are able to place under surveillance those higher up in the network (and often across both jurisdictional and international borders). Where might the tracking of social networks eventually lead? How might suppliers respond to these new means of intervention? Would they become even flatter and less hierarchical, as drug organizations respond to interventions aimed at apprehending drug lords?[2]

This is only one example of the ways the security state has changed policing practices. We can imagine how the mapping of social networks could be used for both good (as a public health intervention) and ill (as an invasion of privacy that would sweep up innocent people in its web). Fittingly, in 2018, the United States Supreme Court ruled that police need a warrant to track a cell phone or other personal devices.[3] Still, we need to ask further questions. What does it mean to sign a waiver shortly after being treated with naloxone/Narcan for an opioid overdose? Conversely, what does it mean when police agents and police stations provide medical assistance and drug rehabilitation in areas that are starved for hospitals, rehab facilities, and early intervention? How, ultimately, have domestic policing practices become inherently transnational, reaching beyond local communities and often beyond jurisdictional bounds that traditionally limited policing activities?

As the scholars in this volume demonstrate, many of the origins of this increased state power can be found in the history of border policing. This volume and its rich new directions will inspire scholars and students about the future of border policing and its real impact on those who live in the borderlands and those who cross it. Moreover, this collection reminds us that how we treat these people defines who we are as nations.

Notes

1. Barry Meier, *Pain Killer: The Empire of Deceit and the Origin of America's Opioid Epidemic* (New York: Random House, 2018 [2003]); Beth Macy, *Dopesick: Dealers, Doctors, and the Drug Company That Addicted America* (New York: Little, Brown & Company, 2018).

2. Michael Kenney, *From Pablo to Osama: Trafficking and Terrorist Networks, Government Bureaucracies, and Competitive Adaptation* (University Park: Pennsylvania State University Press, 2007).

3. "In Major Privacy Win, the Supreme Court Rules Police Need a Warrant to Track Your Cellphone," *NPR's All Things Considered*, aired June 22, 2018, npr.org/2018/06/22/605007387/supreme-court-rules-police-need-warrant-to-get-location-information-from-cell-to; "In Ruling on Cellphone Location Data, Supreme Court Makes a Statement on Digital Privacy," *New York Times*, June 22, 2018, nytimes.com/2018/06/22/us/politics/supreme-court-warrants-cell-phone-privacy.html.

Introduction

HOLLY M. KARIBO AND GEORGE T. DÍAZ

On May 21, 2018, US Customs and Border Protection (CBP) arrested Cedella Roman, a nineteen-year-old foreign woman, for her unauthorized entry into the United States. Although arrests such as this occur every day, the story received national attention because the officers seized the woman not along the Rio Grande but in Washington State, along the US-Canada border. Having arrived from France to visit family in Canada, Roman decided to go for a jog and did not know she needed her passport to exercise. CBP arrested her for literally running across the border. Rather than accept the jogger's explanation, US authorities detained her for two weeks before allowing her to return to her family.[1] This story gained international attention, in part because it challenged the erroneous perception of the US-Canada divide as the "longest undefended border." As Roman experienced firsthand, the 49th parallel of the twenty-first century is in fact policed by an increasingly securitized border apparatus.

Two days after CBP detained the French runner, a US Border Patrol agent operating near Laredo, Texas, shot and killed Claudia Patricia Gómez González, a nineteen-year-old woman from Guatemala. The shooting, which occurred at approximately 12:30 P.M. on a sunny afternoon, drew the attention of a local woman, Marta V. Martinez, who recorded the aftermath of the killing on her cell phone. Contradicting the officer's account that the young woman's group attacked the agent, Martinez stated, "There was no weapon. They were hiding." Martinez added that she "didn't hear any yelling or 'stop' or 'don't run.'"[2] While news agencies covered the shooting, and local protests erupted, it quickly faded from the media spotlight.[3] Subsumed by reports that US president Donald Trump's "zero tolerance" immigration policy had led to the detention, caging, and separation of migrant children from their parents, coverage of Gómez González's death disappeared from the headlines. Justice for Gómez González's family remains uncertain.[4]

Roman's and Gómez González's cases serve as windows into the state of North American border policing in the twenty-first century. Although there are important differences between these two border crossings and the responses by policing agencies, they each demonstrate key developments that shape contemporary approaches to border enforcement. Indeed, nation-states in the twenty-first century police borders through increasingly militarized tactics.[5] Mandatory travel documents; technological innovations such as drones, night-vision goggles, surveillance, and satellite tracking; and the potential use of deadly force by armed policing agents have become current norms.[6] These developments are even more striking considering that nearly two-thirds of US residents live within the "100-mile border zone," an area where Fourth Amendment protections against unwarranted search and seizure can be suspended in the name of border enforcement.[7] These trends, most prominent on the Southwest border between the United States and Mexico, likewise have reshaped life for residents along the northern borderline with Canada. As the journalist Todd Miller documented, since the terrorist attacks on 9/11, policing in regions surrounding the greater US-Canada borderlands has increased. "If you arrive in Erie, Pennsylvania, on a Greyhound bus," Miller observes:

> Odds are you'll run into the Border Patrol authorities eyeing passengers getting off the bus. If you live in Southwest Detroit, the Mexican part of town, you'll probably see the cruising of green-striped vehicles every day. In the north, Border Patrol operations are conducted from Maine to the state of Washington, covering New England, the Rust Belt, and the Pacific Northwest in numbers that take many by surprise.[8]

In short, the expansive power of the security state extends far beyond national divides, potentially subjecting millions of people to the power of border-policing agents.

Since 2016, the Trump administration's immigration and border policing policies have added a new immediacy to these developments. Indeed, in the months that followed Roman's and Gómez González's encounters

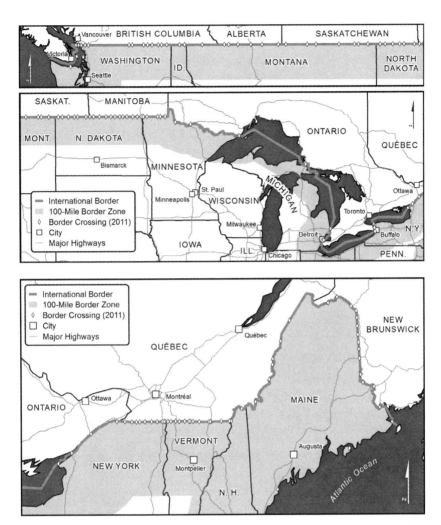

Figures 0.1 and 0.2. Maps of border crossings along the US-Canada border. Some border-crossing locations slightly adjusted for greater clarity. Courtesy of Houston Mount.

with the US policing apparatus, the militarization of the US border escalated further. In the fall of 2018, during the midterm election season, the Trump administration deployed thousands of troops to the Mexican border.[9] And in early 2019, the US president declared a "national emergency," arguing that unauthorized immigration and undocumented immigrants themselves posed a security "crisis."[10] While it may be tempting to see these immigration and policing moves as a radical departure from the past, we argue that doing so only reifies the historical amnesia that often animates public debates over immigration and border enforcement. *Border*

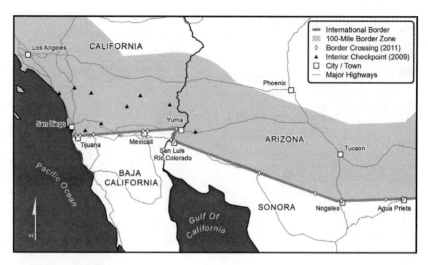

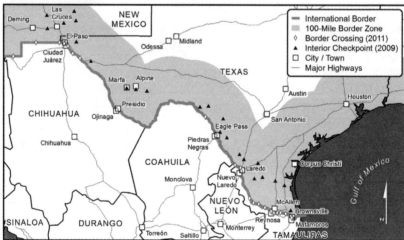

Figures 0.3 and 0.4. Maps of crossing points along the US-Mexico Border. Courtesy of Houston Mount. Data for US Border Crossings provided by United States Department of Transportation, Office of the Assistant Secretary for Research and Technology/Bureau of Transportation Statistics. Data for Interior Checkpoints (2009) provided by United States Government Accountability Office, Report to Congressional Requesters, "Border Patrol: Checkpoints Contribute to Border Patrol's Mission but More Consistent Data Collection and Performance Measurement Could Improve Effectiveness," GAO-09-824 (August 2009), gao.gov/new.items/d09824.pdf.

Policing argues that this move toward an intensified security apparatus has been long in the making, and the chapters that follow reveal how the language around notable "crises" and "invasions" reemerges in moments of political polarization. Tracing their longer histories can provide one important way to critically analyze the security state of the twenty-first century. This book asks and seeks to answer the question of how we got here.

Roman and Gómez González share two other commonalities: both entered the United States as foreign nationals and as women of color.[11] At a time when political leaders (particularly in the United States but also in many European nations) have portrayed the presence of immigrants as an infestation and have decried the supposed hordes of people pouring across the border, the cases of these two women highlight the role that racialization plays in contemporary border-policing practices.[12] For Gómez González, the heated anti-immigrant rhetoric espoused by political leaders turned deadly, and the lack of greater outcry over her death represents the further dehumanization of those who seek refuge in the United States. On the surface, the violence differential between these two cases — one woman was detained, whereas the other was killed — seems to reinforce the popular perception that the US-Canada border is friendlier and more peaceful than the US-Mexico border, but this misses the crucial point. Along both boundaries, these women encountered the expansive force of state border-policing power, and their statuses as national and racial others subjected them to varying degrees of state violence.

We began to compile this volume during a troubled period in North American border enforcement but also with an awareness that current practices are rooted in a much deeper history of state power. In fact, we argue, in order to fully interrogate the unique nature of today's border-policing apparatuses in North America, it is essential to consider how those developments evolved over the previous 200 years. What we experience today is in many ways unique to the historical moment, but it is also rooted in the larger projects of colonialism, nation-building, and securitization that intensified during the nineteenth and twentieth centuries. *Border Policing* explores the key trends and developments that transformed the US-Canada and US-Mexico borders from relatively fluid transnational regions into expansive militarized zones.

Although war and diplomacy established national lines on paper, policing made these boundaries into borders and — in some ways — barriers. *Border Policing* examines how state apparatuses create and regulate national borders and how this impacts communities that cross international divides. This volume is not designed as an all-encompassing analysis of how border policing has shifted over time; nor is it an institutional history of particular policing agencies. Instead, the authors in this volume provide case studies of key moments in North American border policing that shifted either public policy or the experiences of borderland residents in important ways. The following chapters address two key questions: How have states (at the federal, state, provincial, and local levels) attempted to regulate and police people and goods at their geographical and political borders? And how have local communities responded to, been shaped by, and at times undermined particular policing objectives and practices?

Border Policing addresses these questions by analyzing "policing" from multiple perspectives. The chapters explore the actual policies, laws, and procedures that have imbued state authorities with the power to patrol national boundaries. Contributors also trace the informal ways in which individuals have attempted to police, and at times subvert, boundaries of race, gender, and citizenship in the borderlands. While official state policies have played an important role in determining which people and goods could cross the US-Canada and US-Mexico borders, informal economic relationships, evasion of legal boundaries, violence, and vigilantism also played a crucial role in shaping life along North American borderlines. This volume traces both the formal and informal ways in which states have policed national borders and how individuals have contested, complied with, and evaded these policies.

We begin in the nineteenth century, with an examination of the policing of international waterways during the War of 1812. Each subsequent chapter traces how contested jurisdictions and competing interests shaped the practice of border policing into the first decades of the twenty-first century. The collection considers critical historical moments and developments, including the Porfiriato and the Mexican Revolution; the struggles over Indian sovereignty; the creation of immigration laws; Prohibition; the rise of transnational drug trafficking; and the perception of borders in popular culture. In doing so, we examine the powerful ways in which federal authorities impose various political agendas on borderlands and how border residents and regions interact with, and at times push back against, such agendas. By blending political, legal, economic, social, and cultural history, this volume provides new insight into the distinct realities that have shaped the borders dividing Canada, the United States, and Mexico.

Policing Boundaries in North American Historiography

Border Policing explores policing practices in multiple geographical regions in the US-Canada, US-Mexico, and Indigenous borderlands. We take an explicitly connective approach, examining how policing practices emerged in a wide range of transnational regions. In order to do so, this volume joins the small but growing community of scholarship that is working to bring the literature on the northern and southern borders into conversation.[13] Scholarship on the US-Canada and US-Mexico borders tends to reinforce the perception that the borders differ radically from each other. Studies of border policing provide an important opportunity to bring these conversations into direct dialogue. We push for a connective as well as a comparative approach to borderlands studies, demonstrating how state apparatuses in multiple geographic and political locations have attempted to enforce state agendas and how various regional reactions at times develop to undermine those objectives. What happens in one borderland often affects another; thus, bringing these conversations together helps us more fully grapple with the growing power of the state in the nineteenth and twentieth centuries.

If one considers states' creation and maintenance of borders as policing, then a great deal of borderlands history is necessarily the history of policing borders. This certainly predates the nineteenth century, with which this volume begins. The Spanish empire established presidios to police its North American borderlands.[14] These presidios, however, failed to prevent intrusion by rival empires or to police the movement of Indian peoples. When independent American states emerged, they created new apparatuses to wield force on their claims and enforce their sovereignty through policing. The historiography of policing the US-Mexico borderlands ranges from jingoistic hagiographies of Anglo lawmen making the frontier safe for white settlement to critical examinations of state power, its limits, and its impact on those policed.

That historiography began with an epic institutional history of a state police force. First published in 1935, Walter Prescott Webb's *The Texas Rangers: A Century of Frontier Defense* argued that the state police force arose out of a borderland wrought by racial conflict. Ignoring enslaved African Americans whom Anglos brought to Mexico, Webb described Texas in the 1830s as having a "three-cornered racial and cultural conflict" between Mexicans, Indians, and white immigrants from the United

States.[15] Conflict among the groups led each to find a champion, or "its representative fighting man," which for Anglos became embodied in the Texas Ranger.[16] Thus, Webb unabashedly celebrated the Texas Rangers as champions of white supremacy and agents of Indian and Mexican subjugation. Webb's position as a professor at the University of Texas and for a time as president of the American Historical Association cemented his influence on the historiography of border policing, inspiring numerous academic followers and an enduring, if largely erroneous, impression on historical memory and popular culture.[17]

Scholars of color, however, challenged Webb's narrative. Beginning in 1958 with the publication of *"With His Pistol in His Hand": A Border Ballad and Its Hero*, Chicano professor Américo Paredes reexamined the Texas Rangers from the perspective of the policed. Rather than protectors, for ethnic Mexicans of the borderlands, the Texas Rangers were *rinches*, "armed and mounted and looking for Mexicans to kill."[18] Considering Texas Rangers as just one weapon in the state's policing arsenal, ethnic Mexican victims applied the term *rinche* to violent state and state-aligned forces, from posses to the US Cavalry to the US Border Patrol.[19] Mexican American scholars emerging from the Chicano movement of the 1970s picked up Paredes's critique of racist law enforcement, so much so that by the 1980s books like *Gunpowder Justice: A Reassessment of the Texas Rangers* and historians including Arnoldo De León, David Montejano, and others succeeded in not only countering the racist ethnocentrism inherent in the Webb school of border policing but also recovering the voices of those silenced by state violence.[20]

Chicano scholars' success in reclaiming victims' voices prompted historians to reexamine border policing from overlooked perspectives. In 1999, Linda Gordon's *The Great Arizona Orphan Abduction* examined a vigilante mob's removal of lawfully adopted immigrant Irish orphans from their Mexican American parents in 1904.[21] In considering the motivations of the posse, Gordon examined racial construction as well as the role women played in prompting extralegal action. Gordon's book not only won numerous accolades, including the Bancroft Prize; her work in fact helped usher in a cadre of "new borderlands" historians. Calling for "transnational" examinations, new borderlands scholars' research in Mexican and US archives considered border policing binationally, thereby allowing them to shed new light on one-sided accounts.[22] Books like Ben Johnson's *Revolution in Texas*, Samuel Truett's *Fugitive Landscapes*, and Rachel St. John's *Line in the Sand* looked critically at US efforts at border policing while also considering how Mexican state forces at times cooperated in policing a shared border.[23]

Aside from studying how states enforced borderlines and sovereignty through policing, new borderlands historians contemplated the limits of state power. Despite state efforts to define borders and limit the free movement of goods and people across national lines, states discovered that exclusionary laws and trade restrictions did not prevent clandestine crossings. The immigration historians Erika Lee and Mae M. Ngai demonstrated how the Chinese Exclusion Act of 1882 outlawed but did not stop the entry of Chinese immigrants into the United States.[24] Building on Lee's and Ngai's successes, the new borderlands historians Patrick Ettinger, Elliott Young, Grace Peña Delgado, and others showed how Chinese turned away at coastal ports made their way to Canada or Mexico in an attempt to enter the United States overland "through the backdoor."[25] The US Customs Service—the only federal police force regulating the border in the nineteenth century—saw its mission expand from collecting tariffs to enforcing immigration laws across the length of the US-Canada and US-Mexico divides. It is not surprising that mounted inspectors proved inadequate for the task.[26]

As historians of immigration followed restricted immigrants' clandestine journeys across US borders, the fields of immigration history and borderlands history overlapped in considerations of border policing. Kelly Lytle Hernández's *Migra!* provided the first scholarly history of the US Border Patrol.[27] The Border Patrol was established to enforce nativist provisions inherent in the National Origins Act of 1924, and the first agents had little experience and looked to older police forces, in particular to the Texas Rangers, for examples of professional conduct. Although modeled in part on the Texas Rangers, the Border Patrol agents whom Lytle Hernández considered were far different from the men Walter Prescott Webb helped enshrine in lore. Indeed, as Lytle Hernández showed, many of the first Border Patrol agents were poor Anglos who had a personal stake in limiting labor competition. Historians like Kelly Lytle Hernández and Deborah Kang revealed border-policing agents as state resources with some discretionary power but also subject to agency priorities and pressure from growers dependent on the migrant labor that the Border Patrol and Immigration and Naturalization Service policed.[28]

Although new borderlands historians have made great strides in revealing the ways in which states police borders and in uncovering the ongoing porousness of borders despite state efforts, more questions remain.[29] In particular, what does border policing mean for those who are policed? State policing efforts—and their reliance on documents such as privateer licenses, customs reports, consular dispatches, and *matrículas*—make a history of border policing possible. They also, however, bias historians toward examining policing from the perspective of states.[30] The essays in this collection seek to balance this view by considering border policing from multiple perspectives. This includes the lived experiences of border peoples subjected to enforcement on a regular basis.[31] Moreover, gaps remain in the history of border-policing agencies. Excellent histories of the US Border Patrol, Immigration and Naturalization Service, and the Texas Rangers exist, but to date the US Customs Service—the oldest federal police force on the border—remains largely unexamined.[32] Mexican state efforts at border policing are almost absent from historical examination.[33] Historians are only now beginning to examine how states policed sexuality and gendered behavior at the border, opening pathways for further investigation.[34] Moreover, most historians end their examinations of border policing with Operation Wetback in 1954 and leave scholarship on the rest of the twentieth century up to political scientists, anthropologists, sociologists, ethnographers, and other social scientists.[35] We offer this collection as a way to begin to fill these gaps.[36]

In contrast to the expansive literature on policing practices along the US-Mexico border, the scholarship on the US-Canada border remains much sparser. Many of the histories of policing in Canada focus on internal policing policies and on particular agencies. Adopting a case study framework, scholars have focused on municipal or provincial police forces within a given geographical region (such as the West, North, Great Lakes, or Maritimes).[37] The move toward transnational history in the late twentieth century, which challenged histories written around neatly contained nation-states, began to reshape how historians approached studies of policing. The post-9/11 political environment likewise raised new questions about national sovereignty, security, and a longer history of enforcing national interests, bringing a new immediacy to this research. Scholars began to refocus their attention on the nature of national borders, the meaning of citizenship, and ways in which the Canadian and US governments had worked to enforce particular boundaries even before the increasingly militarized environment.[38] Yet, while studies exploring the policing of national boundaries seemed to be a new interest among scholars who study the northern region, historians had in fact been shedding light on various elements of the national policing apparatus for decades.

Three fields in particular laid the groundwork for our understanding of border policing along the 49th parallel: institutional history of policing agencies; northern borderlands studies; and immigration history.

Like Webb's focus on the Texas Rangers, the earliest histories of policing agencies in Canada were also largely institutional case studies of particular agencies. In the early to mid-twentieth century, historians focused their attention on the history of the North-West Mounted Police (NWMP). Formed in 1874, the constabulary agency maintained jurisdiction over unorganized western territories until 1920, when it expanded into a national police force, the Royal Canadian Mounted Police (RCMP). The first studies of the NWMP and RCMP read as celebratory narratives of classic law enforcement heroes and presented the perspectives of the law enforcement officers who worked for the agencies.[39] This work served to reinforce popular mythologies of the brave, noble Mountie who protected law-abiding citizens from dangerous outlaws and Natives on the wild frontier.[40]

By the mid-1970s, reflecting emerging trends within social history, historians challenged this dominant narrative. In 1979, the preeminent historian R. C. Macleod produced one of the most far-reaching and detailed accounts of the RCMP to date.[41] Chronicling the RCMP's transition from a frontier institution to a modern policing force during and after World War I, Macleod places its development in a broader political and social context. Far from writing a celebratory narrative of a "just" institution, Macleod demonstrates the complex colonial roots of the force. He further challenges the stereotypical view of the lawless US frontier and the peaceful Canadian frontier, demonstrating that in fact "there was a good deal of violence in the North-West Territories and equally obviously both police and public expected it to occur."[42]

Following Macleod's critical study, scholars began to draw on the analytic categories of race, ethnicity, gender, and colonialism to create more critical and nuanced evaluations of the agency.[43] Several scholars emphasized the relationship between colonial state power and Indigenous populations under pressure from white encroachment, raising important questions about the nature of the colonial state, Native sovereignty, and boundary creation.[44] This fit with growing attention in the 1980s and 1990s to notions of "state formation," exploring how police forces became important institutions through which liberal democratic states attempted to maintain their hegemony.[45] More recently, scholars such as Greg Kealey, Reginald Whitaker, and Andrew Parnaby have examined the political implications of the national police force, tracing how international developments (such as the Cold War) led to the expansion of the Canadian surveillance state.[46]

Despite attempts to broaden this institutional history, most scholars have examined the RCMP as a national policing body and have downplayed the agency's role in enforcing national borders. Andrew Graybill's *Policing the Great Plains* is one of the few explicitly comparative analyses that examines the RCMP in a transnational context. Graybill provides a connective analysis of the NWMP and the Texas Rangers during the late nineteenth century. Identifying what he terms the "transnational Great Plains frontier," Graybill uncovers the shared objectives and tactics between two parallel agencies.[47] Both used mounted constabularies and armed police forces organized in military-style units. Each was supposed to help control and incorporate a perceived hinterland. And although violence played a more prominent role among the Texas Rangers than in the NWMP, they both enacted forms of state violence in order to displace Indigenous peoples. Graybill's analysis took important steps in considering how emerging police forces in frontier regions—be they "north" or "south"—paved the way for "the development of modern, capitalist state entities."[48] It was, in short, a move away from region and nation and toward a connective and transnational approach.

While institutional histories focused on the development of particular agencies, by the late twentieth century borderlands scholars began to grapple with the many complex enforcement webs that emerged in regions bisected by national boundaries. Since the field of northern borderlands scholarship developed later, and on a smaller scale, than studies of the US Southwest and Mexican North, it remained heavily influenced by that literature. Scholars of the US-Canada border began asking similar questions about northern borderlands identities, the operation of state power, and the role of local actors in shaping what was, by the turn of the twentieth century, an increasingly regulated boundary line. Some scholars examined these issues through the lens of region and identity, asking whether local borderland residents had more in common culturally with their neighbors across the borderline than they did with their respective national cultures.[49] In their 2005 study *Permeable Border*, for example, the authors John Bukowczyk, Nora Faires, David Smith, and Randy Widdis trace how economic integration, cultural ties, and migration helped turn the Great Lakes into a transnational region that connects residents across the national divide.[50] Other scholars, such as Marian Smith, took a policy-oriented approach, examining how the US federal government enacted specific legal policies meant to enforce the national line.[51] Still yet, scholars have explored how Indigenous communities navigated and resisted the increasingly bureaucratized national border as it emerged in the nineteenth and twentieth centuries.[52] Scholars like Gillian Roberts and Dominique Brégent-Heald approached border policing from a pop culture perspective, analyzing how the representation of policing practices in film and literature helped shape national culture in Canada and the United States.[53] When taken together, these conversations helped inform some of the central questions addressed in this volume. How, we ask, did border people react to state attempts to impose national policy throughout their communities? State power may have shaped borders, but to what degree did policies and practices fall short of their actual objectives?

Within borderlands studies, two subfields have been particularly fruitful in thinking through these questions. First, histories of smuggling and cross-border illegal economies provide opportunities to examine how state agencies attempt to control and eliminate particular products, goods, or people from crossing boundaries.[54] They also demonstrate when those projects fail miserably. Studies on Prohibition in the northern borderlands, for example, demonstrate the unintended consequences of federal policies and how attempts at controlling liquor also created much larger—and much more violent—criminal networks that were able to evade state authorities.[55] Second, recent scholarship traces the history of transnational legal regimes, exploring how national policing powers extended beyond the borderline. The work of Katherine Unterman, Ethan Nadelmann, and Brad Miller highlights the extent to which policing agencies became important tools of extending state power into other (supposedly) sovereign nation-states. Through interdiction, extradition, and other legal tools, US agencies such as the State Department, the Federal Bureau of Investigation, US consulates, and customs and immigration enforcement attempted to influence their neighbors and assert a US legal regime whose status, they hoped, would reign supreme.[56]

Finally, the field of immigration studies has played a prominent role in uncovering how the United States and Canada attempted to police national boundaries in the nineteenth and twentieth centuries. Much like the United States, Canada has long cultivated an image as a "nation of immigrants." Indeed, the idea of Canada as a mosaic peopled by "succeeding waves of newcomers" expanded after the 1970s, as multiculturalism became a more widely invoked concept.[57] Critical studies of immigration policy, though, have demonstrated the contours and limits of that mosaic.

In particular, in emphasizing Canada's status as a white-settler society, historians have uncovered the ways in which the process of enacting and enforcing immigration policy played a direct role in shaping the racialized limits of citizenship. While the issues of racial difference and inequality on the US-Mexico border were often taken as accepted realities among borderlands historians, scholars working on the US-Canada border had to uncover just how pervasive racialized perceptions and policies were there. This reflected a broader push among Canadian scholars to grapple with a perceived notion that Canadian history was somehow more color-blind and free of racial strife than that of its American neighbors to the south.[58] Some of the earliest attempts at uncovering racial issues along the northern borderline focused on anti-Asian sentiments in the West and the expansion of exclusionary policies at the turn of the twentieth century.[59] By 2008, Barrington Walker's expansive edited volume, *The History of Immigration and Racism in Canada*, demonstrated the growth in the field of critical race studies and immigration in the Canadian context.

Moving beyond public policy, scholars such as Franca Iacovetta argued that the policing of immigrants both at the border and beyond was performed not solely by immigrant inspectors, customs agents, and enforcement officers but also by a wide range of "gatekeepers." These included middle-class professionals, such as social workers, welfare administrators, mental health experts, dietitians, reporters, and columnists, who worked to integrate immigrants and shape them into proper Canadian citizens.[60] Dovetailing with emerging scholarship on the US-Mexico border, these studies demonstrate how state objectives are often achieved through unofficial channels, which can in themselves become powerful ways of enforcing broader power structures.[61] In all, by studying immigration policies, migration patterns, and enforcement tactics, immigration histories remind us that policing national boundaries in North America has been an inherently racialized project, one that relies on a complex web of enforcement tactics, both formal and informal.

Toward a Connective Approach to Border Policing

The authors in this volume work to place the increasingly parallel literature on border policing in North America into direct conversation. They each highlight the extent to which border policing simultaneously encompasses both broad transnational efforts at nation-building and localized forms of community regulation. While much of the borderlands literature begins in the late nineteenth and early twentieth centuries, this volume traces these developments back to the early nineteenth century. Toward this end, Part I ("Emerging Borders") explores the policing of national and social boundaries at a time when the legal boundary lines of the US, Canadian, and Mexican states were in fluctuation. War and military conflicts in particular played a key role in shaping nineteenth-century policing practices. In chapter 1, "Defining the Acceptable Bounds of Deception," Edward J. Martin examines the use of prize courts during the War of 1812, exploring how local economic interests and cross-border ties in the northeastern borderlands undermined larger state conflicts between the United States and Great Britain. In chapter 2, "Dominance in an Imagined Border," Luis Alberto García likewise explores how war and conflict—in this case, the US Civil War—impacted localized border-policing practices. In particular, García traces the ways in which informal arrangements among regional community leaders determined border policing in South Texas and northeastern Mexico in the middle of the nineteenth century. The final chapter in Part I, Benjamin Hoy's "A Border without Guards," examines the extent to which both the United States and Canada employed indirect border control strategies in order to challenge Indigenous sovereignty and freedom of movement. Rations, annuities, extralegal evictions, and reserve land became important tools both states used to impose national boundaries on Native communities in the prairies and on the West Coast.

Part II ("Solidifying States, Testing Boundaries") examines the shifts that took place in border policing as North American nation-states began to solidify their legal power and jurisdiction over borderlands. The period between the 1880s and the 1920s saw the expansion of a wide range of agencies attempting to police national boundaries, and rising rates of immigration to and across the continent shifted North Americans' attention toward their borders. In chapter 4, "To Protect and Police," María de Jesús Duarte documents the ways in which the Mexican consular network in the United States policed the concepts of belonging to and exclusion from the Mexican nation in the American borderlands before the Mexican Revolution of 1910. By issuing *matrículas* (legal identity documents) and providing legal support and services to Mexican nationals living in the United States, the Mexican state sought to draw thousands of Mexican citizens closer to their home government and away from the US body politic. Thomas A. Klug explores the important shifts in US immigration and cross-border mobility that began at the turn of the twentieth century.

In chapter 5, "Enforcing US Immigration Laws at the US-Canada Border," Klug examines the complexities of enforcing new immigration and customs laws in transnational economic centers. Focusing on the Detroit-Windsor region, the chapter demonstrates that economic and business interests helped determine who was allowed to cross national boundaries and who could benefit from those relationships. Like Klug, James Dupree, in chapter 6, "The Roots of the Border Patrol," explores the relationships between immigration policies, labor laws, and individual enforcement officers tasked with implementing new federal policies. Focusing on the "line riders" that policed the US-Mexico border, Dupree uncovers a complex bureaucratic web that often fell far short of its enforcement goals. Chapter 7 shifts our attention toward vigilantism and informal forms of policing communities in the US-Mexico borderlands during its bloodiest decade. In his contribution, "Home Guard," Miguel A. Levario examines the role that the state played in organizing white civilians as armed protectors of Anglo life and property during the Mexican Revolution of 1910. The chapter demonstrates that vigilantes supported by the state antagonized race relations and embraced a culture of violence that redefined the social and political structure throughout the state of Texas.

The regulation of drugs and alcohol has played a key role in shaping policing practices, border policies, and local economies in the North American borderlands. Part III ("Building and Resisting a Prohibition Apparatus") thus focuses on efforts to build prohibitionist apparatuses in the twentieth century. In chapter 8, "Policing Peyote Country in the Early Twentieth Century," Lisa D. Barnett examines efforts by individuals working for the US Office of Indian Affairs to police peyote commerce through extralegal means in the Indian country of the southern and northern plains. Barnett also demonstrates that both non-Indian borderlands people involved in the peyote industry and Native American consumers resisted federal efforts and found ways to continue the peyote trade. In chapter 9, "Skirting the Law," Carolina Monsiváis examines how the Eighteenth Amendment to the US Constitution allowed for the extension of police powers over women. In South Texas, ethnic Mexican women bore the brunt of this increased scrutiny. While efforts at policing Prohibition reinforced gendered expectations among enforcement officers, they also increased economic opportunities for women who sold and smuggled alcohol. The chapter thus explores how the policing of women and their behavior reshaped both the trajectory of illicit trade on the border and law enforcement tactics. In chapter 10, "Building a Villain/Hero Binary," Holly M. Karibo traces the ways in which Cold War moral politics reshaped approaches to drug smuggling along the US-Canada and US-Mexico borders during the 1940s and 1950s. While state officials attempted to present a unified front against drug traffickers, Communists, and other dangerous individuals supposedly crossing the porous national boundaries, the rhetoric that enforcement officers adopted often undermined states' abilities to build cross-border enforcement collaborations. It turns out that blaming your neighbor for your drug problem was not a particularly effective tool for building international cooperation between policing agencies.

Finally, Part IV ("Expanding State Authority and Its Challenges") examines the contemporary period. It furthermore serves as a bridge between historical considerations of border policing and interdisciplinary examinations of deep-rooted ongoing issues. Adopting multiple methodological approaches—including those utilized within anthropology, Indigenous studies, and media studies—the authors in this part help us better understand how the deep histories of border policing reverberate today. In chapter 11, "Diversity and the Border Patrol," Jensen Branscombe examines the most iconic border police force—the US Border Patrol—directly. In particular, Branscombe uncovers the broad context of dysfunction in the Border Patrol of the 1970s and how corruption and violence in the agency contributed to ineffective and discriminatory policing practices in the US-Mexico borderlands. The chapter focuses specifically on how a lack of diversity in the force influenced the ways immigrants, especially women, experienced life in the borderlands during the period in which the federal government transformed the Border Patrol from a skeletal, unprofessional outfit to a large paramilitary force.

The terrorist attacks of September 11, 2001, led to a consolidation of the US federal police forces examined in this volume as they became part of the newly created Department of Homeland Security in 2003. Though all of the terrorists who participated in the attacks entered the United States lawfully, the strikes exacerbated long-standing US anxieties over the porousness of the country's borders. Moreover, these heightened concerns challenged long-standing practices of transnational border communities. In chapter 12, "Refusing Borders," Devin Clancy and Tyler Chartrand detail struggles between Native communities and settler police forces along the present-day borders of Canada and the United States, while also placing modern developments in their historical context. They argue that the production and policing of borders in North America are contested and resisted by Indigenous concepts of space, which in turn shape the contours of those borderlands. In chapter 13, "Border Surge," Santiago Ivan Guerra examines the impact of national border security concerns on state and local policing practices. In 2015, the state of Texas allocated $800 million for border-security initiatives. The funds allowed for an influx of more than 200 state troopers to the border to aid local and federal forces in policing illicit border activities. In particular, Guerra describes how anxieties about illicit activities, specifically drug trafficking and human smuggling, drove the justification for this surge in policing practices. In chapter 14, "Bordering Reality," Anita Huizar-Hernández considers the content and consequences of media representations of North American border policing by comparing two different reality television franchises: *Border Security*, which depicts the US-Canada border, and *Border Wars*, which depicts the US-Mexico border. Huizar-Hernández contends that these television shows demonstrate the broad power of popular media to not only shape public perception of border realities but also influence public opinion about the kinds of policing practices these border realities necessitate.

We began this book with the stories of two women who encountered police forces in two different North American borderlands. Although these women's border-crossing experiences met very different ends, we hope our book prompts readers to consider the ways border policing along the US-Canada and US-Mexico divides is not only distinct but also related to policies and practices formed over a 200-year history. Indeed, given the expansive growth of the security state, the methods states use to police their borders offer a glimpse of what, if left unchecked, could mark policing practices in communities across the interior of North America.

Notes

1. "Jogger Says US Detained Her after Accidental Border Crossing," *New York Times*, June 23, 2018, nytimes.com/aponline/2018/06/23/us/ap-us-accidental-border-crossing.html.

2. Cristina Caron, "'Don't Treat Us Like Animals': Family of Woman Shot by Border Patrol Denounces U.S.," *New York Times*, May 26, 2018, nytimes.com/2018/05/26/us/border-patrol-shooting-woman.html.

3. Caron, "'Don't Treat Us Like Animals.'"

4. Miriam Jordan and Ron Nixon, "Trump Administration Threatens Jail and Separating Children from Parents for Those Who Illegally Cross Southwest Border," *New York Times*, May 7, 2018, nytimes.com/2018/05/07/us/politics/homeland-security-prosecute-undocumented-immigrants.html; Jeffery C. Mays and Matt Stevens, "Honduran Man Kills Himself after Being Separated from Family at U.S. Bor-

der, Reports Say," *New York Times*, June 10, 2018, nytimes.com/2018/06/10/us/border
-patrol-texas-family-separated-suicide.html.

5. We define "militarization" as state use of military equipment, personnel, tactics, and the rhetoric of war in regard to policing. Although Western historians, most notably Robert Utley, examined the US Army's operations in the borderlands during the nineteenth century, scholarship that considered the border as a militarized zone begins in 1996 with Timothy Dunn's *The Militarization of the U.S.-Mexico Border, 1978– 1992: Low-Intensity Conflict Doctrine Comes Home* (Austin: CMAS Books, 1996). Dunn's examination of how the US military supported the Immigration and Naturalization Service and the US Border Patrol's actions highlighted the ways that law enforcement and national policy agencies utilized military equipment, training, and labor to support or militarize their policing efforts. On militarization and the US-Mexico border, see Dunn, *Militarization of the U.S.-Mexico Border*; and Miguel Antonio Levario, *Militarizing the Border: When Mexicans Became the Enemy* (College Station: Texas A&M University Press, 2012).

6. Scholars of the US-Canada border tend to portray the post-9/11 environment as the crucial turning point on the militarization of the northern border, a phenomenon Peter Andreas terms "the Mexicanization of the Canadian border." As he notes, in the wake of the terrorist attacks, the US Congress tripled the number of Border Patrol agents on the northern border, instructed the Coast Guard to stop all boats crossing the Great Lakes, employed satellite tracking to stop unauthorized entry, and established five US air and Marine bases along the border. On the rise of security apparatuses on the US-Canada border, see Peter Andreas, "The Mexicanization of the US-Canada Border: Asymmetric Interdependence in a Changing Security Context," *International Journal* (Spring 2005): 455; Victor A. Konrad and Heather Nora Nicol, *Beyond Walls: Re-inventing the Canada-United States Borderlands* (London: Routledge, 2008).

7. This includes major ports of entries as well as land borders. ACLU, "The Constitution in the 100-Mile Border Zone," aclu.org/other/constitution-100-mile-border -zone; Margaret E. Dorsey and Miguel Díaz-Barriga, "The Constitution Free Zone in the United States: Law and Life in the State of Carcelment," *Political and Legal Anthropology Review* 38, no. 2 (2015): 204–225.

8. Todd Miller, *Border Patrol Nation: Dispatches from the Front Lines of Homeland Security* (San Francisco: City Light Books, 2014), 22.

9. "Trump Sending 5,200 Troops to the Border in an Election Season," *New York Times*, October 20, 2018, nytimes.com/2018/10/29/us/politics/border-security-troops -trump.html.

10. Rebecca Shabad, Alex Moe, Frank Thorp V, and Kristen Welker, "Trump to Declare National Emergency, Announce $8 Billion for Border Wall," *NBC News*, February 14, 2019, nbcnews.com/politics/congress/government-shutdown-vote-border-bill -trump-n971576.

11. Mattha Busby, "Jogger Crosses US-Canada Border by Mistake," *Independent*, June 24, 2018, independent.co.uk/news/world/americas/french-jogger-crosses-us -canada-border-detained-two-weeks-a8413141.html.

12. Catherine Rampell, "The Real Hoax about the Border Crisis," *Washington Post*,

June 21, 2018, washingtonpost.com/opinions/the-real-hoax-about-the-border-crisis/2018/06/21/5999c96e-7589-11e8-805c-4b67019fcfe4_story.html?utm_term=.f26b426bc4a2.

13. On comparative approaches to the US-Canada and US-Mexico borders, see Benjamin Johnson and Andrew R. Graybill, eds., *Bridging National Borders in North America: Transnational and Comparative Histories* (Durham, NC: Duke University Press, 2010); Elaine Carey and Andrae Marak, eds., *Smugglers, Brothels, and Twine: Historical Perspectives on Contraband and Vice in the North American Borderlands* (Tucson: University of Arizona Press, 2011); Matt Garcia, E. Melanie DuPuis, and Don Mitchell, eds., *Food across Borders* (New Brunswick, NJ: Rutgers University Press, 2017); Sterling Evans, ed., *Farming across Borders: A Transnational History of the North American West* (College Station: Texas A&M University Press, 2017); Laurence Armand French and Magdaleno Manzanarez, *North American Border Conflicts: Race, Politics, and Ethics* (Boca Raton, FL: Taylor and Francis Group, 2017); Brenden W. Rensink, *Native but Foreign: Indigenous Immigrants and Refugees in the North American Borderlands* (College Station: Texas A&M University Press, 2018); and Katrina Jagodinsky and Pablo Mitchell, eds., *Beyond the Borders of the Law: Critical Legal Histories of the North American West* (Lawrence: University Press of Kansas, 2019).

14. David J. Weber, *The Spanish Frontier in North America* (New Haven, CT: Yale University Press, 1992).

15. Webb's book was originally published by Houghton Mifflin in 1935. The University of Texas Press republished the book in 1965 with a preface by President Lyndon Johnson. Walter Prescott Webb, *The Texas Rangers: A Century of Frontier Defense*, 2nd ed. (Austin: University of Texas Press, 1965), 3.

16. Webb, 11.

17. The Texas Rangers continue to be the source of scholarly examination. For a few examples, consider Robert M. Utley's two-volume history *Lone Star Justice: The First Century of the Texas Rangers* (New York: Berkley Books, 2002) and *Lone Star Lawmen: The Second Century of the Texas Rangers* (New York: Berkley Books, 2007); and Charles H. Harris III and Louis R. Sadler, *The Texas Rangers and the Mexican Revolution: The Bloodiest Decade, 1910–1920* (Albuquerque: University of New Mexico Press, 2004).

18. Américo Paredes, *"With His Pistol in His Hand": A Border Ballad and Its Hero* (Austin: University of Texas Press, 1958), 24.

19. Paredes, 24.

20. Julian Samora, Joe Bernal, and Albert Peña, *Gunpowder Justice: A Reassessment of the Texas Rangers* (South Bend, IN: University of Notre Dame Press, 1979); Arnoldo De León, *They Called Them Greasers: Anglo Attitudes toward Mexicans in Texas, 1821–1900* (Austin: University of Texas Press, 1983); David Montejano, *Anglos and Mexicans in the Making of Texas, 1836–1986* (Austin: University of Texas Press, 1987).

21. Linda Gordon, *The Great Arizona Orphan Abduction* (Cambridge, MA: Harvard University Press, 1999).

22. Benjamin Heber Johnson, *Revolution in Texas: How a Forgotten Rebellion and Its Bloody Suppression Turned Mexicans into Americans* (New Haven, CT: Yale University Press, 2003), 4.

23. Samuel Truett, *Fugitive Landscapes: The Forgotten History of the U.S.-Mexico*

Borderlands (New Haven, CT: Yale University Press, 2006); Rachel St. John, *Line in the Sand: A History of the Western U.S.-Mexico Border* (Princeton, NJ: Princeton University Press, 2011); and Katherine Benton-Cohen, *Borderline Americans: Racial Division and Labor War in the Arizona Borderlands* (Cambridge, MA: Harvard University Press, 2009).

24. Erika Lee, *At America's Gates: Chinese Immigration during the Exclusion Era, 1882–1943* (Chapel Hill: University of North Carolina Press, 2003); Mae M. Ngai, *Impossible Subjects: Illegal Aliens and the Making of Modern America* (Princeton, NJ: Princeton University Press, 2004).

25. Patrick Ettinger, *Imaginary Lines: Border Enforcement and the Origins of Undocumented Immigration, 1882–1930* (Austin: University of Texas Press, 2009).

26. Grace Peña Delgado, *Making the Chinese Mexican: Global Migration, Localism, and Exclusion in the US-Mexico Borderlands* (Stanford, CA: Stanford University Press, 2013); Elliott Young, *Alien Nation: Chinese Migration in the Americas from the Coolie Era through World War II* (Chapel Hill: University of North Carolina Press, 2014).

27. Kelly Lytle Hernández, *Migra! A History of the U.S. Border Patrol* (Berkeley: University of California Press, 2010).

28. S. Deborah Kang, *The INS on the Line: Making Immigration Law on the US-Mexico Border, 1917–1954* (New York: Oxford University Press, 2017).

29. Julian Lim, *Porous Borders: Multiracial Migrations and the Law in the U.S.-Mexico Borderlands* (Chapel Hill: University of North Carolina Press, 2017).

30. Scholars have increasingly turned to the history of documentation for insight into state regulation. See, for example, Anna Pegler-Gordon, *In Sight of America: Photography and the Development of U.S. Immigration Policy* (Berkeley: University of California Press, 2009); John Torpey, *The Invention of the Passport: Surveillance, Citizenship and the State* (Cambridge, UK: Cambridge University Press, 1999); and Craig Robertson, *The Passport in America: The History of a Document* (Oxford, UK: Oxford University Press, 2010).

31. Hasina Diner et al., "A Shadow on the Past: Teaching and Studying Migration and Borders in the Age of Trump," *Journal of the Gilded Age and Progressive Era* 17, no. 1 (2018): 41.

32. Carl E. Prince and Mollie Keller, *The U.S. Customs Service: A Bicentennial History* (Washington, DC: Department of the Treasury, 1989).

33. Díaz, *Border Contraband*; Lim, *Porous Borders*; Lytle Hernández, *Migra!*; Carlos J. Sierra and Rogelio Martínez Vera, *El resguardo aduanal y la gendarmería fiscal, 1850–1925* (Mexico City: Secretaría de Hacienda y Crédito Público, 1971); and Paul J. Vanderwood, *Disorder and Progress: Bandits, Police, and Mexican Development*, rev. ed. (Wilmington, DE: SR Books, 1992).

34. Grace Peña Delgado, "Border Control and Sexual Policing: White Slavery and Prostitution along the U.S.-Mexico Borderlands, 1903–1910," *Western Historical Quarterly* 43, no. 2 (Summer 2012): 157–178; and Holly M. Karibo, *Sin City North: Sex, Drugs, and Citizenship in the Detroit-Windsor Borderland* (Chapel Hill: University of North Carolina Press, 2015).

35. Peter Andreas, *Border Games: Policing the U.S.-Mexico Divide*, 2nd ed. (Ithaca, NY: Cornell University Press, 2009); Howard Campbell, *Drug War Zone: Frontline Dispatches*

from the Streets of El Paso and Juárez (Austin: University of Texas Press, 2009); Dunn, *Militarization of the U.S.-Mexico Border*; Tony Payan, *The Three U.S.-Mexico Border Wars: Drugs, Immigration, and Homeland Security*, 2nd ed. (Santa Barbara, CA: Praeger Security International, 2016); David Spener, *Clandestine Crossings: Migrants and Coyotes on the Texas-Mexico Border* (Ithaca, NY: Cornell University Press, 2009); and Chad J. Alvarez, "The Shape of the Border: Policing the U.S.-Mexico Divide, 1848–2010" (PhD diss., University of Chicago, 2014).

36. Recently scholars have examined state use of civilian forces for extralegal border policing and "lynching." For more on lynching, see William D. Carrigan and Clive Webb, *Forgotten Dead: Mob Violence against Mexicans in the United States, 1848–1928* (Oxford, UK: Oxford University Press, 2013); Nicholas Villanueva Jr., *The Lynching of Mexicans in the Texas Borderlands* (Albuquerque: University of New Mexico Press, 2017); and Monica Muñoz Martinez, *The Injustice Never Leaves You* (Cambridge, MA: Harvard University Press, 2018).

37. For regional and municipal policing studies, see Robert Hutchinson, *A Century of Service: A History of the Winnipeg Police Department* (Winnipeg, MB: Winnipeg Police Department, 1974); C. K. Talbot et al., *The Thin Blue Line: An Historical Perspective of Policing in Canada* (Ottawa, ON: Crimecare, 1983); Dahn D. Higley, OPP: *The History of the Ontario Provincial Police Force* (Toronto: Queen's Printer, 1984); Peter McGahan, *Crime and Policing in Maritime Canada: Chapters from the Urban Records* (Fredericton, NB: Goose Land Editions, 1988); Keith Hart, "An Annotated Bibliography of Canadian Police History, 1654–1894" (master's thesis, University of Alberta, 1985); and Michael Boudreau, *City of Order: Crime and Society in Halifax, 1918–35* (Vancouver: University of British Columbia Press, 2012). Greg Marquis provides an important exception to the regional focus in *Policing Canada's Century: A History of the Canadian Association of Chiefs of Police* (Toronto: University of Toronto Press, 1993), and *The Vigilant Eye: Policing Canada from 1867 to 9/11* (Winnipeg, MB: Fernwood, 2016).

38. Peter Andreas, "The Mexicanization of the US-Canada Border: Asymmetric Interdependence in a Changing Security Context," *International Journal* 60, no. 2 (2005): 449–462.

39. A. L. Haydon, *The Riders of the Plains* (Toronto: The Copp Clark Co., Limited, 1910); Cecil Edward Denny, *The Law Marches West* (Toronto: 1939); Ronald Atkin, *Maintain the Right: The Early History of the North-West Mounted Police* (London: John Day Co., 1973); R. C. Fetherstonhaugh, *The Royal Canadian Mounted Police* (New York: Carrick & Evans, 1938); John Peter Turner, *The North-West Mounted Police, 1873–1893* (Ottawa, ON: Edmond Cloutier, King's Printer, 1950).

40. Keith Walden, *Visions of Order: The Canadian Mountie in Symbol and Myth* (Toronto: Butterworth-Heinemann, 1982).

41. R. C. Macleod, *The North West Mounted Police and Law Enforcement, 1873–1905* (Toronto: University of Toronto Press, 1979).

42. Fadi Saleem Ennab, "Rupturing the Myth of the Peaceful Western Canadian Frontier: A Socio-Historical Study of Colonization, Violence, and the North West Mounted Police, 1873–1905" (master's thesis, University of Manitoba, 2010), 16.

43. Robert Thacker, "Canada's Mounted: The Evolution of a Legend," *Journal of Popular Culture* 14 (1980): 298–312; Walden, *Visions of Order*; William M. Baker, ed.,

The Mounted Police and Prairie Society, 1873–1919 (Regina, SK: University of Regina, Canadian Plains Research Center, 1998); Steve Hewitt, *Riding to the Rescue: The Transformation of the RCMP in Alberta and Saskatchewan, 1914–1939* (Toronto: University of Toronto Press, 2006); and Lynda Mannik, *Canadian Indian Cowboys in Australia: Representation, Rodeo, and the RCMP at the Royal Easter Show, 1939* (Calgary, AB: University of Calgary Press, 2006).

44. Elizabeth Furniss, *The Burden of History: Colonialism and the Frontier Myth in a Rural Canadian Community* (Vancouver: University of British Columbia Press, 1999); and Amanda Nettelbeck et al., *Fragile Settlements: Aboriginal Peoples, Law, and Resistance in South-West Australia and Prairie Canada* (Vancouver: University of British Columbia Press, 2016).

45. Hewitt, *Riding to the Rescue*, 7.

46. Reginald Whitaker, Gregory S. Kealey, and Andrew Parnaby, *Secret Service: Political Policing in Canada from the Fenians to Fortress America* (Toronto: University of Toronto Press, 2012); and Gregory S. Kealey, *Spying on Canadians: The Royal Canadian Mounted Police Security Service and the Origins of the Long Cold War* (Toronto: University of Toronto Press, 2017).

47. Andrew Graybill, *Policing the Great Plains: Rangers, Mounties, and the North American Frontier, 1875–1910* (Lincoln: University of Nebraska Press, 2007), 6.

48. Graybill, 203.

49. James Laxer, *The Border: Canada, the US, and Dispatches from the 49th Parallel* (New York: Random House, 2003); Sheila McManus, *The Line Which Separates: Race, Gender, and the Making of the Alberta-Montana Borderlands* (Lincoln: University of Nebraska Press, 2005); and Sterling Evans, ed., *The Borderlands of the American and Canadian Wests: Essays on Regional History of the Forty-Ninth Parallel* (Lincoln: University of Nebraska Press, 2006).

50. John Bukowczyk et al., *Permeable Border: The Great Lakes Basin as Transnational Region, 1650–1990* (Pittsburgh, PA: University of Pittsburgh Press, 2005).

51. Marian Smith, "The Immigration and Naturalization Service (INS) at the US-Canadian Border, 1893–1993: An Overview of Issues and Topics," *Michigan Historical Review* 26, no. 2 (2000): 127–147.

52. Paige Raibmon, *Authentic Indians: Episodes of Encounter from the Late-Nineteenth-Century Northwest Coast* (Durham, NC: Duke University Press, 2005); Lissa K. Wadewitz, *The Nature of Borders: Salmon, Boundaries, and Bandits on the Salish Sea* (Seattle: University of Washington Press, 2012); and Michel Hogue, *Metis and the Medicine Line: Creating a Border and Dividing a People* (Chapel Hill: University of North Carolina Press, 2015).

53. Gillian Roberts, *Discrepant Parallels: Cultural Implications of the Canada-US Border* (Montreal: McGill-Queen's University Press, 2015); Dominique Brégent-Heald, *Borderland Films: American Cinema, Mexico, and Canada during the Progressive Era* (Lincoln: University of Nebraska Press, 2015).

54. For a more general analysis of smuggling in US history, including across land borders, see Peter Andreas, *Smuggler Nation: How Illicit Trade Made America* (Oxford, UK: University of Oxford Press, 2013).

55. Greg Marquis, "'Brewers' and Distillers' Paradise': American Views of Canadian

Alcohol Policies, 1919–1935," *Canadian Review of American Studies* 34, no. 2 (2004): 135–166; Stephen T. Moore, *Bootleggers and Borders: The Paradox of Prohibition on a Canada-U.S. Borderland* (Lincoln: University of Nebraska Press, 2014); and Karibo, *Sin City North*.

56. Ethan Nadelmann, *Cops across Borders: The Internationalization of U.S. Criminal Law Enforcement* (University Park: Pennsylvania State University Press, 2006); Katherine Unterman, *Uncle Sam's Policemen: The Pursuit of Fugitives across Borders* (Cambridge, MA: Harvard University Press, 2015); and Bradley Miller, *Borderline Crime: Fugitive Criminals and the Challenge of the Border, 1819–1914* (Toronto: University of Toronto Press, 2016).

57. Franca Iacovetta, Paula Draper, Robert Ventresca, eds., preface to *A Nation of Immigrants: Women, Workers, and Communities in Canadian History, 1840s–1960s* (Toronto: University of Toronto Press, 1998).

58. Constance Backhouse, for example, details the pervasive role that white supremacy played in the modern Canadian legal system in *Colour Coded: A Legal History of Racism in Canada, 1900–1950* (Toronto: University of Toronto Press, 1999).

59. Kay J. Anderson, *Vancouver's Chinatown: Racial Discourse in Canada, 1875–1980* (Kingston, ON: McGill-Queen's University Press, 1991); Jiwu Wang, *"His Dominion" and the "Yellow Peril": Protestant Missions to Chinese Immigrants in Canada, 1859–1967* (Waterloo, ON: Wilfred Laurier University Press, 2006); Kornel Chang, *Pacific Connections: The Making of the U.S.-Canadian Borderlands* (Berkeley: University of California Press, 2012); Arlene Chan, *Righting Canada's Wrongs: The Chinese Head Tax and Anti-Chinese Immigration Policies in the Twentieth Century* (Toronto: James Loriner, 2014).

60. Franca Iacovetta, *Gatekeepers: Reshaping Immigrant Lives in Cold War Canada* (Toronto: Between the Lines, 2006).

61. For example, Beth Lew-Williams explores how a wide variety of actors—including labor organization and local community members—became part of the impetus for and enforcement of anti-Chinese laws in the western United States. See Beth Lew-Williams, *The Chinese Must Go: Violence, Exclusion, and the Making of the Alien in America* (Cambridge, MA: Harvard University Press, 2018).

PART I

Emerging Borders: Policing Boundaries in the Nineteenth Century

Defining the Acceptable Bounds of Deception

ONE

Policing the Prize Game in the Northeastern Borderlands, 1812–1815

EDWARD J. MARTIN

In 1813 at the height of the war between the United States and Great Britain, the attorney Jonathan D. Weston of Eastport, Maine, had a visitor. This visitor was one Charles Lloyd, a loyalist mariner from Campobello Island, New Brunswick, who came in search of a doctor. In the course of his visit, Lloyd revealed a story that alarmed Weston. Lloyd disclosed that, for eighteen pounds, he had guided the sloop *Experiment* to Little River, where the US privateer *Fly* captured it. Weston learned from Lloyd that the *Fly*'s commander had abused the police powers that came with his privateering commission. Weston also realized that the *Fly*'s captain had attempted to deceive the US district court in Wiscasset, Maine, by paying a British subject to carry a British vessel and its cargo to its capture at a prearranged time and place as a means of illegally importing British goods into the United States.[1]

Lloyd's story revealed that residents of the northeastern borderlands maintained competing allegiances, which undermined the state's effort to tie merchants and mariners to its defense. Attention to policing trade in the northeastern borderlands during the War of 1812 provides borderlands scholars with an early example of how local economic allegiances frustrated the expansion of state power.[2] The US government expected privateers to seize vessels trading with the enemy and not to trade with the enemy themselves. Since the Renaissance, nation-states commissioned privateers as an inexpensive means of supplementing their naval power.

By granting a license to the owners of privately armed vessels, nation-states could increase the number of ships deployed against an enemy without paying for them. The owners, officers, and crew of a privateer were compensated from the proceeds of captured vessels.[3] Even though privateers in the northeastern borderlands brought captured vessels to prize courts, they manipulated their proceedings to maintain economic relationships that predated the war. As George T. Díaz contends in his study of smuggling along the US-Mexico border, residents of borderlands created moral economies of illicit commerce where some forms of smuggling were considered justified in response to government interference with free trade.[4]

When Lloyd told his story at Weston's Eastport law office, he believed a similar moral economy protected his secret. Lloyd did not expect that Weston's identity as an attorney—a professional whose interests were tied to the expansion of state power through the court's jurisdiction—overrode his identity as an Eastport resident. Eastport is situated on Moose Island, adjacent to Saint Andrews, New Brunswick, in the Bay of Fundy. The Bay of Fundy was part of the northeastern borderlands, a transnational region comprising New England, Nova Scotia, and New Brunswick. In the wake of the American Revolutionary War, Republicans settled in Maine, and Loyalists (American colonists who remained loyal to King George) founded the province of New Brunswick. Despite their political differences, Republicans and Loyalists remained tied to each other by kinship and commerce. Although located on the US side of the border, Eastport pledged its neutrality to its Loyalist neighbors when war broke out once again between the now-independent United States and Great Britain in 1812.

As the historian Alan Taylor astutely points out, Maine sat at the center of an international crossroads along a vaguely defined border with New Brunswick. Although the peace treaty of 1783 created a boundary along the St. Croix River between the United States and British North America, local residents ignored it. In the absence of a developed road network, people and goods continuously moved across the waters of the Bay of Fundy as it suited their needs. Therefore, residents of this maritime borderland communicated more frequently with each other than with their fellow citizens or subjects in their nations' interiors.[5]

Under the circumstances, this boundary remained elusive because the United States and Great Britain both disputed the location of the St. Croix River. Once Robert Pagan, a Loyalist merchant and amateur archeologist, discovered the location of Samuel de Champlain's campsite at the mouth

Figure 1.1. Major privateering ports in New England and the Maritime Provinces, 1812–1815. Courtesy of Joshua M. Smith.

of the Schoodic River in 1797, a border commission rejected two other locations for the river. Even though Pagan's discovery determined the border's exact location, boundary enforcement remained difficult. In the absence of organized police forces, both the United States and Great Britain relied on customs collectors to patrol the northeastern borderlands during the War of 1812.[6]

When the United States declared war on Great Britain on June 18, 1812, the commissioning of privateers compounded the lax enforcement of trade regulations. Both countries supplemented their naval forces in the northeastern borderlands by commissioning privateers throughout the War of 1812. The small size of the United States Navy, and the Royal Navy's demands in its global conflict against Napoleon, required both nations to delegate the power to wage war to private individuals. The power to make war included police powers used to detect and stop trade with the enemy. As the United States and Great Britain augmented their naval forces with privateers, delegating these powers to privately armed vessels created a conflict between political and economic allegiances for northeastern borderlands residents. Like the forces authorized to police an international boundary between Mexico and the Confederate States of America (discussed by Luis Alberto García in chapter 2), privateers frequently acted with local interests in mind.

Trade with the Enemy

Trade policy impacted privateers' decisions, prompting some to engage in collusive capture for self-interest. Although privateers on both sides attempted to defraud prize courts by abusing the police powers that came with their commissions, the choice to engage in trade with the enemy or to plunder prizes was determined by restrictions and opportunities created through trade policies. On the US side of the border, the government continued the restrictive system of trade that began with Thomas Jefferson's Embargo Act of 1807. Then during the War of 1812, James Madison's administration hoped to deprive the British of valuable supplies of grain and naval stores through such coercive measures. Unfortunately for Madison, this policy encouraged Maine's privateers to become illicit traders. Collusive capture proved to be a useful ruse for Maine privateers who turned smugglers.

American privateers' self-gain, however, denied the federal government revenue. In order to address this, US prize courts turned to customs officials to detect collusive captures. After Congress passed a prize act on June 29, 1812, privateering commissions, or letters of marque, were granted in the name of the president by the secretary of state. But because the secretary of state had few employees in the nation's ports, he relied on customs collectors to issue and revoke the commissions. Once a collector granted a vessel a commission, the owners were legally authorized to arm it and hire a captain and crew to capture enemy vessels and their cargos. Unlike on a merchant vessel, the captain and crew shared a portion of any prize they captured with the privateer's owners according to their labor. Lawful prizes included enemy vessels, neutral vessels carrying arms and ammunition, and US vessels trading with the enemy.[7]

After customs collectors received copies of blank commissions from the secretary of state, they filled in the requisite information and hastily handed them out to vessel owners who put up sufficient security to ensure their good behavior. Although a collector had limited authority when privateers used excessive force or illegally detained a vessel, he had considerable power to combat collusive captures. Customs collectors were the only federal officials in Maine's ports who had the power to seize a prize or revoke a commission. The authority a customs collector's office gave privateers to combat illicit trade also granted collectors the power to police privateers trading with the enemy. Furthermore, the prize act required privateers to turn over their papers and bring their prisoners to the customs collector. Once the collector examined the prize's papers and the prisoners' responses to standardized questions, known as standing interrogatories, he determined whether the capture was fraudulent or not. If the collector believed the capture was made collusively, the collector entered a claim for it with the prize court.

Few customs collectors realized how much time they would dedicate to combating collusive captures that resulted from their own carelessness during the War of 1812. According to the records of the US district court at Wiscasset, Maine, ninety prizes were carried into the ports in this jurisdiction during the war. The fact that US naval vessels carried in only three of those illustrates that the northeastern borderlands relied on privateers for naval defense. Indeed, a close examination of prize cases reveals that 20 percent of the prizes carried into Maine's ports were captured collusively.[8]

The privateer *Fly*'s fraudulent captures reveal customs collectors' role in combating collusive capture. As the War of 1812 progressed, it became obvious that merchants such as Hugh Kennedy Toler took advantage of a significant smuggling infrastructure that had developed in the northeastern borderlands in the wake of the Revolutionary War. When the British occupied Castine, Maine, in 1779, they created a liminal space where Loyalist privateers captured Patriot vessels carrying provisions. After the war, Patriots and Loyalists who migrated from Long Island Sound to Maine, Nova Scotia, and New Brunswick reinforced the practice of illicit trade. For example, Lemuel Trescott, the customs collector for the Passamaquoddy District, had acquired a comprehensive knowledge of collusive captures as a major in the Continental Army, stationed along the Connecticut shore.[9] Migrants such as Trescott formed part of a large interconnected network that facilitated Toler's illicit ventures.

Toler's schemes became even more elaborate once he began working with Eastport merchants and displaced mariners from Connecticut, such as Henry L. Dekoven and William S. Sebor. During the Revolutionary War, the Connecticut River port of Middletown sponsored numerous privateers. Some of these privateers had engaged in collusive capture, so Dekoven and Sebor knew the police powers that came with a commission could be used to facilitate trade with the enemy. Dekoven and Sebor were brothers-in-law and cousins. Raised in a community with a history of sponsoring collusive capture schemes, in addition to having ties of marriage and blood, the duo made ideal conspirators unlikely to inform on the other.[10]

Before the War of 1812, Dekoven's residence alternated between Middletown and New York City, where he probably met Toler. Both Dekoven and Sebor earned their livings in the European trade until the British extended their blockade to Long Island Sound in 1813. After sailing with his brother-in-law for fourteen years, Sebor had just begun his career as the master of a vessel when the blockade was extended. When Sebor arrived in Newport, Rhode Island, in August 1813, he sought a new source of income and headed east with his brother-in-law to purchase a privateer.[11]

Because both men had made successful voyages in 1812 and 1813, they had ample credit at their disposal when they arrived in Portland and purchased the *Fly*, originally a privateer from Salem, Massachusetts, that had been captured, sold at auction in Halifax, and recaptured.[12] Once they had a suitable vessel, they shipped a crew for wages as a means of deceiving the US district court. Normally, privateers shipped their crews for a share in the prize; however, Dekoven and Sebor were not planning a normal cruise.[13] Rather, they conspired to make a collusive capture in the utmost secrecy. While shipping a crew for wages was an unusual arrangement for a privately armed vessel, many mariners accepted it because they desperately needed money. Alexander Hobbs, an unemployed shipmaster from Portland, joined the crew of the *Fly* in December 1813 for thirty-five dollars per month and thirty-five dollars for each additional prize. Less experienced mariners got twenty dollars per month and twenty dollars for each prize.[14] Despite Dekoven and Sebor's attempts to maintain secrecy, the *Fly*'s crew learned of their captain and lieutenant's illicit intentions. The crew knew that Dekoven and Sebor planned to use the police power granted by their commission to trade with the enemy. The mariner James Crocker later reported in his testimony that the crew of the *Fly* openly discussed the privateer's activities. In his deposition, Crocker remarked, "I did suppose there was an understanding. We used to talk aboard the privateer of our mode of privateering being a most profitable one."[15] Although residents of local communities accepted the wages Dekoven and

Sebor offered, they were not shy about sharing this information with customs collectors and undermining fraudulent captures. In the absence of more reliable sources of income, mariners willingly accepted wages from illicit trade but refused to remain silent about a valuable prize they did not share. The code of silence that shielded trade with the enemy in the northeastern borderlands from lawful authorities was limited by similar self-interested motives.

Next, Dekoven and Sebor made their way to Machias, Maine, and began arrangements to capture two British vessels with valuable cargos of manufactured goods. Sebor made a journey by land to Eastport, Maine, the home of Jabez Mowry, and Mowry traveled to Machias to meet with Dekoven and Sebor at Gates Tavern to coordinate captures with them.[16] Although Mowry later testified that he saw Dekoven and Sebor in Eastport in December or January, he did not mention his own visit to Machias. Mowry claimed that the mariners had business with Lemuel Trescott, the customs collector at Passamaquoddy. He also confirmed that Dekoven and Sebor carried a letter for Toler, who resided in Eastport.[17]

Meanwhile, a group of merchants in Saint Andrews, New Brunswick, loaded a sloop, the *Experiment*, for an intended collusive capture. Shrewd merchants such as Robert Pagan, John Campbell, Thomas Wyer, and David Jack were not willing to part with decent vessels in collusive capture ventures. While the *Experiment* was not fit to make a sea voyage around Cape Sable to Halifax in the winter months, it was the perfect vessel for a collusive capture. The *Experiment*'s dilapidated condition made it inexpensive and easy to part with.[18]

The captain and crew of the *Fly* did not follow the instructions that accompanied their commission when they released Lloyd and the *Experiment*'s crew from custody. The instructions issued to privately armed vessels specified that privateers bring in at least two principal persons with each prize they captured. According to prize law—the branch of the maritime law of nations that established the rules privateers followed when capturing a prize—a "principal person" was someone who possessed an intimate knowledge of the captured vessel and its cargo and could testify about the vessel, its cargo, and the nature of its capture. Prize courts (the courts designated to hear prize cases under the maritime law of nations) used statements from these witnesses as well as the papers found on a captured vessel to determine the fate of a prize. If the witnesses and the papers confirmed that the privateer had followed prize law, then the prize court awarded the prize to the captor. If not, the prize court returned the captured vessel to its owner. If prizes came into port without the requisite witnesses, customs collectors in the northeastern borderlands became suspicious. Since the Department of the Treasury did not employ agents before 1850, customs collectors conducted their own investigations.[19] When Jeremiah Obrien (the customs collector for the port of Machias) learned that the *Experiment* had arrived without the principal persons needed for questioning, he seized the *Fly*'s prize for collusive capture and questioned the prize crew.[20]

As the *Experiment* headed to its place of intended capture, the Saint John merchant Nehemiah Merritt prepared another vessel in the scheme by openly loading goods onto it. Merritt had purchased the *George*, an American schooner, at a prize auction.[21] James Godsoe, the captain of the British privateer *Hare*, brought news that the *Fly* was cruising near Moose Peak while its crew loaded goods onto the schooner destined for capture.[22] David Rodrick, the master of a captured American vessel, overheard Merritt say he was loading it for a Yankee take. A man standing next to Merritt asked what he meant by his remark, and Merritt responded that he was loading the schooner so she could be taken by the *Fly*.[23] When they loaded the *George* with additional goods at a second wharf, Merritt told another witness that he was loading the schooner for the US privateer *Fly*, which awaited it.[24] Merritt spoke freely about loading a vessel destined for a collusive capture because the British government used trade to undermine the American war effort. Neither the Royal Navy nor William Wanton, the Saint John customs collector, intended to stop the *George*. According to Joshua M. Smith of the US Merchant Marine Academy, New Brunswick's customs officers rarely displayed vigilance.[25]

The *George* could not have made a voyage of that distance with a small crew and inadequate sails.[26] Instead, Dekoven and the crew of the *Fly* seized it at Grand Manan on January 13, 1814. The *George*'s crew of three consisted of a Portuguese, a Spanish, and a Greek mariner, whose neutral statuses protected them from detention as prisoners of war.[27] Therefore, no members of the crew were detained as witnesses, which precluded them from answering the questions contained in standing interrogatories.

Although the *George* arrived in Ellsworth, Maine, without the requisite witnesses, Melatiah Jordan, the customs collector for Frenchman's Bay, relied on informants to seize the *George*. Informants played a key role in detecting collusive captures. Eyewitness testimony proved crucial in cases where a fraudulent capture differed only slightly from a lawful seizure. The government recognized the importance of informants by awarding them a third of any prize captured collusively. With a cargo worth more than $100,000, a third of a prize like the *George* provided a powerful incentive for borderlands residents to side with their nation's interests over local economic affiliations. Josiah Hook, the customs collector for the Penobscot District, informed Jordan of the illicit nature of the *George*'s capture. Hook had acquired a packet of papers that included letters in code after a fisherman named John Robinson had captured the US privateer *Lydia*. Although Robinson's actions foiled the *Lydia*'s plan to capture the *Margaretta* fraudulently, Hook excluded the patriotic fisherman from the fruits of his labor. Hook had deciphered the *Lydia*'s papers and now informed Jordan that the *George* was one of several vessels destined for a collusive capture.[28] Hook wanted to keep the informant's share for himself.

Licensed Trade

When British officials in Nova Scotia and New Brunswick began licensing US vessels to carry desperately needed provisions to their provinces, they undermined the self-interested economic motives that made privateers agents of imperial policy. Lieutenant General Sir John Coape Sherbrooke of Nova Scotia and Major General George Stracy Smyth of New Brunswick knew that most of the Royal Navy's resources were committed to defeating Napoleon, which precluded sending reinforcements to the Halifax Station. Therefore, they found it necessary to grant letters of marque under their commissions as vice admirals of their respective provinces. Smyth granted a commission to the owners of the privately armed sloop *General Smyth* on July 28, 1812, while Sherbrooke issued Enos Collins and Joseph Allison a commission for the *Liverpool Packet* on August 20, 1812. They hoped that commissioning their own privateers would reduce the depredations by US privateers.[29]

Ordinarily, the British Parliament passed a prize act after it issued a declaration of war against another nation. Once Parliament passed a prize act, the Admiralty sent instructions to the vice-admiralty court at Halifax empowering it to sit as a prize court. Afterward, the Admiralty delivered a warrant to the lieutenant governors of Nova Scotia and New Brunswick authorizing them to grant commissions to privateers. Although the prince regent issued an order-in-council granting these powers to lieutenant governors and the vice-admiralty courts in October 1812, Sherbrooke and Smyth acted expediently to defend their provinces.[30] Rather than wait for official authorization, both men used their authority as the vice admirals of their provinces to commission privateers. Unlike in the US system of commissioning privateers that required an act of Congress, a lieutenant governor had the authority to arm vessels to defend a British province.

Nova Scotia's and New Brunswick's trade policies prompted privateers to use the police powers of their commissions to capture US vessels protected from seizure. And though the licensed trade reduced the number of New England sailors and vessels that engaged in privateering, it harmed merchants and mariners in Nova Scotia and New Brunswick.[31] In addition to destroying an enemy's commerce, privateering served maritime communities as a form of wartime economic relief. Privateers provided an outlet for unemployed capital and labor. War had disrupted maritime commerce, so merchants invested their money in privately armed vessels to recover their losses. Privateers carried much larger crews than merchant vessels because they needed men to operate them and their prizes. Mariners signed on to privateers with the hope that they would share in valuable prizes. Once a US merchant vessel obtained a license, it ceased to be a lawful prize for Nova Scotia's and New Brunswick's privateers. The placement of US vessels under the protection of British law frustrated merchants and mariners from both provinces as they tried to sustain themselves in a wartime economy. Seventy-one of more than 700 prizes, or almost 10 percent of the vessels adjudicated in the Halifax Vice-Admiralty Court, carried licenses.[32]

Commissions

Whereas a license placed a vessel under the protection of British law, an invalid commission forced a privateer to forfeit its prize to either the Crown or the Admiralty. Only through petitions to the Crown and appeals to the vice-admiralty court could the owners, officers, and crew of a privateer recover their prize. This practice impacted successful privateers such as the *Liverpool Packet* as well as less fortunate privateers. While the *Liverpool Packet* captured at least nineteen of fifty prizes before the order-in-council, the *General Smyth* seized two of four of its prizes before commissions were authorized by the prince regent, the son of King George III who ruled in his name when his father became incapacitated. An additional prize taken by the *General Smyth* was protected by a license to trade.[33] Unfortunately for the *General Smyth*'s crew, the only prize they immediately profited from was a recapture. A recapture entitled the captors to a sixth of a prize rather than the whole. Under the circumstances, the process of paying mariners shares in a prize became even more prolonged, forcing many a sailor to dispose of his share for a fraction of its value. Even though it was not uncommon for mariners to sell their shares before a cruise, uncertain payment dramatically reduced their value.

As one of Nova Scotia's most experienced privateers, Joseph Barss realized that he needed to devise a way to get licensed US vessels condemned in the Halifax Vice-Admiralty Court if he was going to succeed as the *Liverpool Packet*'s captain. In other words, Barss planned to alter the evidence he obtained when seizing prizes to ensure that he and his men profited from the police powers that came with the *Liverpool Packet*'s commission. At least eleven of fifty prizes the *Liverpool Packet* brought into port carried a license to trade. As commander of the *Rover*, Barss knew from personal experience that neutral US vessels had undermined privateering during the Napoleonic Wars. Once US vessels began carrying goods between France and its colonies, privateering ceased to be profitable because neutral vessels were not lawful prizes. When Barss realized that his own government placed enemy vessels outside his reach, he saw history repeating itself. The novel and uncertain circumstances that prevailed in the fall of 1812 led Barss and other privateers to develop deceptive practices to defraud the Halifax Vice-Admiralty Court.[34] These deceptive practices hindered the cooperative relationship both lieutenant governors sought to foster with New England's merchants.

The case of the *Economy* illustrates how British trade policy severed the ties between individual economic self-interest and imperial interest at the heart of privateering. The *Economy* left Boston around September 13, 1812, bound for Alexandria, Virginia. Upon its arrival, the *Economy* discharged a cargo of lime, took on a new cargo, and cleared for Boston. According to Robert Holmes, the *Economy*'s master, his vessel was bound for Halifax but cleared for Boston to allay the suspicions of US privateers. The *Liverpool Packet* seized the *Economy* on November 18, 1812, south of Cape Cod on its voyage to Halifax.[35] Holmes had a license from Sir John Coape Sherbrooke, which William K. Reynolds, a Halifax merchant, procured to protect the *Economy* from seizure. The license was accompanied by a letter from Vice Admiral Herbert Sawyer and covered three voyages to carry flour to Nova Scotia. The *Economy* also carried an American coasting license that revealed the vessel's true nationality. Holmes did not know whether the *Liverpool Packet* was a British or American privateer at the time of the *Economy*'s boarding, because the privateer flew no flag.[36]

The privateer, though, appeared to be American-built. The crew's appearance and dialect also seemed American to Holmes, so he was reluctant to show them the license from Sherbrooke. Revealing a license to a US privateer would provide the crew with the probable cause needed to seize the vessel for trading with the enemy. When Joseph Barss, the captain of the *Liverpool Packet*, told Holmes his vessel was an English tender, Holmes mentioned the license but failed to produce it. Once Holmes learned that Barss intended to send the *Economy* into Saint John, he asked Barss for permission to retrieve a document that would liberate the brigantine. When the captors proposed to send the *Economy* to Halifax instead of Saint John, Holmes requested to accompany the vessel, yet this request was denied even though he was one of the principal persons from the brigantine.[37]

Unfortunately for Holmes, the captain and crew of the *Liverpool Packet* had their own ideas about who should be awarded the *Economy*. They placed Holmes on a previously captured sloop and told him they planned to send the *Economy* to Bermuda. Barss and his crew hoped to disguise the real destination of their prize to ensure its condemnation to themselves as captors.[38] During the early years of the war, Nova Scotia privateers used cartels to facilitate the capture of licensed US vessels. A "cartel" was a vessel employed to repatriate prisoners of war to the enemy. The maritime law of nations allowed privateers to place prisoners on a captured vessel and send them to a friendly port. If a privateer brought in two witnesses who were familiar with the operations of the prize and its cargo, then they were free to release the other prisoners. Originally, this practice had been designed to extend a privateer's cruise. If a privateer captured too many crew members, those same prisoners might recapture a prize or even overwhelm the crew of the captor.[39] Barss and other privateers from Nova Scotia and New Brunswick saw cartels as an opportunity to get rid of witnesses whose testimony might lead to a prize being restored to its owner. By preventing American mariners such as Holmes from appearing at the Halifax Vice-Admiralty Court, privateers obstructed one of the few legal forms of wartime communication that remained in this transnational maritime region. And though the practice of removing witnesses never rose to the level of violence employed by the home guards in Texas (described by Miguel A. Levario in chapter 7), its frequency demonstrates the difficulty British officials experienced enforcing lawful procedures.

The case of the *Economy* exposed the weakness of state power in the northeastern borderlands. Although the lieutenant governors of Nova Scotia and New Brunswick empowered private individuals to supply and defend their provinces, they failed to stop British privateers from seizing licensed US vessels. As a prize court, the Halifax Vice-Admiralty Court determined whether a capture was lawful or not. According to the maritime law of nations, neither lieutenant governor could authorize customs collectors to revoke a commission until the Halifax Vice-Admiralty Court issued its decree. Under the circumstances, the state's ability to regulate privateers depended on the resourcefulness of the captain of a captured vessel.

Once the sloop carrying Holmes landed at Boothbay, Maine, he made his way to Boston, Eastport, and finally to Halifax with the license from Sherbrooke and other documents to prove that the *Economy* was protected from seizure.[40] Despite Holmes's heroic efforts, Judge Alexander Croke rejected the validity of the license from Sherbrooke and Sawyer's letter on two grounds. First, Holmes had not produced the license at the time of capture. Second, Sherbrooke had issued the license before the prince regent's order-in-council granted the lieutenant governors of Nova Scotia and New Brunswick the authority to issue licenses to US vessels.

While Croke's decision dashed Holmes's hope that his vessel and cargo would be restored, the *Economy*'s captors fared no better in the vice-admiralty court. Their prize was condemned as a droit of admiralty because Sherbrooke granted their commission before the king had declared war.[41] (A "droit of admiralty" is a right or privilege extended by the Crown to the Lords of the Admiralty or their representatives to seize the proceeds of a prize captured by a privateer before a formal declaration of war; it also deprived the privateer of the proceeds of a prize without returning it to its owner.) Since Croke's decision awarded the *Economy* to the British government, it failed to deter privateers from seizing US-licensed vessels. His decision deprived the crew of the *Liverpool Packet* of the proceeds of a prize without penalizing the privateers for seizing a vessel protected by a license. On the contrary, it motivated agents for the *Liverpool Packet* to petition the Crown for the prize money and encouraged privateers to continue seizing licensed US vessels.

Conclusion

States' delegation of police powers to privately armed vessels prompted abuse by privateers tasked with enforcing the law. While US customs collectors played a significant role in detecting and reporting collusive capture schemes to prize courts, their counterparts in Nova Scotia and New

Brunswick did not perform a similar function regarding the seizure of licensed vessels. Once a British privateer captured a licensed US vessel, the owner of the captured vessel needed to prove the license protected his vessel from seizure. This process began when the master or owner arrived in Halifax and entered a monition in the vice-admiralty court. (A "monition" is a claim for a vessel filed by either the captor or the original owner in a vice-admiralty court.) Therefore, the captain of a captured vessel played an important role in policing privateers who seized a licensed US vessel.

Frequently, the arrival of a licensed vessel's owner or his representative proved sufficient to convince the captors to withdraw their monition. In a few cases, a private settlement followed between the captor and the owner of the prize. Even though the captured vessel's owner or master had to make a heroic journey to appear before the vice-admiralty court in Halifax, his efforts were often rewarded. The inability of Nova Scotia's and New Brunswick's privateers to prevent unfriendly witnesses from arriving in Halifax illustrates that locals could effectively police some infractions better than others through prize courts. Standing interrogatories functioned better when they were used to collect evidence of an illicit seizure than as a means of detecting collusion. In the case of an illicit seizure of a US vessel licensed to trade with Nova Scotia or New Brunswick, witnesses were willing to testify against an offending privateer. This was not always true in cases of collusive capture, where providing truthful testimony could reveal the guilt of the person being deposed.

Although the United States and Great Britain granted police powers to privateers, the duty of policing these privately armed vessels in the northeastern borderlands fell on judges, customs collectors, and the captains of captured vessels. Government officials on the US side of the border never expected US privateers to use their authority to combat illicit trade with the British to engage in trade with the enemy. On the opposite side of the border, British privateers shocked British officials by seizing US vessels carrying food and provisions to Nova Scotia and New Brunswick protected by British licenses. Perhaps government officials on both sides of the border failed to understand that an unsuccessful cruise was a privateer's greatest enemy regardless of the flag the ship flew. Even though the United States was a nascent republic and Great Britain was a global empire, neither state successfully expanded its influence by delegating to privateers the power to police this transnational region. Both states overestimated the power of economic self-interest to tie merchants and mariners to national or imperial policy. Neither the United States nor Great Britain expanded its control of the territory on its side of this boundary until the 1842 Webster-Ashburton Treaty solidified the border and trade reciprocity eliminated the threat presented by local economic allegiances by normalizing commerce across this vague new boundary. Still, even with normalized economic relations, smuggling and illicit cross-border trade would continue to link residents across the boundaries of these maritime borderlands well beyond the imperial conflicts of the early nineteenth century. Economic self-interest and cross-border ties evident during the War of 1812 would remain central to the cultural life of communities that straddle the northeastern borderlands.

Notes

1. John Barstow, answers, *Dekoven v. Experiment*, Appellate Case Files of the Supreme Court of the United States, Microfilm Publication M214, roll 35, National Archives, Waltham, MA (hereafter cited as Appellate Case Files); Charles Lloyd, deposition, *Dekoven v. Experiment*, Appellate Case Files.

2. Jonathan Weston, answers, *Dekoven v. Experiment*, Appellate Case Files; Barstow, answers.

3. Donald Petrie, *The Prize Game: Lawful Looting on the High Seas in the Days of Fighting Sail* (Annapolis, MD: Naval Institute Press, 1999), 1–13.

4. George T. Díaz, *Border Contraband: A History of Smuggling across the Rio Grande* (Austin: University of Texas Press, 2015), 1–2.

5. The residents of this maritime borderland lived in a binational community that challenged national definitions of space and identity similar to those along the Western border described by Rachel St. John. See Rachel St. John, *Line in the Sand: A History of the Western U.S.-Mexico Border* (Princeton, NJ: Princeton University Press, 2011), 8.

6. Taylor argues that Lemuel Trescott, Eastport's customs collector, cooperated with borderlands residents engaged in smuggling to avoid conflict with his neighbors. See Alan Taylor, "Centers and Peripheries: Locating Maine's History," *Maine History* 39 (2000): 6–9.

7. Joshua M. Smith, "Sentinels of the Republic: Customs Collectors in the District of Maine, 1789–1820" (master's thesis, Eastern Carolina University, 1997), 22–37.

8. Edward J. Martin, Database of Prize Cases from New England and the Maritime Provinces, 1812–1815; Edward J. Martin, "The Prize Game in the Borderlands: Privateering in New England and the Maritime Provinces, 1775–1815" (PhD diss., University of Maine, 2014).

9. Joshua M. Smith, *Borderlands Smuggling: Patriots, Loyalists, and Illicit Trade in the Northeast, 1783–1820* (Gainesville: University Press of Florida), 73.

10. Smith.

11. Jacob Sebor, examination and answers, *Dekoven v. George*, Appellate Case Files.

12. Elisha Marston, examination, *Dekoven v. George*, Appellate Case Files.

13. Alexander Hobbs, deposition, *Dekoven v. George*, Appellate Case Files.

14. Hobbs, deposition.

15. James Crocker, deposition, *Dekoven v. George*, United States District Court for the District of Maine, National Archives, Waltham, MA (hereafter cited as USDC-ME).

16. Elisha Marston, interrogatories, *Dekoven v. George*, Appellate Case Files.

17. Jabez Mowry, deposition, *Dekoven v. Experiment*, Appellate Case Files.

18. John Pendlebury, answers to cross-interrogatories on behalf of the claimant, *Dekoven v. Experiment*, Appellate Case Files.

19. Carl E. Price and Mollie Keller, *The U.S. Custom Service: A Bicentennial History* (Washington, DC: Department of the Treasury, 1989), 120–121.

20. William Preble, claim and answer, *Dekoven v. Experiment*, USDC-ME.

21. David Roderick, deposition, *Dekoven v. George*, USDC-ME.

22. David Roderick, deposition, *Dekoven v. George*, October term, United States Circuit Court for Massachusetts, National Archives, Waltham, MA.

23. Roderick.

24. Oliver Thomas, deposition, *Dekoven v. George*, USDC-ME.

25. Smith, *Borderlands Smuggling*, 77.

26. Nehemiah Merritt, deposition, *Dekoven v. George*, Appellate Case Files.

27. Thomas Trask, interrogatories, *Dekoven v. George*, USDC-ME.

28. Ebenezer Robinson, deposition, *Robinson v. Hook*, USDC-ME.

29. James Stewart, *Report of Cases Argued and Determined in the Court of Vice Admiralty at Halifax in Nova Scotia from the Commencement of the War in 1803 to the End of the Year 1813* (London: J. Butterworth & Sons, 1814), 382–394.

30. Ward Chipman to Jonathan Odell, May 28, 1793, Privateers and Letters of Marque, 1793–1794, RG 1 RS558/G/1, Provincial Archives of New Brunswick, Fredericton, NB.

31. Andrew Lambert, *The Challenge: Britain against America in the Naval War of 1812* (London: Faber & Faber, 2012), 110.

32. Faye M. Kert, *Privateering: Patriots and Profits in the War of 1812* (Baltimore, MD: Johns Hopkins University Press, 2015), 63.

33. Martin, Database of Prize Cases.

34. *Dictionary of Canadian Biography*, s.v. "Barss, Joseph," by Catherine Pross, biographi.ca/en/bio/barss_joseph_6E.html.

35. Examination of the master, *Liverpool Packet v. the Economy*, HVAC, Archives Canada, Ottawa, ON (hereafter cited as HVAC).

36. Examination of the master, *Liverpool Packet v. the Economy*.

37. Examination of the master, *Liverpool Packet v. the Economy*.

38. Robert Holmes, deposition, December 31, 1812, *Liverpool Packet v. Economy*, HVAC.

39. Faye Margrett Kert, *Prize and Prejudice: Privateering and Naval Prize in Atlantic Canada in the War of 1812* (Saint John's, Newfoundland: International Maritime Economic History Association), 103–104.

40. Holmes, deposition.

41. Stewart, *Report of Cases Argued*, 446–469.

Dominance in an Imagined Border

TWO

Santos Benavides's and Santiago Vidaurri's Policing of the Rio Grande

LUIS ALBERTO GARCÍA

On the afternoon of March 10, 1863, a force of sixty Confederate soldiers under the command of Colonel Santos Benavides crossed the Rio Grande and stormed the headquarters of the Mexican army in Nuevo Laredo, Tamaulipas. One hour earlier, one of Benavides's soldiers who resided in that town, Encarnación García, had had a fracas with Mexican forces involving alcohol and guns. News that García died in the altercation unhinged Benavides, who wanted to punish the troops involved in the incident. After an hour of detaining and insulting the Mexican officer in command, Benavides and his force returned to Confederate territory in Laredo, Texas.[1] Benavides's incursion could have led to a diplomatic crisis and war, but beyond a passing alarm among the local military garrisons in Nuevo Laredo and Matamoros, there was no retaliation by Mexican authorities. Benavides's ability to police across international borders stemmed from authority originating from his partnership with Santiago Vidaurri, master of northeastern Mexico at that time. Far from the capitals of Richmond and Mexico City, Vidaurri and Benavides created border policy informally, based on mutual interests and a shared identity that long predated the international divide. Indeed, informal arrangements among regional forces determined border policing in the region until US Reconstruction and Porfirio Díaz's consolidation of power in the 1870s.

This chapter analyzes the way in which regional-local leaderships articulated the policing structure of northeastern Mexico and South Texas during the middle of the nineteenth century and, in doing so, effectively challenged the authority of the nation-state. It also explains how local and state interests vied with the power of the national governments. In order to do so, this study focuses on the political, military, and business relationships between Santiago Vidaurri and Santos Benavides. These figures exemplify local political traditions in transnational Rio Grande borderlands that persisted past the colonial period into the nineteenth century. The local political establishment in this region embraced military leadership because of the isolation of the area and, since the eighteenth century, the presence of Indian groups, such as Comanche and Lipan Apache, whose lifestyles depended on raiding. Moreover, northeastern Mexico was a marginalized and poor area that had no influence over the political decisions made in Madrid or Mexico City. This changed after 1848, when the border moved south to the Rio Grande, creating a commercial hub that integrated the region into the Atlantic economy. Most important, Vidaurri's rise to power in 1855 strengthened the autonomy of Nuevo León and Coahuila. His ability as a leader consisted of bringing together the local figures behind his own authority as governor. Later, Vidaurri used his growing influence to incorporate Santos Benavides and his allies in Laredo into a transnational assembly of *fronterizos* (borderlanders). Therefore, in this way local and state powers joined together to form a powerful transnational political unit. Aligned through common interests, the Benavides-Vidaurri alliance was able to impose its will against federal authority and challenge it effectively.

Because the Vidaurri-Benavides relationship proved crucial to larger border dynamics, this chapter uses their history to explore how personality and contingency can have a dramatic influence on areas of loose state control. Vidaurri and Benavides embraced the traditional borderlands political order, in which political and military leadership were indivisible. They provided stability, which increased the region's wealth through trade and business. This way, the alliance won local support because it achieved what nation-states had not done in half a century. The strong regional interests that Benavides and Vidaurri represented and embodied frustrated Mexico's and the United States' national aims of incorporating their distant borderlands. While they were not the only borderlands caudillos, and many other *norteño* (northern Mexican) leaders challenged their power, Vidaurri and Benavides's association nevertheless set a precedent for how regional powers dealt with national interests. When their alliance collapsed, the political order remained intact into the late nineteenth century.

The ways in which historians treat these two men vary greatly, with Vidaurri receiving far more scholarly attention compared to Benavides. In particular, some historians have pointed out the close and profitable relationship that Vidaurri established with the Confederacy during the US Civil War, one based on geopolitics, commercial interests, and the economic opportunities of the cotton trade. This relationship enhanced Vidaurri's power through access to money and military supplies.[2] Recent biographies have examined the *norteño* leader by focusing on themes such as regionalism, politics, and military organization.[3] Santos Benavides, by contrast, has been the sole focus of only two studies. He has been largely approached as a secondary topic in studies focused broadly on the Civil War and borderlands history.[4] In addition, many studies have analyzed this region through a transnational approach. Most of those focus on the settlements alongside the border or concentrate on the histories of economics, violence, or the nation-state.[5] In doing so, the Rio Grande borderlands historiography tends to consider borderlands policing in binary terms: either violence or cooperation.

This study proposes a middle ground.[6] It considers how alliances among borderlands elites shaped policing and commerce in South Texas and northeastern Mexico. Vidaurri and Benavides represented the local traditions of politics, economics, and defense of the Hispanic population in the North American borderlands; Vidaurri and Benavides were *fronterizos* and *norteños*. Both leaders used their knowledge of the local dynamics of the Rio Grande borderlands to create a powerful transnational structure of political and military power that joined southern Texas and northeastern Mexico under their control as an undivided, quasi-independent state in all but name.

Common Origins and the *Norteño* National Experience

Borderlands elites such as Vidaurri and Benavides shared a common cultural background, one that dated back to the initial colonization of northern New Spain during the seventeenth century. Those first settlements were founded largely by groups of colonists at their own expense in return for Crown land grants.[7] The concentration of political and military leadership in a single figure of authority was another peculiarity of the border-

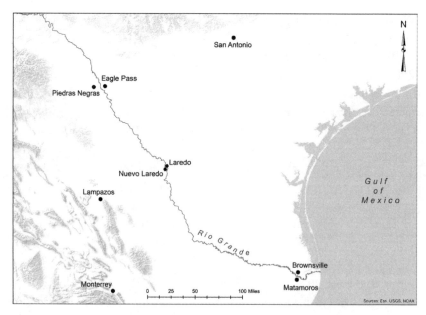

Figure 2.1. Rio Grande borderlands, 1855. Map created by Iván López-Nieto.

lands.[8] Political power depended on the ability to provide defense. These arrangements led to the emergence of an elite class that controlled the region politically and militarily well into the nineteenth century. Vidaurri and Benavides formed part of this social elite and were involved in politics and military affairs. Both figures represented the stereotype of the *norteño* elite class, which over time developed a sense of self-determination regarding local and regional affairs.[9]

Disorder and political instability marked the first decades after Mexican independence. Such circumstances shaped the political thinking of the *norteño* population toward the nation-state. Public debt grew rapidly, and soon there were no resources available to sustain the defense of the northern frontier. The presidio system declined, which reduced the number of troops, who often went unpaid and unsupplied. Moreover, in 1836, the state of Texas won its independence. Frantically attempting to regain control, national authorities diverted the attention of the Mexican army from defending the northern populations to fighting the Texans. During the following years, northern Mexico suffered a wave of Indian attacks of unprecedented severity. Then, in 1846, the Mexican-American War broke out, ending two years later with Mexico's defeat. Mexico gave up not only half its territory but also the populations that lived in those areas.[10] The centralist Mexican government of 1836 restricted voting and regional autonomy. In 1838, this situation ignited a rebellion of the *villas del norte* in the northeast.[11] The rebellion exposed local inhabitants' and northeastern elites' dissatisfaction with the administrative policies of the central Mexican government.[12] Indian attacks were the main concern of the northern populations.[13] At this point, the local population firmly believed that the authorities of central Mexico neither cared about nor understood the needs and particularities of the northern states.[14] This alienation among the local inhabitants toward the Mexican state was one of the reasons that Mexican military power weakened in the northeastern borderlands. During the Mexican-American War, the population was barely involved in the armed conflict, simply because the inhabitants had no sense of nationhood.[15] In this way, the catastrophic first half of the nineteenth century had the effect of distancing the borderland population of the northeast from the political control of the Mexican state. At the same time, a strong sense of regionalism emerged, which revolved around local leadership.

The Emergence of a Transnational Alliance, 1855–1860

After the war, authoritarian and centralist politics caused the Revolution of Ayutla in 1854, bringing a wave of liberal reforms to Mexico. Santiago Vidaurri seized the opportunity and started his own rebellion in 1855, using a regional network of acquaintances and the support of most of Nuevo León's local elites.[16] Vidaurri quickly triumphed and took over the governorship of Nuevo León. At this point, Vidaurri made it clear to the Mexican government that he would rule with complete autonomy.[17] Now for the first time, a *fronterizo* well aware of the local conditions became the most powerful leader of northeastern Mexico. With the support of most of the local inhabitants, Vidaurri built a strong regional coalition that vied for power with the national government.

Ethnic Mexicans north of the Rio Grande faced similar problems with national belonging. Laredo became part of the US territory despite opposition from locals.[18] Mexico and the United States divided communities along the Rio Grande between the two nations in 1848. Local culture and identity remained intact, however, which gave Vidaurri strong empathy for the *norteño* population situated on the north side of the Rio Grande. Tejanos firmly believed that the new political situation would benefit them.[19] Moreover, *norteño* elites were pleased that Vidaurri was a fellow *fronterizo* who did not belong to the political-military establishment of Mexico City.[20] Before Vidaurri, there had been a centralist regime that acted against the local interests regarding trade, politics, and security. Vidaurri planned to improve trade and commerce in the region by reducing duties on imports and reducing insecurity.[21] For the first time, Tejanos dealt with a political authority familiar with their hardships, which helped Vidaurri establish ties with the north bank of the Rio Grande.

The appeal of a shared identity and knowledge of the regional context were the means through which Santos Benavides and Vidaurri began their political interaction. During their first communication, Benavides referred to Vidaurri as a "friend, one like us, who knows how much we have suffered and endured since time immemorial."[22] Benavides, in representing the *vecinos* (settlers) of Laredo, asked for permission to import flour and corn from Mexico. He pointed out that it had been difficult to produce such items because of the drought conditions and the continuous attacks by the Lipan Apache.[23] Thus, Benavides implicitly presented Vidaurri with the two issues Vidaurri most wanted to collaborate on with Texas: trade policing and security.

Vidaurri saw Benavides as an important asset for developing a transnational alliance. Santos Benavides was a prominent leadership figure in Laredo. Benavides had family influence and friendship ties, both of which could provide a useful network of trustworthy allies. This way, Benavides would advise Vidaurri and connect him with people he could trust. For example, Benavides recommended replacing the customs authorities in Nuevo Laredo because they pocketed the income from duties rather than pass the proceeds on to the government. He also suggested that reliable Tejanos serve as customs inspectors.[24] Over time, Benavides referenced myriad people such as doctors, businessmen, ranchers, and military personnel.[25] Benavides also facilitated contact between Vidaurri and Tejano elites such as José Angel Navarro (1828–1876) and Juan N. Seguín (1806–1890).[26] By creating a structure of collaborators, Benavides and Vidaurri dominated the military, politics, and trade of the Rio Grande borderlands independent of federal authorities.

In order to support his position as a transnational caudillo, Vidaurri needed access to financial resources. The political border represented by the Rio Grande provided a solution. Vidaurri controlled the Mexican customs offices along the Rio Grande south of the river, including Camargo, Mier, Nuevo Laredo, Piedras Negras, Reynosa, and Ciudad Guerrero. As the borderland strongman, Vidaurri applied new rules for international trade. He modified import duties by lowering taxes considerably, by between 25 and 60 percent. In doing so, Vidaurri encouraged taxable legal trade instead of untaxed contraband across the region. Increased earnings gave Vidaurri access to credit.[27] This trade-policing measure made Vidaurri the most powerful leader between Austin and Mexico City.

The proceeds of the customs duties generated significant amounts of money for Vidaurri. During the US Civil War, just for cotton imports, the monthly proceeds reached $40,000 to $60,000.[28] Vidaurri controlled such income through the complicity of individuals such as Benavides, who played an important role in establishing and controlling those financial resources. Benavides was part of the new "peace structure" that helped the American authorities govern South Texas after 1848. Tejano elites were accommodated in the new ruling establishment. The Anglos, by contrast, dominated business and trade.[29] Santos Benavides used his position as a political leader to act as an intermediary between Anglo businessmen and Vidaurri. Thus, Benavides built a useful network that included local authorities, posts, muleteers, wagon drivers, and military men, all of whom worked to both benefit and profit from this transnational economic hub.[30] Vidaurri and Benavides effectively policed borderlands commerce and decided who had access to their trading system.[31] As Edward J. Martin demonstrates in chapter 1 of this volume, kinship and trade together proved to be a bond more powerful than national affiliation in North America's northeastern borderlands during the early nineteenth century.

Vidaurri strengthened the region with his remarkable military force: *el ejército del norte*. This northern army originated in 1846, when the Mexican government, desperate because of the insufficiency of its regular army, authorized the creation of the Mexican National Guard. This force was composed of common citizens who elected their own officers. The Mexican army did not have any command over these forces; rather, they were handled directly by governors such as Vidaurri. Even if members of the National Guard did not have any formal military training, in the northeast many accomplished Indian fighters were included among the ranks. Vidaurri used this force as a counterweight against the might of the federal government.[32]

The resources from customs duties helped Vidaurri form this powerful military force. By 1860, his northern army had a register of 11,051 soldiers.[33] Vidaurri's forces were well equipped with supplies, as the border with Texas presented an excellent location for acquiring weapons.[34] Starting in 1856, Benavides contributed to the purchase of rifles, carbines, and powder and also provided transportation.[35] Vidaurri's success and power earned him enemies and rivals. The Mexican national government tried several times—and failed—to undermine his power. Through diplomatic channels, Mexican authorities prompted US authorities to stop and confiscate shipments of weapons bound for Vidaurri. When illicit arms reached Eagle Pass, however, the officer in charge "quietly" ignored the orders and allowed the cargo to pass thanks to Benavides's intervention.[36]

The military power headed by Vidaurri appealed to the population around the Rio Grande. Indeed, at least 400 Tejanos expressed their willingness to enroll in the northern army.[37] Benavides and Seguín established a Tejano recruitment post for Vidaurri's army in San Antonio.[38] Some of those recruits participated in battles in Mexico.[39] Vidaurri also received offers to form military units of Americans willing to participate as mercenaries. Vidaurri and his Mexican officers, however, distrusted Anglo participation in the northern forces.[40] Hence, the military involvement among the Hispanic populations of the region was not merely opportunistic but rather firmly grounded on a shared identity and interests.

Ineffective policing by Mexican and US national forces prompted Vidaurri and Benavides to coordinate security along the Rio Grande. After 1848, the Rio Grande borderlands had become a safe haven for bandits and cattle robbers. But most important, the Texas government had tried unsuccessfully to establish a treaty of military cooperation to fight the Comanche and Lipan Apache.[41] In 1856, after a camp of Lipan Apache had been established in Coahuila, American authorities continuously reported Lipan attacks on US soil. This was a matter of importance for Vidaurri because he could either improve or worsen his ties with Texas and its Anglo merchants. Two days later, on March 11, the northern governor ordered the capture of the Lipan bands. Vidaurri's response was brutal. After his troops captured two bands, soldiers killed almost all the adult men and a large group of women.[42] The massacre established Vidaurri as the dominant power in the Rio Grande borderlands.[43] Also, such action meant the end of the recognition of the bordered domains of Indigenous peoples in the region. Their traditional expression of territoriality through raiding was no longer compatible with the new geopolitical order that Vidaurri and Benavides represented.[44] This action thereby laid the foundation for a different and violent approach toward Indians. Nevertheless, for Vidaurri, the Lipan bloodbath provided a stable relationship with Texan authorities, something that the Mexican government had not been able to accomplish in previous decades and that was of great importance for the inhabitants of northeastern Mexico and South Texas. This was very similar to the case of the US-Canada borderlands during the second half of the nineteenth century, when the transnational movements of Native Americans were perceived as a threat by both the US and the Canadian authorities.[45]

Cooperation in security extended to the policing of cattle rustling in the region. Vidaurri shared information about cattle and horses stolen from Nuevo León with Benavides, who was able to track the animals and discover who stole and sold them in Texas. Vidaurri did the same and returned stolen goods to Texas. This system worked because the border populations reported suspicious activity such as the sudden appearance of foreigners trying to sell animals. Later, Benavides and Vidaurri agreed to regulate the selling of stock from Mexico to Texas. Anyone transporting cattle required official documents signed by local Mexican authorities indicating the number of animals and their brands, otherwise the animals would be confiscated.[46] Corresponding, Vidaurri and Benavides agreed on policing "the multitude of thieves on one and the other side of the river and the several evils that they cause to us."[47]

Difficult Times, 1861–1864

At the start of the US Civil War in April 1861, the Union navy blocked the ports of the Confederacy, isolating the South from trade and supplies. This blockade transformed the Rio Grande into a strategic location. The Confederacy needed to use Mexican territory to trade cotton, weapons, supplies, and food with Europe. Therefore, Vidaurri proved essential to the Southern war effort. During the war, the settlements along the border grew in importance and enjoyed a period of intense economic growth. Near the end of the war, it was estimated that in Matamoros alone some $20 million worth of goods awaited shipment to Europe. Vidaurri engaged in numerous business activities at the same time as he collected customs fees for goods that passed through his domains. He established business houses in Monterrey, Matamoros, Piedras Negras, and other cities along the border. By 1862, there were eight factories capable of handling 1.5 million pounds of cotton annually.[48]

In the middle of this geopolitical and economic struggle, the Benavides-Vidaurri relationship proved extremely profitable. After Benavides became an official member of the Confederate army at the head of a company of 100 men, he regulated the cotton trade in Laredo. In February 1862 Benavides wrote Vidaurri, encouraging him to participate in the cotton business and recommending reliable partners for the enterprise. During this period, Benavides gave priority to cotton shipments belonging to Vidaurri. Even during the later stages of the Civil War, he gave preferential protection to Vidaurri's shipments.[49] Both Vidaurri and Benavides profited from their influence in the region. This commercial boom on the Rio Grande was of common interest to *norteños*, and both leaders gained from the political-business relationship based on their understanding.

The cooperation that emanated from Vidaurri and Benavides's regional authority helped sustain the Confederacy, thereby prolonging the war.[50] Seeing the threat, the US federal government wanted to intervene. At the same time, the national Mexican government was eager to bring the semi-independent caudillo under control. Moreover, and crucially, Vidaurri and Benavides's alliance prompted rivalries with other local leaders. One of them was Silvestre Aramberri (1816–1864), an important officer in Vidaurri's army. Aramberri had serious differences with the northern caudillo, resulting in armed opposition.[51] Benavides's nemesis, in turn, was Juan N. Cortina (1824–1894), a *fronterizo* who opposed the Anglo establishment along the Rio Grande.[52] Cortina destabilized the project that Vidaurri and Benavides represented by fighting them. The US and Mexican governments would try to use these assets for their own interests by enrolling Vidaurri's and Benavides's enemies in their military forces. The mixture of national conflict and regional interest increased violence on the Rio Grande border. Benavides and Vidaurri faced this situation using their own strategies of political-military control. Moreover, both national governments recognized that if they wanted to assert some control and police the region, then they needed local strongmen with the same profile as Vidaurri and Benavides.

In 1861, the Union army worked to destroy the alliance. Juan N. Cortina began to recruit men for the Union who would attack the territory to undermine the interests of the Confederacy and thus Vidaurri and Benavides's trade and military structure. On May 22, 1861, Benavides clashed with "Cortina and seventy of his thieves, leaving in the field seven dead and several wounded."[53] Cortina was defeated but not eliminated. Other figures also soon appeared challenging Vidaurri and Benavides's hegemony. One of them was José María Jesús Carbajal (?–1874), another borderland personage of the Texas–northeastern Mexico region. At different points, Carbajal worked for the Mexican army, the Confederate forces, and the Union army. Like Vidaurri and Benavides, he was more attached to the region and his own interests than to a national project. At some point, Carbajal looked for a commission with the Confederate army to displace Benavides's authority in the region. Failing to do so, he attempted to organize a force in Texas to attack northeastern Mexico and undermine Vidaurri.[54] Octaviano Zapata (?–1863), a local sympathizer of Cortina's, also fought Benavides and Vidaurri's hegemony. Zapata organized forces for the Union army and attacked Benavides's forces using the southern side of the Rio Grande as an operational base. This continued until Benavides and his troops crossed the Rio Grande into Mexico and killed Zapata near Mier, Tamaulipas.[55] This context of incursions and violence brought Vidaurri and Benavides much closer together in military cooperation. But it also meant that their once-hegemonic alliance was now imperiled by external and internal rivals.

Benavides and Vidaurri agreed that their troops could enter Mexico from Texas and vice versa in pursuit of Indians or other hostile actors. Once the armed men reached the opposite shore of the Rio Grande in pursuit of enemies, they cooperated with local allied forces.[56] This measure functioned actively, regardless of the opinion of the national governments. At the same time, the *norteño* leaders did everything possible to eliminate their opponents on both sides of the border. Whenever Vidaurri's enemies attempted to organize an attack from South Texas, Benavides dissolved these forces.[57] Moreover, Benavides even forbade the sale of powder and firearms to these groups, rendering their efforts useless.[58] At this point, the Union army had agents on the Mexican side of the border who monitored and spied on Benavides. They even tried to organize Union forces on Mexican soil.[59] Vidaurri used his power to stop those measures, going so far as to lodge formal complaints against the US government for violating rules of neutrality.[60] Union authorities complained through diplomatic channels when Benavides crossed the river to attack these forces on Mexican soil; Vidaurri shamelessly described these incidents as "inconsequential."[61] Complaints from authorities in Washington, Richmond, or Mexico City were unimportant, however. Along the Rio Grande the only law was what Vidaurri and Benavides decided.

Collapse and Aftermath

The year 1864 brought complications for Vidaurri and Benavides. In the midst of turmoil caused by the French intervention in Mexico, President Benito Juárez was able to unseat Vidaurri from his governorship. Vidaurri went into exile and was executed as a traitor three years later.[62] Benavides continued to fight for his home until 1865, when the Confederacy surrendered. Thus ended the Vidaurri-Benavides alliance. Nevertheless, it did not terminate the political and military control system of local *fronterizos* that the two men had established. Obtaining aid from the local strongmen was vital for any outside power wanting to incorporate the region in a political project. The French recognized this when they bribed Benavides to make peace with the Mexican guerrilla forces headed by his friends. Benavides took the money but gave privileged intelligence about the French army to the Mexican resistance in the northeast.[63] Benavides maintained close relationships with several former Vidaurristas who later filled the vacuum of power. He continued to work in and cooperate with the same framework of politics, armed cooperation, and trade.[64]

From 1867 to 1876, Nuevo León suffered internal conflict between two factions vying to replace Vidaurri. Loyal to Vidaurri until the end, Julian Quiroga (1829–1877) was a close acquaintance of Benavides's. Whenever he needed to, he crossed the Rio Grande to seek refuge or military supplies. When Porfirio Díaz became the new ruler of Mexico, Benavides sponsored the armed opposition headed by Mariano Escobedo and the overthrown president, Sebastian Lerdo de Tejada. Gerónimo Treviño (1835–1914), a former adversary of Vidaurri's, won the conflict with Quiroga and sided with Díaz. But Treviño realized that he needed to make peace with Benavides if he wanted to exert the political control that Vidaurri had in the northeast. In the end, the men became close friends, and Treviño went on to dominate Nuevo León between 1876 and 1890. Porfirio Díaz capitalized on Benavides's relationship with his cousin Manuel González to improve relations with the United States and to pacify the Rio Grande borderlands in the 1880s.[65] By 1890, the region entered a period of peace under the control of national authorities. The age of the warlords ended, and a new era of industrialists and businessmen began.

Benavides and Vidaurri capitalized on the fact that the Rio Grande borderlands existed beyond the control of Washington, Richmond, and Mexico City to establish their own agenda and priorities. Indeed, Benavides and Vidaurri acted as the authorities in a transnational Rio Grande borderland. But military conflicts and an absence of power by nation-states were not the only factors explaining Vidaurri and Benavides's rise in the middle of the nineteenth century; commercial opportunities and the integration of the region in global trade also explain it. The border did not sever these local alliances; rather, it created new opportunities and imposed new limits that made them even more important. This structure of power, however, remained in place after Vidaurri was gone. Even national authorities realized that they had to rely, to some extent, on these regional figures. The Mexican and US authorities effectively incorporated the region into their control by the 1890s, a consummation made possible only through the cooperation of transnational leaders. In this way, nation-states consolidated their territories by using a political-military framework employed and mastered by Santiago Vidaurri and Santos Benavides.

Conclusion

This study demonstrates how inhabitants of the Rio Grande borderlands policed their transnational community. Although confined to a particular geographical area, the case of Vidaurri and Benavides has broader implications for the study of borderlands in other territories. Edward J. Martin demonstrates in chapter 1 how, during the War of 1812, nation-states relied on borderland locals to enforce control, though limited, over the Bay of Fundy. At the same time, the locals found creative ways to benefit from that interaction. Other individuals in similar contexts experienced analogous processes. Such was the case on the La Plata River in the nineteenth century with José Artigas and José Manuel de Rosas and in northwestern Mexico during the Mexican Revolution with Álvaro Obregón and Francisco Villa. All these individuals' *fronterizo* perspectives disregarded state-imposed borders and shaped the ways in which they interacted with the policies of nation-states. Indeed, in some cases, regional transnational leaders shaped national borderlands policing policies in direct and effective ways.

Notes

1. File about Confederate attack in Nuevo Laredo in 1863, May 13, 1873, Comisión Pesquisidora Files, 4-1-4184, box 5, Archivo Histórico de la Secretaría de Relaciones Exteriores (hereafter cited as AHSRE).

2. Mario Cerutti, *Economía de guerra y poder regional en el siglo XIX: Gastos militares, aduanas y comerciantes en los años de Vidaurri (1855–1864)* (Monterrey, MX: AGENL, 1983); and Ronnie C. Tyler, *Santiago Vidaurri and the Southern Confederacy* (Austin: Texas State Historical Association, 1973).

3. Jesús Ávila et al., *Santiago Vidaurri: La formación de un liderazgo regional desde Monterrey (1809–1867)* (Monterrey, MX: UANL, 2012); Artemio Benavides Hinojosa, *Santiago Vidaurri: Caudillo del noreste* (Mexico City: Tusquets, 2012); Luis Medina Peña, *Los bárbaros del norte: Guardia nacional y política en Nuevo León, siglo XIX* (Mexico City: FCE, 2014); Arturo Gálvez Medrano, *Santiago Vidaurri: Exaltación del regionalismo nuevoleonés* (Monterrey, MX: AGENL, 2000); and Edward H. Moseley, "The Public Career of Santiago Vidaurri, 1855–1858" (PhD diss., University of Alabama, 1963).

4. John Denny Riley, "Santos Benavides: His Influence on the Lower Rio Grande,

1823–1891" (PhD diss., Texas Christian University, 1976); Jerry Thompson, *Vaqueros in Blue and Gray* (Austin, TX: Presidial, 1976); and Jerry Thompson, *Tejano Tiger: José de los Santos Benavides and the Texas-Mexico Borderlands, 1823–1891* (Fort Worth: Texas Christian University Press, 2017).

5. Alice L. Baumgartner, "The Line of Positive Safety: Borders and Boundaries in the Rio Grande Valley, 1848–1880," *Journal of American History* 101, no. 4 (March 2015): 1106–1122; Juan Mora-Torres, *The Making of the Mexican Border: The State, Capitalism, and Society in Nuevo León, 1848–1910* (Austin: University of Texas Press, 2001); James Nichols, "The Line of Liberty: Runaway Slaves and Fugitive Peons in the Texas-Mexico Borderlands," *Western Historical Quarterly* 44, no. 4 (Winter 2013): 413–433; and Omar S. Valerio-Jiménez, *River of Hope: Forging Identity and Nation in the Rio Grande Borderlands* (Durham, NC: Duke University Press, 2013).

6. Richard White, *The Middle Ground: Indians, Empires, and Republics in the Great Lakes Region, 1650–1815* (Cambridge: Cambridge University Press, 1991).

7. File about the foundation of Laredo, 1753-1753, Tierras, v. 3519, exp. 7, f. 1–6, Archivo General de Nación (hereafter cited as AGN).

8. José Alfredo Rangel Silva, *Capitanes a guerra, linajes de frontera: Ascenso y consolidación de las élites en el oriente de San Luis, 1617–1823* (Mexico City: COLMEX, 2008), 16; and Sean McEnroe, *From Colony to Nationhood in Mexico* (Cambridge: Cambridge University Press, 2012), 144.

9. "Benavides, Basilio," Texas State Historical Association, tshaonline.org/hand book/online/articles/fbe75; and Jesús Ávila, "En el Reino de Catujanes," in *Santiago Vidaurri: La formación de un liderazgo regional desde Monterrey (1809–1867)* (Monterrey, MX: UANL, 2012), 19–22.

10. David J. Weber, *The Spanish Frontier in North America* (New Haven, CT: Yale University Press, 1992); David J. Weber, *The Mexican Frontier, 1821–1846: The American Southwest under Mexico* (Albuquerque: University of New Mexico Press, 1982); and Brian DeLay, *War of a Thousand Deserts: Indian Raids and the U.S.-Mexican War* (New Haven, CT: Yale University Press, 2008).

11. Josefina Zoraida Vázquez, "La supuesta república del Rio Grande," *Historia Mexicana* 36, no. 1 (July–September 1986): 52; Juan José Gallegos, "Last Drop of My Blood: Col. Antonio Zapata; A Life and Times on Mexico's Río Grande Frontier, 1797–1840" (master's thesis, University of Houston, 2005), 102–103; César Morado, "Aspectos militares: Tres guerras ensambladas (1835–1848)," in *La guerra México-Estados Unidos: Su impacto en Nuevo León, 1835–1848*, ed. Leticia Martínez Cárdenas, César Morado Macías, J. Jesús Ávila Ávila (Mexico City: Senado de la República, 2003), 74–79; and David M. Vigness, "Republic of the Rio Grande," Texas State Historical Association, tshaonline.org/handbook/online/articles/ngro1.

12. Gilberto Miguel Hinojosa, *A Borderlands Town in Transition: Laredo, 1755–1870* (College Station: Texas A&M University Press, 1983); documents about Laredo, January 6, 1838, Laredo Papers, reel 9; Valerio-Jiménez, *River of Hope*, 46, 120; Riley, "Santos Benavides," 44–58; Moseley, "Public Career of Santiago Vidaurri," 52–60; Ávila, "En el Reino," 19–22; documents about Lampazos, September 4, 1839, Mexican Collection, reel 741, vol. 14, Trinity University, San Antonio, TX.

13. DeLay, *Thousand Deserts*, 64–70.

14. Charles H. Harris, *The Sánchez Navarro: A Socio-Economic Study of a Coahuilan Latifundio, 1846–1853* (Chicago: Loyola University Press, 1964), 83–84.

15. J. Jesús Ávila, "Aspectos sociales: Entre la jara del salvaje y el rifle del extranjero," in *La guerra México-Estados Unidos: Su impacto en Nuevo León, 1835–1848* (Mexico City: Senado de la República, 2003), 257, 267.

16. Luis Alberto García, *Guerra y frontera: El ejército del norte entre 1855 y 1858* (Monterrey, MX: AGENL, 2007), 69–81.

17. Newspaper article, June 4, 1855, Official Newspaper, AGENL.

18. Gilberto Miguel Hinojosa, *Borderlands Town in Transition*, 58–59.

19. I define "Tejanos" in this period as people of Mexican descent living in Texas. *El Bejareño* (San Antonio, TX) 1, no. 11 (June 23, 1855), University of North Texas Libraries, texashistory.unt.edu/ark:/67531/metapth178166.

20. *El Bejareño* (San Antonio, TX) 1, no. 16 (August 18, 1855), University of North Texas Libraries, texashistory.unt.edu/ark:/67531/metapth178170.

21. *El Bejareño* (San Antonio, TX) 1, no. 17 (September 1, 1855), University of North Texas Libraries, texashistory.unt.edu/ark:/67531/metapth178171.

22. Benavides to Vidaurri, November 1855, letter 1102, Vidaurri Collection, AGENL (hereafter cited as VC).

23. Benavides to Vidaurri. November 1855, letter 1102, VC.

24. Vidaurri, the governor of Nuevo León, controlled the customs duty of Nuevo Laredo despite being in the state of Tamaulipas. Benavides to Vidaurri, July 14, 1855, letter 1102, VC.

25. Benavides to Vidaurri, May 1854, letter 1190, VC.

26. Benavides to Vidaurri, March 3, 1859, letter 1112, VC; Camilla Campbell, "Navarro, Jose Angel [The Younger]," Texas State Historical Association, tshaonline .org/handbook/online/articles/fna08; Thompson, *Tejano Tiger*, 69; Benavides to Vidaurri, September 23, 1856, letter 1107, VC; Thompson, *Tejano Tiger*, 66; Jesús F. de la Teja, "Seguin, Juan Nepomuceno," Texas State Historical Association, tshaonline.org /handbook/online/articles/fse08.

27. Mario Cerutti, *Propietarios, empresarios y empresa en el norte de México* (Mexico City: Siglo Veintiuno Editores, 2000), 27–35; Octavio Herrera, *La zona libre: Excepción fiscal y conformación histórica de la frontera norte de México* (Mexico City: Secretaría de Relaciones Exteriores México, 2004), 106–115.

28. Tyler, *Santiago Vidaurri*. Isidro Vizcaya Canales, *Los orígenes de la industrialización de Monterrey* (Monterrey, MX: AGENL, 2001).

29. David Montejano, *Anglos and Mexicans in the Making of Texas, 1836–1986* (Austin: University of Texas Press, 1987), 34–45.

30. Benavides to Vidaurri, March 1, July 18, August 17, September 23, 1856, letters 1103, 1104, 1106, 1107, VC.

31. Benavides to Vidaurri, February 1, 1862, letter 1130, VC.

32. García, *Guerra*.

33. García, 55–59.

34. File about weapons purchase, February 23, 1864, Military, box 180, AGENL.

35. Vidaurri to Juan Zuazua, February 28, March 13, September 4, 1856, letters 9960, 9961, 9981, VC.

36. Vidaurri to Juan Zuazua, June 9, 1856, letter 9971, VC; Vidaurri to Benavides, August 17, 1856, letter 1106, VC.

37. Vidaurri to Santos Áviles, August 16, 1856, letter 691, VC.

38. Vidaurri to Santos Áviles, September 23, 1856, letter 1107, VC; *El Bejareño* (San Antonio, TX) 1, no. 17 (September 1, 1855), University of North Texas Libraries, texashistory.unt.edu/ark:/67531/metapth178171.

39. Vidaurri to Ignacio Zaragoza, April 20, 1858, letter 9522, VC.

40. Vidaurri to Benavides, June 9, July 18, 1859, letters 10214, 9510, VC.

41. On October 3, 1855, Captain James Hughes Callahan led an expedition of more than one hundred Texas Rangers into Coahuila for the purpose of "punishing" Indians. Tyler, *Santiago Vidaurri*, 24; Nichols, "Line of Liberty," 430–431; *El Bejareño* (San Antonio, TX) 2, no. 11 (March 15, 1856), University of North Texas Libraries, texashistory.unt.edu/ark:/67531/metapth178192.

42. Vidaurri to Benavides, March 9, 1856, letter 1105, VC; report of Juan Zuazua, March 27, 1856, Lampazos, box 10, AGENL; Isidro Vizcaya Canales, *Incursiones de indios al noreste en el México independiente, 1821–1855* (Monterrey, MX: AGENL, 1995), 331–335.

43. *El Bejareño* (San Antonio, TX) 2, no. 14 (April 5, 1856), University of North Texas Libraries, texashistory.unt.edu/ark:/67531/metapth178195.

44. Juliana Bar, "Geographies of Power: Mapping Indian Borders in the 'Borderlands' of the Early Southwest," *William and Mary Quarterly* 68, no. 1 (January 2011): 5–46.

45. See Benjamin Hoy, chapter 3 in this volume.

46. Vidaurri to Benavides, February 27, April 28, 1859, August 23, 30, 1863, letters 1111, 1113, 1154, 1154, VC.

47. Vidaurri to Benavides, February 27, 1859, letter 1111, VC.

48. Tyler, *Santiago Vidaurri*, 110, 152; Riley, "Santos Benavides," 150–164.

49. Vidaurri to Benavides, May 8, July 12, 1862, December 25, 29, 1863, letters 1139, 1142, 1164, 1167, VC.

50. Gerardo Gurza, *Una vecindad efímera: Los Estados Confederados de América y su política exterior hacia México, 1861–1865* (Mexico City: Instituto Mora, 2001), 73–110; Tyler, *Santiago Vidaurri*; Thompson, *Tejano Tiger*, 80–207.

51. Medina Peña, *Los bárbaros*, 325–356; Tyler, *Santiago Vidaurri*, 59.

52. Jerry Thompson, *Cortina: Defending the Mexican Name in Texas* (College Station: Texas A&M University Press, 2007), 7–33.

53. Vidaurri to Benavides, May 29, June 10, 1861, letters 1124, 1123, VC.

54. Vidaurri to Benavides, February 6, 7, March 28, April 7, 1862, letters 1133, 1136, 1137, VC.

55. James W. Daddysman, "Zapata, Octaviano," Texas State Historical Association, tshaonline.org/handbook/online/articles/fza12.

56. Vidaurri to Benavides, June 10, 1861, April 15, 1862, August 15, 1863, letters 1123, 1138, 1153, VC.

57. Vidaurri to Benavides, March 28, May 8, 1862, letters 1136, 1139, VC.

58. Vidaurri to Benavides, February 1, 1862, letter 1130, VC.

59. Vidaurri to Benavides, January 15, 1864, letter 1168, VC.

60. Reclamations to the US Government, May 18, 1862, 11-H-I-5, folder L-E-2295, file II, AHSRE.

61. Riley, "Santos Benavides," 146–148.

62. Tyler, *Santiago Vidaurri*, 134–144.

63. Juan de Dios Arias, *Reseña histórica de la formación y operaciones del cuerpo de ejército del norte durante la intervención francesa, sitio de Querétaro: Y noticias oficiales sobre la captura de Maximiliano, su proceso integro y su muerte* (Mexico City: N. Chávez, 1867), 15–16.

64. Julian Quiroga File, D/111/598, box 91, Archivo de la Secretaría de Defensa.

65. Thompson, *Tejano Tiger*, 254–255, 276–277, 311–316.

A Border without Guards

THREE

First Nations and the Enforcement
of National Space[1]

BENJAMIN HOY

D
uring the nineteenth century, Canada and the
United States embarked on nation-building campaigns aimed at delineating their shared border
and expanding control over their respective territories. To do so, they
adopted a series of direct and indirect border control strategies. Direct
control focused on monitoring and influencing the ways that individuals
physically crossed the border itself. North-West Mounted Police officers,
border guards, immigration and customs agents, fishery patrols, provincial police forces, and naval units all contributed to this policing. Historical and contemporary accounts of border control often focused on this
naked form of coercion, as it represented one of the most visible ways that
federal governments intervened in daily life.

Direct control, for all its significance, suffered from systemic limitations, particularly when applied to Native American and frontier communities. Army units, Indian agents, North-West Mounted Police officers,
and fishery patrols all complained about inadequate appropriations, insufficient personnel, and the extensive borderland they were forced to
contend with. Canada's small economy created additional impediments
for its border control strategies by limiting the federal presence to little
more than a skeleton force in many regions and by making military
actions—a crucial feature of American Indian policy—prohibitively expensive. The economic, demographic, and military superiority that the
United States maintained over Canada gave the United States additional

options for policing movement, but it still struggled to control an often uncooperative borderland population. Faced with insufficient administrators, troops, and agents, both nations stationed men at areas of heavy traffic and left most of the remaining border undefended. The difficulties of enforcement created room for transnational movement, local variation, misunderstandings, and corruption.

The difficulties Canada and the United States experienced while trying to patrol such an extensive border led them to adopt indirect strategies of enforcement, which attacked the motivations for crossing the border rather than simply the border's physical manifestation. Although this kind of control has received less sustained attention from historians, it was nonetheless essential to extending federal authority throughout the borderlands. Indirect control relied on limiting incentives for movement by restricting access to resources and labor markets. This approach required fewer personnel and allowed agents stationed off the 49th parallel to contribute to border control policies. Although this chapter focuses on indirect control along the Canada–United States border, the approach was not unique to the north. Faced with similar limitations, the United States and Mexico found uses for the same principles in the south as well.

Indirect control came with a distinct set of limitations and was often used to supplement, rather than to supplant, direct control attempts. Controlling the motivations for border crossing worked best when applied at the community and tribal levels and proved inconsistent and ineffective in controlling small-scale movements of individuals and families. Indirect control also could not be applied in a uniform fashion. Dependency, which amplified the effectiveness of indirect control, varied by region and often occurred as the result of a combination of factors over which the federal governments had limited control. The disappearance of the buffalo, changing labor markets, intertribal conflicts, and demographic shifts that took place over the course of the nineteenth century all played important roles. This left both governments with the ability to exploit situational opportunities but prohibited them from imposing consistent and effective indirect border controls on a national scale.[2]

Although indirect control was exercised against all ethnic groups, it was most significant with respect to Native Americans because of their unique legal status within each country and because of the relative inability of either country to control First Nations' movements through checkpoints. Native Americans' knowledge of local geography, the expansiveness of their familial ties, and their ability to slip past federal patrols made enforcing the border at the physical line, more often than not, a lesson in futility. At the same time, the economic, legal, racial, and political statuses of Native Americans in the United States and Canada made them particularly vulnerable to meddling from Indian affairs agents, army units, land surveyors, and treaty commissioners. As Lisa D. Barnett suggests in chapter 8 of this volume, Indian agents' interference with Indigenous spirituality encouraged them to attack broader patterns of mobility across the US borders with both Mexico and Canada. Relying on legal status and vulnerabilities, however, meant that the ability of both governments to exercise indirect control varied by region, tribe, and community. As a result, the strategies that worked on the prairies could not be translated to the Pacific Coast without significant modifications, creating a ragged and inconsistent set of borderland controls that remained in flux throughout the nineteenth and early twentieth centuries.

Indirect Control in the Prairies

In the 1860s and 1870s, the buffalo population, which had served as a principal food source for many plains communities, had become scarce, and by the early 1880s it had all but disappeared. Native American groups responded to the buffalo's destruction in a variety of ways, including selling land in exchange for rations and annuities and engaging in wage labor. In each case, however, the new economic strategies did little to re-create the level of independence that First Nations groups had maintained before the buffalo's destruction, giving Canada and the United States greater ability to interfere in the daily lives of Plains Indians. Canadian and American Indian agents, for example, began using Indian status, rations, and treaty payments as leverage to threaten and punish First Nations who violated the sanctity of national spaces.[3]

Both countries perceived the transnational movements of Native Americans as a financial liability, a diplomatic risk, a challenge to their sovereignty, and a disruption to their Indian policies. Persistent violence made the permeability of the border harder to ignore and provided a strong impetus for new border policies. During the early 1860s, for example, mounting conflicts between the Dakota and the US government created ample concern over border control. The Dakota had ceded parts of Minnesota, Iowa, and the Dakotas to the United States in 1815, 1836–1837, and 1851, but pressure for their land remained. The failure of the United States to pay the Dakota annuities promised under treaty, local traders' reluctance to supply goods on credit, and skirmishes between settlers and the Dakota fanned discontent. Between August 18 and 23, 1862, the Dakota responded to their long-standing grievances by launching a series of attacks in Minnesota that killed hundreds of settlers and threw the surrounding region into disarray. By late September, the US Army had broken Dakota resistance, forcing hundreds to flee from Minnesota to the Red River Settlement in British territory or face arrest. Once across the border, the Dakota refugees attempted to transform their past relationships with the British into contemporary support. The refugees produced flags and medals given to them by the British government during the War of 1812 and requested that Britain set land aside for them north of the border.

The refugees put Britain in a hard position. Britain lacked the troops necessary to evict the Dakota, and the sudden influx of people strained the nearby British and Métis communities. After numerous attempts to remove the Dakota from the Dominion's territory, the government offered the approximately 1,800 Dakota refugees in Canada a permanent reserve with two stipulations. First, Canada maintained that the land being offered was a sign of good faith rather than an obligation on the Canadian government's part. The Dakota would not be considered treaty Indians and would receive no annuities. Second, American Dakota entering Canada after the treaty would not be recognized as Canadian Indians by that country's Department of Indian Affairs (DIA) and would not be given a place on the reserve. Canada attempted to reaffirm the sanctity of the border. Past transgressions could be forgiven, but from this point forward, American Sioux were to remain in the United States. Canadian Sioux were to remain in Canada.[4]

Canada became far more reluctant to grant even partial recognition to American Indians who crossed into its jurisdiction by the late nineteenth century. In the 1870s, the DIA had created complex legal definitions of who qualified as a Canadian Indian, impacting Indigenous people's ability to claim access to land, rations, annuities, and resource-gathering sites. The Canadian Indian Act of 1876, for example, ruled that any Indian who resided for "five years continuously" in a foreign country would lose his or her status "unless the consent of the band with the approval of the Superintendent-General or his agent" was first obtained.[5] This policy divided sanctioned crossings from illegitimate ones, leaving any gray areas to the discretion of the department. Over time, Indian agents pushed to have reserves located farther from the border, increased their commitment to monitoring cross-border movements, and showed greater reluctance to assist Native American groups fleeing conflicts with the United States.[6]

The United States implemented a similar series of indirect border control measures to limit the benefits First Nations from Canada could reap by crossing into the United States. In 1885, Cree militants participated in an unsuccessful resistance against the Canadian government aimed at pressuring Canada to acknowledge the rights of First Nations and Métis. In the rebellion's aftermath, Little Bear's Cree entered the United States seeking sanctuary, much like the Dakota had done in the opposite direction two decades earlier. The Cree received a cold welcome upon their arrival. Local Indian agents prevented the Cree from residing on the reservations of "American" Indians, and the group struggled to find work in the surrounding towns.

In 1896, the US Congress appropriated $5,000 to rid the country of Canadian Cree who had claimed refuge in the United States after the rebellion. Montana's governor, John E. Rickards, argued that the Cree had violated gaming laws, looted cabins, and interfered with cattle grazing. Ultimately the argument rested on the idea that Canada, not the United States, should be responsible for these troublesome "British" Indians. The fact that the Cree had historic ties to land on both sides of the border was lost in the debate. Between June 20 and August 7, 1896, the United States forced Little Bear, Lucky Man, and more than 500 Indians across the line into Canada. The initial roundup included American-born Cree, Ojibwa, Gros Ventre, and Assiniboine. Intermarriages and close associations among some groups added to the confusion. American authorities considered Métis and Cree, for example, to be "Canadian" Indians regardless of their actual birthplace. Congress's orders assumed clarity of tribal identity, race, and nationality that simply did not exist.[7]

By the turn of the century, most of the so-called Canadian Cree had returned to Montana. Soldiers could evict Indians living in the wrong country, but unless a constant force remained stationed along the line, groups like the Cree could easily recross. A. E. Forget, a Canadian Indian commissioner, wrote to the superintendent general of Indian affairs that "it was not possible to do anything beyond the adoption of persuasive measures, to prevent their [the Cree's] exodus."[8]

In 1916, the United States granted Little Bear's Cree a reservation on the military reserve at Fort Assiniboine after conceding that denial of land recognition, annuities, and legal recognition had not deterred the Cree's residence. While the United States had failed to expel the Cree, it had succeeded in gutting the benefits of transnational mobility on the plains and increasing its risks. Little Bear's success in securing suitable land had taken almost three decades of suffering and precluded his ability to claim land and annuities in Canada. The fact that the Cree were willing to endure such great hardships to secure land is more suggestive of the poor treatment they received at the hands of the Canadian government than the ineffectuality of indirect control.[9]

Indirect Control on the Pacific Coast

British, Canadian, and American attempts to control the risks and benefits First Nations gained by crossing the border took a different form on the Pacific Coast than they did on the northern plains. Local circumstances limited the kinds of coercive measures the governments could use. First Nations maintained control over their subsistence along the coast for longer than they had on the plains, and British and American reliance on Native American laborers on the West Coast limited the kinds of economic sanctions the countries could impose until the end of the nineteenth century. Although British, Canadian, and American authority remained limited, each government attempted to restrict only the kinds of transnational movements it found most troubling and left the vast majority of crossings undisturbed. As the demographic, military, and economic contexts changed along the coast, Britain, Canada, and the United States expanded the ways they interfered with transnational identities, attacking the cultural ceremonies, economic opportunities, and familial bonds that spanned national lines. By the twentieth century, they had succeeded in using Indian status and reservation lands as a cudgel with which to enforce the national orderings they had envisioned during the nineteenth century.

During the 1860s, Britain and the United States succeeded in exerting periodic military control along the Pacific Coast, but the border policies they implemented remained limited. When there was no crisis to spur attempts to police the border, the boundary remained open and the national spaces hazy.[10] The Cascades and Rocky Mountains made it easier to travel between the coastal regions of Washington Territory and British Columbia than between the coast and either interior. As a result, businessmen, laborers, smugglers, and even law enforcement officials near the coast found it easy to develop social, economic, and personal ties that transcended national boundaries. They found it difficult to establish such connections within a national framework. The Ne-u-lub-vig, Misonks, Cow-e-na-chino, and Noot-hum-mic living in Washington Territory, for example, maintained strong commercial ties to the Hudson's Bay Company in British territory and weak ones within the United States. By choosing the path of least resistance, people on both sides of the border built regional connections in place of national ones.[11]

The specific labor demands of the canning and hops industries made these production facilities particularly receptive to using Native American and transnational labor. They needed large numbers of workers in the summer when the salmon ran and in September when the hops ripened. When the transnational labor migration of Native Americans peaked in 1885, as many as 6,000 First Nations from British Columbia (approximately 15–20 percent of the First Nations population) migrated seasonally to Washington. The participation of large numbers of Indigenous people in these industries worried Indian agents, because it limited the time the agents had to "civilize" Indians and provided Native Americans with money the US Office of Indian Affairs (OIA) and Canadian Department of Indian Affairs had no control over.

The seasonal nature of the canning and hops industries appealed to groups such as the Stó:lō, Swinomish, and Lummi, because it allowed First Nations to acquire commercial goods without interfering with other seasonal activities. For part of the year, First Nations communities prepared food for the winter. In July and August, these communities left for the canneries, leaving behind only a few individuals to take care of the young children. In September, thousands moved south to the hops fields. In the winter, some groups cut firewood or made woolen socks to sell to European settlers, while others engaged in local wage labor opportunities. The reliance of the regional economies in British Columbia and Washington on Native American labor allowed First Nations to retain their subsistence rights and their mobility. Attacking either risked disrupting the economic arrangements that had been made, and neither Canada nor the United States wished to lose access to an important source of labor.[12] European immigration to the Washington Territory and British Columbia grew during the mid-nineteenth century, decreasing the reliance local industries had on an Indigenous labor force.[13]

If the demographic changes had not been so pronounced, they might have been easy to miss among the complexities of early census-taking. In the nineteenth century, the OIA (United States) and DIA (Canada) produced estimates of the number of Indigenous people in each country that bore little resemblance to the numbers returned by the national censuses. The same government could count the same people in the same year and get different numbers each time. The difficulty of the enterprise and the fluidity of residence explains much of this variation. Differences in definitions, however, played an important role as well. In the United States, the national census initially counted only "civilized Indians," an amorphous category that left significant discretion in the hands of individual enumerators. The Office of Indian Affairs, for its own part, relied on both narrow categories (treaty people) and expansive ones (ethnicity) depending on the circumstances. Attempts to count Japanese and Chinese populations likely fared little better. Distrust created by exclusionary immigration policies provided significant incentives to avoid federal attention. Still, by almost any count, the demographic dominance that Native Americans had held in Washington in the 1860s had completely reversed two decades later. British Columbia experienced a slower but similar reversal. By 1911, First Nations represented well under 10 percent of British Columbia's population; they had been the majority just three decades earlier.[14]

Table 3.1. Washington's Population by Ethnic Origin, 1860–1910[15]

	Census			OIA
Year	White	Chinese	Indian	Indian
1860	11,138	—	426*	est. 31,000
1870	22,195	234	1,319*	est. 16,268
1880	67,199	3,186	4,405*	14,189
1890	340,513	3,260	3,655*	10,837
1900	496,304	3,629	10,039	9,827
1910	1,109,111	2,709	10,997	9,625

*Includes only "Civilized" Indians

Table 3.2. British Columbia's Population by Ethnic Origin, 1871–1911[16]

	Census				DIA
Year	White	Chinese	Japanese	Indian	Indian
1871	—	—	—	—	est. 45,000
1881	16,861	4,350	—	25,661	35,052 to 40,000
1891	65,527	9,386	—	23,257	35,202
1901	127,934	14,885	4,597	28,949	24,576
1911	318,914	19,568	8,587	20,134	24,581

Canada and the United States implemented increasingly aggressive Indian policies as demographic and economic changes eroded the protections that integration into labor economies had afforded groups like the Coast Salish. Indian agents, fishery patrols, and customs agents attacked First Nations' mobility, culture, land, and resource-gathering sites. In doing so, federal agencies began to adopt an interpretation of Indian status that neither granted First Nations the protections due to them under treaty nor aligned Indian policies with policies governing whites or other racial groups. Instead, federal agents in both countries created economic policies that maintained First Nations' separate legal, social, and economic classifications but transformed those classifications from an identity that had once protected Indigenous access to resources through treaty rights to one that used race to restrict their claims. When conflicts emerged between Indians and settlers, the federal governments supported white laborers and businessmen over Native American ones and passed a series of measures, including racially based fishing licenses, that restricted First Nations' ability to work.[17]

Controlling the border, however, remained a tricky proposition. Direct border control strategies struggled to address the needs of Canada, the United States, and Mexico. Military, police, and customs personnel, already swamped with other tasks, including controlling Chinese immigration, could not keep pace. On the Pacific Coast, the border was too long, the transnational connections that First Nations communities maintained were too entrenched, and the geography was too complex to be guarded by a handful of overworked and underpaid personnel. Faced with a difficult situation, federal administrators turned to indirect methods of control to help curtail the benefits Native Americans could gain from moving between national spaces. To do so, Canada and the United States targeted the social and economic bonds that connected transnational communities together on the Pacific Coast and punished those who resisted.

Indirect control showed signs of success. The drive to assimilate First Nations, their exclusion from productive resource sites, and the competition that Native American workers faced from Chinese, Japanese, and white workers all diminished the benefits that groups such as the Stó:lō and Lummi gained from their transnational mobility. The hops industry, which had once encouraged the seasonal migration of thousands of Indians from British Columbia to the United States, stopped being the reliable source of income it had once been. Market fluctuations, labor competition, and the appearance of the hops louse—which ravaged hops production—lessened the industry's reliance on Native American labor and, as a result, reduced the income many communities had come to expect. By 1896, an Indian agent noted in his annual report of the Tulalip Agency in Washington that there existed little inducement for the Indians of the agency to travel to the hops fields because the value of hops and the need for Native American labor had diminished so severely.[18]

The loss of reliable opportunities diminished the economic incentives for border crossings but did not eliminate them entirely. The Kyukahts from the Alberni Agency in British Columbia continued to sell their baskets in Washington in 1902. First Nations found work in the same areas of employment as in the past, albeit in lesser numbers. Labor shortages and short growing seasons in the hops, berry-picking, and canning industries provided periodic surges in employment opportunities. The loss of consistent work, however, eliminated one of the primary motivations for transnational mobility that had been so commonplace in the 1880s.[19]

By the twentieth century, Canada and the United States possessed a variety of viable strategies to pressure First Nations living on the West Coast into adopting a single national identity. The US Army did not forcibly evict "Canadian" Indians living in Washington as it did on the prairies to the east, but economic restrictions eliminated many of the benefits that Native American communities could expect to gain by crossing national lines. As had happened on the plains, economic misfortune allowed the federal governments to use annuities, Indian status, and land recognition to punish those who continued to maintain regional rather than national ties. Both governments began to assault groups such as the Sinixt, who retained ambiguous national identities, by using all manner of inconsistencies—including creating temporary band status, amalgamating and then unamalgamating reserves, and conflating band membership with residency—to strip them of legal protections. Ambiguity ceased to allow Native American communities to play one government against the other. Instead, uncertainty became a liability that allowed federal officials to strip First Nations communities, such as the Arrow Lakes Band, of their title to land and resource-gathering sites.[20]

The Withering of Direct Control

During the early twentieth century, direct forms of control began to impact the transnational movements of non-Indigenous peoples to a much greater extent, owing in part to expanded funding to agencies such as customs and immigration. At the same time, a series of legal challenges brought into question what jurisdiction, if any, these agencies had over Native Americans. In 1924, for example, the United States passed the Indian Citizenship Act and the National Origins Act, which created an unintentional challenge to the transnational movements of Native American laborers along the northern border's entire length. The Indian Citizenship Act made "all non-citizen Indians born within the territorial limits of the United States . . . citizens."[21] Passed the same year, the National Origins Act decreed that "no alien ineligible to citizenship shall be admitted to the United States."[22] Although the drafters of the National Origins Act had intended to use it to keep out Japanese and Chinese immigrants, immigration agents used it to prevent Canadian Indians, who were inadmissible for citizenship under the American Indian Citizenship Act, from crossing the border.

Immigration agents' interpretation of the provisions of the National Origins Act fostered opposition from both the settler communities that still relied on Indigenous labor and groups like the Mohawk that launched legal challenges.[23] A successful legal challenge by Paul Diabo, a Mohawk ironworker from Québec, in 1927 and a subsequent congressional clarification in April 1928 solidified the rights of Indigenous border crossers.[24] The 1928 congressional clarification, however, left gray areas about who fulfilled the criteria of being an "Indian." Nonenrolled mixed-bloods blurred the lines that Indian agents and immigration officials attempted to draw, forcing them to adopt functional definitions of identity based on blood quantum and tribal identity, which were hard to establish in practice. The decision made Indian status and federal recognition an integral facet of the ability of First Nations to cross the border unmolested.[25]

The Bureau of Immigration's defeat in 1928 over the interpretation of the 1924 acts neutered the kinds of direct border control strategies that Canada and the United States could pursue. By that point, however, both countries had ample experience influencing the ways Native Americans interacted with national spaces through other means. Over the course of the late nineteenth and early twentieth centuries, Canada and the United States developed a suite of indirect forms of control that undermined the motivations First Nations had for maintaining transnational connections on the prairies and West Coast. Federal administrators chose reservation locations away from the border to increase the travel times of transnational movements. They withheld treaty goods from groups who disobeyed Indian agents or spent too much time beyond the confines of the nation-state. Both federal governments attacked the cultural and economic practices that drew First Nations communities on both sides of the border together. Indian status and legal recognition became tools that Canada and the United States used to control how Indians moved between national spaces.

Conclusion

Federal policy tore away the connections that Native American communities maintained across the border and encouraged them to adopt a single nationality. Many groups refused to do so and have maintained transnational connections to this day. The kinds of benefits they could gain from this movement, however, eroded over time. The potential risks, as seen by Canada's treatment of the Sinixt and by the Cree's struggle to secure a reservation, grew in significance. Today, battles over tobacco and competing interpretations of the Jay Treaty continue to plague borderland communities at places like Akwesasne and Kahnawá:ke. As Devin Clancy and Tyler Chartrand outline in chapter 12 in this volume, coercive federal control remains. Canada and the United States continue to push the idea that legal recognition as an Indian could be achieved only on one side of the border or the other. Ambiguity—which had once allowed Native American communities to circumvent federal authority—had become a powerful tool to strip groups of their legal title to land and resources.

Notes

1. I would like to thank Andrew Graybill, Stephen A. Aron, Richard White, and three anonymous reviewers for their feedback at various stages of this chapter as well as Stanford University and the Social Science and Humanities Research Council for their financial support. This chapter was first published by the *Journal of the Canadian Historical Association / Revue de la Société historique du Canada* in an unabridged form.

2. Sheila McManus, *The Line Which Separates: Race, Gender, and the Making of the Alberta-Montana Borderlands* (Lincoln: University of Nebraska Press, 2005), 71–74; Andrew R. Graybill, *Policing the Great Plains: Rangers, Mounties, and the North American Frontier, 1875–1910* (Lincoln: University of Nebraska Press, 2007), 61.

3. F. W. Seward to Sir Edward Thornton, February 13, 1879, "Papers Relating to the Sioux Indians of U.S. who have Taken Refuge in Canadian Territory," December 13, 1875–April 14, 1879, microfilm CA1 IA H5P37, 133, University of Waterloo, Waterloo, ON (hereafter cited as Papers Relating to the Sioux); David G. McCrady, *Living with Strangers: The Nineteenth-Century Sioux and the Canadian-American Borderlands* (Lincoln: University of Nebraska Press, 2006), 4, 92, 110; Michel Hogue, "Disputing the

Medicine Line: The Plains Crees and the Canadian-American Border, 1876–1885," *Montana: The Magazine of Western History* 52, no. 4 (December 1, 2002): 4–11; Peter Douglas Elias, *The Dakota of the Canadian Northwest: Lessons for Survival* (Regina, SK: Canadian Plains Research Center, 2002), 57, 83, 222; Andrew C. Isenberg, *The Destruction of the Bison: An Environmental History, 1750–1920* (Cambridge, UK: Cambridge University Press, 2000), 140–143; William A. Dobak, "Killing the Canadian Buffalo, 1821–1881," *Western Historical Quarterly* 27, no. 1 (1996): 33–52; McManus, *The Line Which Separates*, 73; Gerhard J. Ens, "The Border, the Buffalo, and the Métis of Montana," *The Borderlands of the American and Canadian Wests: Essays on Regional History of the Forty-Ninth Parallel*, ed. Sterling Evans (Lincoln: University of Nebraska Press, 2006), 147.

4. "Notes Taken at a Meeting between the Lieut. Governor of the NW Territories Attended by the Officers of the Mounted Police at the Station and a Deputation of About 20 Sioux Indians Headed by a Chief Named White Cap at Swan River on the 29th Day of June '77," June 29, 1877, RG 10, Indian Affairs, Black Series, reel C-10114, vol. 3651, file 8527 [online], Library and Archives Canada, Ottawa, ON (hereafter cited as LAC); Bernard to Alexander Morris, July 16, 1874, Alexander Morris (Lieutenant-Governor's collection) MG 12 B1, microfilm reel M135, no. 811, Archives of Manitoba, Winnipeg, MB (hereafter cited as AM); Elias, *Dakota of the Canadian Northwest*, 18–19, 37–41, 57, 152–159, 205; D. Gunn et al., "Petition," c. 1872, "Manitoba—Proposal for Reservation for Refugee Sioux Indians from the United States," RG 10, Indian Affairs, vol. 3577, file 422 [online], LAC; McCrady, *Living with Strangers*, 16, 105–106; Alvin C. Gluek Jr., "The Sioux Uprising: A Problem in International Relations," *Minnesota History* 34, no. 8 (Winter 1955): 320, 324; J. A. Markle to Superintendent General of Indian Affairs, August 16, 1900, Department of Indian Affairs Annual Reports (1864–1990) [online], 132, LAC (hereafter cited as DIA ARO); John D. Bessler, *Legacy of Violence: Lynch Mobs and Executions in Minnesota* (Minneapolis: University of Minnesota Press, 2003), 25–46; John S. Bowman, *Chronology of Wars* (New York: Infobase, 2003), 86–88; Gontran Laviolette, *The Sioux Indians in Canada* (Regina: Saskatchewan Historical Society, 1944), 31–35.

5. "An Act to Amend and Consolidate the Laws Respecting Indians Assented to 12th April, 1876," in *Acts of the Parliament of the United Kingdom of Great Britain and Ireland* (Ottawa, ON: Brown Chamberlin, 1876), 44.

6. D. R. Cameron to Alexander Morris, April 29, 1874, Alexander Morris (Lieutenant-Governor's collection) MG 12 B1, microfilm reel M135, no. 718, AM; McCrady, *Living with Strangers*, 73–74; Dobak, "Killing the Canadian Buffalo," 48; H. Richardson to Assistant Commissioner Irvine, May 26, 1876, 1–2; G. Irvine to Lieut-Colonel Richardson, July 1, 1876, 2; J. M. Walsh to J. F. Macleod, December 31, 1876, 9–10; and W. T. Sherman to G. W. McCrary, July 16, 1877, 36–37, all in Papers Relating to the Sioux; Hayter Reed to Superintendent General of Indian Affairs, September 24, 1886, in "Northwest Territories—Sioux Indians Crossing the International Boundary and Requesting Direction as to Whether They Will Be Allowed to Stay or Be Sent Back to the United States," RG 10, Indian Affairs, vol. 3766, file 32957 [online], LAC; Indian Commissioner for Manitoba and Northwest Territories, "Indians Enrolled in Canada and United States," May 26, 1908, 3, RG 10, vol. 3573, file 142, reel C-10188 [online], LAC. For examples of sanctioned crossings, see "Alnwick Agency—Request from Allan

and Wellington Salt, for Permission to Reside in the United States," RG 10, Indian Affairs, vol. 2676, file 135, 883; "Alnwick Agency—Application of Hannah Eliza Cox (Mrs. James Cox) and George Cowe for Permission to Reside in the United States," RG 10, vol. 2821, file 168, 097 [online]; and Deputy Superintendent General of Indian Affairs to John Thackeray, December 7, 1895, all in LAC.

7. Michel Hogue, "Crossing the Line: Race, Nationality, and the Deportation of the 'Canadian' Crees in the Canada-U.S. Borderlands 1890–1900," in *The Borderlands of the American and Canadian Wests: Essays on Regional History of the Forty-Ninth Parallel*, ed. Sterling Evans (Lincoln: University of Nebraska Press, 2006), 155–171; Hans Peterson, "Imasees and His Band: Canadian Refugees after the North-West Rebellion," *Western Canadian Journal of Anthropology* 8, no. 1 (1978): 30, 33; "Relief for the Cree Indians, Montana Territory," H.R. Rep. No. 50–341, at 1–6 (1889).

8. A. E. Forget to Superintendent of Indian Affairs, November 20, 1897, 216, DIA ARO.

9. Little Bear to J. D. McLean, March 30, 1905, David Laird to Little Bear, January 24, 1906, Little Bear to Secretary of the Interior, February 10, 1905, Superintendent of Indian Affairs to Governor General in Council, August 1, 1908, and Little Bear to Frank Oliver, November 7, 1905, all in Geneva Stump's Rocky Boy Collection, M7937, Glenbow Archives (hereafter cited as Rocky Boy Collection); Ed Stamper, Helen Windy, and Ken Morsette Jr., eds., *The History of the Chippewa Cree of Rocky Boy's Indian Reservation* (Box Elder, MT: Stone Child College, 2008), 11–16; Brenden Rensink, "Native but Foreign: Indigenous Transnational Refugees and Immigrants in the U.S.-Canadian and U.S.-Mexican Borderlands 1880–Present" (PhD diss., University of Nebraska, 2010), 5–6; Verne Dusenberry, "The Rocky Boy Indians," *Montana Magazine of History* 4, no. 1 (Winter 1954): 10–14; Michel Hogue, "Crossing the Line," 166.

10. M. T. Simmons to Edward R. Geary, July 1, 1860, in "No. 78," 190–191, Office of Indian Affairs Annual Reports of the Commissioner of Indian Affairs, University of Wisconsin Digital Collections, Madison, WI (hereafter cited as OIA ARO); Henry A. Webster to Calvin H. Hale, 1862, in "G4 Territory of Washington—Treaties of Neah Bay and Point-No-Point 1855," 410, OIA ARO; John Lutz, "Work, Sex, and Death on the Great Thoroughfare: Annual Migrations of 'Canadian Indians' to the American Pacific Northwest," in *Parallel Destinies: Canadian-American Relations West of the Rockies*, ed. Ken S. Coates and John M. Findlay (Seattle: University of Washington Press, 2002), 89–94.

11. E. A. Starling to Anson Dart, September 1, 1852, in "No. 71," 171, OIA ARO; Lutz, *Makúk*, 171; Jeremiah Gorsline, ed., *Shadows of Our Ancestors: Readings in the History of Klallam-White Relations* (Port Townsend, WA: Empty Bowl, 1992), 82; Hal J. Cole to Commissioner of Indian Affairs, August 15, 1891, 441, OIA ARO; Lutz, "Work, Sex, and Death," 82; James Douglas to Archibald Barclay, October 5, 1852, in "On the Affairs of Vancouver Island," 101, James Douglas Fond, A/C/20/Vi/2A, British Columbia Archive, Victoria, BC (hereafter cited as BCA); Coll Thrush, *Native Seattle: Histories from the Crossing-Over Place* (Seattle: University of Washington Press, 2007), 41, 47–49, 71; George Swanaset, "George Swanaset: Narrative of a Personal Document," 10, Melville Jacobs Collection (narrative taken by Paul Fetzer, 1951), 1693-91-13-001, box 112, V 206, folder 10, University of Washington Special Collections, Seattle, WA; Elizabeth Rose

Lew-Williams, "The Chinese Must Go: Immigration, Deportation and Violence in the 19th-Century Pacific Northwest" (PhD diss., Stanford University, 2011), 55–56; J. H. Jenkins to Colonel M. T. Simmons, May 27, 1858, in "No. 82," 237, OIA ARO.

12. W. H. Lomas to Superintendent General of Indian Affairs, August 7, 1885, 80, DIA ARO; I. W. Powell to Superintendent General of Indian Affairs, November 5, 1886, 98, DIA ARO; Ira B. Myers to A. W. Bash, August 9, 1883, RG 36, US Customs Service, Puget Sound, box 109, Letters Received from SubPorts and Inspectors, San Juan, file 4, National Archive Pacific Northwest Region, Seattle, WA (hereafter cited as NA PNR); Lissa K. Wadewitz, *The Nature of Borders: Salmon, Boundaries, and Bandits on the Salish Sea* (Seattle: University of Washington Press, 2012), 68–72; Edward Bristow to Charles M. Buchanan, July 15, 1902, RG 75, Annual Reports Tulalip Agency, box 1, 1863–1908, folder 1902, NA PNR; Edward Bristow to Charles M. Buchanan, July 7, 1903, RG 75, Letters Received—Tulalip Agency, Swinomish, box 7, 1899–1904, NA PNR; Russel Lawrence Barsh, "Puget Sound Indian Demography, 1900–1920: Migration and Economic Integration," *Ethnohistory* 43, no. 1 (Winter 1996): 66, 69–70, 77–80; Gorsline, *Shadows of Our Ancestors*, 82; Lutz, *Makúk*, 93, 190; Thrush, *Native Seattle*, 111; A. W. Neill to Frank Pedley, June 30, 1906, 255, DIA ARO; Daniel L. Boxberger, "In and Out of the Labor Force: The Lummi Indians and the Development of the Commercial Salmon Fishery of North Puget Sound, 1880–1900," *Ethnohistory* 35, no. 2 (April 1, 1988): 172.

13. For the geographic distribution of these changes, see Cole Harris, *The Resettlement of British Columbia: Essays on Colonialism and Geographical Change* (Vancouver: University of British Columbia Press, 1997), 149–153.

14. Benjamin Hoy, "Uncertain Counts: The Struggle to Enumerate First Nations in Canada and the United States 1870–1911," *Ethnohistory* 62, no. 4 (2015): 729–750.

15. Decennial Census: United States Bureau of the Census, *Thirteenth Census of the United States 1910: Bulletin Population: United States—Color or Race, Nativity, Parentage, and Sex* (Government Printing Office, 1913), 82; United States Census Office, *Compendium of the Tenth Census of the United States*, vol. 1 (Government Printing Office, 1883), 377; United States Census Office, *Compendium of the Eleventh Census: 1890. Part 1—Population* (Government Printing Office, 1892), 469–470, 474. Office of Indian Affairs: OIA ARO, UWDC, 1860, 21; 1870, 16; 1880, iv; 1890, 544; 1900, 653–654; 1910, 60.

16. Decennial Census: Canada, *The Canada Year Book 1911, Second Series* (Ottawa: C. H. Parmelee, 1912), 16; Canada, *Fifth Census of Canada 1911: Religion, Origins, Birthplace, Citizenship, Literacy, and Infirmities, By Provinces, Districts, and Sub-Districts*, vol. 2 (Ottawa: C. H. Parmelee, 1913), 370; estimates for all populations in 1891 based on BCA, GR-0429, box 3, file 2, British Columbia, Attorney General, Correspondence Inward, B09318 69/94, George Johnson to Minister of Agriculture and Statistics, "Dispute with Ottawa on Indian Census," 1894; BCA, GR-0429, box 3, file 2, British Columbia, Attorney General, Correspondence Inward, 1894, "Re Census of British Columbia." Department of Indian Affairs: DIA ARO, LAC, 1871, 37; 1881, 140, 223; 1891, 253; 1901, part 2, 182; 1911, part 2, 58.

17. Daniel L. Boxberger, "Ethnicity and Labor in the Puget Sound Fishing Industry, 1880–1935," *Ethnology* 33, no. 2 (April 1, 1994): 183; "White Fisherman Are Best for

B.C.," *New Advertiser*, December 17, 1911, in Henry Doyle Collection, acc. 861, box 3, book 1908–1911, University of Washington Special Collections, Seattle, WA; Wadewitz, *Nature of Borders*, 78–87; Daniel L. Boxberger, "The Not So Common," in *Be of Good Mind: Essays on the Coast Salish*, ed. Bruce Granville Miller (Vancouver: University of British Columbia Press, 2007), 60; Lutz, *Makúk*, 239–242.

18. D. C. Govan to Commissioner of Indian Affairs, August 28, 1896, RG 75, Annual Reports Tulalip Agency, box 1, 1863–1908, folder 1896, NA PNR; Jean Barman, *The West beyond the West: A History of British Columbia* (Toronto: University of Toronto Press, 1991), 160; McNeff Brothers to John W. Summers, July 20, 1925, RG 85, INS, entry 9, box 6585, 55466/182, National Archives and Records Administration, Washington, DC (hereafter cited as NARA); Great Britain, Foreign Office, *Diplomatic and Consular Reports. Annual Series. United States, San Francisco*, 1891, 906:27.

19. A. W. Neill to Frank Pedley, June 30, 1906, 255; Alan W. Neill to Frank Pedley, July 26, 1905, 248; and Harry Guillod to Superintendent General of Indian Affairs, August 27, 1902, 265, all in DIA ARO.

20. E. B. Merritt to Secretary of the Interior, November 10, 1923, and C. F. Hauke to D. W. Lambuth, August 14, 1924, RG 75, Tulalip Agency, Records of Court of Indian Offences 1907–1947, folder 1; and Edward Bristow to Jesse E. Flanders, December 30, 1908, RG 75, Letters Received—Tulalip Agency, Swinomish, box 8, folder 4, all in NA PNR; Andrea Geiger, "Crossed by the Border: The U.S.-Canada Border and Canada's 'Extinction' of the Arrow Lakes Band, 1890–1956," *Western Legal History* 23, no. 2 (Summer/Fall 2010): 121–153.

21. "An Act to Authorize the Secretary of the Interior to Issue Certificates of Citizenship to Indians," Pub. L. No. 68–175, 43 Stat. 253 (1924).

22. "An Act to Limit the Immigration of Aliens into the United States, and for Other Purposes [Immigration Act of 1924]," H.R. 7995, 68th Cong. (1924).

23. McNeff Brothers to John W. Summers, July 20 1925, RG 85, INS, entry 9, box 6585, 55466/182, NARA.

24. Gerald F. Reid, "Illegal Alien? The Immigration Case of Mohawk Ironworker Paul K. Diabo," *Proceedings of the American Philosophical Association* 151, no. 1 (March 2007): 72–73; Clinton Rickard, *Fighting Tuscarora: The Autobiography of Chief Clinton Rickard*, ed. Barbara Graymont (Syracuse, NY: Syracuse University Press, 1973), 76–77; United States ex rel. Diabo v. McCandless, 18 F.2d 282, LEXIS 1053 (E.D. Pa., 1927); W. W. Husband to Charles Curtis, October 3, 1927, RG 85, INS, entry 9, box 6585, 55466/182a, NARA.

25. Rickard, *Fighting Tuscarora*, 90, 112–113, 119; McCandless, Commissioner of Immigration v. United States ex rel. Diabo, 25 F.2d 71, U.S. App. LEXIS 2899 (3d Cir., 1928); J. Henry Scattergood to Mr. Hull, September 22, 1930, and John D. Johnson, "Admission into the United States of American Indians Born in Canada," RG 85, INS, entry 9, box 6586, 55466/182b, NARA; "An Act to Exempt American Indians Born in Canada from the Operation of the Immigration Act of 1924," Pub. L. No. 76–194, § 716, 45 Stat. 401 (1928).

PART II Solidifying States,
Testing Boundaries

To Protect and Police

FOUR

Mexican Consuls in the American Borderlands
at the Turn of the Twentieth Century

MARÍA DE JESÚS DUARTE

In the summer of 1891, Montana's district attorney
brought horse-theft and rape charges against Fernando Portillo, an ambitious, young Mexican man
from Texas who sought to expand his horse-trading business into the
US-Canada borderlands.[1] Portillo's legal conundrum had started immediately after he closed his first horse sale with a Mr. Graham. Instead of paying Portillo, Graham accused him of selling a stolen horse and raping his
wife. Montana authorities sided with Graham and apprehended Portillo,
whom they branded as a horse thief. Portillo found out the hard way that
Americans in Montana, just as in Texas, often used horse-theft and rape
accusations to criminalize Mexicans. The way they achieved this, though,
spoke to the social and legal realities in the US-Canada and US-Mexico
borderlands. As the historians Andrew Graybill, William D. Carrigan, and
Clive Webb have contended, in the Southwest borderlands, alleged horse
thieves and rapists often met their fates at the hands of a lynch mob or
were killed by persons unknown as they purportedly tried to escape from
prison or police forces.[2] The extrajudicial violence that particularly characterized Anglo Texas society contrasted with Anglo Montanans' restraint in
using violent tactics toward nonwhite people. Instead, as the Portillo case
shows, Montanans relied on police units and legal institutions to punish
cattle thieves, contrabandists, and rapists from the Cree Indian tribe and
other nonwhites, such as Portillo.[3]

Facing a severe judicial sentence in the hostile Montana courts, Portillo turned to the Mexican government as his best hope to save himself. Portillo presented himself as a worthy citizen of Mexico fluent in English as a result of having lived for around twenty years in Texas. However, he then learned that, in accordance with Mexico's 1886 Nationality and Citizenship Law, he had lost his Mexican citizenship for having resided for more than ten years in the United States without authorization from his home government. As this chapter shows, the 1886 law entitled the twenty-two Mexican consular posts in the United States to act as guardians of Mexican citizenship. This chapter contends that Mexico's consular policies under the Porfirio Díaz administration (1876–1911) exemplify the contradictory yet authoritarian agenda designed to protect and police Mexican emigrants' ties to Mexico and their disenfranchisement from the American body politic. In the process, the ten-year absentee clause left many Mexican immigrants to the United States stateless. Fernando Portillo is one of dozens of Mexicans who endured the dramatic effects of the 1886 law at a time when anti-Mexican hostility in the United States peaked in the late nineteenth and early twentieth centuries.[4] Their cases offer a fascinating lens on consular protection practices and Mexican citizenship and identity formation processes in the American borderlands prior to the nationalist policies brought about by the Mexican Revolution.

Anti-Mexican sentiments in the American borderlands and a hardening of US laws defining the limits of citizenship rights for Mexican immigrants in the United States allowed Mexican consuls to shape and police the parameters of ties of Mexicanness and participation in the American body politic at the turn of the twentieth century. Paralleling immigration enforcement dynamics along the US-Canada border as analyzed by Thomas A. Klug in chapter 5, I show that Mexican consuls adjusted national policing practices to respond to the realities of the US-Mexico border, and as a result immigration and consular bureaucracies extended the power of national governments to the borderlands region. The Mexican government relied on a consular network of twenty-two posts located in the United States that carried out a protective yet controlling agenda toward Mexican nationals.[5] Consuls prevented their compatriots from becoming US citizens, prompting them instead to remain full-fledged Mexican citizens by acquiring a *matrícula* identity certificate. This page-long certificate issued at Mexican consulates in the United States listed the bearer's physical description, his or her literacy status, place of birth, residence in the United States, and signature.[6] A *matrícula* identified its bearer as a Mexican citizen in compliance with the 1886 ten-year absentee clause.

Accordingly, *matrícula* carriers became entitled to consular protective services in the United States.

This chapter draws on borderlands scholarship to examine the ways in which Mexican and US authorities increased their efforts to define the US-Mexico divide and enforce laws in those borderlands.[7] It joins Thomas A. Klug's and James Dupree's contributions in this volume (chapters 5 and 6, respectively) in expanding borderlands historiography by showing the centrality of ground-level enforcement of federal policies in the US-Canada and US-Mexico borderlands at the turn of the twentieth century. It presents Mexican consuls in the United States as central protagonists in President Díaz's efforts to police Mexican communities residing in the border region.[8] While the Díaz administration notoriously used repressive tactics to silence its opponents in the United States during the 1890s and early 1900s, less known are its consular policies to control Mexican citizens there by protecting them from the hostility of US citizens. Thus, these consular policies complicate the common depictions of the Díaz administration as eminently repressive and despotic toward its critics and Mexican emigrants. However, Díaz's consular-led strategies policed Mexicans abroad by reinforcing their ties to Mexico and demanding they remain disenfranchised from the American body politic.

The Díaz government believed that its consular practices nurtured citizens' patriotism. In this view, the acquisition of a consular *matrícula* maintained expatriates' *mexicanidad*, or Mexicanness.[9] Through the 1886 citizenship law, the Díaz government regulated Mexican citizenship, which became contingent on an individual's place of birth and length of absence from Mexico. On the one hand, the Díaz government instructed consular authorities in the United States to revoke the rights of those whose lengthy residencies raised doubts about their patriotism and loyalty to Mexico. On the other, it advanced a notion of Mexican citizenship anchored in a patriotic sentiment of *mexicanidad*, linked to Independence Day, Cinco de Mayo, and an exaltation of national heroes ranging from the Aztec emperor Cuauhtémoc to the Indigenous, liberal president Benito Juárez. The Díaz administration expected Mexican emigrants to express their Mexicanness and embrace the glorious past of the Mexican nation as outlined by their home government.

Despite consular efforts to Mexicanize emigrants, many of them did not learn about the 1886 law or the *matrícula* document until they had the need for consular assistance. Such was the case with Fernando Portillo, who learned of this policy when he asked the Mexican minister in

Washington, DC, for legal assistance with his ordeal in Montana's court system. After twenty years of residence in Texas, Portillo was "not capable of writing myself sufficiently well in Spanish."[10] Nonetheless, he remained a full-fledged Mexican citizen, because "I have never renounced my allegiance to the Mexican Government; never have become a citizen of the United States, or any other country, except Mexico; and still am a subject of Mexico and a citizen thereof, being but temporarily absent and am very desirous of returning there to my native country, my beloved Mexico."[11] Despite this professed patriotism, Minister Matías Romero explained to Portillo that, according to the 1886 law, he had lost his Mexican citizenship rights due to his two-decade residence outside of Mexico and his not having applied for a consular-issued *matrícula* identification. As a result, the Díaz government had no obligation to assist him. This decision rendered Portillo stateless and at the mercy of an unsympathetic justice system far from his homeland.

Mexico's 1886 citizenship law paralleled the 1876 Canadian Indian Act, discussed by Benjamin Hoy in chapter 3 of this volume, which empowered Canada's Department of Indian Affairs officials to determine who qualified as a Canadian Indian based on a five-year residency abroad. Mexican consuls applied the 1886 ten-year absentee clause to monitor emigrants' ties to the Mexican nation. Mexican consuls sought to establish the *matrícula* as an emblem of Mexican identity in the United States. However, records from consulates with large Mexican communities (such as in San Antonio, El Paso, Laredo, Los Angeles, and Phoenix) show that Mexicans did not embrace the *matrícula* program. For the most part, these consulates issued fewer than 200 *matrícula* certificates annually.[12] Scant data notwithstanding, it informed the Díaz administration's consular policies directed at defending loyal citizens and monitoring opposition toward its government from within Mexican communities in the United States.

Consuls to Protect and Police Mexicans beyond National Borders

Throughout the nineteenth century, Mexican authorities established firm policing protocols for government critics and foreign citizens residing in Mexico. Distrust of foreigners seeking to belong to the "great Mexican family" justified meticulous scrutiny of a naturalization applicant's life and activities.[13] Suspicion prevailed for naturalized Mexicans and foreigners despite their demonstration of honest behavior and gainful em-

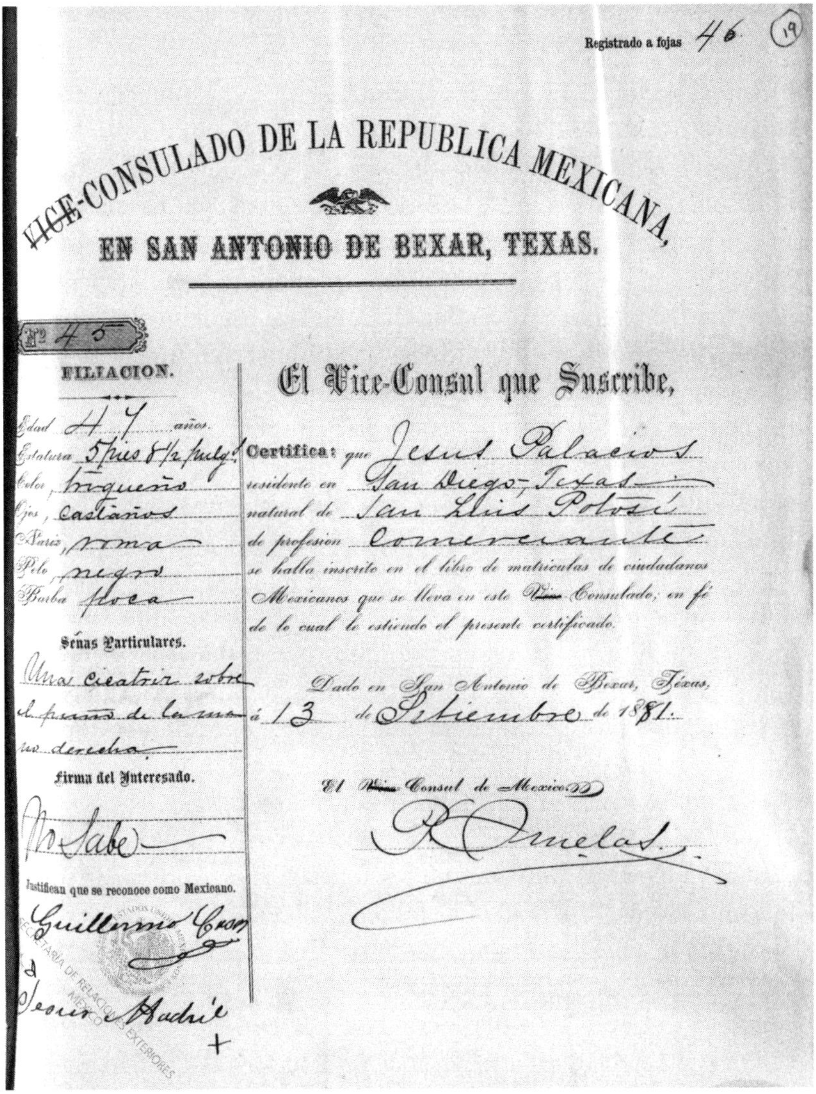
Registrado a fojas 46 (19)

VICE-CONSULADO DE LA REPUBLICA MEXICANA
EN SAN ANTONIO DE BEXAR, TEXAS.

Nº 45

FILIACION.

Edad 47 años.
Estatura 5 pies 8½ pulg.
Color trigueño
Ojos castaños
Nariz roma
Pelo negro
Barba poca

Señas Particulares.
Una cicatriz sobre el puño de la mano derecha.

Firma del Interesado.
No Sabe

Justifican que se reconoce como Mexicano.
Guillermo Cros
Jesus Madrid +

El Vice-Consul que Suscribe,

Certifica: que Jesus Palacios residente en San Diego, Texas natural de San Luis Potosí de profesion Comerciante se halla inscrito en el libro de matrículas de ciudadanos Mexicanos que se lleva en este Vice-Consulado; en fé de lo cual le extiendo el presente certificado.

Dado en San Antonio de Bexar, Téxas, á 13 de Setiembre de 1881.

El Vice-Consul de Mexico
R. Ornelas.

Figure 4.1. *Matrícula* identification certificate issued by the Mexican consulate in San Antonio, Texas, in 1881. Archivo Histórico Genaro Estrada. Acervo Histórico Diplomático. Secretaría de Relaciones Exteriores. México, 28-9-8, Matrículas de nacionalidad mexicana expedidas por el Condado de Bexar y por el Consulado de México en San Antonio, 1881.

ployment.[14] These policing practices informed Díaz's protective yet controlling consular policies toward Mexican citizens in the US borderlands. To identify and quell dissent among immigrants in the United States, the Díaz government redefined the structure of the Mexican consular system. It professionalized the consular corps by requiring strong command of the language of the country in which they aspired to be located, as well as proficiency in Mexican, international, and maritime mercantile law.[15] Although consular appointments often responded to Porfirian nepotism rather than adherence to education and language requirements, most appointees had strong academic credentials and a commitment to Díaz's agenda toward Mexicans in the US borderlands.

A permeable US-Mexico border facilitated the unrestricted entrance of around 70,000 Mexican-born individuals, according to 1880 census figures for the US Southwest.[16] Mexican laborers' arrival coincided with American agricultural cycles or mining and railroad construction work in the US borderlands. Most immigrants came from rural areas where Díaz's modernization policies broke up communal landholdings in southeastern Mexico, transferred them to foreign entrepreneurs, and disrupted subsistence farming and stock-raising activities. These policies forced thousands of peasants to seek employment at local haciendas or migrate to northern Mexico or the United States.[17] The Díaz administration accompanied the influx of emigrants by establishing consular offices in state capitals, main ports, and remote boomtowns in the US borderlands. By 1887, there were twenty-two Mexican consulates in the United States, ten of which served Mexican communities in Texas, Arizona, California, New Mexico, and Colorado.[18] A general consulate headquartered in San Francisco supervised consulates in the Southwest.[19] The consulate general in New York oversaw consular offices in the South, Midwest, and East Coast regions.

During the early 1820s, a newly independent Mexican nation asserted its sovereignty by attaining diplomatic recognition and establishing consular posts in important maritime and commercial centers across Europe, Latin America, and the United States. Mexican consuls collected fees on export certificates, passports, and cargo and passenger ships, which they used to cover consular officials' salaries and maintenance costs.[20] However, not all consulates saw robust commercial activity to provide them with funds for their proper functioning. As a result, the Mexican secretary of foreign affairs sent additional funds to offset the monthly deficits of consulates located in the US borderlands.[21] Mexican consuls prioritized the promotion of commercial relations with the United States, but they also had a mandate to defend "the good name of Mexico [and] inform the government of everything they deem of interest . . . for authorities, and its inhabitants, mainly of those engaged in trade and commerce."[22] During the late nineteenth and early twentieth centuries, widespread hostility toward Mexican immigrants increased the number of consular assistance petitions submitted. In those petitions, Mexicans demanded consuls' attention to cases of possible maladministration of justice toward their compatriots, such as long imprisonment without adjudication or lengthy sentencing for minor offenses.[23] Consular authorities documented immigrants' allegations of impartiality of the US justice system and of violence toward Mexicans.[24]

An examination of consular correspondence records from the turn of the twentieth century reveals the ways in which Mexican petitioners had mastered the Mexicanization discourse promoted by consular officials in the United States. For the most part, Mexican petitioners adopted the role of meek and patronizing supplicants. For example, the Texas prisoner Cipriano Cárdenas asked Consul Plutarco Ornelas in San Antonio, Texas, for assistance to fight bogus claims regarding a misdemeanor that had landed him in jail. In his letter to Consul Ornelas, Cárdenas said he considered Ornelas his only ally because "after God, I place my last hope in You being You the father of the poor, orphans and prisoners, and who else should I plea to if not You and only in You I await the remedy to my affliction."[25] Similarly, another Mexican prisoner, Antonio Llamas, asked Vice-Consul Rufino Vélez in Tucson for immediate assistance in getting a fair trial. He urged Vélez to act as a dutiful father, "because I am Mexican, and all the injustices committed against us it is you, who would remedy them. . . . You, who in this Territory are father to all Mexicans, [you] must consider us and see that no injustices are perpetrated against us."[26] Both Cárdenas and Vélez underscored their Mexican identity as a requisite to accessing Mexico's consular protection services to represent them in American courts of law. Consuls responded to petitioners' with promises to assist them in their legal entanglements, but first they had to prove their Mexican citizenship. In the cases of Cárdenas and Llamas, consuls provided legal assistance, but both men ended up serving prison sentences.

Most Mexican consuls sympathized with the plight of fellow nationals navigating hostile American attitudes in workplaces and courtrooms. For instance, the Mexican consul in El Paso, Texas, Jesús Escobar y Armendáriz, reached out to the Mexican community through local newspapers.

He claimed to understand that "I am here to protect my fellow citizens [because] many are their sufferings. . . . They humbly accept their destiny not being able to raise their voices and make themselves heard."[27] Consul Escobar took it upon himself to give voice to and protect the rights of imprisoned Mexicans and injured railroad workers affected by the inaction of the Twenty-Eighth District Court in El Paso. This stance made him an unpopular figure for *The Republic*, a Texas daily newspaper, which described him as a "conceited and odious diplomat who hates all things American."[28]

To fulfill his consular duty toward his fellow citizens in El Paso, Escobar teamed up with an El Paso legal firm, McGinnis & McGinnis, which offered pro bono legal services to poor Mexican defendants. The McGinnis firm compiled information on dozens of Mexican defendants who had been waiting for more than a year for a trial date or were languishing in jail due to their inability to pay hefty bail sums for minor offenses. The root cause of the irregularities at the Twenty-Eighth District Court was the lack of funds "to pay the expenses of [a] Court with a heavy civil and criminal docket on hand."[29] The Mexican consul lamented that "[the United States] the biggest and most powerful country [failed] to administer expedited justice in courts of law, not only to Americans but also to foreigners who claim their rights under [US] laws."[30]

Escobar's partnership with the McGinnis law firm laid bare the fault lines of the US justice system regarding Mexican immigrants in El Paso. Escobar documented the cases of Mexicans imprisoned for minor offenses and of the destitute families, widows, and orphans of injured workers awaiting their day in American courts. He then requested funds from the Díaz government so that the McGinnisses could defend their clients. In the process, Escobar cemented his reputation as a trusted representative of the Díaz administration in El Paso. However, he also perpetuated patriarchal hierarchies of power and social control among Mexican immigrant families by placing women and children under the care of the Mexican state.

Escobar educated fellow compatriots on their rights and responsibilities as foreigners in the United States. For example, Escobar sought to curb the common practice during Texas elections of casting votes without showing proof of US citizenship.[31] On the eve of the 1889 El Paso mayoral election, he distributed a one-page, typewritten pamphlet written in Spanish, in which he reminded Mexican individuals that "foreigners in this country [Mexican nationals] cannot vote in exchange for any reward whatsoever [because] the right to vote corresponds exclusively to American citizens by birth or naturalization."[32] He alerted his compatriots that those found violating US electoral laws would lose their Mexican citizenship. In this view, El Paso Mexicans maintained their status as disenfranchised from the American body politic because, in that way, they preserved their Mexican citizenship.

In the eyes of Plutarco Ornelas, the Mexican consul in San Antonio, a more effective consular system led by courageous and patriotic consuls was needed to better protect the rights of Mexicans residing in the US borderlands. To achieve such a goal, Ornelas proposed the establishment of a consulate general headquartered in Texas to oversee the Mexican consuls in the US Southwest. Ornelas knew firsthand that, in collecting information on crimes against Mexicans, consuls faced intimidation and even death threats for investigating and demanding justice for Mexican plaintiffs. For these reasons, some consuls resided south of the border and traveled intermittently to their consular offices in the United States. The consulate general that Ornelas proposed would further create "common intelligence and unison actions destined to combat more effectively so many attacks against our nationals."[33] Ornelas envisioned a system in which consuls served as intelligence operatives to neutralize "revolutionary machinations on our border [and] prevent arms and munitions smuggling."[34]

Financial considerations and fear of delegating special powers in a fractious region like the US borderlands prevented the Díaz administration from opening a consulate general in Texas. However, by the late 1890s, Mexican consuls began to follow Ornelas's call for an organized consular surveillance system to abort alleged revolutionary plans formulated by expatriate groups opposed to President Díaz's second reelection in 1888. Consuls identified Catarino Garza, a Mexican journalist living in El Paso, as the leader of "revolutionary machinations" against Díaz. In developing plans to depose Díaz, Garza exalted his Mexicanness. He also asked emigrants not to "sacrifice their national dignity" by taking US citizenship. Consul Manuel Treviño in El Paso, Texas, pointed out that Garza lacked the military and economic capacity to carry out his subversive plans. Nonetheless, Treviño advised consuls in Texas to monitor Garza and the "unemployed individuals . . . with a bad reputation" who supported him.[35] Because Garza attempted to topple a government friendly to the United States from American soil, the Díaz administration instructed consuls to see that American authorities apprehend Garza and his followers for violating US neutrality laws.[36] By 1892, Mexican consuls had turned into covert agents, and with the assistance of Texas law enforcement officials they successfully neutralized Garza's revolt in the US borderlands.

Amid the policing of the Garza rebellion, the Díaz administration hardened its stance toward critics, like Garza, who had lived for decades at a time in the United States. In 1890, the Mexican secretary of foreign affairs, Ignacio Mariscal, instructed consuls in the United States to enforce the ten-year absentee clause of the 1886 Nationality and Citizenship Law. Mariscal asked the consuls to "erase from [their] *matrícula* records those individuals who have lived outside of the Republic [of Mexico] for more than ten years" without permission from the Díaz government.[37] As a result, consular authorities had the power to revoke the citizenship rights of ordinary citizens within their jurisdictions, which limited the number of "true" Mexican citizens eligible for consular assistance.

The 1886 policy was well received by nationalist sectors in Mexico, such as in the liberal Mexico City daily *El Diario del Hogar*. In one editorial, this newspaper demanded that Mexicans in the United States remain free of "all the egoism and practical, utilitarian" attitudes associated with American culture.[38] In addition, *El Diario* advised its readers not to go to the United States, for they might be "treated worse than the Negros."[39] According to *El Diario*, Mexicans in the United States exposed themselves to suffering acts of violence at the hands of Americans and Mexicans alike. It referred to an 1893 case in Cebolleta, New Mexico, where Ireneo González, a Mexican man, fired gunshots at Desiderio Sandoval. A crowd quickly assembled to see that Sandoval had been injured. Then, according to *El Diario*, the angry crowd, integrated by "ex-Mexicans," lynched González. *El Diario* concluded that the lynch mob of former Mexicans "had forgotten much of the noble traditions of their motherland, and have adopted very few of the good qualities of the Americans."[40] *El Diario* explained to its readers how the González case revealed both the absence of ethnic solidarity in the United States and the pernicious influence of American culture on Mexican citizens.[41]

Consul Ornelas concurred with *El Diario* in pointing out the rise of violence perpetrated by Anglos and Mexican Texans against Mexican individuals and the alarming unwillingness of Texas authorities to suppress extralegal justice. The consul drew attention to the ease with which mobs of enraged Americans and former Mexicans "seek to satiate a community's thirst for blood in wanting to avenge the death of one of their own, victimizing . . . innocent people whose only sin is having the same nationality of the one who is said to have committed the crime."[42] Ornelas concluded that an inexistent rule of law in the US borderlands spelled trouble for Mexicans. He specifically referred to anti-Mexican sentiment in Texas: "Not only the lives of the accused are in imminent danger [in Texas], but the sacred code of justice, humanity and international law."[43]

Exclusion and Belonging to the Mexican Nation at the Turn of the Twentieth Century

Throughout the late 1890s, Mexican consuls in the United States continued their protective yet controlling emigrant agenda, prompting their fellow compatriots to visit their nearest consulates and obtain *matrícula* certificates, through which they could ratify their Mexican citizenship. However, Mexican immigrants proved reticent to come under the purview of consular authorities. For many, the process of becoming and remaining a full-fledged Mexican citizen in the United States in the late nineteenth century was a tall order, particularly for rural emigrants affected by the modernization policies of President Díaz.[44] The acquisition of a *matrícula* compelled them to shed their local and regional identities in order to adopt identities as Mexican citizens. A great number of Mexicans struggled to embrace their Mexicanness as a nationality marker and stayed away from consular authorities unless they had a pressing legal issue that required consular aid.

During the 1890s, the enforcement of Mexico's 1886 Nationality and Citizenship Law against expatriates living in the United States widened the gap between the Díaz administration and expatriate Mexican communities in the US Southwest. Díaz's consuls informed emigrants that their rights as Mexicans depended on the length of time they had lived away from Mexico. Thus, it was no longer enough to be born in Mexico; emigrants needed to remain closely linked to the national territory for a decade at a time in order for the Díaz government to consider them full-fledged citizens of Mexico. The ten-year absentee provisions of the 1886 law authorized consuls to disown Mexicans whose decade-long residency in the United States appeared to prove a weakening in patriotic zeal and dissatisfaction with their home government.

Upon learning about the exclusionary rule of the ten-year absentee law, some expatriate Mexican communities questioned the legal basis of such a law and its application in the US borderlands. In one such case, a group of Mexicans from Rio Grande City, Texas, challenged the law. *El Diario del Hogar* reprinted and echoed Rio Grande City's opposition, adding that "no [state or federal Mexican] legislature has had sufficient integrity and energy to represent their offended sovereignty with the issuance of this anti-constitutional decree."[45] Although some Rio Grande City Mexicans had become US citizens "because of their businesses [or] as a last resource of salvation," they insisted that they remained Mexican citizens. Furthermore, because the 1886 law had reduced the number of full-fledged Mexicans in the United States, Rio Grande City critics questioned the reason for the existence of Mexican consulates in some parts of the US Southwest containing a limited number of Mexican citizens to protect.

In 1892, Porfirio Díaz celebrated his third reelection as president of Mexico. He consolidated his grip on power and planned to extend his mandate with the help of Mexican consulates, which he considered his regime's first line of defense in the US borderlands. Consuls received instructions to reintroduce the consular *matrícula* as the official identity instrument for Mexicans residing north of the Rio Grande. In addition, consulates became the official sponsors of Mexican civic holidays such as Independence Day and Cinco de Mayo. These events aimed to bring Mexicans together to demonstrate their Mexicanness in their adopted US borderlands communities. Making sure that Mexicans remained Mexican while living north of the Rio Grande afforded the Díaz regime the ability to stretch its authority across the US-Mexico border to protect its compatriots' rights but also to monitor their political attitudes toward their home government.

Because the ten-year absentee clause in the 1886 Nationality and Citizenship Law empowered Mexican consuls to include or exclude their fellow citizens from the Mexican body politic, a number of ordinary emigrants facing legal troubles in the American justice system saw their Mexican citizenship rights revoked. One such case was that of Fernando Portillo, whose story we introduced at the beginning of this chapter. Portillo found himself stateless while confronting accusations of horse theft and the rape of a white woman in Montana. Like the Rio Grande City Mexicans, Portillo forcefully argued against the revocation of his Mexican citizenship as dictated by the 1886 absentee clause. He insisted that his rights as a Mexican citizen remained intact, despite his lengthy residence in the United States, because he remained disenfranchised from the American body politic. Portillo astutely appealed to President Díaz's policies "to see that I get a fair trial, as the Mexicans in this country are shamefully abused, and never get justice as I can prove."[46] Portillo called on the Díaz administration to use its diplomatic strength to press the US government to see that Mexican defendants receive fair administration of justice.

Racial animus hampered the administration of justice in American courts. In Portillo's case, Matías Romero, Mexico's minister in Washington, hired the attorney J. B. Herford, who informed Romero that racial prejudice weighed heavily against the defendant, even though

> the evidence is not by any means strong against him, but in a country as little settled as most of Montana, a crime of this kind [rape] is naturally more feared and the impulse of a jury is towards conviction on slighter evidence than in many other crimes. . . . There is quite a chance of another conviction particularly since the "lady" in the case is rather good looking and Partello [*sic*] rather the reverse.[47]

Racial tensions abounded in this case. Montana's district attorney (whose name cannot be established based on available records) allegedly referred to Portillo as a "Mexican greaser, baboon, and low down trash."[48] In turn, Portillo claimed "that I came of as good a family as there is, and am as white as [or] whiter than him."[49] For Montana's white community, Portillo's nonwhite complexion represented the embodiment of societal ills.[50] Nevertheless, Portillo's claim to whiteness—intended to counter the offensive slurs from the district attorney—showed his familiarity with whiteness ideologies that regarded African Americans and Mexicans as inferior.

For more than a year Portillo, as a stateless individual, battled his legal troubles in a Montana court. In 1892, Minister Romero unexpectedly revisited Portillo's case. Even more surprising was Romero's depiction of Portillo as a Mexican non–English speaker living in the United States.[51] In this reimagining of Portillo, a *matrícula* was not required. Instead, Romero's depiction of Portillo as a helpless Mexican before an unfamiliar legal system, a victim of injustice who was ignorant of the English language and disenfranchised from the American polity, allowed Romero to rectify a misstep in President Díaz's alleged pro-emigrant consular agenda and use Portillo's case to highlight the protection afforded by the Mexican government to its citizens in American courts of law.

Having Mexicanized Portillo's image, Romero then disbursed twenty-five dollars, apparently from his own pocket, and hired a second attorney, named Garland, to represent Portillo in Montana state court. Portillo was released on bail in mid-June 1892. It is not clear how Garland secured Portillo's liberty given the seriousness of the charge and the racial animosity demonstrated by the district attorney. The consular file on Portillo is silent about the court proceedings and does not include any correspondence among Garland, Romero, and Portillo before his release from prison. Portillo's file ends with a letter from Romero, in which the minister resented not having received a note of gratitude from Portillo. Ultimately—and despite his emancipation from incarceration—Portillo refused to play by the paternalist code of Mexican authorities enforcing Mexican laws against expatriates in the United States.

Minister Romero's intervention in the Portillo case exemplified the power of the Mexican diplomatic and consular corps in the process of making or unmaking Mexican citizens residing in the United States. However, other Mexicans such as Jesús Lares did not have Portillo's luck. A young child in 1882, Lares migrated along with his mother from the northern state of Sinaloa to Arizona. In 1895, more than a decade later, Lares celebrated his twentieth birthday in prison, facing a death sentence for the alleged murder of two US citizens, Frank M. Doll and his son, John.[52] Lares turned to Consul Martin Arce in Phoenix, Arizona, for legal assistance. Arce forwarded Lares's case to Secretary of Foreign Affairs Ignacio Mariscal in Mexico. After examining Lares's situation, Mariscal concluded that "there is no reason for the Mexican government to intervene in this case; since there is no indication of legal violations in detriment of Lares and it is not proven that he maintains the Mexican citizenship. . . . On the contrary . . . it appears that he lost it due to his extended absence from Mexico without government authorization."[53] Similar to Fernando Portillo, Lares had lived for more than a decade in the United States and failed to obtain approval from the Mexican government through a consular *matrícula*. Díaz's diplomatic authorities disowned Lares as a Mexican citizen. He faced Arizona's legal system of justice alone, and he was executed in 1895. He died as a stateless individual. Such were the consequences of the 1886 law for some individuals who failed to live as true loyal Mexican citizens while residing in the United States.

Conclusion

President Porfirio Díaz's administration implemented a nation-building project that prioritized keeping the expatriate Mexican population living in the United States bound to the Mexican nation. The Díaz government relied on a loyal consular network located in the United States that was created to protect the rights of Mexican nationals. Amid racial tensions and instances of maladministration of justice toward Mexicans abroad, providing consular protection services became a priority for consuls in the United States. The signature mark of the Díaz administration became the protective consular agenda toward Mexicans residing throughout the United States, from the Rio Grande to the Montana-Canada region. Indeed, a key part of Díaz's consular protection program focused on affirming "Mexicanization," because Díaz's economic modernization campaign had rendered many Mexicans landless and in search of jobs across the American Southwest.

Displaying a paternalist and patriotic rhetoric, consular authorities compelled fellow nationals to confirm their ties to the Mexican nation by obtaining a *matrícula*, or consular-issued identification, which gave expatriates access to legal services provided by the Mexican consulates. Those without a *matrícula* faced a harsh fate under the ten-year absence provision included in the 1886 immigration law, which rendered a number of Mexicans in the US borderlands stateless.

The application of the 1886 law, along with the requisite *matrícula*, transformed the meaning of Mexican citizenship among expatriate Mexican communities in the United States. These policies were part and parcel of a series of well-orchestrated Mexicanization programs, through which consular officials prompted their compatriots to embrace Mexican citizenship. The process of maintaining Mexican citizenship in the turn-of-the-century US borderlands gave these "true" Mexicans access to consular protection services such as legal counsel. This emigrant-centered approach taken by the Díaz government revitalized the patriotism of many expatriates but disillusioned many others, prompting them to become fierce critics of Díaz or to adopt American citizenship outright. In the process, Díaz's Mexicanization policy allowed some immigrants in the United States to confront the irregular administration of justice, but it also revoked the citizenship rights of Mexicans whose decade-long residence in the United States made them unfit sons and daughters of Mexico. They were thus rendered stateless, vulnerable migrants subject to injustice in the American borderlands.

Notes

1. This chapter uses the term "American" to refer to the United States specifically.
2. Andrew Graybill, *Policing the Great Plains: Rangers, Mounties, and the North American Frontier, 1875–1910* (Lincoln: University of Nebraska Press, 2007); William D.

Carrigan and Clive Webb, *Mob Violence against Mexicans in the United States, 1848–1928* (New York: Oxford University Press, 2017).

3. Graybill, *Policing the Great Plains*; Brenden Rensink, "Cree Contraband or Contraband Crees? Early Montanan Experiences with Transnational Natives and the Formation of Latin Prejudice, 1880–1885," in *Smugglers, Brothels, and Twine: Historical Perspectives on Contraband and Vice in North America's Borderlands*, ed. Elaine Carey and Andrae M. Marak (Tucson: University of Arizona Press, 2011), 24–43.

4. Jaime Aguila, "Protecting 'México de Afuera': Mexican Emigration Policy, 1876–1928" (PhD diss., Arizona State University, 2000); Gilbert G. González, *Mexican Consuls and Labor Organizing: Imperial Politics in the American Southwest* (Austin: University of Texas Press, 1999); George J. Sánchez, *Becoming Mexican American: Ethnicity, Culture, and Identity in Los Angeles, 1900–1945* (New York: Oxford University Press, 1993); Francisco Balderrama, *In Defense of la Raza: The Los Angeles Mexican Consulate and the Mexican Community, 1929–1936* (Tucson: University of Arizona Press, 1982).

5. 30-18-52, Archivo Histórico Genaro Estrada de la Secretaría de Relaciones Exteriores (hereafter cited as AHGESRE).

6. *Reglamento del cuerpo consular: Leyes y disposiciones relativas al servicio consular* (Mexico City: Secretaría de Relaciones Exteriores, 1878).

7. Elliot Young, *Catarino Garza's Revolution on the Texas-Mexico Border* (Durham, NC: Duke University Press, 2004); Samuel Truett, *Fugitive Landscapes: The Forgotten History of the U.S.-Mexico Borderlands* (New Haven, CT: Yale University Press, 2006); Rachel St. John, *Line in the Sand: A History of the Western U.S.-Mexico Border* (Princeton, NJ: Princeton University Press, 2011); George T. Díaz, *Border Contraband: A History of Smuggling across the Rio Grande* (Austin: University of Texas Press, 2015).

8. William D. Carrigan and Clive Webb, *Forgotten Dead: Mob Violence against Mexicans in the United States, 1848–1928* (Oxford, UK: Oxford University Press, 2013); Claudio Lomnitz, *The Return of Comrade Ricardo Flores Magón* (New York: Zone Books, 2014); Kelly Lytle Hernández, *City of Inmates: Conquest, Rebellion, and the Rise of Human Caging in Los Angeles, 1771–1965* (Chapel Hill: University of North Carolina Press, 2017).

9. L-E 1669, AHGESRE.

10. 18-27-17, 8, AHGESRE.

11. 18-27-17, 8, AHGESRE.

12. 28-9-8, 18-27-74, AHGESRE.

13. Erika Pani, *Para pertenecer a la gran familia mexicana: Procesos de naturalización en el siglo XIX* (Mexico City: El Colegio de México, 2015), 19, 38–39.

14. Pani, 51–59.

15. L-E 1599, AHGESRE.

16. Robert John Deger Jr., "Porfirian Foreign Policy and Mexican Nationalism: A Study of Cooperation and Conflict in Mexican-American Relations, 1884–1904" (PhD diss., Indiana University, 1979).

17. *El Diario del Hogar* (Mexico City), April 8, 1891, 2; Lawrence A. Cardoso, *Mexican Emigration to the United States, 1897–1937: Socio-Economic Patterns* (Tucson: University of Arizona Press, 1980).

18. 30-18-52, AHGESRE.

19. 30-18-52, AHGESRE.

20. L-E 1599, AHGESRE.

21. 28-9-131; 14-18-2 (1); and L-E 1864 (VII), AHGESRE.

22. 28-9-131; 14-18-2 (1); and L-E 1864 (VII), AHGESRE.

23. 12-2-30, AHGESRE.

24. Ángela Moyano Pahissa, *Antología: Protección consular a mexicanos en los Estados Unidos, 1849–1900* (Mexico City: Secretaría de Relaciones Exteriores, 1989); Mario T. García, "Porfirian Diplomacy and the Administration of Justice in Texas, 1877–1900," *Aztlán: A Journal of Chicano Studies* 16, nos. 1–2 (1987): 1–25; Carrigan and Webb, *Forgotten Dead*; Nicholas Villanueva Jr., *The Lynching of Mexicans in the Texas Borderlands* (Albuquerque: University of New Mexico Press, 2017).

25. 28-9-104, AHGESRE.

26. 18-27-8, AHGESRE.

27. 12-2-30, AHGESRE.

28. 14-18-2 (1), AHGESRE.

29. 12-2-30, AHGESRE.

30. 12-2-30, AHGESRE.

31. Arnoldo De León, *They Called Them Greasers: Anglo Attitudes toward Mexicans in Texas, 1821–1900* (Austin: University of Texas Press, 1983).

32. 18-27-128, AHGESRE.

33. 18-29-70, 3, AHGESRE.

34. 11-2-38, 1–6, AHGESRE.

35. 2-12-2934 (bis), AHGESRE.

36. Young, *Catarino Garza's Revolution*, 212–213.

37. L-E 1669, AHGESRE.

38. *El Monitor Republicano* (Mexico City), August 8, 1890, 3.

39. *El Diario del Hogar*, August 24, 1890, 3.

40. *El Diario del Hogar*, February 18, 1893, 2.

41. John Nieto-Phillips, *Language of Blood: The Making of Spanish-American Identity in New Mexico, 1880s–1930s* (Albuquerque: University of New Mexico Press, 2004).

42. 18-27-6, AHGESRE.

43. 18-27-6, AHGESRE.

44. *El Diario del Hogar*, April 8, 1891, 2.

45. *El Diario del Hogar*, July 2, 1892, 2.

46. 18-27-17, AHGESRE.

47. 18-27-17, AHGESRE.

48. 18-27-17, AHGESRE.

49. 18-27-17, AHGESRE.

50. Rensink, "Cree Contraband," 24–43.

51. Rensink, 24–43.

52. 18-27-48, AHGESRE.

53. 18-27-48, AHGESRE.

FIVE

Enforcing US Immigration Laws at the US-Canada Border, 1891–1940

The View from Detroit

THOMAS A. KLUG

The difficulty of enforcing US immigration laws along the land borders with Canada and Mexico became evident at the 1915 "Consultation on Immigration" held in San Francisco by the Department of Labor and the Bureau of Immigration. A. Warner Parker, the bureau's chief law officer, spoke on behalf of those calling for firmness in dealing with Canadians and Mexicans who crossed the border without inspection. He brazenly asserted that "we must make these aliens understand that they cannot walk across the border as they please." Parker continued: "I realize that there are cases in which the alien does this thing unknowingly, but there are so many other cases in which the alien does it deliberately . . . and unless we make these people understand as a matter of discipline it does not seem to me that we will get very far with the control of either the Mexican or Canadian border."[1]

At the meeting, Louis F. Post, the assistant secretary of labor, likewise spoke about the practical aspects of policing the land borders. Unlike Parker, however, Post urged immigration officials to be sensitive to the customs and interests of border peoples and communities. This was particularly necessary, he thought, along the northern boundary line. "You have to remember whatever course we pursue, legislative or administrative, that the Canadian border is in many places like any border between two of our states. You couldn't stub your toe against it. You couldn't tell you reached the border unless you had a surveyor along."[2] Post's words of caution applied most acutely to what he called the "peculiar [and] unique" situation in Detroit, where in 1915 immigration officers performed 4.5 million inspections of people entering the United States.[3] "I do not think there is another place on the border that is quite like Detroit," he said. "There is a city on the American side of the river and residential towns on the Canadian side of the river. At Detroit there are two ferries, one brings 500 or 600 people a day; another brings 9,000 people a day, going back and forth. It is the same as between New York and Brooklyn. The people are living in one place and working in another." The daily cross-border commuting-for-labor practice in Detroit had gone on "for years," Post noted. In addition, many Canadians also came over regularly "to shop, to go to the theaters, coming over for one amusement or another or to visit friends." The challenge for immigration law enforcement in Detroit, Post reasoned, was to "regulate the passing of people across the land border without arousing [that which] too drastic laws might arouse." Policing, in other words, had to recognize the well-established "inter-communication" that prevailed among "neighbors." "If you stop that," Post warned, "you are going to have a row. You are going to have a Sherman's idea of war at Detroit. The theater people will rise up, the store people will rise up, for part of their custom is taken away from them."[4]

During the 1890s, the United States began to enforce its Chinese exclusion and immigration laws on the Canadian border. These laws were originally designed to counter the entrance of undesirable immigrants through the northern "back door," but by 1910 the scope of the border bureaucracy's work also applied to Canadians.[5] The historian Bruno Ramirez has examined how the "rise of the border" complicated the lives of Canadians intending to move to the United States either seasonally or permanently.[6] Likewise, the inspections carried out by agents of the US Bureau of Immigration disrupted the ease with which Canadians and Americans had regularly traversed the border. Over time, borderland people learned the rules of the new system, sometimes only after difficult encounters with immigration officers.[7] While scholars have examined how potential immigrants and frequent border crossers adjusted to the border regime, few have focused on the accommodations made by an often underfunded and overcommitted US immigration bureaucracy.[8] As Post's 1915 remarks revealed, the officials charged with implementing federal immigration law operated in particular local contexts, which included considering the impact of their work on local border-crossing customs and entrenched local interests.

Using the Detroit district of the Bureau of Immigration as a case study, this chapter uncovers how the US immigration bureaucracy took policies, laws, and regulations made in Washington, DC, and applied them to the local borderlands context.[9] In doing so, it demonstrates that national policing practices were in fact shaped by local realities and by the economic and political interests of the region in which they were enforced.

Policing the Borderline

The peculiar origins of the American immigration bureaucracy on the US-Canada border help explain its structural vulnerabilities and constraints. With the Immigration Act of 1891, the federal government assumed full control over the enforcement of the country's immigration laws, both at seaports and at land borders with Canada and Mexico.[10] Congress charged the nascent immigration bureaucracy with a mission fraught with tension: imposing barriers to the unregulated movement of people while not paralyzing cross-border traffic. Under section 8 of the act, Congress authorized the secretary of the Treasury (who, at the time, supervised the superintendent—later called the commissioner-general—of immigration) to "proscribe rules for inspection along the borders of Canada, British Columbia, and Mexico." The purpose of such regulations was to ensure that an immigration control system did not "obstruct or unnecessarily delay, impede, or annoy passengers in ordinary travel" between the United States and its neighbors.[11] By this simple language, Congress signaled its sensitivity about undue interference with cross-border traffic and the operations of transportation companies, particularly railroads.

The lack of administrative capacity on the part of immigration law enforcers necessitated making peace with the transportation sector. In the 1890s, it was one thing for the federal government to assume responsibility for enforcing immigration laws in states like New York or Massachusetts—jurisdictions with decades of experience and organizational depth applied to regulating immigration at busy Atlantic seaports.[12] However, no comparable regulatory apparatus existed for the northern land border, obliging the federal government to develop one from scratch. At this moment, however, Congress was unwilling to deploy a costly immigration inspection force along the border.[13] In 1895, just seven immigrant inspectors guarded the line stretching from Sault Ste. Marie, Michigan, to Niagara Falls, New York. In Detroit, immigration inspection was carried out by one man alone.[14]

As an alternative to staffing the borderline, the federal government relied on the Canadian Agreement, first formulated in 1893. American immigration law did not apply in Canada, but that did not preclude US immigration officials from working out a voluntary arrangement with transportation companies operating on the Canadian side. Under the terms of the pact, the steamship lines that brought European immigrants to Canadian seaports permitted US immigration officers to examine people who had declared their intention to travel on to the United States. Those who passed examination received a certificate that allowed them to enter the United States without further interrogation. Railroad companies participated in the agreement, promising not to transport immigrants to the US border unless they possessed certificates.[15] The goal for the United States, as one immigration official described it, was to "bind the companies to a compact" and make them partly responsible for "policing the border."[16] Financial concerns were also paramount. According to Herman Stump, the former commissioner-general of immigration during the Grover Cleveland administration, if the agreement worked and excludable European immigrants could be checked at Canadian seaports, "it would obviate the expense and the necessity of establishing the border line."[17]

The Canadian Agreement, however, proved inadequate as a strategy for stemming the flow of undesirable aliens into the United States, particularly the growing number arriving from southern and eastern Europe.[18] That was the gist of the testimony before the US Industrial Commission in 1899 and the US Senate Committee on Immigration in 1902, and the annual reports of the commissioner-general of immigration. According to the Industrial Commission, the "greatest loophole" was that US-bound immigrants arriving at Canadian seaports learned that they could deprive American inspectors of the right to examine them by claiming "some place in Canada as their destination."[19] Once admitted to Canada, they simply made their way to the poorly policed US border and crossed it at the place and time of their own choosing. If caught, they could only be returned to Canada, where they could bide their time and try again. The Canadian Agreement alone, therefore, could not fend off what the special immigrant inspector Robert Watchorn described as a "tide of pauperism and disease and crime" coming from Europe to the United States via Canada. Instead, argued A. S. Anderson, the passenger manager of the American Line, "strict control at the United States border is absolutely essential."[20]

Anderson insisted that the federal government could manage the Canadian border, citing as precedents the government's customs service operations and periodic quarantine controls.[21] What was missing was a specific strategy and the means to implement "an efficient system of inspection on the border."[22] The answer came in the final report of the Industrial Commission, which offered a vision for controlling the northern border by replicating seaport immigration inspection methods at designated "exclusive ports of entry along the boundary line through which alone aliens should be admitted." Furthermore, "an adequate police force of inspectors" would make these state plans a reality.[23]

The next six years saw the implementation of this vision and a corresponding hardening of the border. With the Immigration Act of 1903, which raised the head tax on arriving passengers from one dollar to two dollars, Congress made a pivotal commitment to allocate personnel and resources to the northern border.[24] In 1908, fifty immigrant inspectors policed the ground between Sault Ste. Marie and Niagara Falls, compared to just nine in 1901. During these same years, the number of inspectors in Detroit grew from two to thirteen.[25] The Immigration Act of 1907 again doubled the immigrant head tax, raising it to four dollars, although it exempted citizens of Canada and Mexico as well as aliens who resided at least one year in either country. Canadians and Mexicans, however, did not escape a new addition to the law, one long sought by champions of a stronger border policy. Congress now required "all aliens" to enter the United States at either an official seaport or a designated "place or places" on the border. Entry at any other site was deemed unlawful and subjected the person to arrest and deportation if caught in the United States within three years following entry.[26]

By 1907, the commissioner-general of immigration was ecstatic about what he said were "almost ideal conditions" on the Canadian border. In just a handful of years, he claimed, the Bureau of Immigration had constructed "a system of administration which could hardly be surpassed."[27] The immigration commissioner John H. Clark noted that in the past year, inspectors had selected 62,823 aliens for examination out of 8 million "regular passengers" who crossed the border from Canada.[28] Bureau officials in Washington enthusiastically recommended this as the model for the troubled southern border, which James Dupree discusses in chapter 6 in this volume. They trusted that F. W. Berkshire, the newly appointed supervising inspector of immigration for the Mexican border, would establish an efficient and effective inspection system, "similar in all essential respects to that so successfully operated for several years in Canada."[29] Indeed, as Dupree notes in his chapter, in the following years

Berkshire worked strenuously to impose bureaucratic order along the Mexican border.

Partnership with Transportation Companies

Over the decade that followed, industrial development, the heightened demand for labor, and population growth in places adjacent to the US-Canada boundary spurred an unprecedented increase in the volume of border crossings. In mid-1913, Commissioner Clark noted an "unusual influx of aliens" into the United States.[30] This was especially true at Detroit, where the development of the automobile industry made the city a magnet for immigrants. During the first two decades of the century, the city's population more than doubled, reaching just under 1 million in 1920. Immigrants accounted for 27.2 percent of the growth. By 1920, the foreign born represented 29 percent of Detroit's population and 44 percent of those employed in the manufacturing sector. Two out of five foreign-born persons in the city originated from southern or eastern Europe or the Middle East.[31] While many immigrants who settled in Detroit arrived in the United States at American seaports, a considerable number made their way to the emerging Motor City via Canada. Clark referred to Detroit as "the Mecca of thousands of aliens from Canada."[32] To handle the influx, he ordered five shifts of inspectors working seven days per week to cover seventeen trains arriving daily in Detroit from Canada. This paled by comparison with the activity at the immigration station at the foot of Woodward Avenue. There, by the spring of 1915, an average of 375,000 passengers entered Detroit every month, the vast majority of them on boats of the Detroit & Windsor Ferry Company. With only a handful of immigration officers assigned to it over the course of a nineteen-hour day, Clark declared that "the Woodward Avenue Ferry . . . presents one of the most difficult problems we have to deal with on the Canadian border."[33]

As budgetary constraints prevented the Bureau of Immigration from aligning staffing levels with the increased intensity of work on the border, immigrant inspectors buckled under the strain. Clark sympathized, warning that "we are exacting from the help hours of labor which are beyond all reason."[34] Most alarming were indicators that the inspection system was failing at ports of entry all along the border. Clark reported that at International Falls, Minnesota, approximately 54,000 people had entered the country by ferry without any examination, while "aliens are constantly getting into the United States at Detroit without proper inspection" because harried inspectors at the Woodward dock could not detect them as vast crowds flowed by during busy hours.[35] All of this, he worried, made a mockery of the law and its enforcers.

Unable to obtain additional personnel, reduce the hours of work for exhausted inspectors, alter the train schedules, or slow the currents of people crossing the border, US immigration officials turned to improving the physical layout of ports of entry, such as the one maintained by the Detroit & Windsor Ferry Company at the foot of Woodward Avenue. Clark, based in Montreal, set the tone in dealing with Detroit's main ferry line. "If our inspection on the Canadian border is not to become farcical," he remarked, "I believe the Bureau will agree that the conditions prevailing at the Detroit ferries must be dealt with in a no half-hearted or uncertain fashion."[36] The issue, as Clark and top bureau officials saw it, was that the company was at fault for permitting chaos to prevail at the Woodward dock. As they understood the Canadian Agreement, the ferry company had neglected its "police duty" to present "passengers for inspection in a systematic and orderly manner . . . rather than permitting them to flock off the boats at their pleasure."[37]

What ensued was a decade of combative negotiations between the government and the ferry company, including instances when immigration officials threatened to eliminate the Woodward dock as a designated place for the landing of aliens.[38] The government eventually obtained from the company the modifications it demanded, including suitable office quarters and physical restraints (such as railings and lane markers) that forced passengers into orderly lines before waiting inspectors.[39] In the process, the ferry company also learned an important lesson: in exchange for making a modest investment in receiving facilities, it could rightly press the government to provide an appropriate number of inspectors to fit its business operations.

During the mid-1920s, the ferrying business in Detroit underwent dramatic expansion as the population and the manufacturing base in the region grew. The number of Canadian residents commuting to work in Detroit reached 15,000 that decade, and automobile traffic also swarmed across the border, particularly during the summer months when Americans traveled to and from their vacation homes on Ontario's shorelines. Detroit's two ferry lines (the Detroit & Windsor and the Detroit & Walkerville) handled up to 95 percent of the cross-border passenger traffic that came into the city, which jumped from 6.5 million entries in 1924 to 10.1

million in 1926; the remaining half-million passengers arrived via railway. The ferry companies coped with this traffic by extending their daily hours of service and by putting additional boats on the river. Aside from the possibility of ice on the Detroit River during the winter months, the only impediments to a high-volume ferrying business were the number and efficiency of government officials at the companies' landings in Detroit. To overcome this potential bottleneck, the companies proactively expanded and rearranged inspection facilities so that immigration officers could perform their duties as quickly as possible.[40]

In early 1926, for example, the Detroit & Windsor Ferry contacted Percy Prentis, the district director of immigration in Detroit, for approval of its plans to open a large intake for automobiles at the foot of Bates Street, one block east of the old Woodward dock. With two large steamers making a total of four landings per hour, the company anticipated a "continuous flow" of automobiles at a maximum rate of 240 per hour. To accomplish this, however, the company needed the government to change the way it conducted immigration examinations. Instead of questioning automobile drivers and passengers as the vehicles left the ferryboats (which delayed the return trips of the boats to Canada), the company proposed that inspection occur after drivers disembarked. With this simple maneuver, the company figured it could increase its automobile business by nearly 50 percent. Of course, increasing the number of vehicles coming through every day meant more work, but the company assured Prentis that it would construct an arrival area that would "give the Government inspectors a much better opportunity of making a thorough inspection." The entire scheme, however, depended on the assignment of "more inspectors to take care of the increased business."[41]

Prentis, together with Inspector in Charge Alexander Doig, lobbied the central office in Washington for additional inspectors in Detroit. Channeling the interests of the ferry companies, they argued that the two firms had invested thousands of dollars to expand their operations with the expectation that the Bureau of Immigration would "furnish the required personnel so that full and complete use may be made of the facilities for inspection afforded."[42] Under pressure, the bureau and the Department of Labor committed more personnel to the city. In mid-1924, there were twenty-five inspectors on duty in Detroit; by the end of 1926, their ranks increased to sixty-six. Over the next five years, there was another gain that brought the total to 115, of which seventy-one were assigned to the ferry landings and train stations and forty-four to the recently opened Ambassador Bridge and the Detroit-Windsor Tunnel. In 1930, nearly 12 percent of the bureau's immigrant inspectors worked in Detroit.[43]

Reading Bodies, Reading the Borderland

Despite the improvements and additions to the ranks, immigrant inspectors could barely keep up with the pressing flow of crowds arriving in Detroit, especially during the morning rush to work and on busy Sunday evenings when large numbers of motorists returned to the city. By law, inspectors were responsible for determining if an alien applying for admission was "clearly and beyond a doubt entitled to land" (that is, to enter the United States).[44] Accomplishing this was no easy task, given the widely held assumption among inspectors that any person crossing the border may be concealing unseemly facts about his or her identity, personal history, or intentions for entering the country. The Immigration Act of 1924 addressed this by imposing upon an alien applicant for admission the burden of proof in establishing that he or she "is not subject to the exclusion provisions of the immigrant laws."[45]

The complex crowds at the border also presented enormous challenges. In conducting examinations, inspectors had to quickly establish an individual's identity and citizenship, immigration status (immigrant, visitor, or alien resident of the United States returning from a visit abroad), whether he or she was the rightful holder of a valid quota or nonquota visa issued by an American consulate, and whether he or she was subject to any of the numerous grounds for exclusion under the Immigration Act of 1917.[46] In stressful contexts such as Detroit, and given the absence of any mandatory identification document (such as a passport) that would apply to all border crossers (including US citizens), inspectors relied on tried and trusted methods of conducting examinations. These informal assessments utilized a stock of shortcuts or tricks of the trade for determining the trustworthiness of border crossers. The assistant secretary of labor, William Husband, indicated as much when he tried to allay the worries of American tourists returning from Canada without proof of their citizenship, informing the public that inspectors "have ways of sizing up an application for admission even when the applicant does not possess what would be regarded as evidence in court."[47]

Given that "on average an examining officer can not devote more than a few seconds of his time to a passenger," as District Director Prentis re-

Figure 5.1. Arriving ferry passengers awaiting their turn with a United States immigrant inspector at Detroit, July 1925. Source: Image 40621, Virtual Motor City Collection, Walter P. Reuther Library, Archives of Labor and Urban Affairs, Wayne State University.

ported in the mid-1920s, "inspectors must make quick use of all their resources in an effort to promptly determine the status of each passenger included in the turbulent mass of humanity surging forward for quick entry from the ferry boats to the gates."[48] Prentis vehemently denied that his inspectors relied on flimsy methods such as giving credence to passengers' clothing labels, "so-called first papers, working checks, baggage checks, return portions of tickets, tax receipts, gas, light, and phone bills, and letters or papers recommending the traveler from persons unknown to our officers."[49] Prentis's examples, however, suggest that the consideration of these very items really was part of the tool kit of immigration officers. Indeed, Husband noted that inspectors often accepted oral statements or written documents, such as membership in clubs or fraternal organizations, as evidence of citizenship.[50]

Prentis considered reading the bodies of passengers to be a much more reliable approach. He declared that "persons whose appearance, talk, carriage, etc., show clearly that they are native US citizens are promptly admitted without unnecessary annoyance."[51] By implication, inspectors were justified in spending extra time on any person who spoke English with even a slight accent. However, inspectors had to be careful. According to one contemporary account, those in the business of advising aliens about how to slip into the United States "will train a man whose knowledge of English is negligible to say 'Chicago' without a trace of an accent and send him out to try and bluff the immigration inspectors at the Detroit ferry docks, who are nearly always rushed, and who often ask no more than, 'where were you born?'"[52]

Attuned to the social, cultural, and economic terrains of the borderland, the immigration bureaucracy enforced the law according to "locally generated knowledge."[53] The typical pattern was for frontline inspectors to enforce the letter of the law only for their superiors to intervene and urge moderation based on a common-sense reading of the borderland. Touring the border-crossing posts along the St. Clair River, for example, Prentis stopped at Marine City and heard a drugstore proprietor complain about an immigrant inspector's interrogations of well-known Canadian residents who frequently crossed the river to shop. One of the Canadians, a farmer and a customer of the drugstore, had vowed he would never return so long as the inspector remained on duty. In brokering a compromise, Prentis reported that he advised the inspector to "avoid unnecessary questioning of Canadian citizens coming regularly to Marine City for legitimate purposes" and then made arrangements to have a border-crossing identification card issued to the customer in question with the hope that it would prevent difficulties in the future.[54]

John Zurbrick, Prentis's successor as district director, likewise took long-standing border-crossing practices into account—such as those adopted by the inhabitants of Pelee Island. Although the island was located in western Lake Erie on the Canadian side of the boundary, Zurbrick observed that "in years past, Pelee Islanders rather looked upon Sandusky [Ohio] as their natural place to go to town." A ferryboat from the island arrived in Sandusky, twenty miles away, every Friday morning, and passengers were examined by an inspector sent over from Toledo. However, Pelee Islanders also arrived unscheduled in small boats "for the purpose of settling for their fish or to see a doctor or dentist." During the winter, they sometimes reached Sandusky, via Kelleys Island, by driving automobiles across the ice-covered lake, and even "a few intrepid travelers ventured across the ice on foot." Although none of these irregular crossers were properly met by US immigrant inspectors, Zurbrick advised officials in Washington not to be alarmed, as the Pelee Islanders returned "as they came" and "the number of non-Canadians on Pelee Island is negligible." Zurbrick had found a technical violation of the law and regulations, but a pragmatic appraisal of this corner of the borderland led him to conclude that there was no need to station an immigration officer in Sandusky.[55]

Canadian musicians performing for pay in American border towns also gave the US immigration bureaucracy occasions to weigh the value of cross-border ties when enforcing the law. In 1929, the city manager of Sault Ste. Marie, Michigan, reported that for quite a number of years, a group of nine or ten members of the municipal band of neighboring Sault Ste. Marie, Ontario, came over twice a week during the summer months to supplement the orchestra in his town; in turn, the Ontario band drew on American musicians. A problem arose when the local chief of immigration forbade the Canadians entry on the grounds that the law required any alien coming to the United States for work to comply with all of the provisions of the immigration law, including procuring a visa and paying the head tax. Zurbrick intervened and held that the law did not apply in this case as no Americans were harmed by the presence of the Canadians. He stressed that the Canadians received the same rate of pay as the American band members and that the musicians had other regular occupations "and perform as bandsmen only when occasion demands."[56]

Zurbrick's instinct was to let custom prevail and allow the issue to "be handled locally" without official interference.[57] But the practice of cross-border commuting for labor had become an explosive issue during the second half of the 1920s, principally due to protests against alien commuters led by the Detroit Federation of Labor.[58] Not daring to make a definitive judgment with wide-ranging political implications, Zurbrick put the case before top immigration officials in Washington. The assistant commissioner-general of immigration replied that "for the time being no change should be made in the manner of admitting these musicians for this temporary employment."[59] This was hardly a firm decision, as it was less an acknowledgement of the border-crossing rights of the Canadian musicians than a momentary toleration of a specific border-crossing custom in an integrated transborder community. Presumably, US officials reserved themselves the right to revisit the issue if and when conditions changed.

Managing the 1940 Border Crisis

Once established by US immigration administrators, the force of immigrant inspectors could serve other national priorities that also required the policing of the country's borders. In the early summer of 1940, for example, the US State Department, motivated by global national security concerns, imposed passport and visa requirements on aliens entering the country along the land borders, including Canadians coming to Detroit to work, shop, and dine. Reaction in Detroit followed immediately. Stressing a long history of cross-border ties, the *Detroit Free Press* condemned the treatment of Canada as a "foreign country" (whereas Mexico, it contended, was "full of Nazis, Stalinists, and other subversive groups"). "The Detroit River is not the Rio Grande," the paper cried. "The fact that here on the border, we Americans and Canadians live and go about our business and pleasure in a social and economic area that virtually ignores the international line, appears to be little understood in other parts of the country. We move into Canada as almost as freely as into Ohio. We work together and play together and intermarry and live together."[60]

Nevertheless, US immigration officers dutifully enforced the new regulations, despite the worries of business interests concerned about depressed holiday travel and protests from US citizens who felt they had an inherent right, "enjoyed for more than 100 years, to cross the border at will."[61] US citizens, while exempt from the order, were startled to discover that upon their return from a Canadian business trip or vacation they would have to prove their identity and citizenship to US immigrant inspectors. According to Zurbrick, native-born Americans in particular had "a mistaken impression that papers showing long residences in the United States are sufficient to answer all questions for those seeking reentry after leaving the United States."[62] To avoid trouble at the border, immigration officials recommended that Americans equip themselves with such vital documents as birth or baptismal certificates or, if applicable, naturalization documents.[63]

The apparent inflexibility of the new regulations spawned tales of frustration and hardship. A cautious man from Indiana decided not to take his family to Canada after learning from American immigration officials at the Ambassador Bridge that an identification card prepared by his hometown police department would not establish his citizenship at the time of reentry to the United States.[64] In a heartbreaking case, border officials prevented the entry of a Toronto woman attempting to reach her dying son in South Bend, Indiana. Immigrant inspectors explained that without seeing the proper documents, "they were helpless and unable to make exceptions."[65] Canadian citizens residing in places such as Michigan faced a unique problem. They found that if they made holiday trips across the border to visit relatives, on their return they would have to present visas obtained from US consulates in Canada and Canadian passports. Attorneys advised most of them to cancel their trips, as Canadian passport officials had a six-month backlog of work. The advice came too late for the Canadian wife of John McNally, a US citizen living in Michigan. Lacking the mandated documents, she was denied reentry at the border on July 1—the same day the regulations went into effect and the same day she was due in federal court in Detroit for naturalization proceedings.[66]

In the midst of a border crisis inflicted by the national government, local US immigration officials managed to keep open some cross-border channels. Instead of demanding passports and new visas, immigrant inspectors in Detroit continued to honor the border-crossing identification cards already in the hands of some 2,000 Windsor commuters who worked in Detroit.[67] The immigration office in Detroit also provided border-crossing cards to anxious Canadian residents of the United States so they could travel to Canada.[68] In early July, in recognition of the "hardships caused by the rigid enforcement of the restrictions," immigration officials in Washington granted Zurbrick "special emergency powers . . . to relieve some of the more serious cases of suffering."[69] One of his top priorities was to permit Canadian citizens to attend the funerals of relatives.

Equally important to Zurbrick was carving out a special exception for the popular Bob-Lo (formally Bois Blanc) Island Amusement Park located on the Canadian side of the boundary at the southern end of the Detroit River. The American company that owned and operated the park also owned the pair of steamboats that annually carried tens of thousands of passengers between its docks in Detroit and the island; Canadians could also reach the island from nearby Amherstburg, Ontario, via the company's ferry service. The State Department's order greatly alarmed company officials. They feared that large numbers of Detroiters would stay away from Bob-Lo if, on their return trips, immigrant inspectors demanded proof of citizenship from US citizens or passports, visas, reentry permits, or border identification cards from alien residents. Early reporting that inspectors posed only "cursory" questions "and seemed to take the passengers' word that they were United States citizens and did not demand proof" hinted at the exercise of discretionary law enforcement on the part of frontline border officials in addressing the problem.[70] But a more complete solution—one that encompassed citizens as well as aliens traveling to the park—awaited authorization from Washington.

In early July, the State Department allowed the Immigration and Naturalization Service to exempt from the passport and visa order all passengers taking the company's boats to Bob-Lo. Building on a precedent established during World War I, when provost marshal regulations prohibited men of draft age from traveling to Canada without the permission of their local draft board, the State Department deemed travel to the island in Canadian waters not to be a departure from the United States; thus, when returning to Detroit, passengers were not required to show any proof of citizenship or immigration status.[71] There was, however, one catch: the company had to discontinue ferry service between Amherstburg and the amusement park. "The ruling," the *Detroit Free Press* noted with some irony, "will close the island, which is Canadian, to all excursionists from Canada, with the exception of those who can enter Detroit first and board the Bob-Lo boat on the American side."[72] By such creative bureaucratic methods, US officials mitigated the effects of a national security measure on important business interests and long-standing patterns of human interaction in the borderland.

Conclusion

Beginning in the 1890s and extending over the next three decades, the United States constructed an immigration control apparatus along its northern boundary in ways that accommodated important business interests and existing border-crossing practices. For example, while charged with applying the immigration laws without unreasonably impeding the movement of people back and forth across the border, the US immigration bureaucracy made arrangements with transportation lines that recognized both the government's authority to conduct examinations of passengers at designated sites and the interests of the companies in achieving an uninterrupted flow of passengers across the border. By facilitating the temporary entries of commuting workers, shoppers, musicians, relatives attending funerals, and others, immigration officials also took into consideration the economic and social ties that had long connected people and communities on both sides of the border. Ultimately, the viability of the system depended on the judgments of immigration administrators at all levels, including frontline inspectors, to balance the political imperative of policing the border with recognition of the complexities of business and life in the border region.

Notes

1. Consultation on Immigration transcript, August 9–10, 1915, San Francisco, CA, 53990/52B, Immigration and Naturalization Service, RG 85, National Archives and Records Administration, Washington, DC, 241–242 (hereafter cited as Consultation on Immigration transcript).

2. Consultation on Immigration transcript, 223–224.

3. John H. Clark, US Commissioner of Immigration, Montreal, to Commissioner-General of Immigration, Washington, DC, April 10, 1915, 53935/6, Immigration and Naturalization Service, RG 85, National Archives and Records Administration, Washington, DC (hereafter cited as INS).

4. Consultation on Immigration transcript, 225–227.

5. Erika Lee, *At America's Gates: Chinese Immigration during the Exclusion Era, 1882–1943* (Chapel Hill: University of North Carolina Press, 2003); Patrick Ettinger, *Imaginary Lines: Border Enforcement and the Origins of Undocumented Immigration, 1882–1930* (Austin: University of Texas Press, 2009); "Guarding Uncle Sam's Back Door," *Detroit Free Press*, January 21, 1912, F8.

6. Bruno Ramirez, *Crossing the 49th Parallel: Migration from Canada to the United States, 1900–1930* (Ithaca, NY: Cornell University Press, 2001), 35–66.

7. Thomas A. Klug, "The Immigration and Naturalization Service (INS) and the Making of a Border-Crossing Culture on the US-Canada Border, 1891–1941," *American Review of Canadian Studies* 40, no. 3 (September 2010): 411–412.

8. For a model analysis pertaining to the southern border, see S. Deborah Kang, *The INS on the Line: Making Immigration Law on the US-Mexico Border, 1917–1954* (New York: Oxford University Press, 2017).

9. In the late 1920s, the Detroit district extended from Port Huron, Michigan, through Detroit to Sandusky, Ohio. Here, the contiguous boundary with Canada was marked by a 120-mile-long line that bisected the St. Clair River, Lake St. Clair, the Detroit River, and Lake Erie.

10. Immigration Act of 1891, 26 Stat. 1084 (1891).

11. Immigration Act of 1891, § 8.

12. Hidetaka Hirota, *Expelling the Poor: Atlantic Seaboard States and the Nineteenth-Century Origins of American Immigration Policy* (New York: Oxford University Press, 2017).

13. Ettinger, *Imaginary Lines*, 74.

14. *Official Register of the United States [. . .] July 1, 1895* (Washington, DC: Government Printing Office, 1895), 154.

15. On the Canadian Agreement, see Herman Stump, testimony, in US Industrial Commission, *Reports*, House Doc. No. 184, 57th Cong., 1st sess. (1901), 15: 17–18 (1901); and Ettinger, *Imaginary Lines*, 78.

16. H. R. Landis, "The Canadian Agreements and Their Scope and Value," January 7, 1929, 4, 6, 55609/550, pt. 4, INS.

17. US Industrial Commission, *Reports*, 15: 18 (1901) .

18. John Higham, *Strangers in the Land: Patterns of American Nativism, 1860–1925* (New Brunswick, NJ: Rutgers University Press, 1963), 87–96.

19. US Industrial Commission, *Reports*, 15: xviii (1901) and 19: 979 (1902).

20. US Senate, Committee on Immigration, *Report of the Committee on Immigration, United States Senate, on the Bill (H.R. 12199) to Regulate the Immigration of Aliens into the United States*, S. Rep. No. 2119, 57th Cong., 1st sess., 138, 155, 446 (1902).

21. Senate Committee on Immigration, *Report* (1902), 155.

22. Senate Committee on Immigration, *Report* (1902), 28.

23. US Industrial Commission, Reports, 19: 979–980 (1902).

24. Ettinger, *Imaginary Lines*, 85, 89.

25. *Official Register of the United States* [. . .] *July 1, 1901* (Washington, DC: Government Printing Office, 1901), 182–186; *Officers and Employees of the Department of Commerce and Labor, 1908* (Washington, DC: Government Printing Office, 1908), 189–233.

26. Immigration Act of 1907, 34 Stat. 898, §§ 1, 36 (1907). The port of entry requirement in section 36 of the law was fleshed out in rule 24 of the regulations, where forty-three ports of entry were identified on the Canadian border; rule 26 identified twenty-one such places on the Mexican border. See US Department of Commerce and Labor, Bureau of Immigration and Naturalization, *Immigration Laws and Regulations of July 1, 1907* (Washington, DC: Government Printing Office, 1907), 48, 52.

27. US Department of Commerce and Labor, Bureau of Immigration, *Annual Report of the Commissioner-General of Immigration for the Fiscal Year Ended June 30, 1907* (Washington, DC: Government Printing Office, 1908), 145.

28. US Department of Commerce and Labor, Bureau of Immigration, *Annual Report for the Fiscal Year Ended June 30, 1907*, 160.

29. US Department of Commerce and Labor, Bureau of Immigration, *Annual Report for the Fiscal Year Ended June 30, 1907*, 146.

30. Clark to Commissioner-General of Immigration, August 6, 1913, 52999/30G, INS.

31. Olivier Zunz, *The Changing Face of Inequality: Urbanization, Industrial Development, and Immigrants in Detroit, 1880–1920* (Chicago: University of Chicago Press, 1982), table 5.4, 106; Joyce Shaw Peterson, *American Automobile Workers, 1900–1933* (Albany: State University of New York Press, 1987), 16–20; US Department of Commerce, Bureau of the Census, *Fourteenth Census of the United States, 1920*, vol. 4, *Population, Occupations* (Washington, DC: Government Printing Office, 1923), 1101–1104.

32. Clark to Commissioner-General of Immigration, November 9, 1915, 52363/34, INS.

33. Detroit immigrant inspectors petition to Secretary of Labor Wilson, April 29, 1913, 52999/61, INS; Clark to Commissioner-General of Immigration, April 10, 1915, March 22, 1917, June 14, 1914, 53935/6, 54261/79, 53935/6, INS.

34. Clark to Commissioner-General of Immigration, June 14, 1913, 52999/30G, INS.

35. Clark to Commissioner-General of Immigration, April 10, December 24, 1915, 53935/6, INS.

36. Clark to Commissioner-General of Immigration, April 10, 1915, 53935/6, INS.

37. Alfred Hampton, Acting Commissioner-General of Immigration, to Clark, January 11, 1916, 52363/34, INS.

38. Arthur J. Tuttle, US district attorney, to G. Oliver Frick, immigrant inspector in

charge at Detroit, March 27, May 27, 1912, letter book 2, box 76, Arthur J. Tuttle Papers, Bentley Historical Library, University of Michigan, Ann Arbor, MI.

39. Klug, "Immigration and Naturalization Service," 400–402.

40. Percy L. Prentis, district director of immigration at Detroit, to Commissioner-General of Immigration, December 27, 1924, November 4, 1926, 55396/11, INS.

41. Detroit & Windsor Ferry Company to Prentis, January 14, 1926, enclosed in Prentis to Commissioner-General of Immigration, January 15, 1926, 55280/11A, INS.

42. Alexander Doig report to Prentis, April 28, 1926, enclosed in Prentis to Commissioner-General of Immigration, May 3, 1926, 55280/11B, INS.

43. Prentis to Commissioner-General of Immigration, August 7, 1924, November 4, 1926, 55396/11, INS; "New Immigration Officers Named," *Detroit Free Press*, November 11, 1930, 8; US Department of Labor, Bureau of Immigration, *Annual Report of the Commissioner-General of Immigration for the Fiscal Year Ended June 30, 1930* (Washington, DC: Government Printing Office, 1930), 32.

44. Immigration Act of 1917, 39 Stat. 874, § 16 (1917).

45. Immigration Act of 1924, 43 Stat. 153, § 23 (1924).

46. Immigration Act of 1917, 39 Stat. 874, §§ 3 (grounds for exclusion), 16 (duty of inspector) (1917). The highly restrictive Immigration Act of 1924, which was a legislative triumph for American nativists, exempted the natives of Western Hemisphere countries (including Canada and Mexico) from the immigration quotas that applied to various European nationalities. However, immigrants from these countries still had to obtain nonquota visas from an American consulate. See Immigration Act of 1924, 43 Stat. 153, §§ 4, 8 (1924).

47. "Answers Criticism by Border Tourists," *New York Times*, July 17, 1929.

48. US Department of Labor, Bureau of Immigration, *Annual Report of the Commissioner-General of Immigration for the Fiscal Year Ended June 30, 1924* (Washington, DC: Government Printing Office, 1924), 15.

49. Prentis to Commissioner-General of Immigration, July 9, 1925, 55280/11A, INS.

50. "Answers Criticism by Border Tourists," *New York Times*, July 17, 1929.

51. On government officials reading the bodies of travelers to glean important information, particularly along the land borders of the United States, where passports were not widely in use, see Craig Robertson, *The Passport in America: The History of a Document* (New York: Oxford University Press, 2010), 185–186, 197.

52. Don Cameron, "Young Canadian Tells of His Adventures 'Running' a Hundred Foreigners," *Detroit Free Press*, April 7, 1929, 9.

53. Robertson, *Passport in America*, 207.

54. Prentis to Commissioner-General of Immigration, March 16, 1926, 55396/11, INS.

55. Zurbrick to the Commissioner of the Immigration and Naturalization Service, August 11, 1934, 55853/258A, INS.

56. Henry Sherman to Zurbrick, April 25, 1929, and Zurbrick to Commissioner-General of Immigration, April 25, 1929, 56013/700C, INS.

57. Zurbrick to Commissioner-General of Immigration, April 25, 1929, 56013/700C, INS.

58. Thomas A. Klug, "Residents by Day, Visitors by Night: The Origins of the Alien

Commuter on the US-Canadian Border during the 1920s," *Michigan Historical Review* 34, no. 2 (Fall 2008): 86–96.

59. George Harris to Zurbrick, May 21, 1929, 56013/700C, INS.

60. "U.S. to Require That Canadians Use Passports," *Detroit Free Press*, June 7, 1940, 1; editorial, *Detroit Free Press*, June 8, 1940, 6.

61. Clifford A. Prevost, "Red Tape in Capital Ties up Border," *Detroit Free Press*, July 2, 1940, 2.

62. "Red Tape Cuts Annual Border Race to a Walk," *Detroit Free Press*, July 5, 1940, 1.

63. Ironically, Zurbrick had no record of his 1874 birth near Buffalo, New York. The city clerk of Detroit agreed to provide him with a voter's certificate. See "Even Zurbrick Caught," *Detroit Free Press*, July 5, 1940, 14.

64. "Red Tape Cuts," 14.

65. "Citizens Warned on Holiday Trips," *Detroit Free Press*, July 2, 1940, 1.

66. "Bar Alien Commuters," *New York Times*, June 30, 1940; "Returning United States Residents Halted by Enforcing of Visa Rule at Canadian Line," *New York Times*, July 2, 1940.

67. "Citizens Warned on Holiday Trips," 1, 3; Frank B. Woodford, "Detroit Feels Lag in Canadian Visits," *New York Times*, July 7, 1940.

68. "US Reaffirms Border Ruling," *Detroit Free Press*, June 26, 1940, 8.

69. "Ban on Canadians to Cost City Thousands in Business," *Detroit Free Press*, July 3, 1940, 3.

70. "Citizens Warned on Holiday Trips," 3.

71. For World War I, see Anthony Caminetti and John Clark, telegrams, May 15–16, 1918, 55410/318, INS.

72. "Ban on Canadians," 3.

SIX

The Roots of the Border Patrol

Line Riders and the Bureaucratization of
US-Mexican Border Policing, 1894–1924

JAMES DUPREE

On the night of December 27, 1906, the US Bureau of Immigration special agent A. A. Seraphic stood in El Paso, Texas, watching the border between that city and Ciudad Juárez, Chihuahua, in Mexico. He saw many people cross back and forth without having to stop for inspection. Earlier that day, in fact, he himself had crossed several times unimpeded. Once, he even went into the immigration station and asked, in Spanish, for a match. He was handed a pencil, as the US border guards did not understand his request.[1] Seraphic had learned in the previous months that despite the presence of an armed federal police force along the US border with Mexico, the border remained essentially open. From what he could tell, it was not, as many inspectors along the border claimed, because there were too few inspectors and the border was too long. Instead, Seraphic believed, it was because agents apparently did not care enough to do their jobs correctly. After all, how could they effectively police the border if many had not even bothered to learn Spanish? Profoundly upset with the performance of immigrant inspectors along the border, Seraphic believed that the situation needed to change. It would, but not in ways Seraphic could have predicted.

At the turn of the twentieth century, nativist fears about a new wave of immigration brought national attention to the North American borderlands. Fears that migrants from eastern and southern Europe, the Middle East, and Asia would use the porous borders of the United States as an entry point into the country began to dominate national political debates.

It was not a new fear. The Bureau of Immigration had patrolled the border for Chinese immigrants since 1894. But in the year leading up to the Immigration Act of 1907, contract labor (foreign workers brought into the United States by American companies) became a concern, especially along the border. Within this context, in 1906, the federal government sent A. A. Seraphic to Texas in order to investigate the actions of immigrant inspectors on the ground. Commissioner-General of Immigration F. P. Sargent gave Seraphic broad latitude in his investigation to find out how restricted Syrians in particular crossed the Mexican border into the United States. His report illuminates problems the US government faced in policing the unauthorized flow of human beings across its borders. Seraphic encountered border stations in disarray as well as inept and untrained officers, confirming for many alarmists that their worst fears of an uncontrolled border had become a reality. Concerned that focus on maritime ports left land borders under-policed, superiors sent Seraphic to the border on a fact-finding mission. The assignment went on to shape how states saw and policed the border.[2] Seraphic's inspection led the bureau to unify the border stations into the Mexican Border District in 1907 as a means of enacting stronger border controls against unauthorized migration and contract labor law violations.

The release of Seraphic's report and the creation of the Mexican Border District coincided with broader political shifts at the national level, including growing political momentum for passage of the Immigration Act of 1907. Aimed at tightening the border and reducing the flow of immigrants into the country, section 24 of the act provided for the hiring of immigrant inspectors (logically referred to as "section 24 agents") whose sole responsibility was enforcing contract labor law, or regulations geared toward restricting immigrant and migrant workers.[3] As the district director, F. W. Berkshire, worked to improve discipline among the local immigration inspectors, the new federal immigration law shifted the bureau's focus from enforcing immigration law to policing contract labor law. In 1907, as the bureau began bureaucratizing the immigration process along the Mexican border by instituting more rigid standards and guidelines, it also began to investigate Canadian and European migrant workers along the Mexican border and throughout the American West. While these policies were initially designed to control workers and immigrants from abroad, they also led to the targeting of Mexican migrant workers in the borderlands. Although attempts to restrict the presence of contract laborers met with little success, these efforts prompted calls for stricter enforcement of immigration law, eventually culminating in the establishment of the Border Patrol in 1924. Seraphic's investigation, when coupled with national legislative shifts, provides a window into how regional enforcement challenges in the borderlands helped fuel stricter enforcement policies at the federal level.

Although Congress passed the Chinese Exclusion Act in 1882 and created the Bureau of Immigration in 1891, the bureau did not place stations along the Mexican border until 1894.[4] Indeed, it took almost a decade after that for an efficient and professional policing force to emerge. Historians have made significant contributions to our understanding of movement across the US border with Mexico and of efforts at policing that movement. The literature on these issues is illuminating. Rachel St. John describes the origins and development of the border itself, and Patrick Ettinger has charted the experiences of migrants crossing both the Mexican and Canadian borders from 1882 to 1930. Similarly, Erika Lee and Grace Peña Delgado have uncovered rich and detailed histories of Chinese communities along the Mexican border, and Theresa Alfaro-Velcamp describes how the Syrian community along the border, as victims of American nativists' fears, found homes in Mexico. Underexamined, though, is the ground-level enforcement of immigration control—and later contract labor laws that restricted migratory labor—in the first decades of the twentieth century.[5] This chapter explores how the Bureau of Immigration, through the "line riders" (a nickname first used by the men who patrolled the border as customs inspectors), became a modern police force.[6] In order to do so, it identifies the important role that inspectors with the Bureau of Immigration played in shaping border-policing policies during the first decades of the twentieth century.

This chapter also explores how ineffective policing prompted further federal oversight of the national border.[7] The distance between frontline bureau agents (line riders) and Washington, DC, meant that casual enforcement of immigration law and inattention to duty—as well as far more serious malfeasance—continued longer at land ports of entry compared to the nation's seaports, which bore greater official scrutiny. Line riders inadvertently made significant contributions to the creation of the border enforcement apparatus by prompting the Bureau of Immigration to intervene and to introduce order and discipline to a police force that was at best incompetent and at worst corrupt. These changes occurred simultaneously with a shift in focus to contract labor enforcement in 1907 with passage of the Immigration Act that year, marking the greater policing of Mexican migrants. For the first time, Mexicans who were enticed into the United States by American companies in order to work were officially stopped at the border. Seraphic's investigation in Texas, and the buildup of enforcement policies that emerged as a result, provide a case study of how local issues can profoundly shape federal enforcement policies.

The Focus on the Border

In 1906, after a series of troubling reports regarding illicit crossings and corrupt low- and midlevel officials, Congress turned its attention to the regulation of the US border with Mexico. Indeed, Bureau of Immigration records from the beginning of the twentieth century are full of reports of agents' corruption and abuse of power, especially along the border near Ciudad Juárez, Chihuahua. This included a wide range of charges, such as incorrectly filling out reports in order to falsify expenses, the abuse of Chinese immigrants, and a scheme with two consecutive customs collectors in Nogales, Arizona, to smuggle Chinese immigrants across the border.[8] Congressional concerns and public fears notwithstanding, the Bureau of Immigration's commissioner-general, F. P. Sargent, was at a loss for how to address the problems.[9] He found his solution in the form of an ethnic Greek special immigration agent with investigative experience by the name of A. A. Seraphic. Not a line rider, Seraphic served as a special agent tasked with investigating politically delicate situations.

Because many migrants who would eventually settle in the United States used Mexico City as their point of departure, Seraphic began his investigation in the Mexican capital on November 15, 1906.[10] The bureau gave Seraphic a specific mission: investigate Syrian immigration emanating from Mexico. Since at least 1879, the US government had been fixated on "controlling diseases associated with immigrants." Syrians, composing part of this "new immigrant" wave, had become a particular concern for the US government and much of the American public due to the fear that they carried trachoma to the United States.[11] Seraphic's report reflects this larger disdain for those considered part of this suspect new immigrant group.[12] And even though this increased scrutiny presented important challenges for migrants hoping to cross from Mexico to the United States, it also at times could create moments of opportunity. Syrian immigrants, for example, sometimes used government officials' racialized view of them to their advantage, portraying themselves as Mexicans in order to cross.[13] Not mere victims, Syrians migrants worked the system with what agency they had. Disguising themselves as Mexicans came easily to Syrians, according to Seraphic, as he believed both tended toward "servility."[14]

In addition to racism and ignorance, a lack of professionalism undermined agents' border policing efforts. In fact, the line riders' resistance to any sort of professional standards insofar as the admission of immigrants made it easier for Syrians to get across. Immigrant inspectors created their own paternalistic fiefdoms and frequently claimed that they knew all the local Mexicans, commenting with some variation of "I know these people" in both Seraphic's report and the responses to it.[15] Syrians could thus cross the border by dressing and acting in ways the inspectors expected of Mexicans. That carelessness was part of a larger pattern of incompetence and racial bias that plagued policing at the Mexican border.[16]

In the wake of his investigation, Seraphic immediately created a list of recommendations addressing what he saw as the core problems along the border. First, he pointed out that Greeks and Syrians who had been debarred (officially prevented from entering the country) rarely returned to Mexico permanently. If one port debarred specific immigrants, preventing them from entering the United States, they often moved on to the next until inspectors allowed them to cross.[17] Second, Seraphic advised that only men who spoke Spanish should be chosen for border duty to better determine if a migrant was Mexican. Indeed, few of the immigrant inspectors before Seraphic's mission were knowledgeable of Spanish, let alone fluent. Along those lines, he recommended that all Syrian interpreters be fired. The bureau could then start over, using stricter hiring guidelines.[18] While American translators could be retrained, Seraphic's report implied that Syrians and other new immigrants could not be trusted.

Finally, Seraphic made what appeared to him the most sensible suggestion: close off the border to all "aliens." He further recommended that the bureau should "deport debarred diseased aliens to the country of their nativity."[19] If both of those options failed, Seraphic suggested that inspectors act on the addresses collected, pursue undocumented immigrants, and deport them.[20] Inspectors should also "be warned with an emphatic circular letter that any proven charge of negligence would result in dismissal."[21] Seraphic was not a sympathetic man; nor was he a patient one. There is no nuance to his report. Immigrants were "illegal" until proven otherwise, and he saw a clear racial hierarchy along the border. While claiming to have no specific animus toward Mexicans (except smugglers), he referred to them as "servile," and none of his recommendations favored immigrants in any way. For Seraphic, there was no path to legal status for *any* undocumented aliens. They were all what the immigration scholar Mae M. Ngai refers to as "impossible subjects."[22]

While many of Seraphic's suggestions required action on the part of Congress, it also provided the bureau with a path forward.[23] In fact, the response to Seraphic's report was immediate and forceful. Sargent was especially pleased with Seraphic's effort, and as a result he sent a strongly worded message to Luther C. Steward, inspector in charge in San Antonio, regarding Eagle Pass.[24] Sargent fumed that apparently just the *appearance* of being Mexican was enough for an immigrant to cross the border. Steward needed to end that practice.[25] Sargent also instructed the inspector in charge in El Paso to hire an assistant, if necessary, to fix his station.[26] Corruption in the enforcement of Chinese exclusion was certainly nothing new. J. T. Scharf, a Chinese inspector for the US Customs Service, was an outspoken critic of the failures of Chinese exclusion at the turn of the century on both a legislative and enforcement level along the borders and in the seaports.[27] But Sargent expressed surprise at the level of misconduct along the border. As the historian Patrick Ettinger has pointed out, the early years of the Chinese exclusion era were focused on the seaports, and while research since has shown that there was considerable activity along both the Mexican and the Canadian borders, that was not the perception of the bureau at the time. Land border crossings paled in comparison to immigrant arrivals at seaports.[28] Seraphic indicated that the line riders were aware that no one kept a close eye on them. After his report landed on Sargent's desk, border enforcement methods and official focus began to change.

Few inspectors lost their jobs because of the report, but there was significant reorganization (records mention at least five important personnel changes, including the demotion of Inspector in Charge Frank Boss and the transfer of an Inspector Searle to Nogales, Arizona).[29] The bureau also ended the use of temporary and voluntary interpreters and carefully reviewed Seraphic's suggestions. Suggestions that were unrealistic usually ended with some form of compromise.[30] For instance, Seraphic wanted interpreters who spoke both Spanish *and* Syrian. The bureau believed that to be virtually impossible, so it agreed to hire more inspectors who spoke one *or* the other. The bureau also realized that it could not send immigrants back to the countries of their nativity, but it *could* send them back to the home ports of the ships on which they arrived.[31] The report's impacts were felt as far away as the Port of New York, as the commissioner of immigration there sent Sargent a letter assuring him that all ships from the Yucatán or South American ports would be more thoroughly inspected.

Seraphic discovered that corruption was not as big a problem as a lack of discipline. As a result, the Bureau of Immigration transformed the line riders into a tightly regulated police force instead of scattered independent inspectors. As civil servants, the line riders went through the same hiring process as any other government employee. The first step involved a civil service exam, a step that was easier to accomplish with a reference from a politician. Each applicant who passed the exam was added to a list that was then forwarded to a border station requesting inspectors. Before 1907, however, job-specific training was left to the inspectors already on the border, thus perpetuating an already flawed system. While the bureau never intended the inspectors to be independent, the distance from Washington, DC, as well as inspectors' isolation while riding the lines, allowed them to develop their own systems and philosophies for running their jurisdictions as they pleased. Seraphic made it clear to the bureau that line riders needed to be watched, regulated, and controlled. They also had to be held to much higher standards by each level of supervision. In other words, they should be treated like members of other law enforcement branches rather than of an administrative agency. Unlike the low-level bureaucrats that seaport inspectors were, line riders were armed, had the power to arrest, and traveled sometimes hundreds of miles by horseback to investigate violations of immigration law. Seraphic's report pushed Washington to shift its view of the immigration enforcement approach along the border from mostly administrative, like it was in the coastal ports, to one more focused on policing. Soon after the report, however, contract labor law took precedent over immigration law.

F. W. Berkshire and the Mexican Border District

After Seraphic's report, Texas, Arizona, and New Mexico were unified into the Mexican Border District under F. W. Berkshire, its supervising inspector. Before, the highest-ranking position in the border states was inspector in charge, and El Paso and Nogales each had more than one.[32] Seraphic's biggest issue with the inspectors along the border was that they were unsupervised and followed few standard rules. Almost immediately after the report, in 1907, the bureau promoted Berkshire, who tightened discipline and instituted stricter regulations and had little patience for those who did not follow them. He also required far more documentation from the inspectors than had been required in the past. Inspectors and supervisors began reporting everything to Berkshire that happened (and much that didn't, by exaggerating their successes) along the border, which Berkshire then reported to the bureau. Steadily, federal oversight grew along the border.

Immigration enforcement was no more successful under Berkshire, but inspectors became much better at creating the illusion of success. Learning to navigate the bureaucracy meant learning what it wanted to hear. Although largely forgotten, Berkshire was also one of the driving forces behind the creation of the US Border Patrol. As early as 1918, he pushed hard to increase the number of inspectors patrolling the border (full-time line riders, also known as "mounted guards," who assisted the immigrant inspectors) to 1,632, in addition to the already present immigrant inspectors.[33] When Congress created the Border Patrol in 1924, the agency rested on Berkshire's groundwork of bureaucratic sensibility that he had instilled in his agents.[34] Indeed, 24 percent of the first Border Patrol officers came from Berkshire's ranks.[35]

In another significant change during the Berkshire era, the focus of enforcement shifted from immigration law to contract labor law violations, which Congress originally had difficulty defining. In the debates leading to the Immigration Act of 1907, Senator Augustus Bacon (D-GA) defined "contract labor" as a man being lured to the United States and signing a contract with an American company. Senator John Spooner (R-WI), however, countered that the report on contract labor given to the Senate stated that anyone who was "seduced or lured to this country by offers of employment" was a contract laborer.[36] Under this interpretation, the signing of a contract was not a necessary component. Congress, and thus the Bureau of Immigration, adopted Spooner's more expansive definition.

Since 1884, immigrant inspectors had concerned themselves primarily with determining whether immigrants met the legal requirements to enter the United States. With the passage of the Immigration Act of 1907, their reports focused more on what those immigrants intended to do once they entered the country. Contract laborers, workers brought in from other countries to work for American companies (with and without signed contracts), became the targets of contract labor inspectors, a position established in section 24 of the Immigration Act of 1907. In 1910, contract labor inspectors—the so-called section 24 agents—began focusing on Mexicans, whose numbers grew along the border as the Mexican Revolution continued. The inspectors found themselves overwhelmed by Mexican immigrants and agricultural- and industrial-sector demands for labor by 1917, however, and the restrictions were loosened, creating tension between agribusiness in the Southwest (which sought Mexican laborers) and groups such as labor unions in the rest of the country (which resented foreign labor).[37] Conflict between border guards and industries along the border endured for decades.[38]

The situation along the border changed for Mexicans following Seraphic's mission. Until 1907, Mexicans could cross the border with few restrictions, but by 1910 the immigrant inspectors focused more on restricting Mexican contract laborers. This focus intensified during the Mexican Revolution, an event that complicated Mexican workers' relationships with white laborers and US companies.[39] White laborers admired a 1914 strike by Mexican laborers at the Guggenheim Mine in Ray, Arizona, for instance, but unions at the national level overwhelmingly supported the Immigration Act of 1907, especially its contract labor provisions. Many Anglo Arizonans believed that Mexican laborers exerting their rights threatened American companies and local law enforcement. White workers' grudging respect for Mexican labor did not prevent Sheriff Harry Wheeler of Bisbee, Arizona, from forcing one-fifth of Bisbee's residents across the border to Mexico in 1917.[40] The combination of World War I, the Zimmermann Telegram (in which a German diplomat secretly offered the Mexican government the return of land lost to the United States in the US-Mexican War in exchange for Mexico joining the Central Powers against the Americans), the Mexican Revolution, and national unions' continued support for the Immigration Act of 1907 changed immigrant inspectors' focus, creating a de facto (if largely unsuccessful) restriction on Mexican laborers immigrating into the United States along the border. The inspector in charge at Brownsville, Texas, for instance, was castigated by his superior in 1915 for not determining if the immigrant Felipe Aranda was intent on working in the United States before allowing him into the country.[41]

Significantly, the Mexican borderlands became a multinational locus of contract labor issues. As mining companies, in particular, brought in Canadians and Europeans to work, section 24 agents attempted to monitor the flow of those workers.[42] There were many instances of inspectors detaining Canadian and European migrants, many of whom were en route to the West, for alleged contract labor violations. In Detroit in 1915, inspectors detained a man headed for the Ford Motor Company in San Francisco; another was headed for the Llano Del Rio Company in Los Angeles; still another, to Albuquerque; a German immigrant was stopped in Laredo; and inspectors investigated a copper mining company in Arizona for bringing in "five or six raw scotchmen."[43]

One case in Lordsburg, New Mexico, provides important insight into the complex battles over contract labor that occurred between immigrant inspectors and the companies who hired migrants. In 1915, five Canadians were recruited by Smith and Travers, a diamond drill–operating contractor based in Canada, to work at the Eighty-Five Mine and the Atwood Mine in Lordsburg.[44] The investigation by the Bureau of Immigration, and then the trial that followed, lasted three years. At the center was the question of whether the drill operators worked for Smith and Travers or for the mines. Debates also focused on whether the mines actively recruited Canadian workers because they would work for lower wages. On August 20, 1918, the US District Court for the District of New Mexico found that the operators worked for the Canadian company and that the mines had *not* sought them out. This ending is not surprising, as courts rarely found companies in violation of federal mandates regarding contract labor. And even though the case alleged against the mines was dismissed, it demonstrated that the new mandate to enforce immigration laws against contract laborers caused tensions between federal authorities and private industries operating in the borderlands. The transnational nature of contract labor left inspectors scrambling to determine who was a "legitimate" worker and who was in violation of the new immigration policies, often much to the frustration of businesses who sought to profit from the labor of temporary migrant workers.[45]

If contract workers from multiple racial and ethnic backgrounds came to the attention of inspectors, there was a significant difference in how they treated those being investigated. Inspectors gave Canadians every opportunity to justify their presence and to testify against the companies accused of luring them to the United States before the authorities released them. Even if inspectors determined that they were inadmissible, Canadians often appealed and wrote letters on their own behalf.[46] It speaks volumes that appeals and letters in the record written by Mexican migrants—whether in Spanish, in English, or through translators—are extraordinarily hard to find. Generally, officials also inspected Canadian workers only when they stumbled on them or were informed of their presence. In contrast, contract labor inspectors sought out Mexican migrants moving back and forth across the border for reasons as varied as looking for daywork or visiting friends and family. Immigrant inspectors likely perceived familiarity in the white faces and common English language of Canadians but differentiated Mexicans as foreign. This made it easier for border guards to transition from monitoring national divides to enacting more targeted enforcement focusing on Mexican laborers. Notably, beginning in 1907, fewer and fewer immigrants were debarred over simple immigration violations; they were more often deported over a contract labor law dispute or a combination of the two. These attempts were largely failures, with Mexicans simply denying they were contract laborers, but the intent of the law is more important than its success. Inspectors' actions in the first decades of the twentieth century provided groundwork for the Border Patrol; for Mexicans migrants, contract labor law took on a deeper significance.[47]

Conclusion

In the late nineteenth century, immigration enforcement along the Mexican border proved ineffective, as border agents were untrained, undisciplined, and inexperienced. A. A. Seraphic revealed that if the Bureau of Immigration had any hope of policing immigration, then it had to more fully police the actions and accountability of inspectors. Placing F. W. Berkshire in charge of the Mexican Border District in 1907 was an attempt to do just that. That same year, the Immigration Act emphasized contract labor violations and created contract labor inspectors, or section 24 agents. Seraphic's report and his suggestions for increasing the efficiency of the inspectors made the transition from focusing on immigration law to contract labor law easier. Initially, inspectors focused on Canadian and European laborers, as well as Mexicans, but after 1910, due to the Mexican Revolution and increased demand for labor in Texas, Arizona, and New Mexico, Mexican migrants predominated. By 1918, Canadians, Asians, and Europeans virtually disappeared from inspectors' reports. None of this should imply that the immigrant inspectors succeeded in stopping undocumented immigration. Indeed, agents were often accused of abetting undocumented border crossings.[48] Even so, while the rest of the country, including those involved in border agribusiness, debated the importance and necessity of Mexican labor in the United States, inspectors stubbornly focused on Mexican contract laborers, reporting that they *were* successfully policing the border. Mexican immigration in the United States increased despite government reports that contract labor violations were significantly curtailed. Focusing on Mexican migrants, enforcing a racial hierarchy, and maintaining the illusion of controlling the border set the stage for the Border Patrol and immigration enforcement for the next one hundred years.

Notes

1. Seraphic Report to Sargent, January 8, 1907, file 514331, 21, National Archives and Records Administration, Washington, DC (hereafter cited as Seraphic Report).

2. James C. Scott, *Seeing Like a State: How Certain Schemes to Improve the Human Condition Have Failed* (New Haven, CT: Yale University Press, 1998).

3. See Immigration Act of 1907, 34 Stat. 898 (1907).

4. Darrell Hevenor Smith and Henry Guy Herring, *The Bureau of Immigration* (Baltimore, MD: Johns Hopkins University Press, 1924), 7.

5. While Deborah Kang looks at the Bureau of Immigration along the Mexican border, she begins in 1917, with Kelly Lytle Hernández picking up the story in 1924 with the Border Patrol. See Theresa Alfaro-Velcamp, *So Far from Allah, So Close to Mexico: Middle Eastern Immigrants in Modern Mexico* (Austin: University of Texas Press, 2007); Patrick W. Ettinger, *Imaginary Lines: Border Enforcement and the Origins of Undocumented Immigration, 1882–1930* (Austin: University of Texas Press, 2009); Kelly Lytle Hernández, *Migra! A History of the U.S. Border Patrol* (Berkeley: University of California Press, 2010); Erika Lee, *At America's Gates: Chinese Immigration during the Exclusion Era, 1882–1943* (Chapel Hill: University of North Carolina Press, 2003); Julian Lim, *Porous Borders: Multiracial Migrations and the Law in the U.S.-Mexico Borderlands* (Chapel Hill: University of North Carolina Press, 2017); Rachel St. John, *Line in the Sand: A History of the Western U.S.-Mexico Border* (Princeton, NJ: Princeton University Press, 2011); and Deborah S. Kang, *The INS on the Line: Making Immigration Law on the U.S.-Mexico Border, 1917–1954* (New York: Oxford University Press, 2017).

6. The legendary inspector George Webb, in fact, took great pride in his past as a line rider with the Customs Service before joining the Bureau of Immigration. See RG 85, HM, 1995, box 1, TX 11, National Archives, Fort Worth, TX (hereafter cited as NARAFW); and Jim Brown and Rand Careaga, *Riding the Line: The United States Customs Service in San Diego, 1885–1930; A Documentary History* (Washington, DC: Department of the Treasury, United States Customs Service, Pacific Region, 1991).

7. "Immigrant" inspector, as opposed to "immigration" inspector, was an inspector's official title.

8. See 1901, RG 85, files 3280–451, National Archives and Records Administration, Washington, DC (hereafter cited as NARA); 1906, file 51402/13, NARA; and George E. Paulsen, "The Yellow Peril at Nogales: The Ordeal of Collector William M. Hoey," *Arizona and the West* 13, no. 2 (1971): 113–128.

9. For congressional rants, see Select Comm. on Immigration and Naturalization, H.R. Rep. No. 51-4048, pt. 2 (1891). Also, congressmen attempted to pass "absolute" exclusion laws multiple times, especially as their attention was drawn to the Mexican border. The first were Senators John H. Mitchell (R-OR) and William Stewart (R-NV)

in 1888 (19 Cong. Rec. 422). Representative Thomas J. Geary (D-CA) claimed that the purpose of H.R. 6185 (the Geary Bill) was no less than "to prevent the coming of Chinese into the country" (23 Cong. Rec. 2912 [1892]). The Geary Bill made no distinctions among Chinese (except diplomats). The final Geary Act was far stricter than the original Exclusion Act, but it was not "absolute" exclusion, a very modest win. It passed on May 4, 1892, two days before the original act expired. For a thorough discussion of the Geary Act, see Kelly Lytle Hernández, *City of Inmates: Conquest, Rebellion, and the Rise of Human Caging in Los Angeles, 1771–1965* (Chapel Hill: University of North Carolina Press, 2017), 64–73.

10. Seraphic Report, 1; see Alfaro-Velcamp, *So Far from Allah.*

11. Alfaro-Velcamp, 31. See *Washington Post*, August 19, 1906, 4; and "Syrians Work Entry Scheme: Afflicted Foreigners Cross from Mexico; Immigration Inspector Finds Case of Wholesale Smuggling of Objectionable Party Whose Members Were Victims of Eye Diseases and Had Been Barred from Entry," *Los Angeles Times*, August 19, 1906, 14.

12. Matthew Frye Jacobson, *Barbarian Virtues: The United States Encounters Foreign Peoples at Home and Abroad, 1876–1917* (New York: Hill and Wang, 2001), 5.

13. Seraphic Report, 6.

14. Seraphic Report, 4.

15. Seraphic Report, 7; Steward to Sargent, February 23, 1907, file 514231, NARA.

16. Steward to Sargent, February 23, 1907, file 514231, NARA; Paulsen, "Yellow Peril," 113; 1901, RG 85, files 3280–451, NARA; 1906, file 51402/13, NARA.

17. Seraphic Report, 23.

18. Seraphic Report, 24.

19. Seraphic Report, 25.

20. Inspectors already traveled quite a bit to track down illicit border crossers, often as far away as Oklahoma City. See Acting Inspector in Charge Henry Brownland to Inspector in Charge W. F. Schlaar, March 30, 1905, RG 85, HM 1995, box 3, E, Tx2, NARA.

21. Seraphic Report, 25.

22. Mae M. Ngai, *Impossible Subjects: Illegal Aliens and the Making of Modern America* (Princeton, NJ: Princeton University Press, 2014), 5.

23. For congressional fears regarding the Chinese, see Select Comm. on Immigration and Naturalization, Chinese Immigration, H.R. Rep. No. 51-4048 (1891); W. S. Chance, "Report of the Supervising Special Agent," *Annual Report of the Secretary of the Treasury on the State of the Finances: Fiscal Year Ending June 30th, 1897*, no. 14 (1897): 755–773; H.R. Rep. 58-758 (1903); *Annual Report of the Commissioner-General of Immigration*, 62; and Lucy E. Salyer, *Laws Harsh as Tigers: Chinese Immigrants and the Shaping of Modern Immigration Law* (Chapel Hill: University of North Carolina Press, 1995). For the media's and general public's fears, see Lon Kurashige, *Two Faces of Exclusion: The Untold History of Anti-Asian Racism in the United States* (Chapel Hill: University of North Carolina Press, 2016), 86–110.

24. Sargent to Seraphic, February 11, 1907, file 514231, NARA.

25. Sargent to Steward, February 11, 1907, file 514231, NARA.

26. Sargent to Schmucker, February 11, 1907, file 514231, NARA.

27. J. T. Scharf, "Chinese 'Exclusion' Laws," *New York Times*, January 16, 1898. See

also J. T. Scharf, "The Farce of the Chinese Exclusion Laws," *North American Review* 166, no. 494 (January 1898): 85.

28. Ettinger, *Imaginary Lines*, 42.

29. F. W. Berkshire, memorandum, February 2, 1907, RG 85, file 514231-A, NARAFW.

30. F. P. Sargent, memorandum, February 23, 1907, RG 85, file 514231, NARA.

31. F. P. Sargent, memorandum, February 2, 1907, RG 85, file 514331-1, NARA.

32. See the *Official Register of the United States*, 1905, vol. 1, and 1907, vol. 1.

33. F. W. Berkshire to Commissioner-General of Immigration, November 3, 1918, file 5002/800-J, pp. 4, 5, Border Patrol Museum Archives.

34. Lytle Hernández, *Migra!*, 37–38.

35. J. Evetts Haley, *Jeff Milton, a Good Man with a Gun* (Norman: University of Oklahoma Press, 1948); Lytle Hernández, *Migra!*, 34; Clifford Alan Perkins and C. L. Sonnichsen, *Border Patrol: With the U.S. Immigration Service on the Mexican Boundary, 1910–54* (El Paso: Texas Western Press, University of Texas at El Paso, 1978).

36. 12 Cong. Rec. 3025 (1907).

37. Paul Ganster and David E. Lorey, *The U.S.-Mexican Border into the Twenty-First Century* (Lanham, MD: Rowman and Littlefield, 2008), 67, 69.

38. Lytle Hernández, *Migra!*, 155.

39. RG 865, HM 1995, box 6, E TX6, folder 5020–99, NARAFW. See also Miguel Antonio Levario, *Militarizing the Border: When Mexicans Became the Enemy* (College Station: Texas A&M University Press, 2015), 97.

40. Katherine Benton-Cohen, *Borderline Americans: Racial Division and Labor War in the Arizona Borderlands* (Cambridge, MA: Harvard University Press, 2011), 205, 216.

41. Acting Supervising Inspector George J. Harris to Inspector in Charge, Brownsville, Texas, August 23, 1915, RG 85, HM 1995, box 6, E TX6, folder 5020–100, NARAFW.

42. Special Inspector Ayers to F. W. Berkshire, June 14, 1911, RG 85, folder 5020–7, NARAFW.

43. Deputy Marshal G. H. Prans to F. W. Berkshire, June 16, 1911, RG 85, folder 5020–7, NARAFW.

44. Inspector Munster to F. W. Berkshire, March 27, 1916, RG 85, HM 1995, box 6, E TX6, folder 5020–107, NARAFW.

45. United States v. Eighty-Five Mining Company. See also A. P. Warner, "Finding of Fact" of the United States District Court of the District of New Mexico, August 20, 1918; and Deputy US Marshal G. A. Franz to F. W. Berkshire, June 19, 1911, both in RG 85, HM 1995, box 6, E TX6, folder 5020–107, NARAFW.

46. "Statement of A. T. Sparks," October 28, 1915, RG 85, HM 1995, box 6, folder 5020–102, NARAFW.

47. Torrie Hester, *Deportation: The Origins of U.S. Policy* (Philadelphia: University of Pennsylvania Press, 2017), 162.

48. Paulsen, "Yellow Peril"; Roberto R. Calderón, *Mexican Coal Mining Labor in Texas and Coahuila, 1880–1930* (College Station: Texas A&M University Press, 1991), 188.

Home Guard

SEVEN

State-Sponsored Vigilantism and Violence
in the Texas-Mexico Borderlands

MIGUEL A. LEVARIO

On the morning of March 9, 1916, the Mexican revolutionary leader Francisco "Pancho" Villa and a small band of men attacked a United States Army outpost in Columbus, New Mexico. After an hour and a half of fighting, Villa and his men were repulsed by US soldiers and armed civilians. Twenty US soldiers and civilians were killed in the attack along with dozens of Villistas. Several of Columbus's male residents quickly took up arms during the attack and pursued straggling Villista soldiers, firing at them as they ran or lay wounded.[1] This group of men, known as the "Columbus home guard," were a vigilante group spontaneously formed in response to Villa's raid. In the aftermath of the attack, the home guard issued a warning to any "strangers" caught around town that they had five minutes to get five miles out of town.[2]

Later that evening, a train returned to Columbus from Deming, New Mexico, and El Paso, carrying several passengers unaware of that morning's events. Among the passengers was an ethnic Mexican from El Paso hoping to open a barbershop in the southern New Mexico town.[3] Members of the Columbus home guard assaulted and killed him when he disembarked the train. More trains arrived from Janos and Asunción, Chihuahua, and many met the same fate at the hands of the Columbus home guard. Approximately twenty-five men were in the civilian posse, and they targeted Mexican men they came across regardless of their association with Villa.[4]

129

In the US-Mexico borderlands and beyond, many Anglos felt compelled to arm and protect themselves from perceived threats from northern Mexico. Since the beginning of the Mexican Revolution in 1910, US border states, such as Texas, experienced an influx of war refugees from Mexico, which overwhelmed the limited resources at ports of entry. Border municipalities grew exponentially, resulting in a demographic shift that favored ethnic Mexicans and worried many Anglos. As a result, many Anglo civilians, like those in Columbus, organized as armed home guards to defend their towns and to pursue suspicious or unwanted ethnic Mexicans. In Texas, Governor Oscar Colquitt authorized their formation, thereby sanctioning state-sponsored policing of ethnic Mexicans by vigilante groups. Texas home guards believed they filled a void left by inadequate law enforcement officers and military personnel in their locales. They did not follow a formal chain of command and were not under the jurisdiction of a recognized local or state authority. Instead, working outside formal legal structures, home guards attempted to assert their superiority over the ethnic Mexican population in their respective towns and cities regardless of any real threat posed to their communities. These home guards perceived their actions to be necessary for security and the protection of the established caste system present in Texas.[5]

A look into Texas home guards provides a lens on how we understand the state's policing of ethnic Mexicans during the Mexican Revolution. Anglo vigilante groups throughout Texas viewed ethnic Mexicans as a danger and threat despite little to no evidence of cause. Moreover, the blanket assertion that ethnic Mexicans were a threat justified latent racist sentiments by many to call for and support vigilantism at and beyond the border.[6] Policing practices offer another lens to understand state control of brown bodies and their movement. More specifically, we understand how the state marks brown bodies in order to control or police their movements.[7] Indeed, the state serves as the perennial security broker between ethnic Mexicans and Anglos in the United States. However, in more rural or sparsely populated areas, a security apparatus did not exist, and white citizens felt compelled to organize and mobilize under the guise of a protective force. Important work by the authors Miguel Levario, Kelly Lytle Hernández, and Alexandra Minna Stern promotes a scholarly trajectory in borderlands studies that seeks to understand the role of the state in restricting ethnic Mexican integration into citizenship through policing. However, few scholars have undertaken the task of understanding how people and communities integrate ethnic Mexicans into the sociopolitical landscape. This chapter examines how Anglo mobs sought and won state support for their attacks on ethnic Mexicans in the borderlands.

This chapter focuses on the early years of the combative phase of the Mexican Revolution, from 1911 to 1914. During this period, several critical events stoked fear and patriotic fervor in the borderlands, including the commencement of hostilities in the northern Mexican states in 1911, the constitutionalist movement of 1913, and the Tampico Affair of 1914. These events and others provide the context of war and its potential reach into the United States. In addition, the displacement of thousands of Mexican refugees and their migration north of the border resulted in the "Mexicanization," or sudden increase of the ethnic Mexican population, of Texas towns and cities such as El Paso, Presidio, Juno, and others. Last, a case study approach provides a lens for the complex nature of law and order on the US side of the boundary and the inability of law enforcement and military officials to adjust to war across the border or to manage unfounded fear among the population. This study contends that the organization of home guards and the calls for vigilance responded not only to immediate concerns of violence and short-staffed law enforcement personnel but also to the perceived threat of Mexican mass migration, demographic shifts, and revolutionary rhetoric, thereby rendering ethnic Mexicans a threat to communities and enemies of the state.[8]

Vigilantism in Texas

In Texas, Anglo residents throughout the state exercised vigilantism under the protection of the state government in order to restrict ethnic Mexican integration. Extralegally mobilized vigilantes, known as "home guards," operated with impunity in the name of security and white supremacy. Texas home guards formed throughout the state and, more notably, away from the conflictive border region. They reported on the activities of resident ethnic Mexicans and patrolled neighborhoods, enforcing curfews and other restrictions. The Mexican Revolution provided perceived cause for vigilantes throughout Texas to identify and target ethnic Mexicans under the guise of patriotism and American self-preservation.

According to the historian Christopher Capozzola, the United States' entry into World War I in 1917 revived a previously dormant organizing effort by home guards in various locales throughout the country. Capozzola contends that "Americans who engaged in extralegal actions to support the war effort insisted that they were exemplars of vigilant citizenship."[9] The Woodrow Wilson administration, along with many local and state authorities, called for a vigilant citizenry in a time of war but was adamantly against vigilantism and home guards.[10] The administration viewed such organizations as incompatible with what President Wilson called the nation's "standards of law and order."[11] However, along the US-Mexico border, especially in Texas, vigilance and vigilantism assumed a far more complicated role than just an expression of patriotic fervor and community defense. On numerous occasions, the Texas governor and the state's top law enforcement official, the adjutant general, blurred the lines between vigilance and vigilantism, contradicting the directive and democratic appeals from the Wilson administration.

Calls for vigilance echoed throughout communities in Texas before the US entry into the war in Europe. The Texas Rangers and the practice of deputizing citizens highlight both the formal and informal practice of keeping vigilance over "others" such as Native Americans and ethnic Mexicans. By 1910, the Texas Rangers, local law enforcement officers, and private citizens mobilized to confront the violent and political complexities of the Mexican Revolution, with revolutionaries and battles at Texas's doorstep along the international border. Home guards formed at the behest of local communities with the support of the governor's office and concerned residents without a clear legal structure or responsibilities. Moreover, many Anglos exploited the volatile international situation to form home guards as a response to their distrust and fear of ethnic Mexicans migrating to Texas and the revolutionary rhetoric that permeated some social and political circles along the Texas-Mexico boundary and inland.

The era of the Mexican Revolution had a profound and complicated impact on Texas. Anglo residents throughout the state wrote to the governor claiming that the "present force of Rangers is entirely inadequate to properly protect the interests of the property owners."[12] The Mexican Revolution ignited the state's support of home guards and vigilant behavior in response to the insufficient number of law enforcement officers and state authorities along the border. More specifically, support for establishing home guards rested on the inability of state and federal institutions and officials to sufficiently manage the flow of refugees into Texas, stem the threat of ranch raids, and apprehend Mexican conspirators violating the United States' neutral stance in the revolution. For example, in April 1913, the commanding general for the Southern Department, Brigadier General Tasker Bliss, wrote to the adjutant general of the army, Brigadier

General George Andrews, that "Mexicans comprised the principal part of the population along the border from Texas to California, and in his opinion the majority sympathized with the constitutionalist movement of 1913 and many remained ardent supporters of the revolution of 1910."[13] The formation of home guards throughout the state, including in areas not immediately affected by the consequences of the revolution, was more than just a reactionary solution to a lack of both security and law and order resources.

The call for civilian organization and heightened vigilance by Anglo citizens and public figures veiled latent feelings of bigotry and fear over the mass migration of ethnic Mexican refugees into the state and the revolutionary fervor of the time. In Val Verde County, just east of Big Bend and along the Texas-Mexico border, Anglo men wrote to Governor Colquitt and the adjutant general calling for Texas Rangers and permission to raise a home guard for the "protection of life and property in case of law emergency." The town of Juno claimed that it "had considerable Mexican population and there are others who would take advantage of existing conditions in order to violate the law."[14] Because of conflated factors like ranch raids, US and Mexican diplomatic conflicts, and mass migration from Mexico, ethnic Mexicans emerged as a perceived threat to Anglo Texas communities. In other words, the formation of home guards in Texas fomented distrust and racial division between ethnic Mexicans and Anglos in Texas. Support from the governor's office, the adjutant general, and other leading law enforcement officials for civilians to take up arms and form home guards rebuffed the democratic pleas for law and order expressed by the Wilson administration. The governor's and adjutant general's active roles in organizing armed civilians for defense indicates their shared view of ethnic Mexicans as enemies of the state. These actions resulted in the bloodiest counterinsurgency by vigilantes and Texas Rangers against ethnic Mexicans in the twentieth century.[15]

Mass Migration

A great consequence of the revolution was the displacement of thousands of refugees and soldiers, especially during the constitutionalist movement of 1913 in Chihuahua. That same year, the border town of Ojinaga saw many people fleeing the atrocities of war and the takeover of Chihuahua City by Francisco Villa's army; those fleeing included members of some of northern Mexico's elite families, such as General Luis Terrazas Sr. and

Enrique Creel. In a span of almost two weeks, Ojinaga absorbed approximately 8,000 refugees, with many crossing the Rio Grande into Presidio, Texas.[16]

Many of the refugees were armed and wounded Mexican soldiers, which posed a security dilemma that added to the challenging logistics of disarming and tending to refugees.[17] Political and legal problems arose since the United States passed the Neutrality Act, which forbade a foreign army to use US territory for its own benefit. Accepting the soldier refugees would clearly violate that mandate; however, refusing their entry almost certainly guaranteed their execution by firing squad by the victorious constitutionalist army.[18] The ill-equipped Presidio port of entry could not house or care for thousands of desperate refugees, perpetuating the crisis.[19] Many more refugees occupied nearby villages across the northern Chihuahuan Desert, hoping for formal entry into the United States. Immigration agents in Presidio provided temporary relief for the complex situation by convincing the refugees to stay in Ojinaga until the constitutionalists attacked. When the rebel army approached the small border town, the refugees made their way across the river into US territory, creating one of the most difficult humanitarian crises in the history of the region.[20]

During the ten-year revolution, immigration contributed exponentially to the population growth of cities and counties along the Texas-Mexico boundary. For instance, the ethnic Mexican population in Brewster, Presidio, and Jeff Davis Counties expanded by 56 percent between 1910 and 1920.[21] The population of El Paso alone increased from 39,279 in 1910 to 61,898 in 1916, with ethnic Mexicans outnumbering the Anglo population for the first time since annexation.[22] The Mexicanization of the Texas-Mexico borderlands and other parts of the state affected racial demographics and led, in many cases, to tenuous race relations between Anglos and ethnic Mexicans. These tensions crossed class lines, uniting professional and working-class Anglos against a common other. For instance, in March 1914 W. E. Ashton, a medical doctor in Presidio, wrote to Governor Colquitt claiming that conditions in Presidio were insupportable because of the nightly indiscriminate firing of pistols by "a lot of drunken Mexicans" and that law and order seemed to be absent in the county.[23] He proceeded to express his grave concern regarding the demographic disadvantage "Americans" had by stating that "the population here is about 300 Mexicans to one American—if necessary I can send a signed petition from the 10 or 11 Americans who reside in [Presidio] in the midst of about 1500 or 2000 Mexicans."[24] The petition would substantiate Ashton's assessment of the situation in Presidio and verify the grave disadvantage "Americans" had to the increased number of Mexicans in the area.

The increased presence of ethnic Mexicans in Texas, especially along the border, caused fear and trepidation among Anglo residents. They, in turn, felt it necessary to raise and mobilize home guards to protect "life and property" and to subdue any "out of line" Mexicans who may be swept up by the revolutionary fervor. Fear, at times, yielded to paranoia, as happened in the small town of Premont in South Texas where O. H. Moyer, manager of the Premont Lumber Company, wrote to the governor asking for "protection" in rifles and ammunition after he noticed that "foreign speaking, and strange people are [in Premont] in abundance buying arms and ammunition."[25] In Bridgeport, just northwest of Dallas, police officer Buck Riley requested a commission as a Ranger or authority to organize a home guard because "[they] have in [their] town and community 900 or 1000 Mexicans."[26] In 1910, Bridgeport claimed 2,000 residents. Riley's assessment of the Mexican population in Bridgeport proposes that Anglos needed protection from a perceived threat of Mexicans despite no indication that there were any disturbances or violence in the town, only that there were more Mexicans in town than Anglos felt comfortable with at the time.

Colquitt received numerous letters like that from Bridgeport requesting permission to form home guards. Demographic shifts favoring a large ethnic Mexican population caused great unease among Anglos throughout Texas. The governor relented and allowed the groups to organize, especially after tensions between the United States and Mexico reached a boiling point when Mexican soldiers captured US servicemen in Tampico, Mexico.

Tampico Affair, 1914

A key motivation for citizens to organize into home guards was the Tampico Affair in 1914. In April, the United States and Mexico nearly came to war when American sailors were arrested and later released by Mexican officials and the sitting Mexican president, Victoriano Huerta, refused to offer a twenty-one-gun salute and raise the US flag on Mexican soil. US president Woodrow Wilson secured congressional permission to use military force to occupy Veracruz and did so on April 30. Along the border, the US Army mobilized a full division at Fort Bliss, near El Paso, and placed two regiments near the international crossing.[27]

Many Anglos felt fear and apprehension over the "status of affairs between our Government and the people across the Rio Grande" before Wilson formally called on Congress to mobilize troops.[28] For example, in late March, residents in Sanderson, Texas, just northeast of present-day Big Bend National Park, organized a "Home Guard Company" of sixty men ready for orders sent by the governor.[29] In Corpus Christi, private citizens asked the governor for permission to raise a company of volunteers in the event of war with Mexico. Governor Colquitt gathered these requests and filed them for "future reference" along with bids to supply arms from private munitions dealers to home guards and volunteers.[30] Towns and cities across the state sought permission from the governor to organize into civilian home guards in order to prepare "should more serious trouble ensue between this country and Mexico," because "no one can tell just what stand the Mexican residents [in Texas] might take against the whites."[31] The question of loyalty among ethnic Mexicans residing in Texas was not lost on many Anglo residents or the US Army.

Letters from willing and able citizens of all occupations flooded the governor's mansion pledging their services for military action against Mexico in 1914. In Palestine, Texas, approximately 112 miles southeast of Dallas, an assistant store manager named Joe Myers claimed he could recruit a full company of men on short notice ready to fight in Mexico, closing his letter with "command me."[32] Some eighty men of the Southwest Texas State Normal School (later Texas State University at San Marcos) informed Governor Colquitt that they were ready to enter military service of any kind if needed.[33] Another letter, from Teague, Texas, not only asked for permission from the governor to organize a company of volunteers but also demanded that "every Texian should show his loyalty to this great Nation and especially to Texas." The term "Texian" echoes the racial divide present during the Texas rebellion of 1836, which aimed to separate Texian Anglos from ethnic Mexican Tejanos.[34] A real estate agent from Houston wrote to Governor Colquitt stating that "patriotism calls upon him to defend a people who fear a lot of 'Greasers.'"[35] The pleas to organize civilian regiments reached Colquitt's desk, and he proceeded to grant permission for the mobilization of home guards throughout the state, insisted they inform the Texas Rangers of their availability, and granted them access to "requisitions for guns through [Texas] Ranger captains."[36] Fear, however, continued throughout the state and along the international boundary. This was especially the case among El Paso's Anglo community. The thought of revolutionary sympathizers operating in the city, the possibility that they would instigate racial violence in El Paso, and the perceived limited presence of the federal military and National Guard deepened the community's concerns.[37]

The assumed threat posed by Mexicans led Colquitt to militarize the border. He rushed sixteen companies of the National Guard to supplement the Texas Rangers already on duty along the Texas-Mexico boundary.[38] El Paso residents offered to aid the National Guard and Rangers by submitting requests to organize volunteer guards for war with Mexico and border protection.[39] The Tampico incident and the militarization of the border, compounded by other political developments, increased security concerns along the border. For example, continued fighting between Mexican revolutionary forces in 1914 led the United States to contribute additional army troops and National Guard forces to border security. Area newspapers added conflicting reports, publishing that thousands of Villa and federal officers and soldiers resided in El Paso and planned to invade the city.[40] Meanwhile, city officials repeatedly downplayed Mexican mobilization by emphasizing their confidence that the city did not anticipate any excitement resulting from the Tampico Affair or any other revolutionary stimuli. Nevertheless, city and military officials moved to militarize downtown El Paso and Chihuahuita, a predominantly ethnic-Mexican neighborhood. Many residents offered to serve as police officers, and the force eventually added fifty men. The number of police officers and mounted men on South El Paso Street and in the lower section of the city (Chihuahuita) doubled.[41] El Paso emerged as an "armed camp largely for the reassuring effect of the troops on the more nervous citizens."[42]

Small towns outside of El Paso took advantage of the governor's call to organize home guards because citizens felt uneasy about Mexicans.[43] The distrust of ethnic Mexicans was so widespread it extended far beyond the international boundary. Citizens in Wichita Falls, located on the border between Texas and Oklahoma, and in Beaumont, a coastal city bordering Louisiana, petitioned Colquitt for the formation of home guards on April 24 and were granted permission to proceed that same day.[44] One concerned citizen named Jacob Adams, in Waco, claimed he heard a Mexican boast that "he had been one of [Huerta's] soldiers and could call up four thousand Mexicans that would get out in arms."[45] Adams suggested that at least 200 to 300 men, along with arms and ammunition, were necessary to "stand ready to protect our homes and family as so that we can put a rush on these Mexicans when they start anything. . . . I understand the treachery of Mexicans."[46] A great number of citizens prepared for a possible war with Mexico before and after the Tampico Affair, and many Anglo civilians requested protection from their hometown Mexican population and sought reinforcements from the Texas Ranger force or permission from the state to form home guards. Although Huerta fled Mexico not long after the events in Tampico, tensions did not subside along the border and neither did the militarization of the region.

Governor Colquitt's compliance and directive in organizing local home guards highlights the dangerous and extralegal action the governor executed in protecting "Americans" from "Mexicans." For instance, when the Terrell County sheriff J. J. Allen received permission to organize a home guard in Sanderson, the governor instructed him that it was not necessary for the county judge to swear in the home guard but to simply have Captain J. M. Fox of the Texas Rangers call upon them and allow requisitions for guns to go through the Ranger company.[47] Colquitt's refusal to legitimize the home guard through a formal and legal process indicates the state's condonation of vigilantism. Throughout this period, Colquitt only sparsely outlined the formal structure of home guards, including their jurisdictions, level of law enforcement authority, and specific role in either local law enforcement or military operations. The ambiguous nature of home guards afforded Colquitt political capital by addressing the perceived safety concerns of his constituency and by granting them law enforcement authority with little to no oversight.

The state's empowerment of the Anglo citizenry allowed armed civilians to act with impunity against ethnic Mexicans, as demonstrated by the increased violence toward ethnic Mexicans throughout Texas and the US Southwest.[48] In 1915, the *La Grange Journal* reported that the infamous Judge Roy Bean of Langtry, Texas, once fined an Anglo man ten dollars for not killing two alleged Mexican bandits when presented with the opportunity.[49] The wholesale categorization of ethnic Mexicans as enemies of the state and a threat to private citizens proved pervasive throughout the US-Mexico borderlands.

Conclusion

The events and consequences of the Mexican Revolution racially delineated enemies and patriots in Texas. By 1914, a military approach to the border and the apparent shortcomings in law enforcement and personnel prompted civilians to arm themselves and organize into vigilante groups known as "home guards." Collectively, they identified Mexicans as an enemy, with little regard for military protocol or distinguishing the guilty from the innocent. Military presence in Mexican neighborhoods resulted in the social categorization of its ethnic residents as a threat to Anglo society and further marginalized this community. Reinforcing the point, a militaristic approach to border violence spread to the civilian sector as home guards felt compelled and justified to organize themselves and fight the "Mexican enemy."

Home guards organized to protect communities from raids and secure justice through extralegal methods. The governor, adjutant general, and other law enforcement officials endorsed and, at times, materially supported the various units sprouting up across the state. Governors Oscar Colquitt and later James Ferguson rallied towns across Texas, especially along the border, to organize able-bodied men and consequentially receive ammunition and other resources from the government.[50] Agencies that included the US military, home guards, and local police attempted to establish order at the same time that they reinforced the idea of the Mexican as the enemy.

The governor's and adjutant general's support of vigilante home guards was an affront to official law enforcement and to federal officials' pleas for citizens not to resort to vigilantism and extralegal activity. The governor directly avoided legitimizing home guards with legal recognition and structure. Still, home guards and the governor's office antagonized ethnic Mexicans, labeling them as enemies of the state with impunity. Scholars suggest that Anglo Texas residents in the early twentieth century straddled the line of maintaining order through legal means and violently securing justice through extralegal methods.[51] For home guards, violence toward ethnic Mexicans was a matter of defending the country from a perceived internal and external enemy.

The "call to duty" by civilians is not contained to the Mexican revolutionary period of the early twentieth century. Ninety years later in the spring of 2005, Jim Gilchrist and Chris Simcox cofounded a civilian border militia known as the "Minuteman Project" in southern Arizona.[52] The organization set up an armed patrol to "do the job our government refuses to do . . . and protect America . . . from the tens of millions of invading illegal aliens who are devouring and plundering our nation."[53] For the Minutemen, the Mexican migrant represented an enemy invading under-resourced American communities that lacked the proper military and law enforcement infrastructure. Hundreds of supporters flocked to the southern Arizona desert to support the project and exercise what they called their "birthright" to secure their homeland.[54] It even inspired smaller groups to organize patrols along the US-Canada border.[55] Although the group disbanded in 2010, splintered factions continue to the present day.[56] Thus, the legacies of vigilantism embraced by the home guards continue to reverberate in contemporary approaches to community policing along the North American borderlands. Ethnic tensions, when fueled by mass migration and demographic shifts, yet again become the pretext in which some try to take the law into their own hands.

Notes

1. "Buck Chaborn, Foe of Pancho Villa and Border Riffraff, Had Adventerous Career," *Southwesterner* (May 1966): 10–11; Miguel A. Levario, *Militarizing the Border: When Mexicans Became the Enemy* (College Station: Texas A&M University Press, 2012), 74.

2. Hector Galán, dir., *American Experience: The Hunt for Pancho Villa* (1993; Boston: WGHB Educational Foundation, American Experience, 2010), DVD.

3. I use the term "ethnic Mexican" to reflect both US citizens of Mexican descent and Mexican nationals because, socially, individuals were identified simply as "Mexicans" regardless of their citizenship status. A perceived shared ethnic quality generalized all who were of Mexican descent. When necessary, I make a distinction regarding citizenship.

4. Levario, *Militarizing the Border*, 73–75. For more on the Columbus raid, see Haldeen Braddy, *Pancho Villa at Columbus* (El Paso: Texas Western Press, 1965); Friedrich Katz, *Pancho Villa y el ataque a Columbus, Nuevo México* (Chihuahua, MX: Sociedad Chihuahuense de Estudios Históricos, 1979); and Eileen Welsome, *The General and the Jaguar: Pershing's Hunt for Pancho Villa; A True Story of Revolution and Revenge* (New York: Little, Brown, 2006).

5. My definition of "vigilantism" draws on Richard Maxwell Brown's monograph *Strain of Violence: Historical Studies of American Violence and Vigilantism* (London: Oxford University Press, 1975), 96–97.

6. Recently, borderlands scholars have furthered the scholarship to understanding the process of policing brown bodies across the international boundary and within the confines of the United States. Levario, in *Militarizing the Border*, traces the process by which the state developed a militarized border using the Texas Rangers, US Army, vigilantes, the National Guard, and the Border Patrol. The increased presence and activity of US police forces exacerbated racial tensions between Anglos and Mexicans in the borderlands and furthered their categorization as an "enemy other." *Militarizing the Border* is part of a longer trajectory of scholarship that seeks to understand the

way the state polices ethnic Mexicans in the United States. See Levario, *Militarizing the Border*; and Kelly Lytle Hernández, *Migra! A History of the U.S. Border Patrol* (Berkeley: University of California Press, 2010), 105.

7. Alexandra Minna Stern, *Eugenic Nation: Faults and Frontiers of Better Breeding in Modern America*, American Crossroads Series, vol. 2 (Berkeley: University of California Press, 2005), 57, ProQuest ebrary.

8. For more on the constitutionalist movement, see Charles C. Cumberland, *Mexican Revolution: The Constitutionalists Years* (Austin: University of Texas Press, 1972); Douglas W. Richmond, *Venustiano Carranza's Nationalist Struggle, 1893–1920* (Lincoln: University of Nebraska Press, 1984); and Adolfo Gilly, *The Mexican Revolution* (New York: New Press, 2005).

9. Christopher Capozzola, "The Only Badge Needed Is Your Patriotic Fervor: Vigilance, Coercion, and the Law in World War I America," *Journal of American History* 88, no. 4 (March 2002): 1356.

10. Capozzola, 1356.

11. Capozzola, 1356.

12. W. N. Pence to Governor Colquitt, April 9, 1914, Records of Texas Governor O. B. Colquitt, Archives and Information Services Division, Texas State Library and Archives Commission, Austin, TX (hereafter cited as Colquitt Records).

13. Bliss to Andrews, April 13, 1913, Records of the Department of State Relating to the Internal Affairs of Mexico, 1910–1929, film 812.00:7229, RG 25; John Eusebio Klingemann, "'The Population Is Overwhelmingly Mexican; Most of It Is in Sympathy with the Revolution . . .': Mexico's Revolution of 1910 and the Tejano Community in the Big Bend," in *War along the Border: The Mexican Revolution and Tejano Communities*, ed. Arnoldo De León (College Station: Texas A&M University Press, 2012), 267.

14. John F. Robinson to Colquitt, April 24, 1914, Colquitt Records.

15. Benjamin Heber Johnson, *Revolution in Texas: How a Forgotten Rebellion and Its Bloody Suppression Turned Mexicans into Americans* (New Haven, CT: Yale University Press, 2003), 2; Charles H. Harris III and Louis R. Sadler, *The Texas Rangers and the Mexican Revolution: The Bloodiest Decade, 1910–1920* (Albuquerque: University of New Mexico Press, 2004).

16. Klingemann, "'Population Is Overwhelmingly Mexican,'" 265–266.

17. Jefferson Morgenthaler, *The River Has Never Divided Us: A Border History of La Junta de los Rios* (Austin: University of Texas Press, 2004), 175.

18. Morgenthaler, 175.

19. Morgenthaler, 175–176.

20. John Eusebio Klingemann, "Triumph of the Vanquished: Pancho Villa's Army in Revolutionary Mexico" (PhD diss., University of Arizona, 2008), 80; F. W. Berkshire to Commissioner-General of Immigration, December 26, 1913, January 29, 1914, RG 85, folders 53108/711, 53108/71J, National Archives and Records Administration, Washington, DC.

21. Klingemann, "'Population is Overwhelmingly Mexican,'" 266.

22. A special census was taken by the Bureau of the Census by order of the president of the United States, issued on October 20, 1915, in compliance with a request by

the chamber of commerce in El Paso. US Department of Commerce, Bureau of the Census, *Special Census of the Population of El Paso, Tex.*, prepared under the supervision of Emmons K. Ellsworth (Washington, DC: Government Printing Office, 1916).

23. Ashton to Colquitt, March 30, 1914, Colquitt Records.

24. In 1910, Presidio County had a population of 5,218. However, by the 1920 census, its population had increased to 12,202. "Texas Almanac: Population History of Counties from 1850–2010," Texas State Historical Association, texasalmanac.com/sites/default/files/images/topics/ctypophistweb2010.pdf; Ashton to Colquitt, March 30, 1914, Colquitt Records.

25. Moyer to Colquitt, April 25, 1914, Adjutant General's Department, April 25–30, 1915, Colquitt Records.

26. Riley to Colquitt, April 23, 1914, Adjutant General's Department, April 25–30, 1915, Colquitt Records; "Texas Almanac: City Population History from 1850–2000."

27. Fort Bliss housed at least 900 soldiers since Victoriano Huerta led a coup d'état against Francisco Madero in February 1913 and well over 1,100 soldiers throughout most of 1914. Levario, *Militarizing the Border*, app. 1, table A.4–A.5, 130–131.

28. Levario, app. 1, table A.4–A.5, 130–131.

29. J. J. Allen, Sheriff of Terrell County, telegram to Colquitt, April 20, 1914, Colquitt Records.

30. Colquitt to Adj. Gen. Henry Hutchings, April 22, 1914, Colquitt Records.

31. Colquitt to Adj. Gen. Henry Hutchings.

32. Myers to Colquitt, April 23, 1914, Adjutant General's Department, July 1, 1914–April 1, 1915, Colquitt Records.

33. Lynton Garrett to Colquitt, April 24, 1914, Adjutant General's Department, July 1, 1914–April 1, 1915, Colquitt Records.

34. Charles O. Adains to Colquitt, April 24, 1914, Adjutant General's Department, April 23–24, 1914, Colquitt Records.

35. J. O. Jones to Colquitt, May 9, 1914, Adjutant General's Department, May 8–15, 1914, Colquitt Records.

36. Colquitt to Adj. Gen. Henry Hutchings, April 24, 1914, Colquitt Records.

37. Shawn Lay, *War, Revolution, and the Ku Klux Klan: A Study of Intolerance in a Border City* (El Paso: Texas Western Press, 1985), 22–24.

38. Harris and Sadler, *Texas Rangers*, 181.

39. Don M. Coerver and Linda B. Hall, *Texas and the Mexican Revolution: A Study in State and National Border Policy, 1910–1920* (San Antonio, TX: Trinity University Press, 1984), 77.

40. Lay, *Ku Klux Klan*, 23.

41. "Citizens Offer to Serve as Policemen," *El Paso Herald*, April 24, 1914, 1.

42. "Soldiers Cover City at Night," *El Paso Herald*, April 24, 1914, 2.

43. "Home Guards in El Paso Not Needed," *El Paso Herald*, April 25–26, 1914, weekend ed., 5-A.

44. Colquitt to L. P. Hammonds, April 24, 1914, and to F. E. Stout, April 24, 1914, Colquitt Records.

45. According to the Texas Almanac and based on the 1910 census, Waco had a

population of approximately 26,425 in 1914. Adams to Colquitt, April 20, 1914, Colquitt Records.

46. Adams to Colquitt.

47. Colquitt to Allen, April 24, 1914, Adjutant General's Department, July 1, 1914–April 1, 1915, Colquitt Records.

48. William D. Carrigan and Clive Webb, *Forgotten Dead: Mob Violence against Mexicans in the United States, 1848–1928* (New York: Oxford University Press, 2013), 21.

49. Carrigan and Webb, 54.

50. Colquitt to Adj. Gen. Henry Hutchings, April 22, 1914; F. E. Stout to Colquitt, April 23, 1914; J. J. Allen to Colquitt, April 23, 1914; and Colquitt to L. P. Hammonds, April 24, 1914, all in Colquitt Records.

51. William D. Carrigan, *The Making of a Lynching Culture: Violence and Vigilantism in Central Texas, 1836–1916* (Champaign: University of Illinois Press, 2004), 3.

52. Meredith Hoffman, "Whatever Happened to Arizona's Minutmen?," *Vice*, March 22, 2016, vice.com/en_us/article/xd7jmn/what-happened-to-arizonas-minutemen.

53. David Holthouse, "Minutemen Project leaders say their volunteers are 'white Martin Luther Kings,' but their anti-immigration campaign is marked by weaponry, military maneuvers and racist talk," *Intelligence Report*, Southern Poverty Law Center, June 27, 2005, splcenter.org/fighting-hate/intelligence-report/2005/minutemen -other-anti-immigrant-militia-groups-stake-out-arizona-border.

54. Tim Murphy, "The Meltdown of the Anti-Immigration Minuteman Militia," *Mother Jones*, August 4, 2014, motherjones.com/politics/2014/08/minuteman -movement-border-crisis-simcox.

55. Janet I. Tu and Lornet Turnbull, "Minutemen Watch U.S.-Canada Border," *Seattle Times*, October 4, 2005, seattletimes.com/seattle-news/minutemen-watch-us -canada-border/?fbclid=IwAR3hNxZEPbvHYEPVJurqb-fbud5MOXAL4fJNewUX3HCZ hF7xqgYYbgf4rUw.

56. "U.S. Militia Groups Head to Border, Stirred by Trump's Call to Arms," *Washington Post*, November 3, 2018, washingtonpost.com/world/national-security/us-militia -groups-head-to-border-stirred-by-trumps-call-to-arms/2018/11/03/ff96826c-decf -11e8-b3f0-62607289efee_story.html?utm_term=.43423d294d1e.

PART III

Building and Resisting a Prohibition Apparatus

EIGHT

Policing Peyote Country in the Early Twentieth Century

LISA D. BARNETT

A 1909 article about peyote in the *New York Sun* both depicted the growing social controversy over the use of peyote by American Indians and described the changing political nature of the US-Mexico border in the early twentieth century. The story focused on the US Customs Service policing the Texas border for articles deemed immoral but not illegal by current laws. The newspaper described the added demands placed upon the "mounted river guards and customs inspectors," who were now required to adjudicate delicate questions about the use of peyote in the religious rites of many American Indians. The account given in the *Sun* referred to the fact that there had been numerous reports of the seizure and confiscation of shipments of peyote "by the United States customs officers at Laredo, Eagle Pass, and other points on the lower Rio Grande."[1] The newspaper also highlighted the growing tension in the United States over the religious use of peyote by Native Americans and the social concerns of non-Indians to protect the country from intoxicants coming across the border.

Peyotism—the religious practice of using the tops of the *Lophophora williamsii* cactus to produce a mild hallucinogenic state—emerged in the United States among the southern plains tribes sometime in the mid-nineteenth century. New practices in the religion developed as it quickly spread among the tribes residing in Oklahoma, the northern plains, and throughout the American West, but the varieties of peyote religious experience all maintained the foundational essence of using peyote as a sacred medicine and a religious adjunct.[2] Coinciding with the rapid dissemination of the Indian peyote religion were Progressive Era reforms targeting intoxicants. Specific legislative acts such as the Pure Food and Drug Act of 1906, which targeted the regulation of patent medicines, the Harrison Narcotics Act of 1914, which addressed opioid use in the United States, and the passage of the Eighteenth Amendment to the Constitution in 1919 prohibiting alcohol expanded federal policing powers. Those powers extended to both the US-Mexico and US-Canada borderlands. As social reformers and policy makers in the United States grew anxious to control alcohol and narcotics, the use of peyote by American Indians also caught their attention in the early twentieth century, and efforts to ban its use in peyote country ensued.

The term "peyote country" has a double meaning. The first use refers to the US-Mexico borderlands, specifically the area between Mexico and Texas along the Rio Grande, which contains the natural growth zone for the plant. The second meaning implied in the phrase is a pejorative synonym for Indian country in the United States, where various tribes adopted peyotism. Indeed, American Indians who opposed the peyote religion promoted the negative connection of peyote country with Indian country. When the leadership of the Society of American Indians discussed a location for the society's annual conference in 1918, they policed their own organization by rejecting Omaha, Nebraska, as a potential site because the Winnebagos used peyote. Gertrude Bonnin, the society's secretary, wrote that she did not believe it advisable to "hold a conference of this Indian organization in a *peyote country*."[3] Policing peyote in Indian country in the early twentieth century not only involved federal control over land and Native peoples but also extended the jurisdiction of multiple federal policing powers and practices to non-Indian populations involved in the commerce of peyote in the borderlands.

In the minds of government reformers, peyote threatened the assimilation efforts in lands throughout Indian country, and this threat came from the borderlands of the Trans-Pecos region of Texas and the lower Rio Grande Valley with its commercial trade of peyote. In line with Anita Huizar-Hernández's observation in chapter 14 that sources often portray the "US-Mexico border as a war zone that threatens to destroy the physical, economic, and cultural foundations of the United States," social reformers in the early twentieth century viewed peyotism as part of a superstitious and ignorant past that prevented American Indians' progress into modernity. Coupled with social attitudes about folkloric traditions prevalent with borderlands peoples, a characterization of "otherness" emerged around attempts to regulate the commercialized trade of peyote and its use among American Indians. The construction of a borderlands identity around peyote significantly impacted the ways the US government (and later the Canadian government) policed peyote country. This chapter examines efforts by individuals working for the US Office of Indian Affairs (OIA) to police the commerce in peyote through extralegal means. In doing so, these US officials exceeded the authorized jurisdictional boundaries of the OIA to police the local communities of the US-Mexico borderlands. It also explores the employment of a discursive racialization of peyote in order to aid efforts to pass peyote prohibition legislation. However, non-Indian borderlands people involved in the peyote industry, as well as Native American consumers of peyote, resisted federal efforts to police the commerce in peyote and also found ways to continue the peyote trade throughout peyote country.

Peyote as a Borderlands Issue

Peyote's habitat along the Rio Grande makes it an intrinsic borderlands issue. The peyote of commerce is native to the northeastern desert region of Mexico and areas close to the Rio Grande in South Texas with small populations in the Big Bend and Trans-Pecos areas.[4] Ethnobotanists also note that peyote coming from the borderlands does not survive well in colder climates north of its native habitat, which is why the practice of drying the peyote tops, or "buttons," became the "key to its diffusion beyond its natural habitat and was crucial to the spread of the peyote religion."[5] The dissemination of peyote across the southern and northern plains of the United States was therefore not possible without a commercialized trade emerging from the borderlands of the Rio Grande.

Peyote trade centers developed in the borderlands, where Indians could come to purchase the dried peyote buttons; Los Ojuelos, Texas, was one of the earliest cultivated areas for commercial purposes. Other key locations in South Texas for the "peyote fields" that supplied the product to Indians included small towns such as Aguilares, Bruni, Encinal, Mirando City, Torrecillas (later in the 1920s called Oilton because of oil discoveries in the area), and Hebbronville.[6] The border crossings at Eagle Pass and El Paso also became important to peyote commerce as entry points for the product from commercial enterprises operating in Mexico. Indian agents noted that peyotist Indians in Oklahoma regularly received shipments of peyote from parties in Mexico. Smaller villages throughout northeastern Mexico participated in the international trade, with some towns along the border "practically supported by the peyote industry."[7]

Laredo emerged as a key distribution hub for the trade because four railway lines had depots in the city.[8] Entrepreneurs took advantage of the transportation network reaching peyotist Indians in the United States and created opportunities to make a profit from the peyote religion. In the late nineteenth and early twentieth centuries, two distributing agents in Laredo controlled the majority of the commercial peyote trade: J. Villegas & Bro. (later called the Villegas Mercantile Company and then L. Villegas & Bro.) and Wormser Brothers. These two firms supplied "most of the peyote consumed by the Indians of Wyoming, Nebraska, Wisconsin, Iowa, and perhaps the Dakotas, and also a considerable part of that used by the Oklahoma Indians."[9] The peyote merchants in Laredo either sold peyote directly to the Indians who made trips to the borderlands or shipped it to dealers in Oklahoma, who supplied the Indian trade. White merchants living alongside Indian reservations and allotment lands assumed the responsibility of getting the product to the peyotist Indians and, in turn, made a profit for themselves.[10] Indeed, the commercialization of peyote allowed many non-Indians to profit from the peyote trade.

The business in peyote evolved into a highly organized commercial enterprise. Mexican and Tejano *peyoteros* earned an average of $2.50 per 1,000 buttons for gathering and drying the peyote, but usually those local suppliers took their pay in trade for groceries and other needed supplies at merchants' stores.[11] The dealers then marked up the price in order to make a profit for themselves. The costs to the peyotist Indians and distributors along reservation borders ranged from $3 to $8 per 1,000 buttons, depending on the availability of the supply and whether the transaction involved railroad or express shipping costs. A sliding scale also took effect depending on the quantity purchased—the more one purchased, the cheaper the cost. Peyotist Indians paid an average of five cents per button in the early period of development of the commercial trade; this cost had decreased to an average of one cent per button by the 1920s.[12] In the eyes of reformers and federal Indian officials, the cheaper prices encouraged greater consumption by peyotist Indians. By 1916, when Congress first introduced legislation to prohibit peyote, Indian agents estimated about 6,000 peyotist Indians among southern and northern plains tribes. The number increased throughout the mid-twentieth century as the peyote religion spread throughout the American West.[13] US officials believed the peyote trade to be a significant problem threatening the moral welfare of the nation; the rationale was analogous to the arguments emanating from the movement for alcohol prohibition in the country and sought the same legislative remedy to stop the peyote trade.

The Policing of Peyote Country

The cultural contestation in the United States over peyote coincided with a renewed assault on the consumption of alcohol and increasing social concerns over the use of unregulated narcotics that led to drug addiction. In the minds of reformers, the evil of intemperance threatened the fabric of the social order. Alcohol prohibition had already been an integral part of Indian policy (though liquor law infractions frequently took place). In 1892, Congress passed a comprehensive prohibition law as part of its Indian policy, but for those Indians wanting to drink alcohol (and those wanting to sell it), federal statutes did not provide enough deterrence. Despite the law, Indians continued to obtain alcohol through a bootleg system, where excessive prices, intimidation, and violence were the norm. The reservation system, which produced "isolation, seclusion, and remoteness," as well as Indians' locations, with easy access to the "Canadian and Mexican borders," made the "introduction of illegal liquors easy."[14] Dubbing it "dry whiskey," social reformers and OIA officials categorized peyote as an intoxicant that demanded regulation under the status quo prohibition laws.[15]

Early efforts to control peyote came under the jurisdiction of Indian agents and superintendents working for OIA, but many Indians and Anglo reformers had long viewed Indian agents with suspicion in their sincerity to solve the "Indian problem" for fear of losing their government-paid positions.[16] Operating with the 1892 prohibition statute in Indian country, which made it illegal for any person to "sell, give away, dispose of, exchange, or barter . . . any article whatsoever, under any label, or brand, which produces intoxication to any Indian," individual agents began to independently interpret peyote as an intoxicant subject to penalties subscribed by the law.[17] Superintendents and agents created their own policies to deal with the peyote problem on their assigned reservations, as well as their own forms of punishment for the violation of such policies. Typically, the most common form of social coercion to adhere to the antipeyote policies centered on economics and the threat from agents to "withhold rations, annuity payments, and lease monies" from Indians who used peyote and to have the confiscated article destroyed.[18] Borderlands peoples and merchants would later experience these same policing tactics of intimidation by federal officials who sought to restrict the peyote trade.

Early attempts by the Oklahoma territorial legislature to restrict peyote concluded that Oklahoma by itself could not stop the traffic in peyote through a ban on the item, as Indians could still buy it in Texas. Many peyote opponents in the territorial legislature believed that "the only way to give proper effect to the law is to induce the states of Texas, Kansas, and Arkansas to pass similar laws and in that way build a wall around Oklahoma."[19] The idea of a symbolic wall around Oklahoma Territory reflected ongoing disputes with the state of Texas concerning the legal boundary line of the Red River. The Red River had long served as the southern international border between the United States and Spain, Mexico, and the Republic of Texas, but doubts over the legal boundary line arose in 1852 with the discovery of the North Fork of the Red River. Texas claimed the area known as Greer County between the North Fork and the main branch. In 1894, the dispute landed before the United States Supreme Court, which ruled that the southern branch of the river designated in the 1819 Adams-Onís Treaty would be the official boundary.[20] Oklahoma territorial officials continued to view Texas with suspicion and identified Texas as the source of the peyote problem for Indians residing in Oklahoma Territory. When the new state legislature of Oklahoma failed in 1908 to amend territorial statutes to prohibit peyote, other measures to curtail the borderlands traffic into Indian lands soon emerged from federal officials. William E. "Pussyfoot" Johnson, appointed "chief special officer" of the Indian Bureau to suppress liquor traffic among Indians, led the charge with his own broad interpretation of the Indian Prohibition Act of 1897.[21]

The 1897 statute (a revision of the 1892 prohibition law in Indian country) prohibited "the furnishing to an Indian or the delivery into the Indian Country, or upon an Indian allotment any article that will produce intoxication," but it did not explicitly mention peyote as an article deemed an intoxicant subject to criminal prosecution.[22] Johnson, who was a Presbyterian active in the Anti-Saloon League's efforts to prohibit alcohol in the nation, criticized the religious use of peyote. In 1906, Indian Commissioner Francis Leupp, with the encouragement of President Theodore Roosevelt, appointed Johnson to a position to stop liquor traffic among Indians in Indian Territory and Oklahoma Territory. Johnson received a promotion in 1908 to chief special officer, and his work now included the suppression of liquor traffic throughout all of Indian country. Johnson began to hear about peyote and convinced himself that it also produced a state of intoxication and was therefore subject to the statute of 1897. Emboldened by his new OIA position, Johnson launched a virtual one-man assault on the supply of peyote into Indian country. Similar to Miguel A. Levario's description in chapter 7 of the Texas "home guards" (state-sanctioned citizen vigilante forces that arose in response to fears over the Mexican Revolution), Special Officer Johnson and Indian agents working for him employed vigilante-like tactics to fill the gap in federal legislative efforts to prohibit peyote.

When Indian agents and the Indian police conducted raids on peyote ceremonies, Johnson also wanted them to obtain information concerning the peyotists' suppliers.[23] Johnson soon discovered that a large commercial network was in place and growing. While some peyotist Indians made trips to the southern borderlands to gather peyote, the majority of them obtained the plant through a commercial shipping enterprise. In Johnson's opinion, this commercial trade, especially peyote coming into the United States from Mexico, possibly violated "certain international laws and treaties."[24] Determined to save the Indians and the country from the evils of intoxication, Johnson systematically began to implement solutions to stop the traffic in peyote.

Though no federal US law existed to stop the importation or commercial sale of peyote, Johnson began to exert the authority of his office to pressure express companies to exclude peyote shipments from their business transactions. On April 28, 1909, Johnson ordered the manager of the Wells Fargo Express Company in Houston to "refuse shipments of peyote to Indians because shipping peyote becomes liable to prosecution" (even though no law was in place that Johnson could legally use to follow through with the threat).[25] Wells Fargo Express instructed its agents in Cache and Fort Sill, Oklahoma, to "be on the lookout for shipments of the kind, and refuse to deliver them to Indians."[26] Johnson also extracted similar agreements from express companies operating in the borderlands in Laredo, Eagle Pass, and El Paso, Texas.[27] Johnson ordered Indian officials to seize and hold any peyote shipments that did make it to Indian country and to advise express agents at Norman, Fort Sill, and Anadarko, Oklahoma, that peyote shipments "cannot be legally delivered to an Indian, or introduced into the Indian Country."[28] Johnson's statement concerning the "legality" of peyote shipments emanated from his broad interpretation of the 1897 statute on alcohol prohibition in Indian country, one that the Oklahoma legislature had already disputed, debated, and settled with the failure to add peyote prohibition to the new state's constitution in 1908.

Realizing that some of the peyote making it to the Indians came from Mexico, Johnson on May 4, 1909, proposed to the OIA that a "prohibitive tariff be imposed upon peyotes to insure that they would not be imported from Mexico."[29] The OIA lacked the jurisdiction to enact such a measure and ultimately never convinced Congress to do so. This did not dissuade Johnson's own attempts to stop the borderland peyote trade by blocking the source of supply. His notable stand against peyote came in late April 1909, when he went to Laredo to deal directly with peyote dealers. Upon his arrival there, Johnson—absent any formal orders from his superiors in the OIA—purchased the entire visible market supply of peyote from the L. Villegas & Bro. and Wormser Brothers merchants and then destroyed it. Johnson estimated that he bought nearly 200,000 peyote buttons with $443 of federal money appropriated to the OIA to stop liquor traffic. In a theatrical style reminiscent of Carry Nation's use of a hatchet to smash illegal saloons to promote temperance, Johnson destroyed the entire supply of peyote buttons by making "a big bonfire of them." Additionally, he "warned the merchants not to carry the beans [peyote] in stock under penalty of severe punishment."[30] Johnson's accounts of the incident indicate that he "obtained from the wholesale dealers agreements that they would no longer engage in the traffic," though this statement was later disputed by Wormser Brothers.[31] While in Laredo, Johnson also contacted the Pacific Express Company, which controlled the express business coming out of the city, and obtained a promise that it would "refuse to accept for shipment any more peyotes from anybody."[32]

Believing in his version of morality that peyote was a harmful intoxicant and in the perceived power of his office with the OIA, Johnson chose to expand his own jurisdictional authority to stop peyote by acting outside of the legislative and executive boundaries. Johnson used his position to begin negotiations with the Mexican consul in Laredo about an agreement to stop the supply of peyote from entering the United States. He reported that Mexican officials "agree to advise all Mexicans to abandon any attempts to pursue this traffic any further."[33] The press soon portrayed the unofficial agreement between the OIA and the Mexican consul as an official State Department policy stating that the US and Mexican governments would "cooperate in an effort to stop the sale of the peyote bean and to eradicate the plant."[34] One report characterized the agreement as a binational war against peyote: "War has been declared by the Mexican and the United States government against the deadly peyote bean. The two governments will cooperate . . . to stop the sale of the bean in both countries."[35] Johnson's actions attempted to change the nature of policing in Indian country and the borderlands.

Utilizing his authority with the OIA, Johnson arranged to send samples of peyote to US Customs officials so that "they can guard against the importation" of the item.[36] Press dispatches soon contained accounts of seizures and confiscations of peyote shipments by "the United States customs officers at Laredo, Eagle Pass, and other points on the lower Rio Grande."[37] For a time, Johnson was successful with the employment of the US Customs Service to police the border in the fight against peyote. When the popular press reported on Johnson's actions in Laredo, stories identified him as a "United States government official" placing a "federal ban" on the sale or shipment of peyote to Indians. In reality, however, Johnson's actions reflected his own personal opinion that peyote was an intoxicant subject to current laws in effect throughout Indian country, and they were merely actions taken by him to police the commercial trade.[38]

Those who profited from the trade, though, soon challenged Johnson's unofficial ban on the importation of peyote. Wormser Brothers questioned the ban on peyote shipments and "wrote to the Secretary of the Interior for a citation of the law."[39] Once it received a clarification of the 1897 law from the commissioner of Indian affairs, both Wormser Brothers and L. Villegas & Bro. became convinced that the ban did not apply to peyote and resumed their commercial trade. For his part, Johnson acceded to this outside pressure and amended his initial "ban" by permitting peyotist Indians to travel into the peyote fields in the borderlands at their own expense to gather the plant. Still, Johnson limited the total amount Indians could gather to no more than 500 buttons.[40] The peyote traffic continued, with Indian pilgrimages to the US-Mexico borderlands as well as the reestablishment of transnational shipments by Laredo merchants. The spread of peyotism and the economic incentive for those involved in the trade proved to be the greatest obstacles in the efforts to stop the commercial trade as non-Indians profited from the Indian religion.

Constructing a Borderlands Identity to Police Peyote Country

Christian reformers and federal officials continued to utilize other means to discredit the peyotist Indians' religious practice. The stories of prohibiting peyote through regulations, laws, and extralegal measures are important in the historical narrative of the religion, but equally important are the Anglo cultural concerns with the "moral economy" around the trade. Convinced that the practice denigrated Indians and delayed their advancement into modernity, reforming activists during the Progressive Era and beyond sought the prohibition of peyote by associating it with a racialized borderland identity.

Peyote prohibitionists highlighted the "otherness" they associated with peyote use. Special Officer Johnson frequently referred to the use of peyote by "ignorant Mexicans along the border," who promoted the use of the article to Indians.[41] Nonpeyotist Indians also promoted a borderlands conspiracy argument claiming that peyotism was "a trick of the Mexican traders to find a market for a poison, which deceives the brain and makes these Mexican traders rich" but did the Indians no good.[42] Others also picked up the race and class identification of peyote users to promote anxiety over the spread of peyotism by arguing that "Indians and the lower class of Mexicans have become addicted to its use and it is gradually extending to the whole country."[43]

Peyote's opponents often linked it to other goods smuggled into the United States from Mexico. Despite the fact that peyote grows on both sides of the US-Mexico border, many times Indian officials attempting to eradicate the trade acknowledged only the supply coming from Mexico. Before the identification of a formal commercial network, Indian agents reported that Indians procured their peyote from "old Mexico."[44] Even after Special Officer Johnson traced the network of supply to areas also located in the Texas borderlands, many federal officials and social reformers continued in their discourse to promote "old Mexico" as the sole supply of peyote to Indians in the United States. Opponents worked to characterize the peyote problem in America as originating in Mexico from where it was then imported into the United States.[45] A borderland identity of peyote also extended to those who distributed the product to peyotist Indians. Johnson assigned traders a racialized characterization when he reported: "The Red man is a schemer, but the bad white man who is responsible for most of his Red brother's troubles is more of a schemer and in all probability, the next move will be to smuggle into the camp of the Indians the peyote bean."[46] Johnson's reference to the issue of "smuggling" peyote after his efforts to ban the product also carried a racial connotation.

By using the term "smuggling," antipeyotists encouraged the expansion of state surveillance along the international boundary line utilizing the US Customs Service. Johnson and other officials even hoped that a language of illicitness around peyote would "eventually result in the installation of a new department of officials in [Laredo] and practically a new department for the United States to prevent the peyote smuggling."[47] In his description of a "moral economy of illicit trade" via smuggling along the US-Mexico border, the scholar George T. Díaz notes: "People became smugglers when they sought something that states wished to regulate or deny them."[48] This, however, was not the case with peyote because no federal legislation during this time prohibited the peyotist Indians from obtaining the product. Regarding the legality of importing peyote from Mexico before the 1924 ban, the US assistant secretary of the interior wrote that there is no provision of law specifically prohibiting the importation: "If the article, when offered for import into this country, is not adulterated or misbranded, or forbidden to be sold, restricted in sale in the country from which exported, within the meaning of the Food and Drug Act of June 30, 1906, it cannot be excluded from the country when properly entered and the duties paid in accordance with the customs law."[49] Use of the rhetoric of smuggling peyote in from Mexico was only a discursive strategy to racialize the plant in an attempt to convince federal lawmakers to enact a total prohibition on the product.[50]

As the peyote religion spread to the peoples of the northern plains, the concern over policing peyote country expanded to include the US-Canada border. The emphasis on policing peyote along the southern borderlands shifted when US policy makers noticed that the use of peyote by Indians had spread "as far as the Canadian border" and was "being used in Canada."[51] The permeability of the international boundary between the United States and Canada during the early twentieth century provided a particular concern for antipeyotists, who, like the supporters of alcohol prohibition, knew the ease with which travelers were able to cross the northern border to obtain products deemed socially unacceptable in American culture. During Prohibition in the United States, "entrepreneurs, temperance workers, tourists, bootleggers, and law enforcement officials often behaved as if no border existed at all."[52] The extent of peyote use in Canada and the commercial trade along the US-Canada border are areas in the cultural history of peyotism open for more study. Anthropologists studying peyote generally concur that the introduction of the religion to First Nations peoples occurred sometime in the mid-1920s, the very era when liquor was prohibited in the United States.[53]

The criminalization of certain drugs in Canada began in 1908 with legislation "to prohibit the importation, manufacture, and sale of opium for other than medicinal purposes."[54] Just as in the United States, the impetus for the 1908 Canadian statute "originated in a racially motivated labor confrontation on the west coast of Canada" involving Chinese immigrants.[55] Canada made changes to the law through the passage of the Opium and Drug Act of 1911, which "added cocaine to the list of prohibited drugs and made possession of either smoking-opium or cocaine an offence punishable by imprisonment."[56] However, unlike the United States' focus on assimilating Native Americans into white culture, the nascent Canadian drug laws did not target peyote, because it simply had not alarmed Canadian officials during the early part of the twentieth century.

In 1954, the Cree Indians of the Red Pheasant reserve established the first Native American Church in Canada (the legal entity to protect peyotism) and imported peyote buttons "from Oklahoma at a price of one cent per button," the same price that Oklahoma peyotist Indians paid for the supply from South Texas with no markup in cost.[57] Even as Canadian border officials instituted their "first crackdown on the import" of peyote buttons to Manitoba in 1954, the lack of any laws prohibiting bringing peyote into Canada prevented a halt in traffic. At best, Canadian border officials could seize only those peyote buttons brought in from the United States "under the section of the customs act which allows confiscation of goods not declared on entry."[58] However, when the Canadian government took an active interest in peyotism "among Prairie Indians" in the mid-1950s, newspapers frequently reported that officials acknowledged the connection to the southern borderlands when they noted that the importation of peyote buttons came from the natural growth region in "Mexico and the valley of the Rio Grande" and that the product had been "filtering into the prairie provinces" for some time.[59] Reports of Cree and Assiniboine peyotists in Canada led the missions committee of the Anglican Church to proclaim that the "Indians have lapsed into paganism with the ceremonial use of peyote," implying that peyotism was a religion of "foolish and stupid people"—similar to arguments made by US officials in discussing peyote use among American Indians.[60] Thus, by the mid-twentieth century, peyote prohibitionists' racialization of the plant to police its trade extended across the breadth of the North American borderlands.

Conclusion

The cultural war on peyote by social reformers and the US government during the Progressive Era reflected Anglo anxieties about Indians entering into modernity without first abandoning some of their Indian identity, which included the practice of the peyote religion. Parallel to later events along the US-Canada border with the Haudenosaunee and tobacco as described by Devin Clancy and Tyler Chartrand in chapter 12, events in the early twentieth century around peyote also represent part of the "long history of settler-colonial policing that conflates the activities of sovereign peoples with criminality and their trade with smuggling."[61] As state and federal government initiatives to prohibit peyote failed, individuals such as Special Officer William Johnson began to police the peyote trade by enforcing their own moral codes through legal and extralegal means. However, the economic reality of the commerce in peyote created a greater impetus to resist efforts to police and control the trade involved with the religious practice. The economic relationship between non-Indian suppliers of peyote and Indian consumers provided a significant force of resistance against policies to police the profitable activity around peyote in the southern borderlands.

Failing to stop the supply of peyote from the southern borderlands to Native Americans throughout Indian country, social reformers turned to a discursive tactic to police peyote country. Framing the need to control the moral economy around peyote for the welfare of the country, supporters of prohibition employed a border racialization tactic to demonize users and traders of the plant. The use of a rhetorical strategy to police peyote served to shame those involved in the commercial trade and persuade them to stop, as well as to convince policy makers of the need for stronger interventionist controls over the product. However, peyotist Indians also utilized the performative power of language to preserve their religious right to use peyote.

Peyotist Indians fought to preserve the sacredness of their faith by arguing for their First Amendment constitutional right to the free exercise of religion. Adding additional support to their argument was the decision in 1918 to incorporate legally as the Native American Church of Oklahoma. While peyotist Indians always considered peyote to be a sacred medicine, Article II of the 1918 Native American Church charter identified peyote as a "sacrament as commonly understood and used among the adherents of this religion in the several tribes of Indians."[62] Through language and other forms of symbolic speech, supporters of peyote worked to transform their own economic and religious identities in the cultural war over peyote. In doing so, they re-presented themselves and peyote in ways that brought both into the modern era and prevented the successful policing of peyote country until the latter part of the twentieth century.

Notes

1. "Sacred, Also Intoxicating," *New York Sun*, June 13, 1909, 2.
2. Omer C. Stewart, *Peyote Religion: A History* (Norman: University of Oklahoma Press, 1987), 17–24.
3. Bonnin to Arthur C. Parker, July 8, 1918, reel 1, Papers of the Society of American Indians (hereafter cited as SAI Papers). Italics added.
4. Servando Z. Hinojosa, "Human-Peyote Interaction in South Texas," *Culture & Agriculture* 22, no. 1 (Spring 2000): 29.
5. Stacy B. Schaefer, *Amanda's Blessings from the Peyote Gardens of South Texas* (Albuquerque: University of New Mexico Press, 2015), 36–37.
6. James Mooney to W. H. Holmes, November 25, 1903, Records of the Bureau of American Ethnology, National Anthropological Archives, Suitland, MD (hereafter cited as NAA–Bureau of American Ethnology).
7. Arthur C. Parker, "Drug-Induced Religion," *Quarterly Journal of the Society of American Indians* 2, no. 2 (April–June 1914): 100.
8. Rev. William H. Ketchum letter, March 9, 1911, in *Peyote: Hearings before a Subcommittee of the Committee on Indian Affairs of the House of Representatives* (Washington, DC: Government Printing Office, 1918), 43 (hereafter cited as *Peyote Hearings*).
9. Bureau of Indian Affairs, *Peyote: An Abridged Compilation from the Files of the Bureau of Indian Affairs* (Washington, DC: Government Printing Office, 1922), 5–6; "Indian Visions Traced to Peyote," *Laredo Times*, May 2, 1909.
10. W. D. Myers, *Report of the Commissioner of Indian Affairs for 1889* (Washington, DC: Government Printing Office, 1889), 191; Thomas & Rives Wholesale and Retail Grocers to Mr. Adams (agent), September 6, 1890, Oklahoma Historical Society, Oklahoma City, OK (hereafter cited as OHS).
11. "Indian Visions Traced to Peyote."
12. Robert Valentine, *Report of the Commissioner of Indian Affairs for 1911* (Washington, DC: Government Printing Office, 1911), 33.
13. Stewart, *Peyote Religion*, 218.
14. Cato Sells to Superintendents, March 29, 1917, OHS.
15. Valery Havard, "Report on the Flora of Western and Southern Texas," *Proceedings of the United States National Museum* 8, no. 29 (September 23, 1885): 449, 521.
16. *Encyclopedia of the Great Plains*, s.v. "Indian Agents," by David Wishar [online], plainshumanities.unl.edu/encyclopedia/doc/egp.pg.032.
17. 27 Stat. 260, quoted in William E. Unrau, *White Man's Wicked Water: The Alco-*

hol Trade and Prohibition in Indian Country, 1802–1892 (Lawrence: University Press of Kansas, 1996), 114.

18. E. E. White, *Report of the Commissioner of Indian Affairs for 1888* (Washington, DC: Government Printing Office, 1888), 99.

19. "The Bean Habit," *Guthrie (Oklahoma Territory) Daily Leader*, March 24, 1899, 1.

20. *Encyclopedia of Oklahoma History and Culture*, s.v. "Texas-Oklahoma Boundary Controversies," by Glen Roberson, okhistory.org.

21. F. A. MacKenzie, *"Pussyfoot" Johnson–Crusader–Reformer–A Man among Men* (New York: Fleming H. Revell, 1920), 81–101.

22. MacKenzie, 67–68, 104–106.

23. Johnson to Charles E. Shell, March 6, 1907, OHS.

24. Charles E. Shell to Express Agent, Geary, OK, April 23, 1909, OHS.

25. Johnson to Charles E. Shell, May 4, 1909, OHS.

26. A. T. Payne to Charles E. Shell, May 4, 1909, OHS.

27. Johnson to Charles E. Shell, May 4, 1909, OHS.

28. Johnson to Charles E. Shell.

29. Stewart, *Peyote Religion*, 139.

30. "Mescal Beans Seized," *Galveston (TX) Daily News*, April 28, 1909, 7.

31. Johnson to Charles E. Shell, May 4, 1909, OHS.

32. William E. Johnson [1909], in "History, Use, and Effects of Peyote in Two Installments—Article I," *Indian School Journal* 7, no. 7 (May 1912): 240, 241, Record Group 75: Records of the Bureau of Indian Affairs, 1793–999, Series: The Indian School Journal, 1904–1926, National Archives at Fort Worth, TX.

33. "To Check the Peyote Habit," *Brownsville (TX) Daily Herald*, August 20, 1909, 1.

34. "Unite to Stamp Out the Deadly Use of Peyote Bean," *San Antonio Gazette and Light*, August 20, 1909.

35. "Governments War on Deadly Bean," *La Crosse (WI) Tribune*, August 21, 1909, 1.

36. "Sacred, Also Intoxicating," *Sun* (New York), June 13, 1909.

37. "Sacred, Also Intoxicating," *Anaconda (MT) Standard*, July 11, 1909; "Peyote Is Not Poison Says Chief Quanah Parker," *Laredo Times*, October 3, 1909.

38. "Peyote Bean Is Double-Distilled Concentrated Jag," *Daily Capital Journal* (Salem, OR), May 10, 1909.

39. William E. Johnson, documents relating to a campaign for the suppression of peyote, Peyote Correspondence, file 2989-1908-126, RG 75, National Archives and Records Administration, Washington, DC.

40. F. H. Abbott to William B. Freer, September 16, 1910, OHS.

41. Johnson to Wormser Brothers, May 14, 1909, in Stewart, *Peyote Religion*, 139–140.

42. Arthur Parker to George Masquequa, October 31, 1914, reel 4, SAI Papers.

43. "Dope Bean to Go," *Oklahoma City Daily Pointer*, August 23, 1909, 3.

44. Louis Meeker to Department of Interior, December 28, 1896, NAA MC 2537, "Meeker, Louis L." folder, NAA–Bureau of American Ethnology.

45. Kiowa Indians to John Blackmon, January 10, 1907, and A. T. Payne to Charles E. Shell, May 10, 1909, OHS.

46. "Peyote Famine Among Indians," *Laredo Times*, May 9, 1909.

47. "Peyote Famine Among Indians."

48. George T. Díaz, *Border Contraband: A History of Smuggling across the Rio Grande* (Austin: University of Texas Press, 2015), 1.

49. C. D. Hilles to Senator T. P. Gore, May 20, 1910, NAA MS 2537, NAA–Bureau of American Ethnology.

50. "Beans May Be Sold," *Fort Worth Star-Telegram*, December 24, 1906, 7.

51. Bureau of Indian Affairs, *Peyote: An Abridged Compilation*, 12.

52. Stephen T. Moore, *Bootleggers and Borders: The Paradox of Prohibition on a Canada-US Borderland* (Lincoln: University of Nebraska Press, 2014), xii, xiv.

53. Stewart, *Peyote Religion*, 258–259.

54. Neil Boyd, *Canadian Law: An Introduction*, 5th ed. (Toronto: Nelson Education, 2011), 47.

55. Boyd, 48.

56. Boyd, 50.

57. "Sask. Crees Set Up Church," *Winnipeg (MB) Free Press*, December 15, 1954, 10.

58. "Indian Rite Narcotics Snatched at Border," *Winnipeg (MB) Free Press*, December 1, 1954, 1, 4; "Indians Lapse into Paganism Use of Peyote," *Medicine Hat (AB) News*, February 3, 1956, 9.

59. "Indian Rite Narcotics Snatched at Border," *Winnipeg (MB) Free Press*, December 1, 1954, 1, 4; "Federal Ban on 'Buttons' Unlikely Despite Manitoba Group's Plea," *Winnipeg (MB) Free Press*, December 6, 1954, 12; "MP Attacks Buttons of 'Beautiful Dreams,'" *Winnipeg (MB) Free Press*, March 22, 1956, 15.

60. "Indians Lapse into Paganism Use of Peyote," *Medicine Hat (AB) News*, February 3, 1956, 9.

61. See Devin Clancy and Tyler Chartrand, chapter 12 in this volume.

62. Articles of Incorporation for the Native American Church of Oklahoma, October 10, 1918, OHS.

Skirting the Law

NINE

Female Liquor Smugglers and Sellers
and Policing through Prohibition along
the Rio Grande

CAROLINA MONSIVÁIS

M aria Velarde's home stood on contested land
near a freight depot, just on the other side of
the Missouri Pacific Railroad tracks edging the
banks of the *estero*, a lush waterway etched by the Rio Grande in Brownsville, Texas.[1] A palm tree marked the entrance to her yard. Velarde's first
documented encounter with law enforcement occurred in 1921, when the
US Customs inspector R. D. Brown, aided by a search warrant, entered
her home. During his search, Brown found two quarts of tequila under
Velarde's bed and one quart of vermouth hidden behind a picture in the
wall. When questioned, Velarde admitted that the vermouth was for her
own personal consumption, but the tequila belonged to another woman
who had placed the bottles under her bed.[2] In October, Velarde faced the
US Customs commissioner H. K. Goodrich, who charged her with harboring contraband with the intent of selling it. Despite the lack of evidence,
she submitted her $100 bond and was released and scheduled to appear
in court December 1921. Over the next decade, law enforcement agents
gathered several times to search Velarde's home as they did other female-
headed households in the Rio Grande Valley.

Though smuggling is often associated with male rumrunners and bootleggers, Velarde's case demonstrates that women also attempted to profit
off the illicit trade that developed during US Prohibition. For women,
especially ethnic Mexican women living and working along the US-Mexico

border, the changes in laws and regulations aimed at curtailing the smuggling and selling of drugs and alcohol inadvertently opened avenues of commerce. While women worked in a variety of industries along the border, smuggling and selling alcohol and drugs proved to be a far more lucrative industry given their limited employment opportunities. Their illicit activities, in turn, brought women into contact with the law on a regular basis, and women found themselves having to negotiate a new policing regime in the borderlands.

This chapter examines the interactions between law enforcement and women who harbored, smuggled, and sold alcohol in the Rio Grande Valley between 1920 and 1933. Drawing on the Preliminary Inventory Records of the US District Court for the Southern District of Texas, it explores how particular gender and racial codes shaped how US federal and local law enforcement policed women's illegal activities. It also examines how women, in turn, asserted their agency during their confrontations with agents. As Lisa D. Barnett uncovers in chapter 8 of this volume, enforcement officers often used extralegal means and an imagined superiority to enforce their authority on marginalized groups. While Barnett's research focuses on the actions taken by the Office of Indian Affairs, this chapter explores similar developments as they affected ethnic Mexican women in the borderlands. Moreover, this chapter provides context on the origins of the culture of abuse among border policing officers that Jensen Branscombe examines in chapter 11.

Contradictory Perceptions and Gendered Performances

As the historians Elaine Carey and Holly M. Karibo have contended in their scholarship, the enforcement of vice codes is about much more than enforcing the law. It also provided the state another way to define appropriate behavior and occupations for women.[3] Examining the records of Prohibition along the US-Mexico border reveals that law enforcement determined whether to arrest female suspects based on women's perceived roles in the home. In particular, policing agents attempted to assess whether a woman's arrest would disrupt internal family dynamics and, by extension, those of their communities and the nation as a whole. Women's presence in suspected liquor violation cases thus influenced how federal and local police forces behaved while attempting to enforce laws. While agents habitually adopted violent tactics when only ethnic Mexican men were involved, their perception of women as the weaker sex often shifted their approaches to female smugglers. In these cases, women not only benefited from their chosen occupation but also were able to negotiate with law enforcement in a manner that deescalated potential violence. Although not always successful, female liquor smugglers and alcohol distributors utilized particular gender and racial stereotypes and created clandestine opportunities for themselves in the Prohibition-era borderlands.

In his 1963 memoir that recounts his tales of adventure as a self-described "frontier lawman," John Peavey, a US Border Patrol agent, included an anecdote about a woman agents referred to as "old Lupe."[4] Peavey described her as a habitual crosser between Matamoros, Tamaulipas, Mexico, and Brownsville, Texas. In the incident at hand, Peavey described Lupe's fashion choices, which included a black, loose-fitting dress that dragged behind her and a faded black shawl—customary attire, he noted, for older Mexican women. The US Customs inspector R. L. Campbell, on watch with him, noticed that her shape seemed odd and ordered her brought into the customs office, where a "lady customs clerk" searched her.[5] Instead of a bustle, officers discovered a horse collar hidden under her long black skirts. During questioning, Old Lupe admitted that she had smuggled many horse collars, usually multiple, and that it was the single horse collar that threw off her gait. Smuggling a horse collar was not necessarily a violation of any US Customs laws (Lupe presumably hid the collar to avoid paying potential tariffs), but Campbell continued his interrogation. She finally confessed to smuggling a little bit of mescal on occasion because it was the "only way she could support herself and the children of a widowed daughter." The agents warned Lupe not to attempt to smuggle again, then released her without charges.[6]

On the surface, this case seems unremarkable. The moment is included as comedic relief in an account otherwise focused on a dangerous and violent occupation. Peavey's memoir, written decades after his years spent policing, includes vignettes detailing his encounters with male smugglers, "bandits," and criminals, which often conclude with violence or tongue-in-cheek descriptions of interrogation tactics that hint at violence. His memoir also highlights the different occupations he held from 1906 through Prohibition in the 1930s, which includes his time as a US scout and Border Patrol agent with immigration services. As a Border Patrol agent, he joined other inspectors and agents, including both of his brothers-in-law, in searching homes for contraband. Indeed, throughout Prohibition it was common for agents to move through different law enforcement agencies and work with agents to whom they were related through either blood or marriage.

A Gendered Approach to Policing Alcohol

Nationwide Prohibition, and the Volstead Act that followed, created or extended policing powers across the nation. In the Rio Grande Valley, some funds were distributed to US Customs with the aim of increasing the number of inspectors, but the funds were not sufficient to hire new agents. Instead, the federal agency extended the power to enforce prohibition laws to Border Patrol agents, the Texas Rangers, and local law enforcement.[7] While Peavey's memoir hints at the extension of policing powers, it also describes the pride he and other law enforcement agents felt in reining in criminals and policing morality. Peavey details his attire and states that, like other agents, he took time with his appearance, including selecting clothes that emphasized his masculinity and that he thought necessary to the job. Peavey considered himself a member of the community he believed his actions protected, reflecting the preference of these agencies for drawing directly from the Anglo public, favoring men with wives, families, and local knowledge.[8]

It is through the male agent's gaze that we learn about Old Lupe. In contrast to the highly masculine imagery Peavey uses to describe himself and his fellow agents, his memoir focuses on the feminine demeanor of this particular interrogation subject. Although Old Lupe's background is not clear, she was dressed in a modest, long black dress that indicated that she was a widow and the caretaker for an extended family. As a woman who performed widowhood and economic need, Lupe fit within an accepted realm and was, at least for that encounter, not deemed a threat to the nation. Her choice of attire hints at both her attempt to skirt the law and her knowledge of agents' notions of proper female behavior.

It is possible, however, that Campbell and Peavey planned to continue their surveillance of Lupe once she returned to the confines of her community. In fact, this was a common practice. In 1926, for instance, the US Customs inspector D. L. Pullin obtained a warrant to search Marcaria Corpus's home in East Donna (which is how agents referred to the "Mexican" side of the town of Donna, Texas).[9] The warrant was granted due to information Pullin received that Corpus was "handling contraband liquor from her home."[10] Additionally, law enforcement resorted to relying on informants to either reinforce their suspicions or uncover homes where

Figure 9.1. Although policing Prohibition largely fell to the US Customs Service, women crossing the border also had to contend with navigating past US immigration inspectors. Brownsville, Texas, c. 1916. Robert Runyon Photograph Collection, RUN03947, the Dolph Briscoe Center for American History, University of Texas at Austin.

alcohol was sold.[11] The warrant, typical of the time, did not have an exact address but rather a description to search "the first house immediately north adjoining the Catholic church building now used as a school in the village."[12] Such vague descriptions granted law enforcement the ability to search houses in a broad area, thereby expanding their policing web. Additionally, law enforcement agents often gathered in groups before entering a person's home. Each case was led by one agent who detailed a narrative of the search, while the other agents provided supporting statements that corroborated the main narrative.

As the agents approached Corpus's house, they spotted her running out the back door, throwing a bottle of mescal in midstride. Pullin noted that some mescal spilled from the bottle and wet the ground where it landed. Inside, the other agents encountered Corpus's son stuffing a bottle under his shirt. In her backyard, they found a gallon jug full of mescal buried underneath some pumpkin vines. When the agents questioned her, she stated that the alcohol was for her and her son because "they enjoyed drinking it."[13] Despite her contention that the mescal was for their own personal consumption, she was arrested and charged with smuggling alcohol in violation of the Volstead Act. The women in these cases were charged with both selling and smuggling alcohol if it was present and deemed foreign, despite a lack of clear evidence that they smuggled it themselves.

In this case, Pullin referred to Corpus as an "old lady." While the agents encountered her son, presumably a young adult, no other male was mentioned, indicating a female-led household. Though Corpus's home did not contain a great quantity of alcohol, the officer chose to arrest her. In this case, Pullin perceived Corpus, unlike Old Lupe, as the kind of threat to the community and the nation that Prohibition was meant to control. In officers' minds, Corpus not only sold alcohol from her home; she was also a poor role model for her son, as it appeared that he also took part in selling and consuming alcohol.[14] Additionally, Corpus's response suggested that she had knowledge of the Prohibition laws. Her actions and confrontation with the officers—a direct challenge to their authority—led them to charge her. The officers' focus on the mother also directed law enforcement's focus away from her son, which reduced chances for any potential violence.

While law enforcement agents' interactions with the women they encountered varied depending on who was present at the time and how the women responded to the agents, the method for attaining a warrant was similar in all cases. In 1926, the Border Patrol inspectors Clifton Brown and John Henley, charged with the authority to rein in liquor violators, obtained a warrant to search Rafela Apersiado's home in the hamlet of Alamo because an informant shared that she "was handling a good deal of contraband alcohol."[15] They went out early on a Friday morning, since it was common for agents to choose an unexpected time of day to catch potential criminals by surprise. In their testimony, the inspectors claimed they encountered Apersiado walking home, hauling a sack filled with bottles. Upon questioning, Apersiado stated, "Well you have caught me, it is booze."[16] She admitted to carrying five quarts of tequila and one of mescal. At this point, Henley demanded that she relinquish any bottles hidden in her home, and the agents claimed she agreed to let them in. They walked with Apersiado to her home, where she gave them a half full bottle of mescal. Henley asked Apersiado what she was doing with the bottle, and officers reported that she replied: "Selling it by the drink."

Many of the documents do not indicate which language the women spoke, nor do the agents note their nationalities. Moreover, the women's statements were funneled through the familiar phrases adopted at the time, such as "I was handling liquor," to support Prohibition-related cases. Due to this goal, law enforcement agents focused on entering homes and finding contraband, which in turn allowed them to tack on smuggling charges. However, the occasional presence of young children cultivated varied responses. In Apersiado's case, even though she operated a makeshift underground cantina, when agents encountered her "family of children" they chose to charge but not detain her.[17] In addition to noting the children as a reason, they indicated that she was not likely to leave her residence. The inspectors were also aware that her husband, Catarino Alvarez, had been apprehended under similar circumstances.[18] Not wanting to leave children without parental supervision, these two factors prompted the officers to show some leniency toward the family.

Three days later, however, the customs inspector D. L. Pullin, who had seized the contraband liquor from Apersiado's home, returned with the Border Patrol inspectors J. P. Cottingham and J. H. Cottingham, who responded more harshly. This time Pullin questioned the husband, Alvarez—who was now back at home—at the door. In his testimony, Pullin claimed he told Alvarez that he had obtained information that the couple had continued to sell contraband alcohol. Alvarez denied it and, according to Pullin, invited him in to look around. Pullin was careful to note that the officers did not enter until they were given permission. On entering the house, the inspector found a bottle between a mattress and the frame. Alvarez stated that he had just been lying there and was drinking from the bottle that he had for his own personal consumption. They also found a quart bottle of mescal in the baby cradle. Apersiado claimed the bottle was hers and added that four days earlier she had purchased two boxes of liquor (twenty-four bottles) and sold each bottle for two dollars. The bottle they found she had kept for herself, she claimed. This time, the couple was charged and detained. Apersiado was released soon after; her husband served three months in jail. While the case resulted in Alvarez serving time, it is important to note the ways in which Apersiado asserted her presence. Perhaps conscious of the danger that law enforcement posed to her husband, she took responsibility for the alcohol and claimed some of it for herself. Nonetheless, Apersiado was released quickly so that she could return to what the state saw as her primary role: being a mother to her children.

Prohibition and Enforcement in the Family Home

As the above cases demonstrate, Prohibition provided law enforcement agents justification for extending patrols beyond the border and into ethnic Mexican neighborhoods. Indeed, if suspected liquor violations enabled lawmen to enter homes, they also provided a pretext for police to enforce a wide range of cultural codes. On Saturday, March 19, 1927, a "Federal Patrol Inspector" named J. P. Murphy, accompanied by a "Federal Patrol Officer" named H. H. Schildt, drove past Maria Librada Lopez's house and noticed a man's feet sticking out over a cot located in her yard. A half-full bottle of tequila rested next to him. Murphy and Schildt stopped and approached the man to ask him where he had obtained the bottle. The man, C. M. Clew, pointed to Lopez's home and stated: "From the Mexican woman who lives there."[19] Already intoxicated, he added that he was currently drinking from the second bottle he had purchased from Lopez. According to Murphy's testimony, he walked around Lopez's house until he found an open door. He looked inside and saw Lopez standing beside a bed, and just inside to the right of the door he noticed two sacks of tequila—twenty-two quarts—which he categorized as "foreign distilled intoxicating liquor."[20] Murphy questioned Lopez regarding the liquor, and she contended that "her boy" found it by the brush and brought it inside. Because her statement is filtered through Murphy's testimony, it is unclear what precisely she meant by the reference to "her boy." Presumably Murphy translated literally, and she was referring to her son, of unknown age, indicating that Lopez was a mother and lived on her own.

Officer Schildt's testimony adds yet another layer to the case. After Lopez denied selling alcohol, Schildt questioned Clew, who openly accused Lopez. At this point, Lopez admitted to selling tequila and asked to be released, promising "not to mix up with anymore tequila." Her plea suggests that she was attempting to elicit sympathy, which she was aware would be much more likely to be extended to a female suspect than to a male suspect. As the officers left with Lopez, her oldest son approached them and asked what was happening. Schildt noted that her son, who had been recently shot, appeared to be in "bad health." Schildt shared with Lopez's son that she had sold alcohol to Clew and warned him that if he had any alcohol in his own home he needed to relinquish it. Schildt threatened to wait all night to receive a warrant to enter his home. When he did, Lopez's daughter-in-law opened the door to their home, pointed to the thirteen bottles of tequila they were harboring, and stated: "There it is, take it." Schildt confiscated the thirteen bottles, although he was careful to note that they were not to be included in the charges against Lopez. He merely wanted to record what "the whole family were doing."[21] The officers chose not to arrest Lopez's son due to his poor health and because he had small children, thereby leaving his family intact. The officers, however, arrested Lopez because she disrupted the family dynamic by being a poor role model.[22]

Here, the conflicting definitions of motherhood become apparent. While officers were often reluctant to separate mothers from their children, they also sometimes punished women precisely for being the wrong type of mother, one that might expose her children to lawlessness, vice, and crime. In these cases, agents acted as moral enforcers and arrested women when they felt it reified the idea that women should serve as better role models. Unlike when men were the primary targets, law enforcement varied their approaches to investigating and apprehending women, leaving officers less likely to use violence as a means of enforcing the law. Women, as the above cases show, were aware of this contradiction and attempted to shape the outcome.

Perceived Gender Transgressions as Threats to the Local Community

If officers were willing to show some leniency toward mothers, there was another category applied to women who not only sold alcohol as a form of family income but also, according to law enforcement, disrupted the community by acting as "public nuisances." Nuisance charges granted law enforcement officers another means to police women and their homes. Agents targeted women who, from their point of view, stepped beyond accepted social boundaries by either failing to meet familial expectations or inadvertently disrupting the family dynamics of others by selling alcohol to men. Indeed, many implications can be drawn from such a vague term as "public nuisance." One reason for this is that the term, rooted in black codes and enacted in the southern United States following Reconstruction, was created to criminalize the behavior of African Americans.[23] Utilized during Prohibition, this phrase stigmatized ethnic and working-class neighborhoods throughout the United States and particularly in the borderlands.

In 1926, law enforcement agents acting on this concern took deliberate steps to establish Maria Mancillas's business and adjoining home, which she shared with her husband and daughter in the city of McAllen, Texas, as a "place of public nuisance."[24] In May, Deputy Sheriff Lorenzo Garcia arrested two groups of "Mexican" men, one group in the morning and one in the evening, who were leaving her restaurant drunk and carrying alcohol. The men were fined for being drunk and disorderly. The incident occurred just a few months following a previous search of Mancillas's residence, during which law enforcement agents found thirty-two bottles, which they confiscated and destroyed. On that occasion, the judge presiding over her case gave Mancillas a warning.

Garcia notified Peavey and Pullin of the May arrests, which provided justification for another warrant to search Mancillas's premises. When they returned to her residence, the law enforcement agents searched areas where bottles had been previously hidden, such as in the yard between her home and store. There they came across a tub planted with flowers that hid a bottle of tequila. During this search, they also found three freshly emptied tequila bottles tossed in the yard. Additionally, they encountered a tub with freshly planted flowers, placed over a recently excavated hole two feet deep inside a small enclosure near the front of her house. In his testimony, J. P. Cottingham compared the hole to others found in "boot-legging" joints used for concealing alcohol from law enforcement. Cottingham also noted that the mounds of dirt that should have accumulated due to the size of the dug-out hole were conspicuously missing. Ultimately, they found one bottle of tequila and a small amount of mescal.[25]

The women in these cases rarely chose to answer officers' questions. Mancillas, however, participated in the interrogation. Throughout her answers, Mancillas contended that she did not sell alcohol and added that the local sheriff and deputy sheriff often came around to check on her despite knowing that she did not handle contraband liquor. The questioning also focused on the holes dug out beneath the tubs. J. P. Cottingham was eager to have Mancillas explain the purpose of each hole. According to Mancillas, the tubs served as flower beds and the holes were intended to catch rainwater.

When the officers questioned Mancillas about the men they had arrested, she clarified that it was not two groups but rather two men, whom her husband had ushered from her store because they were intoxicated. They reminded her that she had been previously charged and warned that she was not to have any alcohol on her premises. She argued that the small amount of mescal the officers found, which she had not thought would be a problem, was given to her by one of the men who had been taken from the store to rub on her head because she often suffered from headaches. The tequila bottle, she added, was thrown there by the local police because, as she stated, "the Mexicans here are sore at me because the judge did not fine me."[26] The officers reiterated that her yard was enclosed and that, despite her argument, it did not seem possible for someone to hide a bottle in her tub of flowers. Throughout the interrogation, Mancillas maintained her innocence and argued that, despite the judge's conditions for her release, she kept a small amount of mescal for her headaches. She added that she was sleep deprived due to working long hours and this had caused her to forget the judge's warning. For the judge presiding over her second case, the evidence was strong enough to sentence Mancillas to serve sixty days in the Cameron County Jail and to declare her home a place of public nuisance.[27] In Mancillas's case, agents took steps to build a case against her with the help of local community members. Under the guise of "public nuisance," Mancillas was not only guilty of breaking the law but also punished for cavorting with intoxicated men who were not her husband and for leading other members of the community down their paths toward deviancy.

Despite law enforcement officers' connections to local communities and their reliance on informants, they turned to other methods to enter homes. In addition to declaring a residence a place of public nuisance, law enforcement agents often added the phrase "Christian Surname Unknown" to their warrants. Here, the religious moral overtones are apparent: if a woman was unable to prove her church-sanctioned title, then officers could use this as a pretext to challenge her place in the community. In 1929, for instance, the customs inspector C. H. White obtained a warrant to search Josefa Gonzalez's home because an informant claimed she was selling alcohol, especially on Sundays. Law enforcement agents applied the phrase "Christian Surname Unknown" to her warrant because, as White explained, it was otherwise impossible to enter a neighborhood and make useful inquiries. This was the case because community members often gave false names or warned neighbors that law enforcement agents were in the process of obtaining a warrant to search their homes. Additionally, law enforcement agents were frustrated by ethnic Mexican women's usage of both their married and maiden names. Provided in conjunction with vague descriptions of homes, the phrase allowed officers to significantly broaden their searches depending on what they found on the ground.

In this case, White, accompanied by the US Customs inspector Paul Wright, searched Gonzalez's home, which was located in an area they noted as "Tule Town" in Edinburg, Texas, with a warrant stating "Christian Surname Unknown."[28] The inspectors did not find any "foreign distilled liquor" but rather home-brewed beer and the materials to brew beer. They also found empty mescal bottles in a tub in her home's backyard and fifty-two bottles of beer on ice sitting in another tub in the kitchen. Next to that was another tub with an additional fifteen to sixteen beer bottles, both empty and full, "pelted" with water from the ice melting around them. Additionally, the inspectors found five gallons of "crook," which was used to make beer, and a capping machine they presumed capped the bottles once filled.

Because the alcohol had clearly not been imported, the inspectors charged Gonzalez with being in possession of alcohol without proper documentation but not with smuggling. Unlike in Maria Librada Lopez's case, the inspectors did not have definite proof that Gonzalez sold alcohol. She claimed that the beer was for her and her husband's personal consumption. The large quantity of alcohol, however, granted law enforcement agents the ability, in addition to declaring her home a place of public nuisance, to charge Gonzalez with possessing and manufacturing intoxicating liquor. The ultimate disposition of an individual case depended on the perception of the presiding judge. During Gonzalez's hearing, for instance, the judge was reluctant to detain her because, as court testimony indicated, she was a woman, and this made the judge feel "loathe" to fix a bond.[29] This was particularly the case because she came to court with her two small children, one of which was a "baby in her arms," which added to the judge's discomfort. Gonzalez ultimately agreed to attend her court date of her own volition.[30] Similar treatment was a national trend as judges proved hesitant to immediately jail women who were clearly trying to maintain a household or had small children. Moreover, despite the high number of women arrested during Prohibition, judges, and to a certain extent the public at large, treated cases involving women as anomalies.[31]

Finally, a careful examination of the cases reveals another tactic law enforcement agents employed during this era: intimidation. Although more difficult to identify, the ways in which women responded to or behaved regarding questions and searches indicated that intimidation played a key role. The narratives contained within the cases are riddled with statements claiming law enforcement was granted immediate access to homes where alcohol often lay out in the open. This surrender is understandable given the violence unleashed on ethnic Mexican communities by American law enforcement in the previous decade.[32] Moreover, the women managing cantinas from their homes knew that officers killed the male liquor smugglers who supplied them.[33] This underlying threat, which police documents silence, explains why Rafela Apersiado readily admitted to selling alcohol when agents returned to her home.

That intimidation was evident in a 1928 case in which the US Customs inspector W. B. Hopkins attained a warrant to search Rosa Morales's home in Rio Grande City. A few days before his arrival, Hopkins had received "reliable information" that Morales handled liquor from her home. He requested that the Border Patrol agents Jesse Perez and Bland C. Durham accompany him. A World War I veteran and the son of a Texas Ranger, Perez approached Morales's home with a history of violence behind him.[34] The group traveled down a dirt road off the main highway to a home described as a frame construction with shingles, gables, and roof, painted white with green trim. In their search, the agents found two one-gallon bottles of mescal, one quart of mescal, six quarts of *aguardiente*, and six quarts of tequila hidden in various parts of Morales's home. They promptly charged her with possession of and transporting alcohol, and the court set her bail at $200. During the proceedings, Morales admitted that her mother and children had implored her to stop selling alcohol but that she "would not quit."[35] This type of admission was rare. The women in these cases generally adopted phrases commonly used at the time that exploited the loopholes in Prohibition laws, such as that the alcohol was for medicinal purposes or for their own personal consumption. As agents of the state, the officers were empowered to act as both legal and moral enforcers. This type of confession specifically points to the questioning of Morales's behavior — not just whether it was legal but also what it indicated about her character. Moreover, her response hints at a personal dilemma about working in an illicit occupation out of necessity and choice.

Conclusion

Prohibition in the United States granted federal, state, and local police forces greater power to monitor and regulate Americans' behavior. In South Texas, the policing of Prohibition extended beyond the borderline and into suspect homes. In particular, Prohibition granted law enforcement agents another way to extend their surveillance of ethnic Mexican communities in South Texas, injecting it into the most intimate space: the family home. Conscious of their intrusion into women's domestic spheres, officers enforcing Prohibition took a gendered approach to policing that shaped their interactions with ethnic Mexican women suspected of smuggling or selling alcohol. How officers perceived particular women and their roles in the local community had a direct impact on how they chose to enforce liquor policies. Enforcement officers used the categories of "mother" and "breadwinner" as lenses to assess what type of punishment individual female smugglers and liquor sellers should receive. On the one hand, when officers perceived a woman as the primary caregiver to her children or the breadwinner in the family, they tended to mete out warnings or milder punishments. Reinforcing the notion of women as the weaker sex, they took a paternalistic approach in which individual officers seemed to view their roles as being the protectors of individual families. On the other, mothers and wives who failed to meet officers' standards of proper female behavior were also often labeled "public nuisances" and faced harsher penalties. Their perceived gender transgressions were framed as threats to the local community and the nation as a whole, and such women often faced harsh scrutiny, surveillance, and longer sentences.

A close study of the case files suggests that women who lived in the borderlands were aware of these contradictory perceptions and used them to their advantage whenever possible. Often, when faced with these intrusions, women resisted through gendered performances that could protect them and their families from the coercive forces tasked with enforcing Prohibition laws. Although in their appeal for sympathy and lenience these women's performances reinforced state and community expectations of proper female conduct, they also provided a strategic path forward for women who made money through illicit means. Ultimately, these cases illuminate women's efforts to exercise agency over their homes in the face of police intrusion and the threat of state violence. Officers exerted increasingly invasive powers in the Prohibition-era borderlands, but those powers were not all-encompassing. Women and their families found creative means to evade, resist, and play the gendered system, often enabling them to continue to smuggle, sell, and consume illegal liquor in contravention of US federal law.

Notes

1. Benjamin Heber Johnson, *Revolution in Texas: How a Forgotten Rebellion and Its Bloody Suppression Turned Mexicans into Americans* (New Haven, CT: Yale University Press, 2003), 276–277.

2. *United States v. Maria Velarde* (1921), Criminal Case Files for Brownsville, Texas, RG 21, Preliminary Inventory Records of the United States District Courts for the Southern District of Texas, National Archives, Fort Worth, TX (hereafter cited as NARAFW).

3. Elaine Carey, *Women Drug Traffickers: Mules, Bosses, and Organized Crime* (Albuquerque: University of New Mexico Press, 2014); Holly M. Karibo, *Sin City North: Sex, Drugs, and Citizenship in the Detroit-Windsor Borderland* (Chapel Hill: University of North Carolina Press, 2015).

4. John R. Peavey, *Echoes on the Rio Grande* (Brownsville, TX: Springman-King, 1963), 172.

5. George T. Díaz notes that female customs inspectors were often tasked with

searching women under suspicion of smuggling across the border. It is important to note that in these cases only male agents searched the homes. George T. Díaz, *Border Contraband: A History of Smuggling across the Rio Grande* (Austin: University of Texas Press, 2015), 68.

6. Peavey, *Echoes*, 172–173.

7. Lisa McGirr, *The War on Alcohol: Prohibition and the Rise of the American State* (New York: Norton, 2015), 69–71; William James Sheeran, "The Enforcement of Prohibition in South Texas 1919 to 1933" (master's thesis, Texas A&I University, 1970), 49.

8. Sheeran, "Enforcement of Prohibition," 63–65. See also Peavey, *Echoes*.

9. *United States v. Marcaria Corpus* (1926), Criminal Case Files for Brownsville, Texas, NARAFW.

10. *United States v. Marcaria Corpus* (1926), Criminal Case Files.

11. Sheeran, "Enforcement of Prohibition," 44. Peavey also mentions his reliance on embedded community members for information.

12. *United States v. Marcaria Corpus* (1926), Criminal Case Files.

13. *United States v. Marcaria Corpus* (1926), Criminal Case Files.

14. *United States v. Marcaria Corpus* (1926), Criminal Case Files.

15. *United States v. Marcaria Corpus* (1926), Criminal Case Files. Law enforcement frequently relied on local informants to attain search warrants. According to James Sheeran ("Enforcement of Prohibition," 44) officers struggled to enforce Prohibition without using informants. Informants in turn were paid one-fourth of all fines and penalties that resulted in an arrest.

16. *United States v. Marcaria Corpus* (1926), Criminal Case Files.

17. *United States v. Rafela Apersiado* (1927), Criminal Case Files for Brownsville, Texas, NARAFW.

18. *United States v. Rafela Apersiado* (1927), Criminal Case Files; *United States v. Catarino Alvarez and Rafela Apersiado* (1927), Criminal Case Files for Brownsville, Texas, NARAFW.

19. *United States v. Maria Librada Lopez* (1927), Criminal Case Files for Brownsville, Texas, NARAFW.

20. *United States v. Maria Librada Lopez* (1927), Criminal Case Files.

21. *United States v. Maria Librada Lopez* (1927), Criminal Case Files.

22. The fact that two widows, Rosa Scroggins and Librada Garza de Gonzalez, posted bail on Lopez's behalf (two hundred dollars each) by using lots they owned indicates the degree to which women could appeal to community networks for support. *United States v. Maria Librada Lopez* (1927), Criminal Case Files.

23. McGirr, *War on Alcohol*, 91.

24. *United States v. Maria Mancillas* (1926), Criminal Case Files for Brownsville, Texas, NARAFW.

25. The cases often include agents' forensic abilities to justify their entrance into homes. This included comparing homes where alcohol was sold, or "tracking" smugglers' paths into homes. See Alexandra Minna Stern, "Nationalism on the Line: Masculinity, Race, and the Creation of the U.S. Border Patrol, 1910–1940," in *Continental Crossroads: Remapping U.S.-Mexico Borderlands History*, ed. Samuel Truett and Elliott Young (Durham, NC: Duke University Press, 2004), 299–323.

26. *United States v. Maria Mancillas* (1926), Criminal Case Files.

27. *United States v. Maria Mancillas* (1926), Criminal Case Files.

28. *United States v. Josefa Gonzalez* (1929), Criminal Case Files for Brownsville, Texas, NARAFW.

29. *United States v. Josefa Gonzalez* (1929), Criminal Case Files.

30. *United States v. Josefa Gonzalez* (1929), Criminal Case Files.

31. Lisa McGirr in *The War on Alcohol*, 97, notes that, nationally, judges tended to dole out either warnings or reduced sentences to first time female offenders with children. Repeat offenders, however, were more likely to be fined and sentenced to prison.

32. From 1915 to 1919, hundreds, possibly thousands, of ethnic Mexicans were killed in South Texas during an era known as "La Matanza," primarily by the Texas Rangers. See Trinidad Gonzales, "The Mexican Revolution, *Revolución de Texas*, and *Matanza de 1915*," in *War along the Border: The Mexican Revolution and Tejano Communities*, ed. Arnoldo De León (College Station: Texas A&M University Press, 2012).

33. Díaz, *Border Contraband*, 99–101.

34. Jesse Perez Sr. details his son's time as a soldier in World War I. Additionally, Perez Sr. was directly linked to the era of violence in the Rio Grande Valley. Jesse Perez, "The Memoirs of Jesse Perez, 1870–1927" (unpublished typed manuscript), Center for American History, University of Texas, Austin.

35. *United States v. Rosa Morales* (1928), Preliminary Inventory Records of the United States District Courts for the Southern District of Texas, NARAFW.

Building a Villain/Hero Binary

TEN

Public Rhetoric, Smuggling, and Enforcement
in the Postwar Borderlands[1]

HOLLY M. KARIBO

On January 5, 1952, a front-page *Washington Post* article reported on a nationwide crackdown on narcotics trafficking, describing it as "the greatest criminal roundup in the Nation's history." "The raids stretched from Canada to Mexico" and included border cities like Buffalo and New York—a "key gateway" to the drug market in Canada—as well as "a scattering of cities in Texas and New Mexico near the southern border." In this massive federal raid, American authorities attempted to "break the backbone" of the illegal drug trade that, by the early postwar period, stretched across North America and beyond. The porousness of the national line, and the gall of the criminal underworld that congregated around it, the paper reported, was increasingly making life difficult for federal policing authorities and dangerous for law-abiding citizens.[2]

As the *Washington Post* article demonstrates, during the late 1940s and 1950s the issue of illegal drug smuggling along the US-Canada and US-Mexico borders was hotly debated in the public arena. In publications ranging from nationally circulated papers like the *New York Times* and the *Globe and Mail* to local papers like the *Windsor Daily Star* and the *Arizona Republic*, Canadians and Americans regularly read about drug traffickers and crime syndicates bringing large quantities of narcotics into North America. Blaming the smuggling problem on the rise of organized crime and Communist conspiracies from abroad, these stories presented an image of racial and ethnic others subverting national laws and sneaking across North American borders.

If the domestic drug problem was a result of global criminals and porous borders, Americans and Canadians began to wonder what their governments were doing to protect citizens. In 1955, the American and Canadian federal governments took up this question, forming special Senate committees to investigate the drug problem. Through their testimonies before the committees, officials like the heads of the Federal Bureau of Narcotics (FBN), the Royal Canadian Mounted Police (RCMP), and immigration and customs departments worked hard to demonstrate that they were in fact in control of the drug problem and were effectively working together with neighboring nations to enforce stringent drug policies. In doing so, their testimonies reaffirmed the image of heroic federal officials fighting racial and ethnic others at each nation's boundaries. At a time when the Canadian and American governments were attempting to project a unified front in the fight against Communism and other subversive forces, fighting vice networks was about more than simply eliminating a particular illegal activity.[3] It was also a way for the federal governments to enact what the scholar Kenneth Meier terms "morality politics," in which federal officials asserted themselves as the proper authorities to define productive citizenship and protect their nations' boundaries from dangerous interlopers.[4]

Yet a closer look at the complex representations of border enforcement in the Senate committee debates also highlights the contradictions inherent in attempting to control spaces that operate simultaneously as barriers and connecting points. Although the simplistic dualism of "heroes" and "villains" sometimes enabled federal enforcement officials in the United States, Canada, and Mexico to work together to fight an identifiable "other," it also often led local enforcement officers to blame the trafficking problem on the lax policies of their neighbors. American customs and border agents publicly accused the Mexican government of failing to stop the flow of drugs out of Mexico, while Canadian law enforcement officers likewise complained about the influx of drugs from their American neighbors to the south. Despite lofty attempts to present a unified prohibitionist front in the fight against cross-border smuggling and crime at the federal level, the realities of life in border cities often blurred the line between "good guys" and "bad guys" that was so central to postwar antivice rhetoric. Ultimately, the exclusive definitions of citizenship that allowed the public and government officials to blame vice and illicit cross-border activities on dangerous outsiders also undermined the effectiveness of nation-building projects, diplomacy, and border enforcement in the postwar years.

Public Debates: Setting the Context for the 1955 Senate Committees

As several chapters in this volume demonstrate, antidrug discourses were not unique to the postwar period and indeed have a long genealogy in North American history. However, the postwar environment shaped public perceptions of illegal drugs and drug users in key ways. Growing fears over two international conspiracies — the Mafia and Communism — helped transform national antidrug narratives into global struggles against much larger sinister forces. This transformation was bolstered by high-ranking federal officials who stressed the need to remain vigilant against the infiltration of these menacing forces into North American society. Organizations like the FBN and the Federal Bureau of Investigation, under the direction of Harry Anslinger and J. Edgar Hoover, respectively, misleadingly depicted both the Mafia and Communism as coherent and centralized international conspiracies, arguing that they were the two most dangerous threats facing North American society.[5] Their claims were reinforced by several government investigations into the growing power of organized crime and its negative effects on North American life.[6]

Throughout the late 1940s and 1950s, newspapers, magazines, films, and television shows, drawing on "evidence" provided by law enforcement officials and politicians, created sensational stories about the connection between the illegal drug trade and transnational syndicates. Anslinger and other FBN agents collaborated with journalists who printed stories based solely on the information they received from the enforcement officers. They regularly leaked stories about their agents standing bravely against the Mafia and the People's Republic of China, suggesting that the objective of both was to speed up the moral degeneration of the American people through the spread of drug addiction.[7] Similarly, national publications in Canada printed stories of large-scale syndicates trafficking dope across the national border and subsequently harming thousands of Canadian citizens. "The individual racketeer has gone," one 1954 *Maclean's* magazine article reported, "and the traffic is controlled today by 'syndicates' headed by [men who are] clever, suave, outwardly well-mannered, but inwardly as vicious and dangerous as the old-time gangster."[8]

Widely circulated media representations of the Italian mobster shaped public perceptions of the clever and cunning, yet extremely dangerous, drug trafficker. One article, written by the investigative reporter Drew Pearson in 1950 and reprinted in newspapers across the country, explained to the American public: "A total of 50 men control most of the big rackets in the United States. All are members of the mysterious Mafia, and all but one are either Italian-born or of Italo-American descent. . . . Like a plate of spaghetti the connections of the Mafia members are tangled and twined together."[9] Similarly, a *Chicago Defender* article provided a brief history of the organization, describing its transition over time from a group of Sicilians forming an underground economy in the eighteenth century to a sophisticated organization that used violence and intimidation to infiltrate legitimate businesses and unions across North America. According to the article, ethnicity and blood lines were key, with pedigree "being handed down from father to son in the strict baronial manner." "Essentially," the Mafia was "just one big law-breaking family."[10] Contemporary reports likewise noted that this violent, patriarchal "family" controlled the narcotics traffic in North America by using lower-level peddlers to do the actual work of moving the illegal products. The higher-ups rarely got their hands dirty, instead relying on a series of midlevel dealers who pushed drugs in designated urban neighborhoods, especially among racially segregated African American and Latino communities.[11] As a result, federal officials had to use increasingly sophisticated tactics to pin narcotics, racketeering, or prostitution charges on them.

The danger of the white ethnic mobster could be matched only by that presented by Chinese Communists, who—according to the media—trafficked dope into North American cities as part of an agenda designed to undermine the moral and physical health of citizens. A long history of associating men of Chinese descent with opium use and other forms of vice lent credence to the argument that Chinatowns were hotbeds of both drug use and Communist subversion in the postwar years.[12] One *Spokane Daily Chronicle* article, for example, told the story of Pon Wai, a "smiling 64-year-old operator of the Fragrant Flower Garden shop in San Francisco's Chinatown," who "was peddling the white death called heroin." The article explained that "day after day" the FBN had watched the florist, whom they suspected of drug trafficking, in an effort to ascertain how he was moving his illegal products. When a search of one of Pon Wai's messengers revealed that he was smuggling "pure heroin" in green capsules attached to the stems of roses, the FBN agents finally had the evidence needed to arrest the florist and eight of his messengers on smuggling charges.[13] In these media narratives, federal agents emerged victorious over smugglers who used sophisticated and violent tactics to evade arrest.

As the power of these global drug networks increased, postwar media narratives began to report on cities along the US-Canada and US-Mexico borders, framing them as the first sites of contact between transnational smugglers and vulnerable citizens. In the United States, national discussions about border towns tended to center on Mexico, due in part to the growing amount of heroin and marijuana being imported from that country.[14] Images of Mexican border towns, though, were also rooted in a longer history in which Americans perceived the border as a racialized space that enabled criminality and violence.[15] In the postwar years, public panics over illegal immigration likewise fueled American perceptions that the US-Mexico border enabled lawlessness. Large-scale immigration enforcement efforts, most significantly Operation Wetback in 1954, were highly publicized and had the effect of bolstering perceptions that countless illegal immigrants were pouring across the border on a daily basis.[16] Newspapers often explicitly linked the "illegal Mexican aliens" with vice problems in American cities. As one report explained it: "Because these people live outside the law . . . they have become victims of lawless elements in Southern California where dope and prostitution rings are causing serious local problems."[17]

American newspapers regularly described Mexican border towns as lawless places whose locations next to large American markets enabled extensive vice industries to flourish. One *Milwaukee Sentinel* article described Baja California as "the gate to hell." The article explained that the city's "gaudy night clubs and half hidden dives attract Americans in droves. Tourist dollars spent on lurid pastimes—and on bullfights and horse and dog racing—provide the border population with just about its only income." In a city with only 100,000 residents, the article maintained, there were as many as 8,000 prostitutes. "Their customers were Americans— 'who come here every time they need drugs, easy women, or to satisfy whatever insane desire they may have.'"[18] The ease with which Americans could travel back and forth between American cities and Mexican border towns was central to this problem. As a *Los Angeles Times* article explained, many Americans were "only a hop, skip, and a fix away from pushers in [towns like] Tijuana."[19]

The notion of the wide-open border town likewise shaped public perceptions of cities along the northern border. A description of Windsor,

Ontario, painted the city as a gateway to hell, where even "the devil him-self lack[ed] the persistency, defiance, and outright gall of bordello and bootleg operators," who profited from their positions along the national line. In these narratives, northern border towns like Windsor, Niagara Falls, Buffalo, Toronto, and Detroit also functioned as fluid spaces that united the central tropes of the postwar drug panic—race, mobility, and the power of organized syndicates. As one *Maclean's* magazine article explained to its readers, the headquarters of the "underworld lords" in Canada was "said to be in Toronto, hooked up with supply lines passing from Mexico through New York and Minneapolis. In boom years, their transactions have run in the millions."[20] Papers regularly reported coordi-nated antidrug efforts between American and Canadian officials, such as the 1959 sting that netted criminals from Montreal to New York and con-stituted the "biggest criminal narcotics case in Canadian history."[21]

Contemporary publications stressed the interconnected nature of the drug trade between Canada, the United States, and Mexico. News stories explained that nefarious traffickers often used the legal divide that sepa-rated border cities as a way to evade arrest. As one South Carolina news-paper warned: "Good Neighbor Canada will wake up any day [now] with as hard a headache as ours, over a national dope and crime scandal." Claim-ing that cities across Canada were seeing a rise in drug use, especially among young people, the author stated that the problem was caused by the extensive smuggling networks that successfully brought heroin into Canada from either Mexico or the "Orient." "The reason is," the article ex-plained, "the executive (mobster controlled) work of the Canadian under-world is done in Detroit and Buffalo, which are beyond the jurisdiction of the Mounties and other law enforcement agencies north of the bor-der. And the parallel executive affairs for much of Buffalo, Detroit, and other nefarious traffic are headquartered in Canada, beyond the jurisdic-tion of the US Federal and other policing." Traffickers "shrewdly operated in this fashion," according to the author, "so that books, witnesses, collat-eral data, etc. can't be subpoenaed on either side of the line." In this way, sophisticated drug networks used the legal divides separating the cities along the borders as a way to evade detection and arrest, subsequently opening up a relatively free flow of illegal goods across North America and beyond.

The 1955 Senate Committees:
Projecting Consensus at the Federal Level

The consistent outpouring of news stories depicting a growing drug problem convinced many North Americans that something needed to be done to stop it. Within this context, the Canadian and American federal governments decided to assess the extent of the drug problem and to study how they could eliminate the social evil from their respective nations. In 1955, each country's Senate established special committees designed to do just that. As the largest federal investigations into illegal narcotics in the postwar years, these massive undertakings were conducted over the course of several months and in more than fifteen major North American cities — from Montreal to Vancouver and New York to Los Angeles. The hearings were well publicized, and North Americans could read highlights from the hearings as the testimony moved from city to city.

The Senate committees purported to take a comprehensive approach to the drug problem, one that would help cut through the escalating public rhetoric, which, in the words of one RCMP officer, "favored sensationalism rather than accuracy."[22] They heard testimonies from a variety of witnesses on the extent and nature of the drug problem, including breakdowns by city, state, and province. The senators also reviewed the current law to determine what policies were working and what changes needed to be made. Overall, as one Canadian official explained, the hearings were designed to provide "sober, factual, and objective examinations." The use of the word "sober" here is telling. Despite their professed "balanced approach," the committees collected information in large part from legal authorities and federal enforcement officers who were tasked with enforcing antidrug laws and with punishing users and sellers on a daily basis. Rather than countering popular rhetoric that framed drug traffickers and addicts as dangerous and unwanted outsiders, these supposedly neutral investigations served to reinforce the perception that upstanding federal officials were needed to fight a growing problem across North America.[23]

Given the global nature of the drug trade, as well as the extensive media coverage of organized crime and transnational smugglers in both countries, it is not surprising that the hearings discussed their nations' borders in detail. The senators heard testimonies from a wide variety of individuals about where heroin was produced, how it was imported, and who was in charge of these activities. Canadian and American law enforcement officials generally agreed on the sources of illicit narcotics, which were produced externally in Mexico, the Middle East, the Mediterranean, and China and trafficked through various trade routes, usually through European countries like France and Italy or from Hong Kong.[24] There was some evidence that the main sources of heroin had shifted from the Middle East in the early postwar period to mainland China by the mid-1950s, in part the result of the opening of global trade routes following the war. In the case of marijuana, supplies tended to originate in Mexico and were smuggled across the border and, occasionally, up to Canada.[25]

Although drug networks were expansive and stretched across many different countries, federal officials paid particular attention to imports from Communist China. Linking these imports to larger sinister political objectives, the committees heard a wide range of evidence that China was attempting to sneak heroin into North America as a way to destroy its free and prosperous nations from the inside.[26] In his testimony before the US Senate committee, the FBN's Anslinger explained that a recent increase in the importation of potent heroin on the West Coast from Communist China had already been responsible for the death of several users across the country. The Chinese government was purposefully trying to harm North American citizens, Anslinger claimed, and the problem would continue to grow over the coming years if the federal government failed to act swiftly.[27] Senator Price Daniel's remarks at the hearings in Texas stated the problem more bluntly: "[Drug addiction] is a vicious thing, it is a cancer on our society. We have to do something to stop this drug traffic if we want to save our boys and girls and communities and country. It is tied into subversion. Red China is pushing this heroin here."[28] The image of Chinese Communists threatening the safety of the nation's children fit well with the villain/hero binary because it enabled federal officials to frame the fight against drug trafficking as part of a larger moral battle between "good guys" and "bad guys," between harmful outsiders and innocent citizens.[29]

The Senate committees also heard detailed testimony about the complex web of agencies involved in antitrafficking efforts. Though the enforcement of prohibition policies was officially under the purview of the RCMP and the FBN, immigration and customs authorities were often considered the first line of defense in narcotics cases. As General J. M. Swing, commissioner of the Immigration and Naturalization Service at the time, explained to the US Senate committee: "In performance of their regular duties [immigration officers] are called upon to make still watches at known crossing points along the international boundary; they must inspect pedestrian traffic, automobiles, rail, and air traffic travelling inland from the border—thus, they normally come into contact with many persons of questionable character."[30] Although a larger portion of American resources and attention was spent policing the Mexican border, the United States also had officers regularly stationed in Canada who worked closely with Canadian officials to reduce illegal smuggling.[31] This included a "flying squad" of six plainclothes officers who patrolled the Great Lakes region to detect smugglers. The RCMP also had a liaison officer stationed in Washington, DC, who regularly met with "all enforcement agencies in the United States," including frequently with the FBN on "joint problems."[32]

Canadian and American federal officials praised the congenial relationship between their respective enforcement officers, promoting their mutual dedication to drug prohibition as a sign of close diplomatic ties. This relationship was seen as early as the opening day of the hearings, when American senators warmly welcomed the chairman of the Canadian Senate committee and its chief counsel. The Canadian senator was asked to provide the first comments before the US Senate committee. He spoke of the significance of the drug problem, the common situation facing Canada and the United States, and the appreciation he felt for being invited to work with the American senators.[33] The language of affection and close neighborly ties continued throughout both hearings. In his description of the various agencies involved in enforcing narcotics legislation in Canada, the head of the RCMP claimed that it "would be discourteous if I did not mention as well the close link we have with the US Bureau of Narcotics and the great help we get from that agency. We get the very best type of help from that Bureau."[34] Similarly, George McClellan, commander of the Ontario division of the RCMP, asserted that "the R.C.M. Police have been most fortunate in the quality of the co-operation which we receive from the United States Bureau of Narcotics, and in particular, the Agents of that Bureau at the border points" throughout Southern Ontario.[35]

Several high-level American officials likewise praised the cooperation they received from Mexican authorities, arguing that what was once a troubled relationship had much improved by the postwar years. As the head of the FBN explained, "There was a time when there were gun battles along the border there among the smugglers and the enforcement officers." Thanks to close cooperation, this was no longer the case. Indeed, Anslinger criticized newspapers in American border states for blaming the drug problem on Mexican officials, arguing instead that they deserved praise for their ability to reduce drug-related crime over the course of the previous decade.[36] Similarly, the US commissioner of customs described the cooperation his agency received from Mexico as "excellent." "I was tremendously impressed," he said, "with the relations between our customs men, our forces there, and the Mexico police authorities. . . . Our reports from Mexico City are very voluminous and very wonderful, in my opinion. I think that is probably our best . . . representation abroad." Indeed, the highest officials in Mexico, including the minister of health, the attorney general, and President Adolfo Ruiz Cortines, all publicly supported enforcement efforts, and it was "because of their support that [the FBN was] able to get some of the big gangsters."[37]

To demonstrate a united front, senior enforcement officials provided numerous examples of specific cases in which cross-border interaction had facilitated drug-related busts and arrests of smugglers operating across the American, Canadian, and Mexican borders. One of the most impressive examples of interagency cooperation led to the arrest of Antoine D'Agostino, who according to committee transcripts was "considered by international law enforcement authorities as one of the most important international narcotics violators." In 1937, D'Agostino moved from his native Bône, Algeria, to Marseilles, France, where he began working with a group of notorious Corsican criminals who specialized in narcotics, international jewelry robberies, counterfeiting, and gold smuggling. In 1948, he fled his death penalty conviction in Toulouse (after being charged with treason for supplying French troops with heroin during the war) and subsequently began a large smuggling network out of Montreal, Québec. Once busted by Canadian authorities, D'Agostino left Canada and headed for New York City, where he joined another gang of Corsicans. After the FBN cracked down on this smuggling network, D'Agostino went underground. Though his whereabouts were unknown between 1951 and 1953, he resurfaced in Mexico City, where he was arrested on March 7, 1955, and sent back to New York City to face narcotics charges. Canada likewise filed extradition charges to bring D'Agostino back to Montreal, after which the French government indicated that it would extradite him for execution upon termination of the charges in the United States and Canada. In what was a truly international effort, federal authorities working in Canada, the United States, and Mexico were able to track down this notorious and dangerous drug trafficker and subsequently bring him to justice.[38]

Much like the news stories of cross-border drug smuggling, the testimonies of federal officials served the dual purpose of delineating particular images of dangerous drug smugglers and presenting federal enforcement officers as the heroes needed to fight them. Federal officials discussed the problem of organized syndicates and Communist subversion, framing antitrafficking efforts as a struggle between nefarious outsiders and upstanding enforcement officers. The highly visible public hearings of the Senate committees provided an ideal platform for federal officials to promote their prohibitionist agendas and to boast about their successful sophisticated tactics.[39] For agencies whose operating budgets depended on both a perceived need for their services and a positive success rate, projecting images of cross-border cooperation and success was clearly important.

Officials' testimonies before the committees, though, also had broader implications for definitions of citizenship in the postwar years. By perpetuating images of heroes and villains along the border, American and Canadian officials were engaging in a discourse of state-making that drew a line between acceptable and unacceptable behavior and between desirable and undesirable community members. Situating these lines within a prohibitionist framework, which emphasized criminalization over treatment, federal agents reinforced racialized images of dangerous outsiders and vulnerable citizens to solidify their agencies' importance within the global struggle against Communism. In this way, federal enforcement officers presented their mission not only as stopping the spread of drug trafficking and addiction but also as facilitating close diplomatic ties with their neighbors, whom they saw as integral to their ability to be successful in the fight against the global drug trade.

The Villain/Hero Binary and the Realities of Policing on the Border

While stories of federal agents taking down key members of the underworld made for good publicity and helped project a positive image of federal enforcement agencies at the Senate investigations, they often failed to reflect the daily experiences of many officials tasked with enforcing the national line. The testimonies of law enforcement officers working on the ground in border cities often undermined the image of cross-border cooperation and consensus. Ironically, the very villain/hero binary embedded in antidrug rhetoric facilitated this divide between federal objectives and local approaches. Expressing frustration with the wide-open nature of border cities and a perceived lack of cooperation coming from the governments across the line, local officers sometimes offered testimonies that proved damaging to federal diplomatic objectives. The rhetoric of prohibition highlighted an inherent problem: it was tricky to cultivate a close relationship with neighboring nations while framing one's domestic drug problem as an import from dangerous outsiders.

One of the most blatant divides between the testimonies of senior federal officials and those of officers working on the ground was the language they used to describe lawbreakers. The representations of transnational smugglers, in which the media and federal officials afforded the high-level traffickers some degree of agency, stood in stark contrast to the images of demoralized addicts, peddlers, and prostitutes with whom lower-level officers dealt on a regular basis. Rather than portraying drug users as "sophisticated" and "cunning" criminals, local police officers, Border Patrol agents, and immigration officials defined them as pathetic individuals who inhabited the lowest levels of society. As Commissioner Leonard Nicholson of the RCMP vividly described: "From the standpoint of the police who see them day to day, they are a dreary lot of parasites supporting themselves . . . by crime and prostitution. . . . They are in truth the dregs of society."[40] Another RCMP officer similarly explained that drug peddlers "contribute nothing to society" but instead "prey on society in conditions of degradation, filth, and depravity."[41]

These morally bankrupt individuals were, according to local officials, right at home in border towns, which officials claimed attracted the lowest type of criminals. This was especially true, they testified, along the US-Mexico border. In the hearings held in Texas and Southern California, Border Patrol officers, immigration inspectors, and local law enforcement officers described the situations in cities like Juárez and Tijuana, emphasizing the ease with which even the most novice tourist could find any type of illicit good or service he or she desired. In his discussion of Juárez, a local news reporter stated that one need only head over to the "slum" area known as the Bellavista District, which was home to more than fifteen establishments where one could purchase heroin. The reporter's discussion of these slum areas was reinforced by photographs of city streets where Americans could easily locate heroin dealers and prostitutes. Two photos show the Baños Jordan, a bathhouse run by La Nacha ("the queen of the border"), a notorious trafficker and madam who had been operating out of Juárez since the 1920s (see figures 10.1 and 10.2).[42] These pictures, which were accompanied by fifteen mug shots of Mexican and Chinese smugglers who operated out of the region, helped solidify racial connec-

Figure 10.1. Home of La Nacha, "the queen of the border."

Figure 10.2. Baños Jordan, a bathhouse run by La Nacha.

Figure 10.3. Several mug shots of Mexican and Chinese smugglers appeared in the US Senate committee report.

tions between traffickers on the Mexican border and the illicit spaces in which they operated (see figure 10.3).[43]

Notions of racial and cultural difference often led American enforcement officers on the ground to criticize the way Mexican authorities handled the drug issue. Bernard McLeaish, a customs agent working out of Brownsville, Texas, testified that Mexicans were culturally much more tolerant of vice than Americans. As he explained to the committee: "If you stay on the Mexican border for any length of time you will understand the Mexican philosophy is quite different from ours. What is immoral to us in the United States is not immoral to them in Mexico." This was true, McLeaish asserted, of both the Mexican people and Mexican authorities.[44] Further, in wider public discussions, American authorities called heroin originating in Mexico "Mexican Brown heroin," likewise creating an implicit connection between the production of the illegal substance and a perception of racial difference with their southern neighbors. The term "Mexican Brown heroin" angered Mexican authorities so much that they appealed to the United Nations to ban members from using it at UN meetings.[45]

American senators found themselves walking a fine line between soliciting feedback from local officers working on the ground and being careful not to cause further damage to the relationship between American and Mexican authorities. The senators seemed aware that any suggestion of racial or cultural difference between Mexicans and Americans risked straining diplomatic tensions between the two nations. This is precisely what occurred after the testimony of Walter Naylor, the chief narcotics division officer for the state Department of Public Safety in Texas. Naylor had blamed much of the drug problem on Mexican traffickers and on Mexican authorities from whom he received very little cooperation. He described the ease with which anyone could purchase drugs in Mexican border towns and the willingness of Mexican authorities to turn a blind eye. This problem went all the way up the chain of command, according to Naylor. He described one instance when high-ranking Mexican officials had backed out of a meeting to address this issue and refused to reschedule. Naylor claimed with a condescending tone: "We thought we might be able to assist the Mexican Government in their problems, if they do have a problem, and we think they do. I offered the Mexican consul the use of my men to use as undercover agent[s] . . . [but w]e haven't heard any more [from them]."[46] When Senator Daniel asked Naylor what he thought of the Mexican officials and whether he received any cooperation from them, Naylor responded flatly: "No, sir."[47]

Much to the US Senate committee's frustration, Naylor's testimony sparked outrage on the part of Mexican officials and forced the American senators to do damage control.[48] Daniel brought Naylor back to testify so that he would have a chance to explain the evidence he used in making his accusations about Mexican authorities. Although Naylor for the most part stood by his original assertions, Daniel insisted emphatically that the goal had not been to offend Mexican officials, whom senators considered great allies in the fight against trafficking. Yet, beneath even such conciliatory words, Daniel also struck a tone that blamed this misunderstanding on Mexican authorities, who had been invited to sit in on the hearings in Texas but had declined. "Had they been there . . . I am sure they would have known that every time anything was said about Mexico," he said, "about 10 times as much was said about our own citizens and our own people and our own laws. We have a mutual problem on the border."[49] "I wish they had done like Canada . . . and be present and here."[50]

Senator Daniel's lamentation that Mexican authorities had declined an invitation to participate in the Texas hearings reflected a larger trend in which American and Canadian authorities used their relationship as the example of sophisticated cross-border ties that Mexican authorities should work to emulate. FBN head Anslinger suggested paternalistically in his opening remarks before the US Senate committee that "those men who are down there on the firing line" along the US-Mexico border get together for informal meetings similar to those held by officials working along the US-Canada border. He openly contrasted the violent and unpredictable nature of the southern border with the peacefulness and orderliness of the northern border, suggesting that Mexican authorities could learn much by emulating the cooperation provided by Canadian officials.[51] He made no suggestion of racial, ethnic, or cultural differences between Americans and Canadians. Instead, the world's "longest undefended border" was once again upheld as the example of how modern states should interact with their neighbors.

Yet a close examination of the testimonies of local enforcement officers working along the US-Canada border likewise suggests that they too were often frustrated with the situation in northern border cities. Ironically, while Mexican officials were concerned with the overemphasis Americans placed on Mexico as the source of the US drug problem, Canadian authorities expressed frustration that they received *too little* attention from their American counterparts. Indeed, American officials spent considerably less time trying to assess the problems along the northern border. Although the senators interviewed enforcement agents as well as former users about their experiences with smuggling along the US-Canada border, they did not pursue the issue with nearly as much zeal as they did when interviewing users along the southern border.[52] There were no accompanying photographs or maps of Canadian border towns, nor did the issue of cross-border smuggling in cities like Detroit and Buffalo dominate the investigations as it did in cities like El Paso and San Diego.

The tendency of American authorities to downplay the cross-border issue along the northern border frustrated Canadian authorities. After all, the United States was Canada's main source of heroin and marijuana in the postwar years, much as Mexico was a key supplier for the American drug market. In his testimony before the Canadian Senate committee, McClellan of the RCMP expressed the frustrating and at times hopeless situation local law enforcement agents faced when trying to curtail cross-border vice in cities like Windsor, Hamilton, and Toronto. Their proximity to major American cities and the long "undefended" border between the countries were central enforcement challenges for local agents. As McClellan explained: "There is a heavy flow of international traffic in both directions, by rail, air, and automobile. This . . . free flow of traffic in accordance with the mutual trust and understanding between the two countries . . . poses many problems for both Canadian and US Immigration and Customs Officials."[53] McClellan said that it would be completely impossible "to establish any rigid system of checking traffic without completely tying up the free movement of people and goods essential to our international commerce and tourist trade." For McClellan, this heavy traffic, combined with the fact that "most affluent elements of the criminal underworld on the United States side reside in areas easily accessible to the Ontario and Quebec borders," made smuggling relatively easy for traffickers and made regulation extremely difficult for Canadian officials.[54]

The veiled frustrations expressed by Canadian authorities like McClellan to the 1955 committees had erupted explicitly five years earlier, when the Kefauver Committee (named for its chair, Senator Estes Kefauver of Tennessee) passed through the city of Detroit. In many ways a precursor to the expansive 1955 investigations, the Kefauver Committee's hearings in Detroit were well publicized across Canada and raised concerns about the relationship between organized crime in the United States and Canada. Tensions between American and Canadian officials arose in November 1950 when a Canadian newspaper printed a story titled "Windsor Wire Service: Predict US Senate Will Rap Ontario." The article claimed that the US Senate was going to reprimand the Ontario government's response to vice activities and suggested that the US Senate would take a strong-arm approach to dealing with its Canadian neighbors. This had broader implications for illegal industries in the region, the article asserted, because "the same people who are involved in the gambling rackets are mixed up with narcotics and prostitution." According to the article, "Speculation by police officials here is that the Ontario Provincial Government will receive a severe condemnation by the US Senate" and would be expected to take strong action to "clean up Windsor."[55]

The premier of Ontario, Leslie M. Frost, considered this to be a diplomatic affront and quickly contacted Senator Kefauver to prevent a public lashing by the US Senate. Frost took this one step further, using it as an opportunity to suggest that in fact American authorities had failed to do their duty to prevent cross-border vice and smuggling. In a letter sent to Kefauver in November 1950, Frost defended the work of Canadian agents, blasted the lack of cooperation from American officials, and suggested further meetings be held between Canadian and American police forces to deal with the problem. After providing a detailed account of the approach taken by Ontario officials over the previous couple years, Frost asserted that "the problem is international in nature. . . . May I draw your attention to the fact that the problems in regard to gambling and vice which we have in the Province of Ontario have their origin in the United States in nearly all cases. Our Forces here cannot effectively deal with the problem without the cooperation of the United States law enforcement agencies." According to Frost, if the Detroit side gave the Windsor police as much cooperation as the Ontario provincial government gave its American counterparts, then vice in Windsor, which the premier characterized as "difficult if not impossible to cope with," could be very much curtailed.[56]

Though nothing serious came of this exchange—the Kefauver Committee did not publicly "rap" Ontario enforcement officials—it does provide some insight into the frustrations that occurred between American and Canadian authorities tasked with regulating vice in cities near the nations' common border. Though Canadian and American authorities held similar goals, and both recognized the importance of effectively policing their shared border, each side emphasized different priorities. Authorities in the booming metropolis of Detroit were primarily concerned with the ways in which drugs were brought into their city from other large American cities like New York and Chicago in addition to cities along the US southern border with Mexico. In contrast, Ontario officials were keenly aware of their position along the national line, in that American-run criminal syndicates often enabled narcotics and other vice operations to flourish in adjacent Canadian cities. Canadian officials often felt they had little chance of curtailing vice in their own cities without the help of their neighbors to the south, and this cooperation was not nearly as extensive as Canadians officials would have liked.

The diplomatic ruptures that occurred between Canada, the United States, and Mexico suggest that, despite lofty rhetoric voiced by federal officials, a cohesive prohibitionist agenda was extremely difficult to enact along the borders running across North America. The tendency to blame the drug problem on "others"—be they racial and ethnic outsiders, lax Mexican authorities, or American criminals—which is so prevalent in the villain/hero binary, profoundly shaped the perspectives of local officers working in border cities. Dealing daily with the permeability of the border, these officers rarely spoke of a comprehensive cross-border strategy in the fight against transnational crime. Instead, officers working to try to stamp out illicit, cross-border crime were keenly aware of the inefficiencies in cross-border policing tactics that made their jobs difficult. Prohibition policies were much more difficult to enact than federal officials let on and interagency cooperation was often undermined by local officers' tendencies to blame the drug problem on the lax efforts of seemingly lazy enforcement officers on the other side of the national line.

Conclusion

As the 1955 committees drew to a close, the senators put forward a series of recommendations for how best to address the drug problems in their respective nations. These recommendations ultimately reflected the committees' dedication to a prohibitionist ideology that defined illegal narcotic use as immoral and drug users themselves as undesirable citizens. In the end, both bodies recommended increased policing, harsher sentences, and other punitive measures such as aggressive enforcement of drug-related crimes like theft and prostitution.[57] The US Senate committee's recommendations were implemented the following year in the Narcotic Control Act of 1956, which raised the minimum sentence on some drug offenses to five years and allowed a jury to impose the death penalty on anyone over the age of eighteen convicted of trafficking heroin to minors.[58] Likewise, the Canadian Senate committee's recommendations were implemented in the 1961 Narcotic Control Act, which increased the maximum penalty from fourteen years to life for trafficking, possession for the purposes of trafficking, and importing and exporting.[59] By the end of the postwar period, blaming social ills on unwanted outsiders clearly had very real effects on people involved in the drug trade. Now subject to the harshest penalties enacted to date in each country, traffickers ultimately bore the brunt of the blame for North America's drug problem.

Public debates played a crucial role in creating a climate in which the federal governments of the United States and Canada, as well as Mexico, could enact harsher penalties. Indeed, throughout the late 1940s and 1950s, news stories and federal hearings had effectively created links between transnational drug trafficking, racial minorities, and Communist subversion. Working within a Cold War moral framework, these disparate groups established the villain/hero binary, which perpetuated the notion that North Americans were increasingly susceptible to the dangerous wiles of unwanted outsiders. By constantly depicting violent confrontations between drug traffickers and law enforcement officers, these deeply racialized images likewise underscored the notion that a strong enforcement presence was needed along the borders. Drug traffickers, Mafia bosses, and Communist agents had to be stopped at the borders, and federal officers were just the ones to take on this job.

Yet, if the emphasis on traffickers as dangerous criminals enabled federal officers to push for stricter enforcement policies that would bolster the political importance of their respective agencies, the very success of the villain/hero binary sometimes worked against larger diplomatic objectives. An examination of the testimonies of local law enforcement agents before the 1955 Senate committees highlights the contradictions inherent in trying to pin the drug problem on racial, ethnic, and political others while trying to maintain close diplomatic ties with neighboring nations. When Texas officers blamed the "wide open" nature of southern border towns on the supposed moral weaknesses of their Mexican counterparts, they made it much more difficult for federal officials to project a united front in the struggle against crime on the southern border. Likewise, though American and Canadian authorities often touted the bonds of friendship and shared cultural values that enabled enforcement officers to work together across the northern border, Canadian officials were also often frustrated by the lack of attention they received from their counterparts to the south. In these moments, the rhetoric of cross-border friendship and cooperation clearly did not match the reality of enforcing prohibition policies in local border communities.

The very fact that illegal drug trafficking continued across the US-Mexico and US-Canada borders despite these prohibition policies, and that it would actually grow substantially in the next decade, suggests that we need to be skeptical of federal proclamations about the effectiveness of antidrug policies in the postwar era. The authorities' inability to police the long borders that connected Canada, the United States, and Mexico demonstrates the resilience of illicit economies and their ability to adapt to local environments, especially in the border towns that brought North Americans together during the postwar years.

Notes

1. An unabridged version of this chapter was first published by *Histoire sociale/ Social History* 47, no. 95 (November 2014).

2. "Nation-Wide War on Dope Launched by Authorities," *Washington Post*, January 5, 1952, 1.

3. John Herd Thompson and Stephen J. Randall, *Canada and the United States: Ambivalent Allies* (Athens: University of Georgia Press, 2002), esp. chap. 7, "Canada in the New American Empire, 1947–1960," 184–213.

4. Kenneth Meier, *The Politics of Sin: Drugs, Alcohol, and Public Policy* (New York: M. E. Sharpe, 1994), 4.

5. Michael Woodiwiss, *Organized Crime and American Power: A History* (Toronto: University of Toronto Press, 2001), 248; Lee Bernstein, *The Greatest Menace: Organized Crime in Cold War America* (Amherst: University of Massachusetts Press, 2002), 9.

6. Stephen Schneider, *Iced: The Story of Organized Crime in Canada* (Mississauga, ON: John Wiley and Sons, 2009), 227.

7. Woodiwiss, *Organized Crime*, 244–245.

8. Alan Phillips, "The Case of the Drug Peddling Priest," *Maclean's*, August 1, 1954, 15.

9. Drew Pearson, "Fifty Members of the Mafia Control Big Rackets in United States," *St. Petersburg (FL) Times*, October 10, 1950, 6.

10. "Says Mafia Is Just One Big Family," *Chicago Defender*, July 19, 1958, 11.

11. Rufus Schatzberg and Robert J. Kelly, *African American Organized Crime: A Social History* (New York: Garland, 1996), 108.

12. "US Agents Smash Big Narcotics Ring," *New York Times*, April 6, 1954, 26.

13. "San Francisco Agents Seize Narcotics from China," *Spokane (WA) Daily Chronicle*, December 6, 1955, 9.

14. Erick Schneider, *Smack: Heroin and the American City* (Pittsburgh: University of Pennsylvania Press, 2008), 77.

15. Steven W. Bender, *Run for the Border: Vice and Virtue in US-Mexico Border Crossings* (New York: New York University Press, 2012), esp. chap. 1, "El Fugitivo," 11–26.

16. Juan Ramon Garcia, *Operation Wetback: The Mass Deportation of Mexican Undocumented Workers in 1954* (Westport, CT: Greenwood, 1980); Kelly Lytle Hernández, *Migra! A History of the US Border Patrol* (Berkeley: University of California Press, 2010); Ronald Mize, *Consuming Mexican Labor: From the Bracero Program to NAFTA* (Toronto: University of Toronto Press, 2011); Don Mitchell, *They Saved the Crops: Labor, Landscape, and the Struggle over Industrial Farming in Bracero-Era California* (Athens: University of Georgia Press, 2012).

17. "Ike Endorses Strong Policy on 'Wetbacks,'" *Oxnard (CA) Press-Courier*, August 18, 1953, 4.

18. "Baja California Offers Sun, Fun," *Milwaukee Sentinel*, November 24, 1958, 8. See also "Fictional Picture of Mexico as Crime Sanctuary False—Unless You're Mexican," *Ocala (FL) Star-Banner*, May 1, 1955, 3.

19. Gene Sherman, "Border Dope Traffic Swells," *Los Angeles Times*, November 17, 1951, 1. See also "Narcotics Smugglers Out of Control," *Oxnard Press-Courier*, April 20, 1954, 2; "Opium Pours across Rio Grande," *Washington Post*, February 29, 1948, B5; "Narcotics Running from Mexico Rises," *New York Times*, March 1, 1953, 13; and "'Wetbacks' Cross at Two a Minute: Linked to Narcotic Trade," *New York Times*, April 16, 1953, 11.

20. Robert Francis, "Hopheads," *Maclean's*, February 15, 1947, 50.

21. "Big Narcotics Haul Made in Montreal," *New York Times*, July 10, 1959, 8. See also "RCMP Reviews Careers of Canada's Crime Kings," *Winnipeg (MB) Free Press*, January 6, 1955, 22.

22. Canada Senate, *Proceedings of the Special Committee on the Traffic in Narcotic Drugs in Canada* (1955), 20.

23. Nancy D. Campbell, *Using Women: Gender, Drug Policy, and Social Justice* (New York: Routledge, 2000), chap. 5; Schneider, *Smack*, 73; David F. Musto, *The American Disease: Origins of Narcotic Control* (Oxford, UK: Oxford University Press, 1973), 261.

24. Canada Senate, *Proceedings of the Special Committee*, 63.

25. US Senate Committee, *Illicit Narcotics Traffic* (Washington, DC: Government Printing Office, 1955–1956), 4492.

26. Musto, *American Disease*, 231.

27. US Senate Committee, *Illicit Narcotics Traffic*, 43.

28. US Senate Committee, 3410.

29. US Senate Committee, 3410.

30. US Senate Committee, 148.

31. US Senate Committee, 129.

32. US Senate Committee, 107.

33. US Senate Committee, 107.

34. Canada Senate, *Proceedings of the Special Committee*, 21.

35. Canada Senate, 314.

36. US Senate Committee, *Illicit Narcotics Traffic*, 106.

37. US Senate Committee, 108.

38. US Senate Committee, 81.

39. Lytle Hernández, *Migra!*, 211.

40. Canada Senate, *Proceedings of the Special Committee*, 28.

41. Canada Senate, 28.

42. US Senate Committee, *Illicit Narcotics Traffic*, 3310.

43. US Senate Committee, 3314.

44. US Senate Committee, 2818.

45. US Senate Committee, 314–315.

46. US Senate Committee, 2383.

47. US Senate Committee, 2382.

48. US Senate Committee, 3318.

49. US Senate Committee, 3784.

50. US Senate Committee, 3318.

51. US Senate Committee, 107.

52. US Senate Committee, 75, 107, 150, 216, 1593, 2138, 2134, 4519, 4290.

53. Canada Senate, *Proceedings of the Special Committee*, 313.

54. Canada Senate, 312.

55. "Windsor Wire Service: Predict U.S. Senate Will Rap Ontario," *Globe and Mail*, November 23, 1950, 3.

56. Leslie Frost to Estes Kefauver, November 23, 1959, RG 3-23, box 213, Windsor Police Commission, file 313 G, B292181, Archives of Ontario, York University, North York, ON.

57. Robert R. Solomon and Melvyn Green, "The First Century: The History of Non-medical Opiate Use and Control Policies in Canada, 1870–1970," in *Illicit Drugs in Canada: A Risky Business*, ed. Judith C. Blackwell and Patricia G. Erickson (Scarborough, ON: Nelson, 1988), 104.

58. Musto, *American Disease*, 231.

59. Solomon and Green, "First Century," 105.

PART IV

Expanding State Authority and Its Challenges

Diversity and the Border Patrol

ELEVEN

Race and Gender in Immigration Enforcement along the US-Mexico Border

JENSEN BRANSCOMBE

While working for the US Border Patrol in the 1970s, Fred Drew reported several of his fellow officers for violent crimes including the abuse and rape of immigrants. He was dismayed when the charges resulted in only minor reprimands. More perplexing, Drew was the one fired by the Border Patrol, while his more violent colleagues stayed on the job. Another officer, Edward Begley, was similarly frustrated by the brutality he witnessed in the Border Patrol during his service from 1976 to 1978. One "notorious" officer in San Ysidro, California, "dragged a guy out through the window of a car," Begley reported, "and beat him half to death."[1] Drew and Begley shared their experiences with journalists from the *New York Times* investigating accusations of fraud and abuse in the Immigration and Naturalization Service (INS). The result of the investigation was a series of five lengthy articles published in January 1980 that condemned the graft and violence that characterized INS law enforcement practices, especially along the US-Mexico border.[2] After interviewing current and former immigration officials like Drew and Begley, *Times* reporters concluded that the INS deserved its "bruised reputation" as a law enforcement agency because of "the refusal of the agency to police itself, and corruption, malfeasance, and brutality."[3]

Reporters and whistle-blowing immigration officers were not the only critics of the INS and the Border Patrol in the 1970s. Although public criticism of the Border Patrol dates back to its creation in 1924, discontent with immigration law enforcement reached unprecedented levels in the 1970s.[4] Troubling stories of corruption and fraud in the INS, as well as accounts of violence and racial profiling in enforcement procedures, drew the attention of activists inspired and informed by the civil rights movement to stand up for the rights of immigrants. Civil liberty groups like the American Civil Liberties Union (ACLU) joined the burgeoning immigrants' rights movement to bring the issue of abusive practices in the treatment of immigrants, especially those without documentation, to national attention. Activists decried the same abusive practices later described in the *Times* series.

Responding to the public outcry, the Department of Justice (which housed the INS), Congress, and the US Commission on Civil Rights (USCCR) investigated the Immigration Service throughout the 1970s. While the federal investigations focused on policy matters, congressional hearings and USCCR reporting reveal that policy makers identified violence as a major problem in the INS. Malpractice revealed by government and activist attention makes clear that the US-Mexico border could be a place of violence and oppression for immigrants and communities of color. This reality emerged despite the hopes of the Lyndon Johnson administration that immigration reform passed in 1965 would result in a more humane and equitable system.[5]

Critics of the INS identified the treatment of women and minorities as one of the disturbing areas of immigration policy enforcement. While discriminatory and abusive practices were national problems encompassing INS operations along the northern and southern borders as well as in major cities, the INS stationed the majority of its personnel in the Southwest in the 1970s. Those agents policed a population that was largely Mexican and male, though increasing numbers of women also entered the United States from Mexico to take advantage of new job opportunities in the service sector. Few people of color or women, however, were involved in crafting immigration policies or enforcing them. Accounts of racism and sexism in immigration policies and enforcement in the Southwest demonstrate that the racial and gender disparities between immigrants and agents policing them contributed to larger immigration enforcement problems in the 1970s and gave an inherently authoritative law enforcement agency even more power.

Although advocates of immigration enforcement reform varied in goals and tactics in the 1970s, they shared the common goal of eradicating violence and corruption. Disparate groups from government, media, and concerned communities each identified a lack of diversity in the Border Patrol as a primary factor in the ineffective and inhumane enforcement practices. By the early 1970s, the expanding women's liberation movement introduced a new language of sexual harassment and violence at the same time the Black Power and Chicana/o movements illuminated the long-standing hostilities between law enforcement and communities of color. Activists held a national conversation on law enforcement and concluded that police forces should be more representative of the communities they patrol.[6] A growing public awareness of how the social location of people with policing power affects the way they wield power informed those troubled by the culture and practices of the INS. In response to critics of the immigration agency, the government attempted reform, but its half-hearted efforts failed to alter the demographics or culture of the agency. Rather than prompting real change, the troubles of the 1970s fortified the culture of power and prejudicial practices that existed within the Immigration Service and Border Patrol.

Policing the Borderlands in the 1970s

During the 1970s, economic woes, political scandal, and the disastrous war in Vietnam eroded many citizens' trust in government institutions. The decade also proved a particularly challenging one for the INS. Although much of the agency's trouble was self-inflicted, some of it resulted from a changing immigration landscape in the Southwest. Most notable, the numbers of unauthorized border crossings increased after the end of the Bracero Program in 1964 and the implementation of the Immigration and Nationality Act of 1965 (known as Hart-Celler), which set numerical limits on migrants entering the United States from Western Hemisphere countries.[7] Contributors to this volume have described other times in INS history when it struggled with a lack of resources. In chapter 5, for example, Thomas A. Klug describes the challenges of enforcing immigration laws along the US-Canada border at the turn of the twentieth century with an "often underfunded and overcommitted US immigration bureaucracy."[8] As the numbers of immigrants entering the United States without documentation increased in the 1970s, immigration officers "buckled under the strain" as they had earlier in the century and called for more resources and public awareness of law enforcement challenges.[9] One particularly effective voice in the 1970s was Leonard Chapman, who served as INS commissioner from 1973 to 1977. To draw attention to his agency and win additional funds from Congress, Chapman launched a publicity campaign to alert the public to what he framed as the dangers of undocumented immigration, often overestimating the numbers of undocumented immigrants in the United States and blaming them for social problems like unemployment and crime.[10] As a result, immigration in the Southwest borderlands—particularly undocumented immigration—became a national issue. A growing immigrants' rights movement, galvanized by the Chicana/o movement and public calls for "tougher" immigration policies targeting Mexican immigrants, further focused national attention, most of it negative, on the service's treatment of immigrants.

One consistent factor cited by investigators, journalists, and activists concerned by the problems of violence in immigration enforcement was the lack of diversity within the INS. In an era of the Black Power, Chicana/o, and feminist movements, immigrants' rights activists were familiar with national conversations and debates over police brutality and sexual exploitation. Many activists linked the numerous charges of brutality in the INS to racial disparities between the police and communities of color. As one activist put it, the abusive treatment of immigrant populations resulted from the Border Patrol hiring "biased Anglos" and "ex-military types."[11] Likewise, a representative for the National Council of La Raza bemoaned the "bigotry" in the INS and denounced white officers for acting disparagingly toward people of Mexican descent.[12]

INS employee demographics support claims of minority underrepresentation. In 1976, a member of Congress wrote to President Gerald Ford to update him on an investigation into equal employment opportunities in the INS. The data, he asserted, "raised serious questions that the minimal minority and female representation in the INS workforce severely inhibits the agency from discharging its statutory obligations."[13] Racial and ethnic minority representation in the Border Patrol was "abysmal," according to the letter. Out of approximately 10,000 service employees, Hispanics—the largest minority—made up a mere 15 percent of Border Patrol personnel in the mid-1970s and represented only 5 percent of INS investigators and 9 percent of immigration inspectors. This was "despite the focus of INS efforts to halt the illegal entrants who are predominantly of Spanish heritage."[14] Nearly seventy years after Special Agent A. A. Seraphic, as described by James Dupree in chapter 6, decried the lack of Spanish speakers employed by the agency along the US border with Mexico, INS overseers were still puzzled by INS hiring practices. African

Americans held just seven positions in the Border Patrol in 1972 and represented only 4 percent of INS personnel. Women represented less than 5 percent, with only eleven female agents and sixteen investigators.[15]

Critics of the lack of diversity in law enforcement organizations like the Border Patrol had evidence to support their belief that white-majority police forces in communities of color resulted in oppression and discrimination. As accusations of violence and abuse by immigration police forces galvanized immigrants' rights activists in the 1970s, memories lingered in their minds of the race riots of the late 1960s and the movement to push for the hiring of more minority officers that followed.[16] Moreover, the Black Power and Chicana/o movements petitioned for police reform in order to address the historic brutality these communities faced. Big-city police forces gradually started minority-officer recruitment efforts, and immigration reformers caught on to the idea.

Civil liberty groups lodged other complaints against the INS in the 1970s associated with the lack of minority representation, such as the brutal roundup-style raids and racial profiling used by the agency. A 1974 report published by the ACLU outlined examples of mistreatment perpetrated by the INS against documented and undocumented immigrants of Hispanic descent during a raid in Los Angeles.[17] The author of the ACLU report determined that

> one might well conclude . . . that the quarry in this INS "crackdown" was a population of murderers, thieves, and rapists instead of people who might— or again might not—be present in this country illegally. In fact, had the "suspects" indeed been accused of murder, theft, and rape, they could not have been subjected to this kind of treatment at the hands of the police.[18]

The attention the ACLU gave to INS policing practices rallied civil liberty advocates across the nation. Concerned Citizens for Justice for Immigrants, for instance, was a New York–based immigrants' rights group that petitioned the federal government to change enforcement practices and issue amnesty to undocumented immigrants. A member of the group, Sean Ferguson, wrote to the Ford administration to complain that INS "mass round-ups, dragnets and strongarm tactics" violated the civil rights of all immigrants regardless of status.[19] Immigration officials' use of racial profiling was a frequent complaint from immigration lawyers, such as one who wrote to the government in February 1976 alleging the INS based many of its investigations solely on "the appearance of the person interrogated."[20]

Like civil liberty advocates, local and regional organizations in the Southwest also targeted racist INS search tactics and treatment of immigrant detainees through their own protests. The Chicana/o movement prompted many young Mexican Americans to find racial solidarity with immigrants of Hispanic descent in the United States. These young activists formed their own organizations and persuaded traditional Mexican American rights groups to embrace the immigrants' cause.[21] The cooperation of Chicana/o activists, traditional Mexican American groups, and pro-immigrant allies solidified after 1975 when national calls for immigration reform increased and the country geared up for a presidential election year. Albert Garcia, for example, who was president of the United California Mexican American Association, wrote to an INS regional commissioner in 1975 to lodge a complaint against the Border Patrol based on its "abusive and prejudiced attitude towards the Mexican-American population in the Southwest region."[22] The most notable achievement of immigrants' rights activism occurred in 1977 when attendees of the First National Chicano/Latino Conference on Immigration and Public Policy met in San Antonio and, in a remarkable show of solidarity with immigrants, passed a series of resolutions that demanded "full civil and human rights" for all immigrants regardless of status.[23]

Human rights violations of immigrants were a galvanizing issue for activists in the 1970s, as were reports that some officers participated in extralegal policing. A few officers, particularly in the high-traffic states of Texas and California, allegedly organized or offered support to vigilante groups that systematically brutalized undocumented immigrants, carrying on a legacy of violent vigilantism dating back to the "home guards" of the early twentieth century (as documented by Miguel A. Levario in chapter 7). Vigilantes favored extralegal actions because they believed undocumented immigrants would not otherwise receive "proper" punishment.[24] When Ku Klux Klan Grand Wizard David Duke organized the Klan Border Watch program in 1977, for example, he claimed to have the support of Border Patrol officers who believed the INS did not have the manpower or resources for the enormous task of policing the US-Mexico border.[25] Though the immigration agency denied involvement in the Klan's program, there were other instances of vigilantism's connection with the Border Patrol. Four officers in California faced federal brutality charges for organizing a vigilante group with the intention of assaulting undocumented immigrants, and former agents reported knowledge of other vigilante activity.[26] Belligerent officers, furthermore, used beatings to intimidate immigrants or shot them using unregistered weapons, which one officer called "throw-away guns." "I've seen many such shootings," the officer noted, "and these are unarmed people [Mexican immigrants]."[27] Physical attacks of immigrants occurred in more formal interview settings too. One inspector at the San Ysidro, California, station reported that a supervisor there forced immigrants to listen to religious sermons and would "punch him out" if an immigrant acted disinterested in the message.[28] With few exceptions, these crimes went unpunished, according to witnesses and whistle-blowers.[29]

Women were particularly susceptible to violence and exploitation when they encountered state agents patrolling the border. Treatment of these women differed significantly from the paternal actions of law enforcement agents toward female smugglers in Prohibition-era Texas that Carolina Monsiváis uncovers in chapter 9. "The giving of cards and entry permits to female aliens, including prostitutes, in exchange for sexual relations is apparently . . . common along the border," the New York Times series reported in 1980.[30] The articles did not offer quantitative data on the number of alleged rapes, but all of the former agents interviewed mentioned that rape or sexual exploitation was a routine part of the job for some officers. It was not only women crossing the border who were subjected to sexual extortion. Nicholas Estiverne, who worked as a Border Patrol officer in McAllen, Texas, in 1975, recalled a restaurant there as a "haven for female aliens," where it was common practice for Border Patrol agents on "inspection tours" to arrest one of the women and demand sexual relations in return for her release.[31] Grace Halsell, a journalist who toured the US-Mexico border with the US Border Patrol in the late 1970s, recounted a similar phenomenon. One of the Border Patrol officers she talked to told her about a pastime enjoyed by some of his coworkers. He explained,

> Sometimes we organize a "pussy posse" and go out at night with some of the sheriff's men and city police and round up 150 illegal Mexican women in the small bars. Of course, there's not much we can do with them. There are no detention centers for women. We put them in the county jail, write them up, and then release them.

Halsell concluded that it was "a bit of a diversion for the men," but such practices created fear among women of Mexican descent living and working in border communities.[32]

The numerous atrocities illuminated by concerned citizens in the 1970s led to a series of formal inquiries into the immigration service. The Department of Justice initiated an investigation of the INS dubbed "Operation Cleansweep" that ran through the early years of the decade and shed light on the culture of corruption and abuse within the agency.[33] The Cleansweep team gathered evidence that more than 150 past and current service employees, including several top officials, facilitated "the smuggling of illegal aliens and narcotics; [took] hundreds of thousands of dollars in bribes and kickbacks from government contractors; [and] engaged in perjury, fraud, and obstruction of justice." The team found "every federal crime" except "bank robbery," said investigator Alan Murray.[34] Rarer than cases of graft, but also more damning, were instances of violence. Years before the 1980 *New York Times* series, the Cleansweep team turned up accounts of "gross physical abuse of immigrants," including instances when Border Patrol agents "raped female aliens and systematically brutalized others with such devices as lead-filled gloves, thumbcuffs and even garrotes."[35] Congress initiated its own hearings in 1973 and 1974 to investigate the regional operations of the INS. Later in the decade, the USCCR also examined INS practices. These inquiries uncovered many of the same abuses discovered in the Cleansweep investigation. The USCCR, for example, heard complaints about the "hostile attitudes" of the Border Patrol toward immigrants, including the "sexual coercion by members of the Border Patrol against females attempting to cross the border."[36]

Despite the staggering number of abuses brought to light in these investigations, only a handful of immigration officials faced serious punishment. While INS officials claimed that there was not enough evidence to bring charges against officers accused of crimes, the reporter John Crewdson argued that the lack of indictments was due to the fact that the investigation was underfunded and lacked a clear process. There was also the larger distraction of the Watergate scandal and its aftermath and the challenge of getting immigration employees to testify against one another.[37] A general lack of support for whistle-blowers compounded the problems of corruption, abuse, and racism- and sexism-driven practices.

Reform Efforts

The INS did take action to address one persistent criticism. Facing pressure at the national and local levels from government officials and grassroots activists, the INS initiated a recruiting campaign to attract more women and racial minorities. This effort occurred at a time when many law enforcement agencies in the United States attempted to diversify their ranks. Members of various social movements at the time successfully spread the message that, in order to achieve a more equitable society, historically oppressed groups needed better access to education and jobs and more representation in government and the criminal justice system. Federal laws supported these efforts. The 1964 Civil Rights Act and the 1972 amendments to Title XII prohibited discrimination based on race or sex in the public and private sectors. Affirmative action programs in police departments aimed to achieve better opportunities and increased representation for marginalized groups.[38]

Like other police forces, the Border Patrol did not have an established track record of hiring women or racial minorities. Although a few patrolmen of Hispanic descent had served throughout the history of the Border Patrol, the government denied positions for women and African Americans until the late 1960s.[39] Diversity among service employees working as immigration inspectors was only slightly better. Women did work in immigration offices but held secretarial positions until 1920, when the Bureau of Labor—then overseeing immigration—created a "Woman's Section." The commissioner subsequently directed that women "be admitted on equal terms with men hereafter to inspectorships" so that they could "deal with matters peculiarly affecting women and children."[40] There was apprehension among regional immigration directors who believed women were unsuited for inspection work. This was especially true in remote areas like the US-Mexico borderlands. A letter from the district headquarters in El Paso, Texas, to the immigration commissioner outlined the demands of an inspector working in the region. "By their very nature, women are unfitted to undertake" the duties required, he concluded.[41]

Even though there were skeptics of the abilities of women in law enforcement, the INS in the late 1970s recognized the lack of diversity among its employees and sought to extol agency efforts to hire underrepresented groups.[42] A 1977 edition of the *INS Reporter*, the agency's official public newsletter, included an article titled "Minorities and Women in the INS" that praised diversification efforts. The article explained that almost 30 percent of the roughly 10,000-person agency consisted of ethnic and racial minorities. Just over 3,000 employees were women. The first women graduated from the Border Patrol academy in 1975, and by the summer of 1977 there were eleven female officers. The article also reported that by 1977 there were eleven African American Border Patrol agents, 321 agents of Hispanic descent, nine Native Americans, and two agents of Asian descent. Finally, the article noted the opportunities for advancement for women and racial minorities in the INS, citing the Equal Employment Opportunity Act of 1972 as an important impetus for the changes in employment practices.[43] While the INS highlighted its employment data as a sign of progress, others cited similar figures as evidence of the dearth of opportunities for women and minorities in the INS. The member of Congress who wrote to President Ford in 1976 and described minority representation in the Border Patrol as "abysmal" cited similar figures.

Putting diversity initiatives into practice, especially incorporating more women into the Border Patrol, necessitated some procedural changes. In the fall of 1975, the INS's *Information Bulletin* included a section titled "Tips for Male Supervisors" that provided guidelines on how to treat female officers and instructions on assumptions about women to avoid. Advice included a reminder to "treat women as adult persons," to "ask [women] their opinion before making your decision," and to avoid the assumption that women "really don't want a career."[44] These instructions reflect the institutional assumptions that women could not be serious about a career or were not suited for leadership.

Despite attempts to diversify, the INS failed to employ significant numbers of women and made only small advancements in hiring racial minorities. The lack of racial and gender diversity in the service contributed to its ongoing enforcement problems. In 1980, the United States Commission on Civil Rights issued a 158-page report titled *The Tarnished Golden Door: Civil Rights Issues in Immigration* that concluded several years of investigations and highlighted the widespread discrimination in US immigration policies and enforcement practices. One solution proposed by the USCCR was for the INS to hire more racial and ethnic minorities as well as more women. "Few INS employees staffing the Service's contact points with the public have racial or ethnic backgrounds similar to those of many immigrants," the commission found. The report stated that although women and racial minorities made up a "significant portion" of the INS workforce, they had "little or no participation in policy formulation and decision-making within the INS."[45] It concluded: "This has contributed in part to a strong public perception that persons, particularly those of minority background, are often treated rudely or insensitively by INS employees."[46] Reformers were disappointed by the failed diversification effort. The INS carried out reform efforts halfheartedly, and its meager attempts proved ineffective in resolving entrenched violence and complacency. Not sure where or how to reach more interested minorities or women, the INS continued to rely on traditional sources of manpower: military veterans and those with a law enforcement background. There were few women in these recruiting pools at the time, and INS leadership did not demonstrate enthusiasm for overcoming recruiting challenges.

Other reform efforts of the 1970s sought to address more general complaints about the treatment of immigrants in the Southwest. In the aftermath of the Cleansweep investigation, the Justice Department created an internal corruption unit in the INS. Within a few years, though, most employees of the service conceded that the unit was incompetent and ineffective.[47] The INS routinely fired whistle-blowers, and supervisors meted out light punishments to officers caught committing crimes against immigrants, additional evidence that the INS was intentionally avoiding reform. Three former immigration officials—Fred Drew, Edward Begley, and Nicholas Estiverne—who agreed to talk to reporters were all dismissed from the Border Patrol after filing complaints about other officers' behavior. Estiverne, who was disturbed by the use of "throw-away guns" and the sexual exploitation of immigrant women in South Texas, claimed he was fired for failing to properly shine his shoes.[48] Other officials that *New York Times* reporters talked to asked to remain anonymous out of fear of retribution from colleagues and supervisors.[49]

The election of a new president focused on human rights, and his appointment of a new INS commissioner, offered reformers real hope. Jimmy Carter spoke about immigration during the presidential campaign of 1976 and proposed a set of policy reforms in the first year of his administration. He also appointed Leonel Castillo to head the INS. Castillo was the first Hispanic commissioner of the INS and only the second from a border state (Texas). He emphasized his desire to improve the reputation of the Border Patrol by mending the relationship between patrol officers and border communities. He launched an investigation into violence along the border, for example, and announced that his goal for the INS was the "humanization" of its services.[50] In correspondence with the journalist Grace Halsell, Castillo commented: "I am trying to change the INS— make it humane and effective, or as human and effective and decent as we can."[51]

Despite these notable changes, Carter's proposals for immigration reform were widely criticized by immigrants' rights activists, and Castillo held the position for just under two and a half years. Castillo left office frustrated by ongoing problems with violence in the Border Patrol and criticisms that he was too "soft" on undocumented immigrants. He was dismayed when officers at both the federal and local levels complained to the press. "They thought I was giving the country away to Mexicans, or that I was spending too much money on low priorities and I should be spending money on enforcement," he explained. Illuminating the racism among some service employees, Castillo recalled that there were "little jokes about how everybody [would] have to learn how to speak Spanish in the Central Office or how you [would not] get promoted if you didn't have a Spanish surname."[52]

Thus, little had changed in the INS by the time the *New York Times* sent its reporters to investigate the agency. Bribery remained the most frequent offense, but more egregious problems such as physical and sexual brutality toward immigrants continued. Immigrants' rights groups succeeded in raising awareness about abusive practices, but the *Times* series exposed persistent troubles within the agency. Among the array of problems in 1980 were "suspicious deaths, shootings, beatings, rapes, and forced confessions; incidents of torture, emotional abuse, unlawful arrests and deportations and other violations of legal and human rights" carried out by Border Patrol officers and immigration officials.[53] One former immigration inspector reported that "the most common statement a person of brown skin hears during interrogations is, 'In this place you have no rights.'"[54]

Conclusion

The public outcry and subsequent reform effort by the INS during the 1970s echoed an earlier episode in the agency's history. A similar public backlash to inhumane deportation practices during the 1930s led the agency to clean house and attempt reform. As in the 1930s, reform efforts during the 1970s aiming to shift public perceptions of the INS were limited, revealing the ongoing tensions between local and federal officials.[55] An area where the INS attempted change—diversification of its employees—failed due to institutional prejudice and haphazard effort. When Ronald Reagan was sworn in as president in 1981, the Border Patrol employed roughly 2,000 officers, but only twenty-five of them were women. A few years later, Congress passed the Immigration Reform and Control Act (known as Simpson-Mazzoli), which included a provision to double the number of Border Patrol officers on the southern border. The number of employees increased fivefold through the 1990s and early 2000s. Despite the overall increase in employees, however, the percentage of female Border Patrol officers remained low. As of 2018, women made up only about 5 percent of the workforce in the Border Patrol, despite some moderate efforts in the agency to target women in recruitment efforts.[56] Racial and ethnic diversification efforts have been more successful, with Hispanics making up significant portions — as much as half in some cases — of Border Patrol sectors.

Activists blamed many of the abusive practices in the Border Patrol during the 1970s on the fact that it was primarily a white, male institution. They believed more women and racial minorities in the Border Patrol would curb some of the racist and sexist behavior in the agency. And though diversity was a noble goal for those wanting to achieve more equitable job opportunities in law enforcement in the United States, diversification alone could not rid the INS of racist or sexist attitudes. Its leadership did not think that more Hispanic or female officers would prevent the abuse and exploitation alleged by immigrants' rights activists. Instead, agency leaders argued that the violent behavior was limited to a few bad actors and that the majority of officers maintained proper ethical standards on the job. The culture of violence in the Border Patrol, however, also meant that many well-intentioned officers turned a blind eye to bad behavior. A few new token employees could not change a culture that embraced power and was increasingly militarized, but an overhaul of the training and discipline and significant demographic changes in the agency could have altered employee attitudes.[57]

INS officials policed an incredibly vulnerable population in the Southwest borderlands during the 1970s, a population that found growing support among many US communities. Immigrant supporters and whistleblowers made a strong case to reform immigration practices and created a model for the twenty-first-century immigrants' rights movement. But their campaign could succeed only if there was a reciprocal and sincere internal effort to root out brutality, racism, and misogyny in the Immigration and Naturalization Service. Lacking that, as they did, immigration reformers could only look to a new decade and redouble their efforts to achieve more humane policies and enforcement.

Notes

1. Quoted in John M. Crewdson, "Violence, Often Unchecked, Pervades US Border Patrol," *New York Times*, January 14, 1980.

2. The series, titled "The Tarnished Door: Crisis in Immigration," ran in the *New York Times* January 13–17, 1980. It won a Pulitzer Prize for National Reporting.

3. Bernard Weinraub, "Immigration Bureaucracy Is Overwhelmed," *New York Times*, January 17, 1980.

4. Kelly Lytle Hernández, for example, argues that violence pervaded the Border Patrol since its formation in 1924. See Kelly Lytle Hernández, *Migra! A History of the US Border Patrol* (Berkeley: University of California Press, 2010), 57–65. For other early problems in the Border Patrol, see Erika Lee, *At America's Gates: Chinese Immigration during the Exclusion Era, 1882–1943* (Chapel Hill: University of North Carolina Press, 2003); and Mae Ngai, *Impossible Subjects: Illegal Aliens and the Making of Modern America* (Princeton, NJ: Princeton University Press, 2014).

5. The 1965 Immigration and Nationality Act is rightly credited with abolishing the racist and nativist national origins quota system established in 1924 and with opening the United States to a more diverse group of immigrants from Asia and Latin America. Despite the positive consequences, the 1965 act also had many unintended consequences, including the increase in undocumented immigration to the United States.

6. See Wesley G. Skogan and Kathleen Frydl, *Fairness and Effectiveness in Policing: The Evidence* (Washington, DC: National Academies Press, 2004), 149–150; and Ronald John Weitzer and Steven A. Tuch, *Race and Policing in America: Conflict and Reform* (New York: Cambridge University Press, 2006), 96.

7. The 120,000 annual numerical limit for Western Hemisphere immigrants, a figure many immigration officials feared would be too low and reached quickly, went into effect in 1968. When officials turned away applicants for failure to meet immigration criteria or because they exceeded the numerical limit, many of those denied entry found alternative extralegal means to enter the United States. For more on the effects of the ending of the Bracero Program and the 1965 immigration act, see Douglas S. Massey and Karen A. Pren, "Unintended Consequences of US Immigration Policy: Explaining the Post-1965 Surge from Latin America," *Population and Development Review* 38, no. 1 (2012): 1–29.

8. See Thomas A. Klug, chapter 5 in this volume.

9. Klug, chapter 5.

10. Douglass S. Massey, Jorge Durand, and Karen A. Pren, "Why Border Enforcement Backfired," *American Journal of Sociology* 121, no. 5 (March 2016): 1561.

11. Albert Garcia to Fernando E. C. De Baca, November 23, 1974; and Albert Garcia statement for the press, September 15, 1975, both in "Illegal Aliens—Garcia, Al" folder, box 4, Public Liaison Office, Fernando E. C. De Baca files 1974–1976, Gerald Ford Library, Ann Arbor, MI (hereafter cited as Ford Library).

12. *Immigration Policy and Procedure: Hearing before the United States Commission on Civil Rights* (1978) (statement of Michael Cortez, vice president for research, advocacy, and legislation, National Council of La Raza), 21.

13. Don Edwards to Gerald Ford, May 24, 1976, "Immigration Matters (1)" folder, box 4, Counsel to the President Bobbie Greene Kilberg files, 1972–1977, Ford Library.

14. Don Edwards to Gerald Ford.

15. Don Edwards to Gerald Ford.

16. Riots occurred in cities across the United States in the late 1960s, including in Watts (Los Angeles) in 1965 and Detroit in 1968. In the context of such riots, a 1968 presidential commission, the National Advisory Commission on Civil Disorders (known as the Kerner Commission), recommended that police departments hire more

minority officers as a solution to the distrust between communities of color and law enforcement. Roddrick A. Colvin, *Gay and Lesbian Cops: Diversity and Effective Policing* (Boulder: Lynne Rienner, 2012), 34–35.

17. See Trudy Hayden, *The Immigration and Naturalization Service and Civil Liberties: A Report on the Abuse of Discretion* (New York: ACLU, 1974), 12–13, 17.

18. Hayden, 12–13, 17.

19. Ferguson to "Senator," n.d., "Ames, Fred" folder, box 7, Public Liaison Office, Thomas Aranda files, 1976–77, Ford Library.

20. Leon Rosen to Fernando de Baca, February 20, 1976, "Illegal Aliens (2)" folder, box 3, Public Liaison Office, Thomas Aranda files, 1976–77, Ford Library.

21. David Gutiérrez, *Walls and Mirrors: Mexican Americans, Mexican Immigrants, and the Politics of Ethnicity* (Berkeley: University of California Press, 1995), 188, 189.

22. Albert R. Garcia to L. W. Gilman, May 1, 1975, "Illegal Aliens — Garcia, Al" folder, box 4, Public Liaison Office, Fernando E. C. De Baca files, 1974–76, Ford Library.

23. *Dallas Morning News*, October 31, 1977; Gutiérrez, *Walls and Mirrors*, 201–203.

24. Crewdson, "Violence, Often Unchecked."

25. Bob Bast, "Klan Watching Border," *Brownwood Bulletin*, October 26, 1977; "Klan Warned against Plans to Patrol Mexican Border," *Independent* (Long Beach, CA), October 19, 1977.

26. Crewdson, "Violence, Often Unchecked."

27. Crewdson.

28. Crewdson.

29. The 1980 *New York Times* series documented numerous cases of light or non-existent punishments for violent crimes and fraud.

30. John M. Crewdson, "US Immigration Service Hampered by Corruption," *New York Times*, January 13, 1980.

31. Crewdson.

32. Grace Halsell, *The Illegals* (New York: Stein and Day, 1978), 102.

33. For an overview of Operation Cleansweep, see the reporting of John Crewdson in the *New York Times* series "The Tarnished Door: Crisis in Immigration," January 13–17, 1980. Crewdson expanded the articles into a book, *The Tarnished Door: The New Immigrants and the Transformation of America* (New York: Times Books, 1983).

34. Crewdson, "Hampered by Corruption."

35. Crewdson; John M. Crewdson, "Wide Corruption in Immigration Service Suspected," *New York Times*, October 8, 1979.

36. *Immigration Policy and Procedure*, 21–22.

37. Crewdson, "Wide Corruption in Immigration Service"; Crewdson, "Hampered by Corruption."

38. Skogan and Frydl, *Fairness and Effectiveness in Policing*, 149.

39. Lytle Hernández, *Migra!*, 42, 226–227.

40. Commissioner-General to commissioners of immigration, inspectors in charge of officials of the immigration service, September 29, 1920, folder 54933/185&185A, box 4024, RG 85, Records of the Immigration and Naturalization Service Subject and Policy Files, 1893–1957, 54933/089–54933/201, National Archives and Records Administration, Washington, DC (hereafter cited as INS Records).

41. Supervising Inspector to Commissioner-General of Immigration, December 13, 1920, folder 54933/185&185A, box 4024, RG 85, INS Records.

42. For examples of contemporary arguments made for and against women on police patrol, see Deirdre Carmody, "Police Divided over Assignment of Women to Street Patrol Here," *New York Times*, July 15, 1974; "Female Fuzz," *Newsweek*, October 23, 1972, 117; and "Arresting Preconceptions," *Time*, May 27, 1974, 8.

43. "Minorities and Women in the INS," *INS Reporter*, Summer 1977, 2–3.

44. "Hints for Male Supervisors," *INS Information Bulletin*, nos. 9–12 (September–December, 1975), 25–26.

45. US Commission on Civil Rights, *The Tarnished Golden Door: Civil Rights Issues in Immigration* (Washington, DC: Government Printing Office, 1980), 133.

46. US Commission on Civil Rights, 133.

47. Crewdson, "Hampered by Corruption."

48. Crewdson.

49. Crewdson.

50. Leonel J. Castillo, interview by Oscar J. Martínez, June 23, 24, 1980, interview transcript number 532, Border Labor History Project, University of Texas at El Paso Institute of Oral History, El Paso, TX (hereafter cited as Castillo interview).

51. Halsell, *Illegals*, 122.

52. Castillo interview, 24–25.

53. Crewdson, "Violence, Often Unchecked."

54. Crewdson.

55. For an account of the reform efforts during the 1930s, see chapter 3 in S. Deborah Kang, *The INS on the Line: Making Immigration Law on the US-Mexico Border, 1917–1954* (Oxford, UK: Oxford University Press, 2017).

56. See Alan Neuhauser, "Border Patrol Has a Problem with Women: Current and Past Agents Recount Stories of Harassment and Unfair Working Conditions," *US News and World Report*, August 3, 2018; and Department of Homeland Security, "Careers for Women in US Customs and Border Protection," cbp.gov/careers/careers-women-us-customs-and-border-protection.

57. Militarization resulted from fears of terrorism and undocumented immigration as well as the War on Drugs and includes the "use of military rhetoric and ideology, as well as military tactics, strategy, technology, equipment, and forces." Timothy J. Dunn, *The Militarization of the U.S.-Mexico Border, 1978–1992: Low-Intensity Conflict Doctrine Comes Home* (Austin, TX: CMAS Books, 1996).

Refusing Borders

TWELVE

Haudenosaunee Resistance, Tobacco, and Settler-Colonial Borderlands

DEVIN CLANCY AND TYLER CHARTRAND

O n March 30, 2016, the provincial police force Sûreté du Québec (SQ) carried out Operation Mygale, the largest coordinated police action against contraband tobacco in Canadian history. Seven hundred officers from the SQ, Royal Canadian Mounted Police, Ontario Provincial Police, Canadian Border Services Agency (CBSA), US Immigration and Customs Enforcement, Drug Enforcement Administration, and Department of Homeland Security conducted seventy raids in the borderlands between Québec, Ontario, and New York State; 52,800 kilograms of tobacco were seized and sixty people were arrested.[1] Despite the fact that only four of the accused had links to Kahnawá:ke and Six Nations of the Grand River, the SQ described the events as a victory against highly structured "Aboriginal organized crime."[2] Initial reports also falsely indicated that raids were carried out in both Indigenous communities, leading band representatives and Aboriginal police forces to quickly dispel the alarming misinformation. "Tobacco is not an illegal activity," reads a joint statement from the Mohawk Council of Kahnawá:ke and the Elected Council of Six Nations. "It's disheartening to read statements, like the one recently issued in the MYGALE project, attempting to criminalize our tobacco industry. . . . Tobacco is a historical trade that supports the growth and economic prosperity of our communities. As sovereign Nations, the federal and provincial governments have no jurisdictional right to tax and regulate tobacco on our Territories."[3] Understanding these raids as an attack

219

on the legitimacy and sovereignty of their communities, both councils denounced Operation Mygale as another episode in a long history of settler-colonial policing that conflates the activities of sovereign peoples with criminality and their trade with smuggling.

Border policing activities that target Indigenous communities are conducted and justified within the context of settler-colonialism. Settler-colonialism emerges when a new society is imposed on occupied territory and is accompanied by the dispossession, displacement, extermination, and control of the territory's Indigenous communities. The scholar Patrick Wolfe contends that we must understand settler-colonialism as a structural relation and not a historical event of the past.[4] Present-day struggles over sovereignty, natural resources, and the restitution of Indigenous homelands in Canada and the United States demonstrate that settlement is not a finished project. The material and social reproduction of settler society is an ongoing process that involves the continual renewal of settler society's legitimacy and the erasure of Indigenous peoples' own legitimate claims to their territory. This renewal and erasure is precisely what is at stake in the policing of Indigenous communities, particularly in the borderlands. As part of effacing the crimes of colonialism, settler police criminalize Indigenous peoples and their activities, such as the tobacco trade, which predates European settlement and persists to this day.

Despite protests from the band councils of Kahnawá:ke and Six Nations, US and Canadian police agencies criminalize Haudenosaunee (Six Nations) trade through specialized tobacco task forces and other provincial- or state-level initiatives that facilitate information sharing and coordinated policing operations in contested borderlands.[5] Efforts to securitize the US-Canada border draw upon and extend joint policies like the 2011 Beyond the Border Action Plan, which emphasizes the use of new surveillance technologies, the collection and sharing of biometric information, and preemptive policing strategies to eliminate the risk of potential terrorist and criminal activity.[6] While certain economic interests, including multinational tobacco corporations, are able to circumvent these stringent measures through preclearance programs and expedited passes, Indigenous communities split by the international borderline endure the violence of border policing and state surveillance.[7]

The Mohawk territory of Akwesasne, which straddles the border between Ontario, Québec, and New York State, has been a particularly dense target for militarized surveillance. Described as a "jurisdictional vacuum" by conservative policy analysts, Akwesasne has been consistently vilified and misrepresented as lawless by commentators on both sides of the international border.[8] During an increase in tobacco smuggling in the 1990s, for instance, news media frequently referred to Haudenosaunee reserve communities as "lawless enclaves and havens for criminal gangs."[9] In media projections of criminality, Indigenous rights to cross-border mobility and trade are threats to the integrity of the US-Canada border. Paranoid settler narratives of Akwesasne as a porous, unprotected, and liminal space are deployed in order to justify increased policing and surveillance, while unspecified claims of terrorist financing are used to delegitimize the Indigenous tobacco trade.[10] Indeed, the so-called smuggling hot spot of Akwesasne has been one of the justifications for the US Congress's 2016 commission of a northern border security review by the Department of Homeland Security.[11] Canadian authorities claim that, in the two-year period leading up to the Operation Mygale raid, the smuggling it targeted represented fraud of more than US$400 million.[12]

Contestation over the circulation of tobacco across North America has defined the contours of its borderlands. As such, this chapter examines the policing of tobacco in the borderlands of Canada, the United States, and their colonial predecessors and how Indigenous communities have resisted these developments. We begin by examining the colonial foundations of modern borderlands, which include contestations over tobacco in Virginia and other colonies that established ongoing settler-colonialism in northeastern North America. We then extend these genealogical foundations to discuss contemporary forms of settler policing in the New York, Québec, and Ontario borderlands that split traditional Haudenosaunee territory. Focusing on the resistance of Haudenosaunee communities in the tobacco trade reveals the various ways Indigenous sovereignty resists settler borders. The Native tobacco trade, then, is not, as settler policing agencies tend to emphasize, a "criminal enterprise" but a site for the actualization of resurgent anticolonial Indigenous nationhood.

Tobacco and Settler-Colonial Borders

Indigenous peoples in Canada and the United States have a unique relationship to the border, as they were present before any settler-colonial boundaries were drawn. Their resistance to settler-colonial borders in fact goes back to before settler societies had the legitimacy to label their violent border practices as "policing." Before modern states stretched across North America, their colonial predecessors policed the borders between their territorial claims and the Indigenous lands beyond. Settlers enforced early borders *against* Indigenous sovereignty, using the violent process of dispossession, displacement, and often murder. Thus, the way states police Indigenous peoples today has dimensions that stretch back to before North America's settler-colonial states took their current form. The Akwesasne and various other Haudenosaunee communities that straddle either side of the US-Canada border today continue to demonstrate this living tension between colonial past and nation-state present. In order to fully contextualize the present-day struggles of these communities in continuing their historic tobacco trade, this section recovers key historical dynamics related to tobacco, borders, and policing.

As the Mohawk Council of Kahnawá:ke and the Elected Council of Six Nations state, tobacco is a "historical trade" that has long nurtured Indigenous and Native communities.[13] Tobacco's contemporary status as property and commodity exists in tension with its status in what Indigenous people consider a living relationship between all things, without stark distinctions between humans and the natural world. Therefore, dispossessing land is not just a matter of appropriating territory or resources; it also represents the dispossession of a living relationship that developed over many generations in order to sustain agriculture.[14] As colonial settlements populated northeastern shorelines and pushed inland, Indigenous peoples who primarily relied on agriculture for subsistence were the first dispossessed.[15] This dispossession of the land for tobacco sustained the English colony of Jamestown, Virginia.

The English legal traditions that inform modern ideas of policing, criminality, and borders in Canada and the United States were transposed to North America with the founding of colonial Virginia. Whereas Spanish and French colonialism required Indigenous people to be "participants" facilitating circuits of trade with their labor, English settler-colonialism was the first to view Indigenous people as "hindrances upon" trade.[16] As English settler society spread, European colonialism in North America shifted from extractive trades to settler-colonialism oriented around agricultural commodities. The first major agricultural commodity to sustain English settler-colonialism was tobacco.

Early colonial settlements defined their boundaries through a process that the scholar Charles Tilly suggests is characteristic of European state development: distinguishing coercive force that is internal to the territory from that which is external.[17] This distinction first appears in 1609, two years after Jamestown's founding, when the English settler John Smith began killing members of the Powhatan Confederacy to extract food and supplies.[18] In order for Jamestown to survive, the settlers reasoned, the Powhatan had to be cleared from the area with brute force and political assassinations that forced surrender.[19] The settlement spread rapidly, with 1620 figures estimating a population of 2,200 settlers and 119,000 pounds of tobacco delivered to England.[20] With each subsequent year, the growth increased the size of the settler society and, therefore, the scale of Indigenous dispossession. In 1622, the Powhatan Confederacy responded by declaring war on the settlers.[21] And though the settlers had initiated previous clashes of violence, they responded to this action by targeting Powhatan communities in a series of massacres and a campaign of "systematic destruction of all . . . agricultural resources."[22] The force that carried out this violence was an early forebear of modern police, which the scholar Kristian Williams contends developed in both England and North America out of such ad hoc and "military functions."[23]

After these clashes, English settler-colonies carefully policed the movements of Indigenous peoples within their territories. Guarding against "Indians" in Charleston, South Carolina, was among the official duties for the first town watch, established in 1671, in addition to its more infamous concern with slave controls.[24] By 1680, Indigenous people as well as slaves were required to carry passes in Virginia.[25] These controls on Indigenous presence and movement became the foundation for further controls placed on every aspect of Indigenous life.

As settler-colonial borders expanded to envelop most of the present-day eastern US-Canada border, particularly those portions that intersect the remaining lands of the Haudenosaunee, settler controls over movement and trade intensified with more modern means of violence and the significance of an international border. As both the United States and Canada developed into modern industrial nations, the control over the circulation of tobacco remained paramount. The earlier tactics of violent dispossession and movement controls transformed into regulations associated with national economies around taxation, distribution, and advertising of this special commodity. The case of ongoing Akwesasne resistance to tobacco control demonstrates that both historic and contemporary controls rest upon dispossessing Indigenous peoples and disrupting their own trade in tobacco.

Smuggling and the Circulation of Tobacco

The Mohawk community of Akwesasne and other Haudenosaunee communities along the current US-Canada border still conduct trade along their own Indigenous borders, thereby resisting settler-colonial claims over Indigenous lands. Indigenous activists have challenged the criminalization of their cross-border movements by invoking the Jay Treaty of 1794, which finalized the eastern US-Canada border. Signed by the United States and Great Britain, this treaty established jurisdiction among sovereigns and harmonized trade relations along the US-Britain border. In a concession to Indigenous nations, Article III of the Jay Treaty acknowledged the preexisting right of Indigenous peoples to traverse the border freely without levy and without paying duty, tax, or excise on any goods passing with them.[26] Like most treaties, however, the Jay Treaty has been subject to persistent revaluations and drawbacks by the Canadian and US governments. As the Mohawk scholar Audra Simpson explains, the Jay Treaty "leaves the legal regimes of Canada and the United States with the power to define who those Indian nations are and how that right to pass shall be rendered and respected. As well, and very critically, the regimes of the United States and Canada were bequeathed the power to choose whom they would recognize as members of these communities."[27] In other words, the Canadian nation-state justifies its control over Indigenous trade with reference to its own narrow channels of state-based recognition that reify and ossify Indigenous culture and offer little protection for self-government in modern circumstances.[28] As Benjamin Hoy explains in chapter 3 of this volume: "Indian status and legal recognition became tools that Canada and the United States used to control how Indians moved between national spaces."

This is especially clear when considering the limitations and conditions applied to "recognized" Indigenous rights to cross-border trade and travel. In 1956, the Supreme Court of Canada ruled that Jay Treaty Native tax exemptions applied only to personal possessions and not to expensive items like cars and appliances or items being traded.[29] To challenge this ruling, in 1988, the Akwesasne grand chief Mike Mitchell traveled across the US-Canada border to trade with the Tyendinaga reserve. He declared his goods at the border, but his rights to trade within Mohawk territory were denied and he was ordered to pay duty. In the final 2001 court ruling, the Crown used archeological evidence to claim that trade north of the St.

Lawrence, where Tyendinaga sits, was *not* a significant part of Mohawk culture and that the right to trade could therefore not be upheld.[30] Accordingly, although Indigenous peoples and nations may have *some* sovereign rights within the legal framework of Canada, settler state actors retain the right to determine what is "truly integral" to one's "distinctive culture." In the context of tobacco trade, this cultural racism is echoed by a Mackenzie Institute report that states: "When the Jay Treaty was signed in 1794 to allow Natives to bring goods across the border without paying taxes, king size, filter-tipped menthol flavored cigarettes were a long way off."[31] These sentiments relegate "authentic" Indigeneity to a foregone past, transforming Natives who trade and sell commercial cigarettes into criminal smugglers simply because cigarettes are an industrialized commodity.

In citing the Jay Treaty, Mohawk traders *refuse* Canadian law that renders them smugglers and instead assert their rights to trade as members of a distinct sovereign polity that predates the United States and Canada. The Canadian government and the media, however, have consistently erased this refusal. In 1993, a *Globe and Mail* article warned of "Indian masterminds making links with organized crime," and a 1994 editorial in the paper argued that a reserve "mobocracy" conspired to mobilize sovereignty to "obstruct police in the enforcement of Canadian law on Canadian land."[32] As Audra Simpson describes: because "rights" are understood only in a liberal capitalist sense—as wedded to private property and capital accumulation, and linked to nation-state legality—alternative appeals to sovereignty are misrepresented as an abuse of special rights afforded Indigenous peoples by Canada.[33]

The crime of smuggling itself relies upon a state's claim to possess authority and control over the flow of all goods, people, and capital through its territory. Authorizing particular means of transportation and distribution has long been associated with taxation practices. Taxation on exports such as tobacco not only raised revenue for emergent North American states but also constituted claims of national sovereign force at their borders. In the United States, excise taxes on tobacco funded much of the federal government before the twentieth century.[34] The administration of such taxes involved highly contested concentrations of force and coercion at key points of entry under the authority of a central government and rendered illegal any trade that did not pass through authorized channels. This included trade conducted by sovereign Indigenous nations, which the Canadian and American states criminalized in defiance of inherent Indigenous rights and histories. Thus, the collection of excise taxes is also a claim against Indigenous trade sovereignty, particularly in the case of the cross-border tobacco trade examined here.

In recent decades, the administration of excise taxes has taken on even more complex relationships with Indigenous tobacco trade and control. In 1991, the Canadian federal government raised excise taxes on the domestic sale of cigarettes by 140 percent.[35] At the same time, however, it applied no similar taxes to exported products. In an attempt to avoid taxes, Canadian tobacco manufacturers used this loophole to export untaxed cigarettes to the United States and then smuggle them back into Canada for the illegal market. Many of the cigarettes flowed through Haudenosaunee reserve communities split by the US-Canada border.[36] By 1993, contraband cigarettes accounted for 40 percent of Canada's $12 billion tobacco market. With their revenue diminished due to smuggling, owners of convenience stores worked with big tobacco corporations to pressure the government to lower taxes. After years of lobbying and with increasing losses to tax revenue, Prime Minister Jean Chrétien agreed to lower the taxes on tobacco.[37] In his parliamentary address on February 8, 1994, Chrétien stated: "Smuggling is threatening the safety of our communities and the livelihood of law-abiding merchants. . . . It is a threat to the very fabric of Canadian society."[38] Unable to face Canada's settler-colonial foundation, the government viewed the free trade of tobacco as smuggling and as a breakdown of settler law.

The 1994 plan emerged at a time when popular media accounts represented Indigenous trade as the borderless chaos of "Native smugglers." Similar to the situation in the US-Mexico borderland, which Lisa D. Barnett explores in chapter 8, Canada utilized the discourse of "smuggling" and illicitness to justify an expansion of state surveillance and control. Sensationalist media accounts, like the 1996 CBC documentary *Witness* episode "The Dark Side of Native Sovereignty," obscured alternative Indigenous mappings that predated the US-Canada border and conflated Indigenous sovereignty with criminality.[39] Despite the fact that tax evasion by big tobacco corporations fueled smuggling, these reports scapegoated Indigenous traders as the primary cause of the problem. In her analysis of these reports, Audra Simpson describes the Native cigarette as unsettling: "The images of criminal 'warriors' were set side by side with *contraband* cigarettes, cigarettes that were contraband because they eluded being taxed, they were not providing revenue for Canada, and, as such they were themselves the synecdoche for unsettling settlement, the unbounding of the place of Canada, as Canada itself—a claim of property, of seizure through law and citizenship without consent."[40] These Canadian media accounts mirror the discourse of "war" that is emblematic of depictions of the US-Mexico border in American reality television shows that Anita Huizar-Hernández describes in chapter 14. In attempts to control this unsettling trade, anti-contraband campaigns reproduced normative arguments about settler law and social order. By recasting Indigeneity as existing within these colonial borderlands, such representations reinforced nation-state sovereignty to normalize settler dispossession.[41]

Canadian authorities' efforts to directly police Indigenous communities sparked public confrontations. When the town of Oka, Québec, tried to expand a nine-hole golf course onto contested Kanehsatà:ke lands, for example, Mohawk land defenders began a peaceful blockade to stop the encroachment on their sovereign and sacred territory. Tensions rose when the Sûreté du Québec tried to forcibly remove the land defenders and when the Canadian military took over negotiations. In response to this escalation of force, other land defenders from Kahnawá:ke blockaded the Mercier Bridge, blocking southern access to Montreal. Negotiations lasted seventy-eight days, until the land defenders decided to destroy their weapons in a bonfire and burn ceremonial tobacco before leaving the site peacefully.[42]

Due to this wide-scale coordinated defense of Indigenous territory, settler enforcement has been displaced to the in-between spaces of transit and transport, while graphic media campaigns have littered urban areas warning passersby that "illegal cigarettes fund criminal activity in [their] neighborhood." Discursively, this campaign sought to reproduce the law-abiding citizen through fear of death. Paired with already existing health campaigns against the dangers of smoking, contraband cigarettes became an insidious product that not only poisoned bodies but also corroded the very law and order settlers depended upon for their security.

In response to Indigenous assertions of trade sovereignty across the US-Canada border, the US and Canadian governments have worked to criminalize and eliminate the Native tobacco trade through unprecedented coordination between settler institutions of state and capital. In Canada, the National Coalition Against Contraband Tobacco (NCACT) collectively represents the interests of big tobacco corporations, retailers, and police institutions and has been instrumental in drafting legislation that further criminalizes Indigenous peoples involved in the production, sale, and distribution of Native tobacco products. The controversy sur-

Figure 12.1. Crime Stoppers billboard depicts a hooded figure with a smoking gun in an attempt to link illegal cigarettes to violence in "your community." Photo taken in Toronto, Ontario, by the author, November 2016.

rounding Bill C-10, the Tackling Contraband Tobacco Act, is emblematic of their efforts.[43] Introduced by the Conservative minister of justice Peter MacKay on November 5, 2013, this tough-on-crime approach introduced greater fines and mandatory prison penalties to deter Native traders while also supporting the intensification of police task forces that target the tobacco industry.[44] Through an interplay between taxation, distribution control, and advertising, North American settler states continue to treat the control over the circulation of tobacco as paramount.

Tobacco Sovereignty against Settler Police

While a Royal Canadian Mounted Police investigation into the 1990s contraband "crisis" linked big tobacco companies like JTI-Macdonald Corporation to tax evasion and smuggling, in the early 2000s the majority of contraband tobacco production and policing shifted to First Nations communities.[45] Active during the initial tobacco boom of the 1990s, the Mohawk community of Tyendinaga in Ontario has since seen incredible growth in its own production and sale of cigarettes.[46] Canada considers this industry illegal, however, because many of the factories and retailers operate without federal licenses. Shawn Brant, a community activist involved in the tobacco trade, explained that monies from this growing industry have been instrumental in lifting Tyendinaga out of poverty, providing employment for its members and revenue separate from that allocated by the Department of Indian Affairs.[47] Accordingly, profits from tobacco have gone toward food security and health awareness programs and toward building a longhouse, which is the seat of traditional Haudenosaunee governance outside of the band council system.[48] For Brant and others in Kahnawá:ke and Six Nations of the Grand River, the development of a Native tobacco industry is both an economic and political project that draws upon and redeploys Indigenous sovereignty separate from the Canadian nation-state.[49] Notably, some tobacco manufacturers have used their capital to fight for Indigenous sovereignty rights in the Canadian legal system. Whereas in the 1990s the federal government launched court battles against big tobacco and focused on lost tax revenue, contemporary struggles over contraband place Native sovereignty at the forefront.

When Bill C-10 was introduced to Parliament, it faced intense criticism and protests from Native reserve communities. At a forum held in Grand

River, the Tyendinaga lawyer Stephen John Ford expressed his frustration with the bill: "It's about denying First Nations peoples their own industries, their own sources of income. . . . It's about federal control of First Nations people. They don't want you to make money. It's continued colonial oppression. This is a microcosm of that broader picture."[50] Quickly, opposition campaigns gained broad support from a number of organizations across the country. The Chiefs of Ontario issued a statement of rejection, the Law Union of Ontario critiqued the bill for infringing on Indigenous sovereignty rights, and the grassroots social movement Idle No More spoke to the dangers of Bill C-10 in its May 14, 2014, National Day of Resistance.[51] These groups condemned the bill for its writers' lack of consultation with First Nations communities and the reluctance on the part of the government to consider the adverse effects it would have on Native communities. In its public statement, the Law Union of Ontario likened Bill C-10 to illegal economic sanctions that "criminalize much of the First Nations tobacco industry, and further impoverish peoples impacted by colonialism and dispossession."[52] Despite these protests, however, the Tackling Contraband Tobacco Act received royal assent on November 6, 2014.

There were, however, serious limitations to the government's crackdown on contraband tobacco. Even though the NCACT and police task forces were aware of unlicensed cigarette factories operating across First Nations territories in Ontario and Québec, they could not effectively raid these operations. Such a move would be understood as an attack on Indigenous sovereignty and galvanize Native protest. In other words, the specters of Oka and other instances of resurgent Native resistance limit the actions of government agencies on reserve territory, especially when it comes to attacks on economic self-determination. Law enforcement agencies and the NCACT are aware of this reality, which is why their policy recommendations refer back to Aboriginal communities as "partners" in any long-term solution. Unable to effectively undermine Native tobacco at its source, government policy documents and agencies appealed to Native communities through limited forms of recognition. However, these paradigmatic moves to recognition remained structurally committed to settler-capitalist dispossession as state initiatives aim to co-opt Indigenous peoples' assertions of nationhood through limited negotiations over land settlements, economic development, and self-government.[53] In attempts to curtail contraband tobacco, for instance, the importance of "working with First Nations communities and leadership" is highlighted and creative forms of "Aboriginal administered taxation-schemes" are proposed.[54] The issue of the inherent sovereignty of Indigenous nations, however, does not appear.

And even though government and policing agencies appealed to Indigenous nations as partners, settler institutions increased their surveillance of Native communities. Since September 11, 2001, for instance, the border has hardened, making it difficult and dangerous for Indigenous peoples to enact their inherent rights to trade and travel.[55] Indigenous people are expected to prove their "Indianness" to border guards using settler identity categories of blood quantum and status that echo past ambiguities of membership and alienage.[56] Indigenous people's documents are questioned, while border guards' interpretations of Native mobility rights can lead to long waits, increased interrogation, harassment, and the outright denial of entry. As much as settlers attempt to police and control movement across the border, however, it is not a site of transgression for Native peoples. Rather, as Audra Simpson asserts, the border is a site for the activation and articulation of Natives' rights as members of reserve nations; it is a site of sovereign refusal.[57] To travel on one's own political documentation and to insist upon treaty rights is to refuse the settler state's colonizing claims to absolute authority.

The people of Akwesasne openly challenged misrepresentations of their community and continued to fight against the restriction of their mobility rights and the militarized police presence on the border. When it was announced in 2009 that CBSA guards at the Kawehno:ke (Cornwall Island) border crossing on Akwesasne territory would begin carrying 9mm handguns, community members started an encampment and closed the border altogether.[58] As a result, the customs office was relocated to the city of Cornwall proper, yet when Akwesasne residents travel within the reserve — from the United States to the Canadian side — they are still required to check in at the crossing. Like Starr County in Texas on the US-Mexico borderland, as Santiago Ivan Guerra explains in chapter 13, increased militarization of the borderlands has increased the burden on local communities and exposed them to more encounters with law enforcement officers. When community members of Kawehno:ke refuse this encroachment on their sovereignty, they are criminalized in the name of national security. A recent Ontario court ruling, for instance, denied two Mohawk women their mobility rights for dropping off relatives at

Kawehno:ke before checking in first with border agents. The defendants cited the hardships experienced by Akwesasne residents who cross the border multiple times a day, often facing increased suspicion from guards. According to the judge, however, these hardships are "self-imposed" because the community forced the checkpoint to relocate.[59]

Increased attacks on Indigenous tobacco, as well as unsubstantiated claims about its connections to terrorist financing, only worsened tensions at the border and brought Indigenous travelers under increased suspicion. When Antoine Delormier, a sixty-seven-year-old resident of Kawehno:ke, fell ill and attempted to drive himself to the hospital in Cornwall, he was stopped by CBSA guards. Despite not having traveled to the United States that day, he was questioned, sent for further inspection, surrounded by guards, and ordered to exit his truck. When Delormier protested these excessive measures, guards forcefully pulled him from his vehicle and knocked him to the ground. He was then detained in a cell after telling the guards that he had a heart condition and could not breathe. The CBSA eventually called an ambulance, but his truck was impounded. Officers justified Delormier's harassment because an agent supposedly caught a whiff of tobacco emanating from the truck; no tobacco was ever found.[60]

Conclusion

Indigenous resistance to US and Canadian border enforcement affected the implementation of colonial border policy. Far from unilineal processes, Canadian and US border practices have varied historically in their responses to Indigenous assertions of sovereignty. In this chapter, we have unmapped the settler-colonial bordering practices of Canada and the United States and drawn genealogical connections between contemporary policing and the violent origins of settler colonialism in British North America. In doing so we have focused on the settler attempts to regulate and control the circulation of tobacco. Historically, control of the growth and sale of tobacco has coincided with the earliest bordering practices of colonial powers. These initial forms of alienage and accumulation by dispossession have shifted in response to Indigenous resistances but remain central concerns in the establishment and reproduction of settler-colonialism. While controlling tobacco at the borders initially meant dispossessing tobacco fields and disrupting Indigenous trade, it eventually came to revolve around issues of taxation, distribution channels, and advertising.

In the contemporary context, a unique coalition of big tobacco companies, tax-law advocates, settler business associations, health-care officials, and policing agencies have collectively targeted Indigenous communities and their trade in tobacco as a threat to the nation. The notion that Indigenous tobacco is illegal, illicit, or contraband, however, relies upon the exclusive legal domains of Canada and the United States. These domains are products of and are structurally wedded to the maintenance of settler-colonial power and the dispossession and disavowal of Indigenous sovereignty. Still, as members of nested sovereign communities strangulated by Canada and the United States, Native peoples involved in the tobacco trade refuse to be criminalized. Until Native sovereignty is adequately addressed, conflicts over tobacco will continue to disrupt the settler social order that Canada and the United States seek to enforce.

Notes

1. Kalina Laframboise, "SQ Targets Contraband Tobacco, Money Laundering in Raids," *CBC News*, March 30, 2016, cbc.ca/news/canada/montreal/quebec-raids -contraband-tobacco-operation-international-1.3511876.

2. Sûreté du Québec, "Contrebande de tabac — Importante frappe de la Sûreté du Québec et de ses partenaires," press release, March 30, 2016, sq.gouv.qc.ca/nouvelles /contrebande-de-tabac-importante-frappe-de-surete-quebec-de-partenaires.

3. The Mohawk Council of Kahnawá:ke and the Elected Council of Six Nations of the Grand River, "Kahnawake and Six Nations Exercising Inherent Right to Participate in Tobacco Trade," press release, April 6, 2016, sixnations.ca/PressRelease_JointKahn awakeandSixNationsSetRecordonTobaccoStraght.pdf.

4. Patrick Wolfe, *Settler Colonialism and the Transformation of Anthropology* (New York: Cassell, 1999), 2.

5. Ministry of Community Safety and Correctional Services, "Ontario Creating New Enforcement Team to Combat Contraband Tobacco," press release, January 25, 2016, news.ontario.ca/mcscs/en/2016/01/ontario-creating-new-enforcement-team -to-combat-contraband-tobacco.html.

6. "Beyond the Border: A Shared Vision for Perimeter Security and Economic Competitiveness" was an initiative announced in a joint declaration by the US president and Canadian prime minister on February 4, 2011. The Canadian government describes it as a "joint long-term partnership between Canada and the United States (U.S.) which outlines specific initiatives that support a perimeter approach to security . . . while facilitating the legitimate movement of people, goods and services into our countries and across our shared border." "Beyond the Border Action Plan," Public Safety Canada, publicsafety.gc.ca/cnt/brdr-strtgs/bynd-th-brdr/index-en.aspx.

7. For more on the influence of capital in the development of border policies and the contradictions of open borders for capital and closed borders for people, see Thomas A. Klug, chapter 5 in this volume.

8. Jean Daudelin, Stephanie Soiffer, and Jeff Willows, *Border Integrity, Illicit Tobacco, and Canada's Security* (Ottawa, ON: Macdonald-Laurier Institute, 2013), 6.

9. Lysiane Gagnon, "Inside Quebec: The Violent Mohawk Faction Seems to Be in Control Right Now," *Globe and Mail*, February 19, 1994.

10. Christian Leuprecht, *Smoking Gun: Strategic Containment of Contraband Tobacco and Cigarette Trafficking in Canada* (Ottawa, ON: Macdonald-Laurier Institute, 2016), 29.

11. Northern Border Security Review Act, S. 1808, 114th Cong. (2016).

12. Laframboise, "SQ Targets Contraband Tobacco."

13. For geographic approximations of precontact agriculture, see R. Cole Harris, ed., *From the Beginning to 1800*, vol. 1 of *Historical Atlas of Canada* (Toronto: University of Toronto Press, 1987).

14. Roxanne Dunbar-Ortiz, *An Indigenous Peoples' History of the United States* (Boston: Beacon, 2014), 16–17.

15. Harris, *From the Beginning*.

16. Francis Jennings, "Virgin Land and Savage People," in *Early American History: Indians and Europeans; Selected Articles on Indian-White Relations in Colonial North America*, ed. Peter Hoffer (New York: Taylor and Francis, 1988), 101.

17. Charles Tilly, *Coercion, Capital, and European States, AD 990–1992*, rev. ed. (Cambridge, MA: Blackwell, 1992), 70–75.

18. Dunbar-Ortiz, *Indigenous Peoples' History*, 60.

19. David F. Marley, *Wars of the Americas: A Chronology of Armed Conflict in the Western Hemisphere*, 2nd ed. (Santa Barbara, CA: ABC-CLIO, 2008), 153.

20. *Historical Statistics of the United States, Colonial Times to 1970*, bicentennial ed., ser. Z 457–459, 1–19 (Washington, DC: Bureau of the Census, 1975), 1191, 1168.

21. Marley, *Wars of the Americas*, 209–210.

22. Dunbar-Ortiz, *Indigenous Peoples' History*, 61.

23. Kristian Williams, *Our Enemies in Blue: Police and Power in America*, 3rd ed. (Oakland, CA: AK Press, 2015), 56–57.

24. Williams, 76.

25. Williams, 68.

26. Audra Simpson, "Subjects of Sovereignty: Indigeneity, the Revenue Rule, and the Juridics of Failed Consent," *Law and Contemporary Problems* 71 (2008): 201.

27. Simpson, 202.

28. Bonita Lawrence, *Fractured Homeland: Federal Recognition and Algonquin Identity in Ontario* (Toronto: University of British Columbia Press, 2012), 57.

29. Viviane Namaste, "Francophone Discourse Analysis: A Case Study of Representing Native Peoples and 'Contraband' Cigarettes in Anglophone and Francophone Quebec Media, 1993–1994," *Social Semiotics* 9, no. 1 (1999): 28.

30. Simpson, "Subjects of Sovereignty," 210.

31. John Thompson, *Sin-Tax Failure: The Market in Contraband Tobacco and Public Safety* (Toronto: Mackenzie Institute, 1994).

32. Peter Moon, "Smuggling of Cigarettes Grows into Big Business: Indian Masterminds Making Links with Organized Crime," *Globe and Mail*, May 29, 1993; editorial, *Globe and Mail*, February 11, 1994.

33. Audra Simpson, *Mohawk Interruptus: Political Life across the Borders of Settler States* (Durham, NC: Duke University Press, 2014), 126.

34. William J. Bernstein, *A Splendid Exchange: How Trade Shaped the World* (New York: Atlantic Monthly Press, 2008), 320.

35. Stephen Schneider, "Organized Contraband Smuggling and Its Enforcement in Canada: An Assessment of the Anti-smuggling Initiative," *Trends in Organized Crime* 6, no. 2 (2000): 6.

36. These series of events reveal that Indigenous trade networks—which cross the US-Canada border—remain relevant distribution channels for both Indigenous communities and settler capital.

37. Jim Poling Sr., *Smoke Signals: The Native Takeback of North America's Tobacco Industry* (Toronto: Dundurn, 2012), 149.

38. Jacob Sullum, *For Your Own Good: The Anti-smoking Crusade and the Tyranny of Public Health* (New York: Free Press, 1998), 137.

39. *Witness*, season 5, episode 13, "The Dark Side of Native Sovereignty," aired August 20, 1996, by Canadian Broadcast Corporation.

40. Simpson, "Subjects of Sovereignty," 214.

41. Namaste, "Francophone Discourse Analysis," 34.

42. For more on the Mohawk people's defense of their sovereign territory, see Leanne Simpson and Kiera L. Ladner, eds., *This Is an Honour Song: Twenty Years Since the Blockades* (Winnipeg, MB: Arbeiter Ring, 2010); and Alanis Obomsawin, dir., *Kanehsatake: 270 Years of Resistance* (Montreal: National Film Board of Canada, 1993).

43. Tackling Contraband Tobacco Act, R.S.C. 2014, c. C-10.

44. "Contraband Tobacco Bill Sets Mandatory Minimum Sentences," *CBC*, March 5, 2013, cbc.ca/news/politics/contraband-tobacco-bill-sets-mandatory-minimum-sentences-1.1302812.

45. Peter Cheney and Victor Malarek, "Tobacco Executives Charged in $1.2-Billion Fraud," *Globe and Mail*, March 1, 2003; Robert Schwartz and Teela Johnson, "Problems, Policies, and Politics: A Comparative Case Study of Contraband Tobacco from the 1990s to the Present in the Canadian Context," *Journal of Public Health Policy* 31, no. 3 (2010): 346.

46. Audrey Huntley, dir., "Mohawk Smokes," CBC News Sunday, aired 2006 by Canadian Broadcasting Corporation, youtube.com/watch?v=Tcw6qHoqgQo&spfreload=10.

47. Huntley, 4:40.

48. Huntley, 6:15.

49. Jeff Dorn, dir., *Smoke Traders* (Vancouver, BC: Rezolution Pictures, 2012), DVD, 7:25.

50. Noaman G. Ali, "The Looming 'War' on the Native Tobacco Trade," *BASICS Community News Service*, February 24, 2014, basicsnews.org/bill-c-10-attacks-indigenous-economic-sovereignty.

51. Chiefs of Ontario, "Chiefs of Ontario Reject Bill C-10 That Will Criminalize the Tobacco Trade, Calling It a Direct Attack on First Nation Constitutional and Treaty Rights," press release, June 10, 2014, chiefs-of-ontario.org/node/866; "Law Union of Ontario Statement on Bill C-10," Law Union of Ontario, April 21, 2014, lawunion.ca/2014/law

-union-of-ontario-statement-on-bill-c-10; "Join in the National Day of Resistance," Idle No More, May 13, 2014, idlenomore.ca/join_in_the_national_day_of_resistance.

52. "Law Union of Ontario Statement on Bill C-10."

53. Glen Coulthard, *Red Skins, White Masks: Rejecting the Colonial Politics of Recognition* (Minneapolis: University of Minnesota Press, 2014), 151.

54. "Contraband Tobacco in Canada: An Assessment of the Fifth Anniversary of the RCMP's Contraband Tobacco Enforcement Strategy," National Coalition Against Contraband Tobacco, May 7, 2013, self-published policy document on file with the author; "Anti-Contraband Tobacco Working Group Meets in Ottawa," Macdonald-Laurier Institute, December 1, 2014, macdonaldlaurier.ca/anti-contraband-tobacco-working-group-meets-ottawa.

55. Bruce Granville Miller, "Life on the Hardened Border," *American Indian Culture and Research Journal* 36, no. 2 (2012): 27.

56. Simpson, *Mohawk Interruptus*, 115–146.

57. Simpson, 116.

58. "Border Authorities Shut Down Akwesasne Crossing," CBC News, June 1, 2009, cbc.ca/news/canada/montreal/border-authorities-shut-down-akwesasne-crossing-1.776854.

59. Douglas Quan, "Mohawks' Right to Freely Cross the Canada-U.S. Border Trumped by National Security," *National Post*, October 28, 2015, news.nationalpost.com/news/canada/mohawks-right-to-freely-cross-canada-u-s-border-within-akwesasne-territory-trumped-by-national-security-judge.

60. Jorge Barrera, "Akwesasne Man, 67, Says He Was Brutalized by Border Guards over Whiff of Phantom Tobacco," APTN *News*, September 24, 2015, aptnnews.ca/2015/09/24/akwesasne-man-67-says-he-was-brutalized-by-border-guards-over-whiff-of-phantom-tobacco.

Border Surge

THIRTEEN

Drug Trafficking and Escalating Police
Power on the Rio Grande

SANTIAGO IVAN GUERRA

n 2015, the state of Texas allocated $800 million for
border security initiatives. The funds allowed for an
influx of more than 200 state troopers to the border
to aid local and federal forces in policing illicit activities. In testimony to
the Texas House Appropriations Committee, the director of the Texas Department of Public Safety (DPS), Colonel Steve McCraw, stated: "[In] the
two counties that represent the most significant threat to this nation as
it relates to organized crime and transnational crime, Starr County in the
Rio Grande Valley and Hidalgo County, we dramatically increased the detection coverage [and] the interdiction capacity, and it has had an impact
on that area. It's a different game right now."[1]

As a result of the increased police presence in the Rio Grande Valley,
citations and warnings in both Hidalgo and Starr Counties increased
dramatically. In response, McCraw stated that it was a necessary outcome since "[cartel operatives] deliberately engage law enforcement on
our roadways as decoys."[2] The increased policing impacted all members
of these border communities, not just the cartel operatives and migrant
smugglers. As Rio Grande City's state representative Ryan Guillen articulated: "It's not fair that families in Starr County are being scrutinized at a
greater level than families in pretty much any other county in the state."[3]

The escalation of border policing that culminated in Texas's dramatic
2015 investment in border security was entwined with the growing recognition of Starr County as a significant site of illicit drug importation and

distribution. In particular, the increase in large-scale marijuana smuggling through the rural South Texas county resulted in dramatic drug seizures publicized through local, state, and national media outlets. In mid-2011, these busts of more than 1,000 pounds of marijuana generated attention among the multiple policing agencies involved in drug interdiction. In June 2011, authorities discovered 1,100 pounds of marijuana in a hidden bunker. About a month later, drug investigators executed a search warrant on a property with multiple bunkers housing nearly 7,000 pounds of marijuana. Over the next couple of years, several more bunker discoveries, typically with more than a ton of marijuana each, generated enough concern for local, state, and federal authorities to initiate strategic, collaborative operations in an attempt to disrupt drug-trafficking operations in the area. By 2013, these efforts garnered a significant outcome for the police forces. Through a coordinated effort, Operation Cassanova, local and federal authorities targeted a major Starr County–based drug-trafficking organization, culminating in the seizure of more than 25,000 pounds of marijuana and the imprisonment of nineteen members of the organization in 2014.[4]

In this chapter, I rely on an ethnographic case study of Starr County, as a site of intense drug trafficking and a target of the ongoing Texas DPS border-policing operations, to explore how border communities become sites of intensified policing and how these communities then are affected by, and respond to, these types of policing practices. My primary mode of methodological inquiry is ethnography. As such, I have conducted participant observation, oral history, and interviews (formal and informal) with members of the border communities of Starr County affected by drug trafficking. I rely on this ethnographic data set, as well as primary and secondary sources, to construct this narrative of the impact of policing escalation and drug trafficking along the South Texas border. In particular, I describe how anxieties about illicit activities, specifically drug trafficking and human smuggling, drive the justification for surge policing practices exemplified by the Texas state-based policing operations.

Policing and Smuggling: The South Texas–Mexico Border Context

Starr County is the largest rural county in South Texas, and it is situated between two of the fastest-growing metropolitan areas in the United States: Laredo to the north and the Mission–McAllen–Edinburg metro area to the south. Starr County's population of just more than 60,000 is about 96 percent people of Hispanic/Latino origin, the majority being individuals of Mexican descent. Along with consistently being one of the US counties with the highest percentage of Hispanic/Latino people, it is also often ranked as one of the counties with the highest rates of poverty in the nation. It is also often cited as a main transit area for illicit drugs and is officially designated under the Drug Enforcement Agency's High Intensity Drug Trafficking Areas program (HIDTA) on the South Texas border.[5] As a result, Starr County has received increased scrutiny and intensified policing activities from local, state, and federal law enforcement.[6]

The federal government allocates most of the drug control budget, upward of 70 percent, to interdiction. According to reports by the US Office of National Drug Control Policy, Inter-American Commission on Drug Policy, and the US General Accounting Office, only 30 percent of federal drug monies are allocated for drug treatment and drug prevention programs. Over the years, the federal government has directed important initiatives to cut off the flow of illegal drugs into the United States. In September 1969, the government launched Operation Intercept in response to the expanding international drug trade driven by increasing drug demand in the US market. In June 1986, Operation Alliance directed efforts at drug enforcement to the US-Mexico border and allowed for the growth and expansion of the US Customs Service. Such federal interdiction missions have led to the contemporary militarization of the border, whereby local and federal government agencies employ military tactics to combat drug-trafficking organizations. The implementation of the military tactic of low-intensity conflict doctrine on the US-Mexico border has contributed to the use of military strategies and weapons by local police forces, including the Border Patrol, county sheriff's departments, and departments of public safety or state police.[7]

Scholars have devoted significant attention to the issue of policing along the US-Mexico border. Timothy Dunn and Peter Andreas in particular have framed the issue of border enforcement within the correlated processes of escalation and militarization. Joseph Nevins has devoted significant attention to how undocumented immigration has fueled intensive border-policing operations, most notably Operation Gatekeeper. Additionally, David Shirk has investigated the significant law enforcement challenges posed by immigration and drug trafficking along the US–Mexico border in the twenty-first century. These scholars, among many others, have contributed significantly to our understanding of the politi-

cal processes that fuel policing initiatives along the border, both historically and into the present.[8]

In addition to these social scientists, ethnographers have also interrogated the subject of border policing by documenting the effects of the
aforementioned border-policing practices on communities along the US-
Mexico divide. Alejandro Lugo demonstrates how inspections at ports of
entry and border crossings more broadly differentially affect individuals based on particular identity markers, most significantly complexion,
gender, and class status. Jonathan Xavier Inda employs ethnography of
the border to demonstrate how the prophylactic technology employed in
border-policing practices bring together an array of practical mechanisms
in an effort to affect the conduct of unauthorized immigrants in a way that
forestalls illicit border crossings. In his ethnography of Ambos Nogales,
Gilberto Rosas highlights how border policing has impacted young people.
In particular, Rosas chronicles how criminalized youths interact with, and
are victimized by, policing officials along the border. Finally, newer research by Margaret Dorsey and Miguel Díaz-Barriga has documented the
problematic ways in which border residents' constitutional rights are suspended along the Rio Grande border as a result of the refocusing of border policing as a national security imperative. In this chapter, I attempt to
draw from these perspectives in border-policing studies through an integration of ethnography and policy analysis.[9]

In Texas's lower Rio Grande Valley (LRGV), the border has been subject to a process of surge policing practices that rely on the triangulation
of local, state, and federal authority. The inception of Operation Strong
Safety, a Texas DPS border-policing initiative, in 2014 along the LRGV signaled a culmination of the escalation of border policing, a border surge
that has saturated parts of the LRGV with local, state, and federal policing
agents. While many scholars have theorized about the militarization and
policing of the US-Mexico border, many of these studies have neglected
to consider how the experiences of border residents, drug traffickers, and
policing agents are shaped by the militarization of the border within the
context of the US War on Drugs. The border is undergoing significant
policing and militarization as narc (narcotic agent) activities invade the
lives of drug traffickers and the general border population. As drug traffickers react to drug policing, young and old border residents get drawn
into their activities to varying degrees.

Policing and Prosecuting the Border Drug War:
A Local Perspective

Prosecutors in Starr County who appear on behalf of the government in criminal cases before district and county courts are, for the most part, natives of the area. They are individuals from the community who were fortunate enough to pursue a higher education and attain a law degree. As a group, they constitute an important sector of the criminal justice system in Starr County. Whereas law enforcement officers are charged with policing and apprehending drug offenders, and probation officers are charged with monitoring these offenders, prosecutors are responsible for making sure that drug offenders and other people engaged in criminal acts are held accountable for their actions. They represent, and are in service to, the local, state, and federal governments. Yet they are also members of the community and are predominately Mexican Americans. The perspective of local law enforcement officers and prosecutors situates the concerns about drug trafficking and public safety within a local cultural context that recognizes the inadequacies of policing for significantly impacting drug traffic through this area.

In 2009, Horacio Bazan, a native of Rio Grande City, served as district attorney of Starr County. First elected to office in 1989, he was the district's only prosecutor at the time, and he employed only one secretary and one investigator. Today, however, his office grew considerably to employ six assistant attorneys, eight investigators, and administrative secretaries. Bazan also served on the executive board of the HIDTA task force, which is staffed by members of local and federal law enforcement agencies and determines how money is dispersed for drug policies. When he was first elected, the district attorney handled the court's entire caseload. But with the expansion of his office he focuses his attention on the major cases. The office's assistant district attorneys handle the rest of the office's caseload.

While serving as district attorney, Bazan revealed that a majority of the cases the office handled were drug related, an assertion echoed by two of his assistants. One of the assistant district attorneys, Tomás Garcia, concluded:

Without doing any kind of statistical analysis, I would have to guess that, you know, roughly 80 percent [are drug-related]. Eighty percent of our cases here, at least the cases that I handle and I would have to say that the office at large handles, is related to drugs in some way or another. Whether thefts, burglary, possessions of narcotics, murders, assaults. A lot of these things, a lot of these types of crimes are gonna at some point, kidnappings, are gonna be related in some way or another to drugs. Now, whether it's that they are under the influence of drugs, okay, or they owe money, okay, or a particular victim is accused of stealing dope or owing money, or just some cases are mistaken identity by people in the narcotics business. A lot of these crimes are sort of gonna revolve around the drug trade, or drugs, in some way or another. But otherwise I would say that the majority of the cases are gonna be dealing with narcotics. In some way or another they deal with narcotics.[10]

The offenders prosecuted in the district court today are, for the most part, young and middle-aged men. Some are women, juveniles, and even older individuals. Bazan highlighted that the oldest individual he prosecuted for a drug case was a sixty-eight-year-old man. But as Garcia makes clear:

Yeah, I mean, most of the offenders that you are gonna see, or that I have seen, are gonna be ages, let's say, between eighteen to thirty-five, you know, that range there. But you've got old people, too, you know, fifties, using drugs, sixties, using cocaine, so, I mean, you see it all the way around, but by and large most of them are gonna be between eighteen and thirty-five. That's where most of your offenders, that age group, is gonna come in.[11]

The Starr County district court handles felony charges, especially drug possession cases and cases of drug possession with intent to distribute. However, as Eduardo Alvarez, one of the assistant district attorneys, made clear, the court does not handle the conspiracy cases that target drug-trafficking organizations. Alvarez stated:

Yeah, but that's how we prosecute them mostly, but we really don't do conspiracy. The feds do that. What we do is we take out the spokes. If the criminal organization is like this [draws wheel], and we take one of the spokes out. And that's how we prosecute. Eventually if we can, we will. It's just that these organizations, they're evolving. They're sophisticated now in the fact that most of the head honchos sort of, almost, you can't even relate the drugs back to them. So that's where we're at. We know that they're operating, we just can't get to them.[12]

However, when Garcia handled cases that involve drug trafficking rather than drug abuse, he modifies his prosecution approach:

Narcotics traffickers are a little bit different. Those people, like, the bigger narcotics traffickers, will go up, like, federal, they will go to the federal court. We'll prosecute them here, but there's a whole different list of considerations to deal with when you deal with people who are caught with bigger loads of narcotics. So that's the general approach we take to drug cases.[13]

Despite their best efforts, the team of Starr County district attorneys faces dilemmas when prosecuting members of its own community. The most difficult part of being a prosecutor in this small community is that, as Bazan states, "people in this office face the difficulty of knowing the people that are prosecuted in the courtroom." Bazan recalled that, in the entire time he has served as the office's chief prosecutor, he has had to prosecute his peers, including neighbors, classmates, and childhood friends. Having grown up as a farmworker, he has had to prosecute people he grew up with and worked alongside in the fields of South Texas. Beyond the difficulties attorneys faced in prosecuting drug cases, Bazan argued "that jury selection for these cases is a difficult process because 70 to 80 percent of the jurors are likely to be related to someone [in the drug business], so there is sympathy for the defendants."

But regardless of the difficulties Starr County's prosecutors faced, they expressed that their work is vitally important to the safety and integrity of the community. As Alvarez stated: "The problem is that if we don't do our jobs, then crime just keeps escalating and people lose faith in their community; it starts spiraling downwards." Garcia agreed about the importance of their positions:

I mean, there is a certain amount of authority that goes with the position 'cause we have discretion with what we can do with our cases that we handle. So it is a position with a certain amount of importance, but, you know, in the end we realize that what we try to do is we try to dispose of the cases fairly and in a way that's fair to the defendant and to the state and to the victims and the community. So I view it as an important position in the community, one of the important positions.[14]

The district attorney's office's best efforts, however, did not significantly deter or reduce drug trafficking in Starr County. As evidence of the failure of the War on Drugs, local and federal law enforcement officials have not succeeded at eliminating large-scale drug trafficking. Alvarez reminds us about the reality of combating drug trafficking at the local level:

"I mean we're just doing a drop in the bucket. There's a lot of crime out there, a lot of drugs [still] getting through."[15]

Targeting Traffic(king): The Local Effects of Border Policing

It is within the social and political context highlighted by the prosecutors of Starr County that the state of Texas initiated its border-policing surge. As the governor of Texas, the Republican Greg Abbott, articulated on Twitter: "I've already sent the Nat'l Guard, 100s more public safety officers, boats, planes, cameras, etc. Texas is doing all it can to do Feds job."[16] The surge was the culmination of Texas's efforts to triangulate police power on federal, state, and local law enforcement fronts. In June 2014, the Texas DPS launched Operation Strong Safety along the South Texas border, primarily in Hidalgo and Starr Counties, which was followed up by Operation Secure Texas. As the DPS director Steve McCraw stated, the policing initiatives were an effort "to deny Mexican cartels and their associates unfettered entry into Texas, and their ability to commit border-related crimes, as well as reduce the power of these organizations, whose success depends on their ability to operate on both sides of the border."[17]

McCraw highlighted in testimony to the Texas House of Representatives, once the operations were under way, that Texas was responsible for stepping up its policing efforts because of local and federal law enforcement failures. McCraw asserted:

Texas Governor Greg Abbott and the Texas Legislature understand that securing our nation's border with Mexico is the sovereign responsibility of the federal government, they recognize that the federal government has failed to adequately provide the appropriate resources to secure our international border with Mexico. That failure has forced the State of Texas to spend millions of dollars of state money to fulfill what is a federal responsibility.[18]

Furthermore, in his March 2016 testimony, McCraw articulated the key components of the policing surge:

Governor Abbott has long-recognized the gravity of this situation and in his first year in office, he signed into law the toughest border security program in the nation. As part of that plan, more than $800 million has been appropriated over the next two years to add more resources, more manpower and more assets toward securing our border. This includes state-of-the-art aerial assets, enhanced land and maritime patrols, advanced monitoring technology, enhanced communication capabilities, 250 new state troopers, a new company of Texas Rangers, pilots, additional support personnel, increased overtime and funding to conduct sustained surge operations in high threat areas.[19]

The surge was a response to perceived threats of unfettered drug smuggling and an influx of Central American migrants coming through the Rio Grande Valley sector of Texas, specifically female and child migrants in late 2014. The Texas border comprises fourteen border counties across 1,254 border miles. As part of a state border security assessment, the DPS designed a four-point-scale threat-level-category system for each of the counties. The tiered system was devised to assign each county a threat level based on the amount of drugs and number of people smuggled through it, with Tier I representing the highest threat and Tier IV representing minimal threat. In a 2016 unclassified report on Operation Secure Texas, eight of the fourteen counties were designated as Tier IV, or minimal threat, two were designated as Tier III, two as Tier II, and only two as Tier I, the highest threat level. The two counties representing the greatest threat level were Starr and Hidalgo Counties in the Rio Grande Valley sector. With 146 border miles, these counties together had just over one-tenth of the state's border mileage, with Starr containing sixty-eight border miles and Hidalgo seventy-eight.

As the report makes clear, along with Cameron County, the border counties of the Rio Grande Valley sector account for more than half of immigrant apprehensions and more than one-third of drug seizures along the entire Rio Grande border. At the county level, however, Starr County represents a significant proportion of drug seizures. In 2014, for example, Starr County seized more than twice as many drugs than the next leading border county (Hidalgo), at a total of 164,122 pounds of various drugs. As a result of Operation Secure Texas, drug seizures dropped by nearly 27 percent in Starr County and nearly 29 percent in Hidalgo County. The total number of drug seizures in Starr County in 2015 after the implementation of Secure Texas amounted to more than 120,000 pounds. Moreover, as drug seizures dropped in these target counties, drug seizures increased in neighboring counties: by 11 percent in Webb County, 18 percent in Zapata County, and 25.5 percent in Cameron County.[20]

US Route 83 runs along the Rio Grande and is the main traffic artery of Starr County. After the initiation of Operation Secure Texas, the impact of border policing became evident along this highway. Most noticeably, the roughly fifteen miles of US 83 between the Starr-Hidalgo county line and the eastern edge of the Rio Grande City limits were saturated with state trooper units on patrol. The Texas DPS officers were positioned at virtually every highway crossover, roughly a quarter mile from one another. The state agents were not the only policing agents positioned on the highway; Starr County sheriff's officers patrolled along this section, and numerous US Border Patrol units also traversed the highway. The Border Patrol's substation is situated along this highway at almost the exact midpoint in the county in Alto Bonito, Texas. Observations along this stretch during the first week of February 2017 recorded a minimum of twenty total patrolling units at various times throughout the day and week, more than one patrol unit per mile. The heavy police presence raised concerns for many Starr County residents, and in the following text I provide examples of three important concerns residents raised about the intensified policing that resulted from Operation Secure Texas.

A significant issue raised by Starr County residents focused on the inconvenience of the increased traffic stops as a result of the border surge. Residents and lawmakers alike were concerned with the potential for racial profiling, harassment, and civil rights abuses as a result of the increased traffic patrols and stops. Indeed, state lawmakers from Starr and Hidalgo Counties pointed out that many of their constituents voiced dissatisfaction with the increased levels of scrutiny due to the operation. Many residents, including a Starr County judge named Eloy Vera, complained that the state trooper presence negatively impacted their quality of life. The judge was frustrated that he had also been swept up in the excessive traffic stops. The question of racial profiling was further complicated by the fact that the population of Starr County is composed almost entirely of people of Hispanic origin, at more than 95 percent, and the troopers required for the operation came from elsewhere in the state. As one high-ranking state trooper stated: "I'm from East Texas. When I get sent down there, it's like I'm in a whole 'nother country."[21] As a result of the charges, the Texas DPS made greater efforts to hire more Hispanic state troopers. However, with respect to charges of harassment and racial profiling, the DPS director Steve McCraw replied: "That's garbage, that's the bottom line."[22] The story of Eleazar Garza, a young man from Starr County, however, provides more insight into this.

At the time of our interview, Eleazar Garza was eighteen years old. He had lived in one of Starr County's small communities his entire life. Tattoos covered Garza's forearms, and a couple of shiny studs pierce his left eyebrow. He drove "a badass truck," as he reminded me—a four-door Chevy with twenty-two-inch wheels that rides low, just a few inches off the ground. Garza liked to spend his evenings cruising through the small towns that pepper the highway in Starr County, sometimes to visit friends, other times just to be out of the house. Prior to the surge of policing that resulted from Operations Strong Safety and Secure Texas, Garza had minimal problems going on his cruises. The local police and sheriff's deputies knew him and would often just wave as he passed them. When the state troopers arrived in Starr County, however, the situation changed. Garza was sixteen years old at that time and only recently obtained his driver's license, having completed the necessary requirements after securing his learner's permit a few months earlier. He complained that the state troopers often stopped him and that he was harassed and often told that he "fit the description." Eventually, Garza had to limit his cruising to avoid these police encounters, and, like many other residents of Starr County, he avoids driving too much. As John Michael Torres, the spokesperson for a local civil rights organization, stated: "Our members in Starr County have said the 'surge' has changed their lives. You don't go out, they tell us, except when you have to, to go work or to buy groceries. Anything non-essential—the things that make life more enjoyable and boost the local economy—they decide not to do them, opting to stay home rather than risk traffic fines or immigration checks."[23]

A second community concern about intensified policing was its impact on community safety. The increased police presence in Starr County also resulted in more drug seizures and immigrant apprehensions. However, policing also relied more heavily on pursuits to make many of these seizures and apprehensions possible. Often, these pursuits endanger not only the lives and safety of the offenders but also the police officers themselves and border residents nearby. Border police pursuits in the last decade have turned more deadly for all parties involved. In 2013, a state trooper–initiated chase in Hidalgo County resulted in the death of a couple and their four children. Instances of pursuits have also resulted in perpetrators crashing through private properties, endangering the residents, and in numerous officer-involved collisions.[24]

However, officer-involved collisions are not always the result of pursuits like these. The experience of Delia Lopez illuminates some of the unintended community consequences of intensive border policing. In March 2016, Lopez was driving to a local grocery store in Alto Bonito. Her shopping trip took her past the Rio Grande City Border Patrol substation, which she passed as an agent group's shift ended. When she pulled up to a stop sign behind a couple of other cars, Lopez felt the quick and heavy thud of a vehicle slamming into the rear of her vehicle. A Border Patrol agent— either exhausted or distracted from the border-policing work shift—had rammed into her. As a result of this collision, Lopez experienced severe back and neck pain, requiring time off work, serious injection-based treatments, and high medical costs.[25]

Lastly, border residents also expressed major concerns about the economics of the surge in border policing. As the implementation of Operation Secure Texas made clear, the state of Texas prioritized the funding of border policing—officers, overtime, and technology—at the expense of other actions requiring state financial support. Residents had mixed reactions about this final issue. The presence of state troopers did increase economic activity in the Rio Grande Valley, as troopers stayed in local hotels and ate at local restaurants. Yet even though this represented a windfall for some individual businesses in the area, there was little long-term economic benefit. As Michael Siefert, a border community leader and Brownsville resident, articulated in an online guest column and a personal blog post, Operation Secure Texas did little to improve the lives of border residents or increase security in their communities. Siefert contended that the resources could be more properly invested in community clinics, health care, and education.[26]

This last point especially is salient when discussing the reduction of illicit activity in Starr County. The county is among the poorest in the nation, with roughly half the population living below the poverty line. Moreover, educational outcomes in Starr County drastically impact the potential for social mobility for young adults. As a result, state investment in economic development in the county and region could have a profound impact on community nonparticipation in illicit economies. Indeed, as the anthropologist Gilberto Rosas has argued, delinquent activities along the border are as much a product of intensified neoliberal policing as they are a failure of the state to generate opportunities for youths and young adults in the area.[27]

Conclusion

Operation Secure Texas, an ongoing policing endeavor along the South Texas border, is the culmination of border-policing efforts that have triangulated police power among local, state, and federal authorities at unprecedented levels. As evident from this ethnographic case study of Starr County, Operation Secure Texas demonstrates that border policing, though often incomplete, can take on more invasive and complete forms when social and political factors around criminality and security intersect to justify these policing actions. The experiences of Starr County residents reveal that policing and security do not always work uniformly for the national body politic. As Texans and Americans are persuaded to believe that these initiatives make them more secure, border residents sacrifice their security and quality of life in the process.[28]

The consolidation of police power along the South Texas–Mexico border has significantly impacted the lives of the largely Hispanic/Latino border residents of these communities, resulting in what the anthropology scholars Margaret Dorsey and Miguel Díaz-Barriga refer to as a "permanent state of carcelment."[29] In particular, the case of Starr County reveals concerning trends in the escalation of policing as well as the consolidation of police power along the South Texas border. Like Arizona's infamous SB 1070 legislation resulted in the increased policeability of the Hispanic/Latino community, so too have the Texas-based police projects resulted in the precision targeting of border residents of Mexican descent.

The strong presence of drug trafficking through Starr County has been cited as a justification for the expansion of police power in that community. However, the chief policing strategy employed through these operations has relied on a deterrence strategy grounded in what I refer to as "intimidation-saturation." The surge of police power and the intimidation presented by this strong police presence, however, has not targeted drug traffickers with precision. Rather, the policing strategy has effectively converted all border residents—and specifically those of Mexican descent—into possible suspects, or policeable subjects, not only disrupting drug trafficking through the area but also expanding in a way that impacts all levels of border life.[30]

Notes

1. Julian Aguilar, "DPS Border Surge Saps Officers from the Rest of Texas," *Texas Tribune*, July 19, 2016, texastribune.org/2016/07/19/dps-makes-progress-border-rest -texas-feels-void.

2. Tom Benning and Andrew Chavez, "After 2 Years and $800M, Texas' Border Boosts One Solid Outcome: More Traffic Tickets," *Dallas Morning News*, November 22, 2016.

3. Benning and Chavez.

4. Ildefonso Ortiz, "Starr County Drug Kingpin Gets 27 Years; 18 Others Sent to Prison," *Monitor* (McAllen, TX), March 6, 2014; Sergio Chapa, "Smugglers Lead Border Patrol Agents to Drug Bunker in Starr County," *ValleyCentral*, November 21, 2012, valleycentral.com/news/local/smugglers-lead-border-patrol-agents-to-drug-bunker -in-starr-county; "2,400 Pounds of Marijuana Found in Roma Drug Bunker," *Valley- Central*, October 25, 2011, valleycentral.com/news/local/2400-pounds-of-marijuana -found-in-roma-drug-bunker; Jared Taylor, "DPS Finds More Than 3 Tons of Pot Stashed in Underground Bunkers in Starr County," *Monitor*, July 22, 2011; US Immigration and Customs Enforcement, "ICE Seizes 1,100 Pounds of Marijuana from Bunker under South Texas Garage," press release, June 2, 2011, ice.gov/news/releases /ice-seizes-1100-pounds-marijuana-bunker-under-south-texas-garage.

5. "High Intensity Drug Trafficking Areas (HIDTAs)," United States Drug Enforcement Administration, dea.gov/ops/hidta.shtml.

6. "Quick Facts: Starr County, Texas," United States Census Bureau, census.gov /quickfacts/starrcountytexas; "South Texas High Intensity Drug Trafficking Area Drug Market Analysis," National Drug Intelligence Center, justice.gov/archive/ndic /pubs22/22796/index.htm.

7. Timothy Dunn, *The Militarization of the U.S.-Mexico Border: Low-Intensity Conflict Doctrine Comes Home* (Austin: University of Texas Press, 1996); Peter Andreas, *Border Games: Policing the U.S.-Mexico Divide* (Ithaca, NY: Cornell University Press, 2009); Lawrence A. Gooberman, *Operation Intercept: The Multiple Consequences of Public Policy* (Elmsford, NY: Pergamon Press, 1974); United States Office of National Drug Control Policy, *US/Mexico Bi-National Drug Threat Assessment: May 1997* (Washington, DC: US Department of Justice, Drug Enforcement Administration, 1997).

8. Dunn, *The Militarization of the U.S.-Mexico Border*; Timothy Dunn, "Border Militarization via Drug and Immigration Enforcement: Human Rights Implications," *Social Justice* 28, no. 2 (2001): 7–30; Andreas, *Border Games*; David Shirk, "Law Enforcement and Security Challenges in the U.S.-Mexican Border Region," *Journal of Borderlands Studies* 18, no. 2 (2009): 1–24; Joseph Nevins, *Operation Gatekeeper: The Rise of the "Illegal Alien" and the Making of the U.S.-Mexico Boundary* (New York: Routledge, 2002).

9. Alejandro Lugo, "Theorizing Border Inspections," *Cultural Dynamics* 12, no. 3 (2000): 353–373; Alejandro Lugo, *Fragmented Lives, Assembled Parts: Culture, Capitalism, and Conquest at the U.S.-Mexico Border* (Austin: University of Texas Press, 2008); Jonathan Xavier Inda, "Border Prophylaxis," *Cultural Dynamics* 18, no. 2 (2006): 115–138; Gilberto Rosas, *Barrio Libre: Criminalizing States and Delinquent Refusals of the New Frontier* (Durham, NC: Duke University Press, 2012); Gilberto Rosas, "The Managed Violences of the Borderlands: Treacherous Geographies, Policeability, and the Politics of Race," *Latino Studies* 4, no. 4 (2006): 401–418; Margaret E. Dorsey and Miguel Díaz-Barriga, "The Constitution Free Zone in the United States: Law and Life in a State of Carcelment," *PoLAR* 38 (2012): 204–225.

10. Tomás Garcia, personal interview by Santiago Guerra, Rio Grande City, Texas, March 1, 2009.

11. Garcia, personal interview by the author.

12. Eduardo Alvarez, personal interview by Santiago Guerra, Rio Grande City, Texas, March 5, 2009.

13. Garcia, personal interview by the author.

14. Garcia, personal interview by the author.

15. Alvarez, personal interview by the author.

16. Abbot quoted in Benning and Chavez, "After 2 Years."

17. Steve McCraw, testimony before the Subcommittee on National Security and Subcommittee on Government Operations, Texas House Committee on Oversight and Government Reform, March 23, 2016 (hereafter cited as McCraw testimony).

18. McCraw testimony.

19. McCraw testimony.

20. *Operation Secure Texas: Texas Border Security Performance Measures*, ver. 2016. 07.19.6 (Austin: Texas Department of Public Safety, 2016); "Southwestern Border Sheriff's Coalition and Texas Border Sheriff's Coalition," Border Sheriff's, bordersheriffs.us.

21. Marty Schladen, "In Rio Grande Valley, Officials Question Reason for DPS Stops," *El Paso Times*, March 28, 2015; Tom Benning, "DPS Is Hiring More Hispanic State Troopers, and Texas' Border Surge Is a Big Reason Why," *Dallas Morning News*, June 28, 2016.

22. Benning.

23. Steve Taylor, "DPS: We're Going to Triple the Number of Troopers in Starr County," *Rio Grande Guardian* (McAllen, TX), October 2, 2015.

24. Ildefonso Ortiz and Jared Taylor, "After Pursuit Kills South Texas Family, DPS Policies Questioned," *Monitor*, August 13, 2013.

25. Ethnographic fieldwork by the author, August–September 2016, Starr County, TX; Delia Lopez, personal interview by Santiago Guerra, Rio Grande City, Texas, August 28, 2016.

26. Michael Siefert, "Border Security," *Views from alongside the Border* (blog), October 12, 2016, alongsideborder.com/2016/10/02/border-security.

27. "Quick Facts: Starr County, Texas"; Santiago Guerra, "*La Chota y los Mafiosos*: Mexican American Casualties of the Border Drug War," *Latino Studies* 13, no. 2 (2015): 227–244; Rosas, *Barrio Libre*; Rosas, "Managed Violences," 401–418.

28. Santiago, *La Chota*, 227–244; Rosas, *Barrio Libre*; Rosas, "Managed Violences," 401–418; Inda, "Border Prophylaxis," 115–138.

29. Dorsey and Díaz-Barriga, "Constitution Free Zone," 204–225.

30. Dorsey and Díaz-Barriga, 204–225.

Bordering Reality

FOURTEEN

Dramatizing Policing the North American
Borderlands in Reality Television

ANITA HUIZAR-HERNÁNDEZ

When it comes to border policing, the US-
Mexico and US-Canada borders seem worlds,
not miles, apart. Filmmakers, news outlets,
politicians, and vigilantes endlessly paint the US-Mexico border as a war
zone that threatens to destroy the physical, economic, and cultural foundations of the United States. As the cultural studies scholar D. Robert De-
Chaine contends, "Public attitudes regarding migrants, border inhabitants, and other border-crossing subjects are conditioned by prevalent
narratives and imagery that depict the US-Mexico border as a badlands
that is out of control."[1] Contrasting dramatically with this reputation
is that of the US-Canada border, which, as the cultural studies scholar
Gillian Roberts notes, "has traditionally been referred to as 'the world's
longest undefended border.'"[2] Though neither of these depictions captures the complex realities of either space, they nonetheless shape the
justifications for and implementation of policing along both borders.

Popular culture is a key site where stereotypes about these borders are
developed and disseminated. As Holly M. Karibo makes clear in chapter 10
of this volume, sensationalistic portrayals of border policing in the media
are not new. These depictions have nevertheless evolved into new forms
of entertainment in the early twenty-first century.[3] Since 2010, the rising
popularity of reality television has led to the development of two different franchises that depict border policing.[4] The first, *Border Wars*, follows
the actions of US Customs and Border Protection (CBP) agents as they

police the border between the United States and Mexico. The second, *Border Security: Canada's Front Line* and *Border Security: America's Front Line*, both part of the *Border Security* franchise, follow Canadian Border Services Agency (CBSA) officers and US CBP agents as they police the border between the United States and Canada.[5] Working in close partnership with the border-policing agencies they depict, all three series purport to objectively document the day-to-day work of the officers who control the flow of people and goods across North America's borders.

Nevertheless, as the contrasting titles of *Border Wars* and *Border Security* suggest, the episodes offer carefully constructed visions of policing along their respective borders, guiding viewers to see the US-Mexico border as a dangerous war zone and the US-Canada border as a benign space of commerce and exchange. Through a comparative analysis of the programs' audiovisual environments, this chapter examines how production choices manipulate the border-policing realities portrayed. A close reading of the shows' starkly contrasting images, music, voice-overs, and interviews reveals that they are highly mediated, despite being marketed as "reality," and provides a window into how stereotypes about borders, the officers who police them, and the people and goods who cross them are popularly perceived.

Reality Check: Policing the US-Canada and US-Mexico Borders

Border Wars and *Border Security* depict the US and Canadian agencies charged with managing the daunting balancing act of facilitating trade while maintaining security in the aftermath of NAFTA and 9/11.[6] *Border Wars* and *Border Security: America's Front Line* both portray the US border-policing agency known as CBP, following its officers at work along the border between the United States and Mexico in the case of *Border Wars* and along the border between the United States and Canada in the case of *Border Security*. CBP is a relatively new agency within the US federal law enforcement structure. After 9/11, calls for improved border security prompted President George W. Bush to increase the nation's border security budget by 1,000 percent and to streamline government oversight by merging twenty-two existing agencies to form the Department of Homeland Security.[7] In March 2003, the Department of Homeland Security merged several of its internal agencies to form the Bureau of Customs and Border Protection.[8] As the disparate settings of *Border Wars* and *Bor-*

der Security: America's Front Line demonstrate, CBP is responsible for policing both US borders.

Border Security: Canada's Front Line portrays the Canadian equivalent of CBP, the CBSA, a relatively new agency tasked with securing Canada's borders. Following 9/11, like the US government, the Canadian government also reorganized the structure of its border security operations. Throughout the 1990s, border policing in Canada fell under the jurisdiction of the Department of Trades and Public Works, but by 2002 its oversight had been transferred to the minister of citizenship and immigration. In 2003, Canada created the CBSA within a new department, the Public Safety and Emergency Preparedness Department, the Canadian equivalent of the US Department of Homeland Security.[9] As *Border Security: Canada's Front Line* shows, CBSA officers regulate the movement of people and goods in such varied locations as Canadian land crossings, airports, mail facilities, and ports.

Considering the primacy of border policing within recent US and Canadian politics, it is not surprising that *Border Wars* and *Border Security* are both popular and polemical. *Border Wars* first aired on the National Geographic Channel in 2010 and was an instant success. The show, which had the highest-rated premiere in the history of the network, went on for five seasons from 2010 to 2013 and at the time of this writing continues to air regularly as reruns.[10] It used a documentary-like style to present CBP agents at work on the border between the United States and Mexico. As the producer Nicholas Stein explained, CBP granted *Border Wars* unprecedented access "to tell their story in a serious way and to tell it in an accurate way."[11] This access, however, raised questions about the show's claims of objectivity. Although National Geographic marketed *Border Wars* as a documentary, Stein admitted that its purpose was to "look at the work and the dedication of the men and women [who police the US-Mexico border]. . . . this is a look from the point of view of the federal law enforcement folks."[12] Journalists and academics contended that the show was less of a documentary and more like free CBP propaganda conveniently funneled directly into viewers' homes.[13]

Border Security: Canada's Front Line first aired in 2012 on the immensely popular channel National Geographic Canada, with its US spin-off, *Border Security: America's Front Line*, debuting in 2016.[14] Like *Border Wars*, *Border Security* was also marketed as a documentary.[15] Nevertheless, *Border Security: Canada's Front Line* was produced in overt collaboration with the CBSA, which maintained final approval over each episode.[16] The CBSA also provided financial support for the show in the form of additional staff salaries, travel, and communications support, adding up to a total contribution of at least $200,000 per season.[17] Unsurprisingly, journalists, academics, and eventually a broad community of concerned Canadian citizens contended that the show was, like *Border Wars*, not a documentary but rather not-so-free publicity designed explicitly to bolster public support for the CBSA.

The concerns *Border Wars* and *Border Security* provoked revolve around the slippery separation between reality television and other closely related genres like documentaries, which also claim to depict what is real.[18] As the media studies scholar June Deery argues, the line between the reality that more "objective" media genres portray and the highly manipulated image portrayed in reality TV is not always so easy to distinguish.[19] Because *Border Security* and *Border Wars* walk this fine line between the objective reality of a documentary or news program and the more sensationalized narratives of reality television, the impact of their representations of border policing on public opinion and on the actual practice of policing borders is magnified. Though the highly manipulated content of these different programs is *not* transparent, their influence on perception and policy *is* real, as they all contribute to a broader (mis)recognition of the risks associated with border crossings and crossers as well as the appropriate responses to those perceived risks. *Border Wars* and *Border Security* represent some of the most recent—and most dangerous—iterations of mediated representations of border policing in popular culture, with potentially far-reaching consequences.

Alternate Realities: Documenting Policing in *Border Wars* and *Border Security*

In season 1, episode 1, of *Border Wars*, ominous pulsating music with heavy bass accompanies rotating images of the US-Mexico border wall, Border Patrol vehicles, cars waiting to cross the border line, and desert landscapes. The booming baritone voice of the male narrator begins:

> It runs for 2,000 miles, through cities, mountains, and some of the most inhospitable terrain in America. The US-Mexico border: an imaginary line that separates two peoples, two languages, two economies. And in recent years, it's become a kind of battleground, a place where every day a high-stakes game of cat and mouse is played out between those who want to cross the

border illegally and those whose job it is to stop them. . . . Like every war, this one evokes passions. It splits families apart and causes casualties. New weapons have been brought in to fight it. New tactics have been introduced, measures and countermeasures deployed. Over the past few decades, the conflict has intensified. Now, with rare access, National Geographic takes you inside the border war.[20]

The opening voice-over narration highlights the exceptionality of the time and place of the contemporary border between the United States and Mexico, which is so uniquely dangerous that it demands an extraordinary response that is both technologically advanced and heavily militarized. The fact that there is no actual war along the border between these two nations is hardly relevant. Rather, from the opening moments, it is clear that the look, sound, and feel of *Border Wars* delivers exactly what the title promises: high-stakes combat along the boundary that separates the two nations.

In the first fifty-minute episode, *Border Wars* presents an in-depth portrayal of the US-Mexico borderlands that highlights a diverse group of participants who hold multiple and conflicting perspectives. Most of the recorded action takes place away from the official points of entry at airports and land crossings and focuses on the inhospitable Arizona desert. These desert scenes highlight the danger the landscape represents, from snakes and spiders to cacti and sudden shifts in weather. Within this context, the show introduces a broad spectrum of actors. In addition to interviews with Border Patrol agents and border crossers, *Border Wars* incorporates many other voices that provide a wider context for understanding the causes and consequences of who and what crosses the border. Interviews with Mike Wilson, a Tohono O'odham man who refills water stations throughout the desert to aid struggling migrants, and Dr. Bruce Anderson, a forensic anthropologist who identifies migrant remains at the Pima County Office of the Medical Examiner, serve to humanize migrants and underscore the difficulties inherent in their journeys across the desert. On the other end of the spectrum, an interview with a woman named Cindy, a vigilante who combs the desert for migrants to alert Border Patrol of their whereabouts, shows the anger and fear that the topic of border security so often inspires. Overall, the first episode of *Border Wars* is less about policing and more about documenting the complex context within which these movements occur.

The complexities that mark the perspective of episode 1 of *Border Wars*, however, are nowhere to be seen in episode 2. A two-year break separates the 2008 *Border Wars*, which appeared as a stand-alone documentary, from its continuation in the second episode and subsequent five seasons. The launch of *Border Wars* as a series marked a decisive shift away from the journalistic, documentary-style approach of the first episode and toward the sensationalized entertainment of reality television. Nick Stein, producer of the relaunched version, explained:

> There was an original show that National Geographic did called "Border Wars" that was a one-hour show that was done by their Explorer Unit and it was sort of a—more of an overview of all the things that go on there. But, really, this is a look from the point of view of the federal law enforcement folks. There is, I think, many opportunities for many filmmakers of every stripe and news organizations to do a more comprehensive look at all of the issues here. There's so many points of view. But we decided that a lot of people really didn't understand what these men and women are being asked to do on our behalf and with our tax dollars. And we thought that it was important to get on the ground and really see that happening.[21]

Stein's comments confirm that the relaunched *Border Wars* consciously moved away from the multiperspective style of the first episode to focus exclusively on the experiences of the "men and women" charged with protecting the border. The show's description on the National Geographic Channel's website further underscores this one-sidedness, advertising *Border Wars* as an opportunity to "follow the Department of Homeland Security's federal law enforcement agents and officers as they defend and protect America's borders."[22] This description promises viewers a front-row seat to a classic battle between good and evil, as seen through the eyes of the unequivocally good side.

In the first relaunched episode, "Last Defense," *Border Wars* follows agents again working in the Arizona sector as they intercept cars smuggling illicit goods and track migrants through the desert.[23] At the Nogales port of entry, agents intercept a car heading north into the United States carrying $18,000 worth of marijuana hidden in a compartment above the gas tank. Later, they intercept a car heading south into Mexico with a hidden compartment filled with US dollars. As the agents explain, drugs go in and profits come out. Away from the official port of entry, agents pursue groups of migrants of varying sizes through the desert by day and by night using a variety of techniques, from high-tech sensors, helicopters, and ATVs to low-tech methods like horseback riding or even walking. By the end of the episode, the agents have successfully intercepted three separate groups of unauthorized migrants.

The postproduction editing of these apprehensions strategically quells potential viewer ambivalence or uneasiness about the agents' actions. In each of the three cases, the agents are portrayed in an unambiguously positive light. In the first two cases, they are depicted rescuing migrants from imminent danger. One group requires immediate medical help, which the agents provide in the form of water, food, IV drips, oxygen tanks, and other medical interventions. The agents provide lifesaving help to these men, who would likely die without some kind of outside intervention. The other "rescue" is more disputable. Agents intercept a group they have been tracking, which includes two eight-year-old girls and a man who claims to be their godfather. He explains to the agents that he is supposed to take them to New York, where they will reunite with their parents. The narrator repeatedly suggests, without evidence, that the girls may be the victims of sexual trafficking. In this case, the otherwise unsettling image of Border Patrol agents intercepting migrants who pose no perceivable threat is recast as the welcome sight of agents saving young girls from a life of sexual slavery. The show never clarifies if this was in fact the case, although it repeatedly does provide follow-up information for other plotlines, leaving the viewer to wonder whether this is a rescue or the forced separation of two daughters from their parents.

In the final case, agents pursue a group of people at night in a highly dramatic scene. The narrator repeatedly sets up the confrontation as a potentially lethal encounter with dangerous drug smugglers. The drama is heightened by night-vision camera shots that follow the agents as they run through the desert and whisper updates to the camera. When the agents finally intercept the group after an intense chase on foot and horseback with the aid of a helicopter, they discover that the travelers are not drug smugglers but rather another group of migrants in search of work. Once more, the show positions the Border Patrol agents as unequivocally good, this time by casting doubt on the intentions of the migrants. Again with no evidence, the show implies that these migrants might *say* they are coming for work but are in actuality dangerous criminals. As the agents handcuff the group and lead them into a van to be taken to a detention center, one of the agents says: "We don't know their history, we don't have access to their criminal records. . . . You'd be surprised, you can't just relax. . . . A lot of these people do have criminal records." The show provides no follow-up information about this particular group, leaving the audience to wonder whether they are truly guilty of any crime more serious than pursuing a better life.

This one-sided perspective prompted questions about the appropriateness of policing agencies joining up with television production companies to publicize their activities. Shortly after *Border Wars* relaunched, the television critic Jon Caramanica wrote an article for the *Los Angeles Times* criticizing its partiality. He observed that the show criminalizes "practically everyone" when it comes to migrants yet always "paints the officers as benevolent," blurring the line between a television show and a CBP public relations campaign that comes dangerously close to propaganda.[24] Because *Border Wars* is a *reality* television show, its partiality is even more pernicious. Viewers watch, react to, and interpret reality television differently from other programming because it makes truth claims that other genres do not. As a result, when *Border Wars* criminalizes (without evidence) *all* migrants who appear in the show, it guides the audience to do the same. As the cultural studies scholar Lisa Cacho contends, the social consequences of this blanket criminalization are steep: "To be stereotyped as a criminal is to be misrecognized as someone who committed a crime, but to be criminalized is to be prevented from being law-abiding."[25] By criminalizing all the migrants it depicts, *Border Wars* prevents the audience from viewing migrants as anything but dangerous criminals, regardless of their specific circumstances.

Season 1, episode 1, of *Border Security: Canada's Front Line* immediately establishes an audiovisual environment that contrasts sharply with that of *Border Wars*. The episode opens with a message typed by an invisible hand, rapidly appearing letter by letter. It reads: "Thousands of men and women dedicate their lives to protecting Canada's border crossings." As the message disappears, it is replaced with a collage of images: Canadian flags waving, planes landing, border agents interrogating passengers, cars waiting to cross a border checkpoint, and people being handcuffed all flash across the screen to the tune of an electric guitar riff that swells to a sustained high note just as the show's title, *Border Security: Canada's Front Line*, appears.[26]

The combination of the fast-paced guitar rhythm and the quick interspersing of familiar images of border policing creates a sense of immediacy and drama. However, this drama is quickly diffused as the episode cuts to the more mundane images of a plane landing and luggage being hauled off and loaded onto moving conveyor belts. The music shifts from the guitar riff to a pulsing background rhythm as a narrator begins to speak. The cadence of the male voice is cheerful, and some viewers might even recognize this particular narrator, Jeff Cole, who also narrates the Canadian version of the popular US show *Say Yes to the Dress*.[27]

As the episode progresses, the show follows border agents at the Vancouver airport and the Douglas land border crossing. At the Vancouver airport, agents pull aside an Australian passenger traveling to visit his girlfriend and check suspicious baggage from China. After briefly interrogating the Australian, the airport agent discovers that he is traveling with more than the permitted amount of alcohol and has a history of drunk driving and drunk and disorderly convictions back home. Though minor chords in the background music indicate tension, the drama is quickly interrupted by a cut to a more lighthearted montage of passengers retrieving their luggage from a conveyor belt at baggage claim. Here, a dog named Whiskey picks out suspicious bags that the agents pull for further inspection. The luggage belongs to three Chinese students and contains prohibited meat products. The episode then cuts to the Douglas land border crossing, located between Washington State on the US side and British Columbia on the Canadian side. The agents pull aside two snowboarders from Nevada and California and discover that they possess marijuana. At the same land border, agents pull aside a Texan coming with a permit to work as a mechanic and who is also carrying a gun. By the end of the episode, the Australian passenger is sent back home, the snowboarders are temporarily placed under arrest and then sent back to the United States without their marijuana, the Chinese students are fined $800 each, and the Texan is told to keep his gun in the United States until he secures a permit to have it in Canada.

The seriousness of the situations shown is undercut by the breeziness of the episode's editing. In reality television, the invisible postproduction editing process is what shapes hours of footage into something interesting and enjoyable for the audience and also what distances the final product from the reality it supposedly portrays. Deery notes that "on RTV [reality television] there are often high shooting ratios of 100:1 or even 300:1," meaning that production crews sometimes take 300 hours of footage to produce a one-hour show.[28] With such high shooting ratios, what appears in an episode is only very loosely based on what actually happened. In this episode of *Border Security*, the postproduction shaping of the show's sound, pace, and voice-over narration molds the gravity of the circumstances into lighthearted entertainment. The energetic rhythms and bright sounds of the background music that transition one scene to the next alleviate whatever stress may have built up, while the fast pacing of the show also diffuses tension as the levity of one narrative thread is quickly interrupted with a jump cut to a different story line. The playful voice-over narration also relieves tension and maintains amusement. As it becomes clear that the Australian passenger may be denied entry into Canada due to his history of alcohol abuse, the narrator glibly jokes: "A young Aussie's plan to visit his girlfriend appears to be going bottoms-up."[29] Later, the narrator minimizes the potential gravity of the snowboarders transporting drugs across an international boundary when he teases: "An American snowboarder finds himself on a slippery slope after a jar of pot is found in his vehicle."[30] Whereas *Border Wars* characterizes someone carrying illegal drugs across international lines as a drug smuggler, *Border Security* tellingly portrays the snowboarders as harmless tourists. Despite depicting crime, *Border Security*'s postproduction editing ensures that the overall tone of the show remains upbeat, implying that the criminal activity portrayed does not undermine the overall safety of the US-Canada borderlands.

These postproduction choices mark *Border Security* as a reality show meant to entertain its audience and not as a documentary intended to inform, although as noted previously, the line between the two is often blurry. The media studies scholar John Corner proposes thinking of reality shows as existing along a continuum in which "the legacy of documentary is still at work, albeit in a partial and revised form."[31] *Border Security* belongs to what Corner calls "the 'postdocumentary' culture of television."[32] He describes the "decisive shift toward diversion," noting that while there has long been a "requirement for documentary to do some entertaining to gain and keep a popular audience," this is subtly and significantly different from "a piece of work in documentary format [that] is entirely designed in relation to its capacity to deliver entertainment," provoking "radical changes . . . both to the forms of representation and to viewing relations."[33] Because the show is intended to entertain its audience, the postproduction editing of *Border Security: Canada's Front Line* creates an enjoyable viewing experience, purposefully presenting sometimes serious content in a relaxed and humorous format.

The question of where *Border Security* fell on the spectrum from documenting to sensationalizing reality prompted major controversy and the show's eventual cancellation. In 2013, the show filmed six people who were detained and arrested in an immigration raid. The men's lawyer argued that their consent to allow the recording of their arrest was coerced and represented a violation of their privacy rights. An online petition to cancel the show quickly gained more than 22,000 signatures. Nevertheless, various Canadian politicians responded with support for the show, which they characterized as a "public awareness effort."[34] One year later, despite mounting criticism, the CBSA made the controversial decision to approve a third season of the show. A spokeswoman for the CBSA stated that "the benefits of the series warranted continued participation," as viewers could "witness the professionalism with which the agency performs every day."[35] This response prompted even more debate about the show, which some contended was no more than a CBSA public relations campaign.[36] Finally, in 2016, the CBSA ended its controversial relationship with *Border Security* following the privacy commissioner Daniel Therrien's finding that the show breached the Privacy Act when it filmed the undocumented migrants' arrest in 2013.[37]

Border Security: Canada's Front Line is not the only reality TV show to invite ethical controversy. Many debates center on the issue of exploitation, which, as the media studies scholar Wendy N. Wyatt notes, is the "one criticism . . . routinely leveled against the reality television genre."[38] Intentional or unintentional, Wyatt cites reality programs' degrading portrayal and commodification of participants and blatant neglect for their well-being as indicative of an exploitative system. The ethical stakes and exploitation that form the backbone of *Border Security*, however, are even more unsettling precisely because of the show's close relationship to the CBSA and its depiction of vulnerable populations. Whereas other shows may exploit their participants in order to enhance profit, *Border Security* is invested in not only profit but also public opinion.

Border Security's representation of the CBSA corroborated the Canadian view of its border security apparatus as more civil and approachable than its US counterpart. As the urban geographer Yolande Pottie-Sherman and the sociologist Rima Wilkes contend, the Canadian *Border Security* explicitly avoided the sensationalized fearmongering of shows like *Border Wars* in order to present Canada "as a generous, evenhanded and diverse nation" that was diametrically opposed to the United States and its border enforcement practices.[39] Statements made by Canadian politicians and the CBSA in support of the show affirm that they understood the political value of such a program, which allowed them to maintain such a benevolent image.

The 2016 cancellation of *Border Security: Canada's Front Line* did not mean the show had seen its last days. Instead, the franchise moved south and became *Border Security: America's Front Line*, looking at the same border but this time from the US perspective. In the opening scene of season 1, episode 1, of the US spin-off, the nearly identical structure makes clear that little has changed. The same message flashes across the screen (with "protecting Canada's border crossings" changed to "protecting America's borders") as the same music plays and the same narrator's voice introduces the episode. The focus continues on the same border, although a different side, with no episode focusing on the more notorious southern border. Episode 1 features agents at New York's JFK Airport investigating cargo they suspect includes drugs, an unemployed Dutch traveler entering through Detroit's airport who agents suspect intends to work illegally, an American traveler of Iraqi descent who is denied entry into Canada at the Pacific Highway crossing because his name triggers an "armed and dangerous" alert, and a Canadian bachelorette party heading to Seattle that agents suspect might have drugs.[40]

The largely similar postproduction editing techniques of *Border Security: America's Front Line* create a televisual tone analogous to its Canadian predecessor's. By the end of episode 1, some of the suspicious cargo found at JFK turns out to be *dulce de leche* (a dessert), while other packages include a banned substance used to cut cocaine and illegally imported primate skulls. The Dutch traveler is denied entry and returns to the Netherlands. The US traveler, who is returning from Kurdistan, is in fact a United States Army veteran who was flagged because his identity was mistaken for someone else's. The Canadian bachelorette party, which is all laughs, is allowed to continue on to Seattle after the only item agents find is an inflatable male doll. Despite varying greatly in gravity, the way the show is edited equalizes the different story lines, which are all neatly resolved by the end of the thirty-minute episode.

By far the most remarkable and disturbing plotline centers on the veteran attempting to cross the border to visit his girlfriend in Vancouver. After pulling the man off a bus heading north, the CBSA denies him entry to Canada. As the narrator clarifies, "that's a red flag" for US CBP officers. A CBP officer explains that before allowing this "US passport holder" back into the United States, he has to verify that the man "is an American coming back" and "that there's no wants or warrants, or that no one's looking for him." As dramatic drumbeats play in the background, the CBP officer asks the man to place his hands on the desk and subsequently handcuffs him and takes him to a holding cell. The narrator clarifies that "the traveler's name has triggered an armed and dangerous alert."[41] Following a luggage exam, the CBP officers discover that the man has recently returned from a trip to Kurdistan, his birthplace, where he was visiting family. When officers question him about how he ended up in the United States, the man explains that he was an exchange student who later enlisted in the US Army and fought in Afghanistan. After looking at the man's passport more carefully, agents realize that his name and birth date are not in fact a match for the armed and dangerous alert. Even though the man is not found to be a threat, he is still fingerprinted and photographed by CBP agents before being released from custody.

Though its tone is diametrically opposed to *Border Wars*, this episode of *Border Security* nevertheless points to how race shapes interactions along not only the US-Mexico border but also the US-Canada border for both agents and potential crossers. The episode's dramatic tension is predicated on the assumption that the audience will imagine the man is a terrorist. Though his name is never given, the narrator tells viewers that it triggers an armed and dangerous alert (although this ends up not being true) and that he has recently returned from Kurdistan, a place viewers are assumed to associate with terrorist activity. The episode purposefully constructs the man as a potential terrorist threat in order to heighten the impact of the dramatic twist: not only is the man not a terrorist, he is a US war veteran, a revelation that would be less striking if he were white. It is precisely because he is Iraqi American that his status as an American veteran proves to be a shocking surprise.

Once the truth is revealed, the show quickly wraps up his narrative. The narrator nonchalantly comments that, despite the situation's threatening appearance, "it looks like a case of mistaken identity." A man who appears to be a CBP supervisor then explains why the innocent man was handcuffed and jailed. He states: "This is just a routine action we take each and every day in protecting the homeland." The traveler remarks with a tone of marked resignation: "I was born in Iraq so every time I come and leave, this is how I get treated."[42] Though racialized policing practices are more often associated with the US-Mexico border, the fact that both agent and traveler characterize this encounter along the US-Canada border as routine points to the fundamental role that race plays in policing along *both* borders.

Conclusion

Despite their overt investment in portraying the border agencies they depict in a positive light, both *Border Wars* and *Border Security* reveal how criminality is racialized in the borderlands. In *Border Wars*, the show's editing suggests that each border crosser is not only undocumented but also a dangerous criminal associated with powerful drug cartels. Even after agents intercept crossers and find that they are not in fact smuggling drugs but are simply migrating in search of work, the show continues to frame them as potential criminals. In *Border Security*, the suspense that holds the episode with the Iraqi American traveler depends on the presumed threat posed by the Middle Eastern man. Even after agents realize that they were mistaken and the man is not a terrorist but in fact a US Army veteran who served in Afghanistan, the show still applauds them for their careful attention to detail and commitment to protecting the homeland.

These unsettling scenes point to the ways that popular culture shapes border policing in formal and informal ways. As the criminologists Anna Pratt and Sara K. Thompson have demonstrated, the combination of broad discretion and ambiguous risk assessment makes racial profiling a fundamental part of border policing, despite official policies to the contrary.[43] When agents rely on their instincts to assess risk, Pratt notes that "racialized/nationality-based stereotypes are often not far away."[44] Both *Border Wars* and *Border Security* document this border-policing reality, as each show celebrates agents using stereotypes about undocumented migrants and Middle Easterners as an appropriate metric to inform their policing.

The shows' close relationships with the agencies they represent confirm that the viewing experience they offer only borders on reality, as all three blatantly attempt to shape public opinion about the borders, crossers, and officers they depict. By masquerading as neutral, fly-on-the-wall representations of border policing, *Border Wars* and *Border Security* encourage audiences to interpret the mediated portrayals they offer as real and impartial. Although the thirty-minute or hour-long stories they tell are far from objective, they nevertheless powerfully shape public perception of border policing.

Notes

1. D. Robert DeChaine, "Introduction: For Rhetorical Border Studies," in *Border Rhetorics: Citizenship and Identity on the US-Mexico Frontier*, ed. D. Robert DeChaine (Tuscaloosa: University of Alabama Press, 2012), 8.

2. Gillian Roberts, *Discrepant Parallels: Cultural Implications of the Canada-US Border* (Montreal: McGill-Queen's University Press, 2015), 4.

3. See, for example, Lee Bebout, *Whiteness on the Border: Mapping the U.S. Racial Imagination in Brown and White* (New York: New York University Press, 2016); William Anthony Nericcio, *Tex[t] Mex: Seductive Hallucinations of the "Mexican" in America* (Austin: University of Texas Press, 2007); and Arnoldo De León, *They Called Them Greasers: Anglo Attitudes toward Mexicans in Texas, 1821–1900* (Austin: University of Texas Press, 1983).

4. June Deery defines reality television as "pre-planned but mostly unscripted programming with non-professional actors in non-fictional scenarios." "Reality TV" is a broad term that encompasses many different subcategories, including contest shows, self-improvement shows, and day-in-the-life programs about particular families, regions, or occupations. Both *Border Security* and *Border Wars* fall under this last designation, depicting both a region (the US-Canada or US-Mexico border) and an occupation (border security agent). See June Deery, *Reality TV* (Cambridge, UK: Polity, 2015), 13.

5. Both shows are spin-offs of *Border Security: Australia's Front Line*, aired as *Nothing to Declare*. See IMDb, "*Nothing to Declare, Border Security: Australia's Front Line (original title)*," imdb.com/title/tt0439351.

6. For more on the changing security context along these borders, see Karine Côté-Boucher, "The Diffuse Border: Intelligence-Sharing, Control and Confinement along Canada's Smart Border," *Surveillance & Society* 5, no. 2 (2008): 142–165; and Peter Andreas, "The Mexicanization of the US-Canada Border: Asymmetric Interdependence in a Changing Security Context," *International Journal* 60, no. 2 (2005): 449–462.

7. Emmanuel Brunet-Jailly, "Security and Border Security Policies: Perimeter or Smart Border? A Comparison of the European Union and Canadian-American Border Security Regimes," *Journal of Borderlands Studies* 21, no. 1 (2006): 7, 10.

8. Brunet-Jailly, 9.

9. Côté-Boucher, "Diffuse Border," 153.

10. Reece Jones, "Border Wars: Narratives and Images of the US-Mexican Border on TV," *ACME: An International E-Journal for Critical Geographies* 13, no. 3 (2014): 531.

11. Maureen Cavanaugh and Sharon Heilbrunn, "Behind the Scenes of National Geographic's 'Border Wars' Documentary," *KPBS*, January 5, 2010, kpbs.org/news/2010/jan/05/border-wars.

12. "Border Security," National Geographic Channel, natgeotv.com/ca/border-security/about; Cavanaugh and Heilbrunn, "Behind the Scenes."

13. See Jones, "Border Wars"; and Jon Caramanica, "'Border Wars' Looks at Illegal Immigration and Efforts to Stop It," *Los Angeles Times*, September 5, 2010.

14. Yolande Pottie-Sherman and Rima Wilkes, "Visual Media and the Construction

of the Benign Canadian Border on National Geographic's *Border Security*," *Social & Cultural Geography* 17, no. 1 (2016): 83.

15. "About CBS Reality," CBS Reality, cbsreality.tv/uk/about.php.

16. Pottie-Sherman and Wilkes, "Visual Media," 83.

17. Pottie-Sherman and Wilkes, 87.

18. For an in-depth discussion of the relationship between documentary filming techniques and reality television, see John Corner, "Performing the Real," *Television & New Media* 3, no. 3 (2002): 255–269.

19. Deery, *Reality TV*, 15.

20. *Border Wars*, season 1, episode 1, "No End in Sight," aired April 1, 2008, by National Geographic Channel.

21. Cavanaugh and Heilbrunn, "Behind the Scenes."

22. "Border Wars," National Geographic Channel, channel.nationalgeographic .com/border-wars (accessible on March 19, 2017); see, alternatively, video.national geographic.com/video/border-wars.

23. *Border Wars*, season 1, episode 2, "Last Defense," aired January 10, 2010, by National Geographic Channel.

24. Caramanica, "'Border Wars.'"

25. Lisa Cacho, *Social Death: Racialized Rightlessness and the Criminalization of the Unprotected* (New York: New York University Press, 2012), 4.

26. *Border Security: Canada's Front Line*, season 1, episode 1, "Episode 1," aired September 6, 2012, by Force Four Entertainment.

27. "Jeff Cole," IMDb, imdb.com/name/nm6042680.

28. Deery, *Reality TV*, 50.

29. *Border Security: Canada's Front Line*, season 1, episode 1.

30. *Border Security: Canada's Front Line*, season 1, episode 1.

31. Corner, "Performing the Real," 257.

32. Corner, 257.

33. Corner, 262–263.

34. Kate Webb, "Lawyer Questions if Border Security TV Show Is Really 'Documentary,'" *Toronto Metro*, March 28, 2013.

35. Douglas Quan, "Canada's 'Border Security' Reality TV Series Filming Third Season Despite CBSA Concerns, Public Complains," *National Post* (Toronto), May 7, 2014.

36. These same concerns arose regarding the original series on which the Canadian spin-off was based. Documents emerged showing that the Australian Border Force and immigration department maintained extensive control over what *Border Security: Australia's Front Line* depicted, leading to concerns about the manipulation of information in order to gain public support. See Paul Farrell, "Border Force and Immigration Officials Have Final Say on Reality TV Show," *Guardian US*, September 21, 2015.

37. Jim Bronskill, "'Border Security' TV Show Cancelled after Watchdog Finds Privacy Violation," *Star* (Toronto), June 12, 2016.

38. Wendy N. Wyatt, "Exploitation: When Reality TV Becomes Degradation TV," in *The Ethics of Reality TV*, ed. Wendy N. Wyatt and Kristie Bunton (New York: Continuum, 2012), 159.

39. Pottie-Sherman and Wilkes, "Visual Media," 95.

40. *Border Security: America's Front Line*, season 1, episode 1, "Episode 1," aired January 10, 2016, by Force Four Entertainment.

41. *Border Security: America's Front Line*, season 1, episode 1.

42. *Border Security: America's Front Line*, season 1, episode 1.

43. Anna Pratt and Sara K. Thompson, "Chivalry, 'Race,' and Discretion at the Canadian Border," *British Journal of Criminology* 48, no. 5 (2008): 620–640.

44. Anna Pratt, "Between a Hunch and a Hard Place: Making Suspicion Reasonable at the Canadian Border," *Social and Legal Studies* 19, no. 4 (2010): 472.

Within and Without Borders

KARL JACOBY

O ne of the central paradoxes of modern borders is
their existence as places marked by simultaneous
extremes of law and lawlessness. The contempo-
rary border functions as a "space of exception" where the state allows itself
extraordinary police powers.[1] It is no accident that the largest law enforcement arm in the federal government today is Customs and Border Protection (CBP) and that its officers along with agents of Immigration and
Customs Enforcement have far broader powers to stop, search, and seize
individuals at the border than do police elsewhere. At the same time, because one of the most fundamental features of modern sovereignty is the
control over a defined geographic space, borders are locations that reveal
the limits to the nation-state's police powers.[2] The existence of such limits
give rise to particular forms of lawbreaking, above all the covert movement of goods or peoples from one jurisdiction to another, an activity that
state authorities have come to criminalize as smuggling. Powerful cultural
tropes accentuate such realities, casting the borders as uncertain arenas of
disorder and violence—a trend that runs from nineteenth-century dime
novels such as *Bob Woolf, The Border Ruffian* (1899) through Orson Welles's
Touch of Evil (1958) to such recent Hollywood releases as *Sicario: Day of the
Soldado* (2018).

How should we make sense of this peculiar amalgam of law and lawlessness that swirls around borders like those between the United States and

269

Mexico and the United States and Canada? It is not enough to assert that one causes the other—that because borders are inherently lawless zones, the state must be given exceptional police powers within them. After all, as the essays in *Border Policing* illuminate in telling detail, the very categories of law and lawlessness can in their own ways be as arbitrary as the geographic lines sketched on maps that have become our international boundaries. What the state terms "lawlessness," such as the importation of peyote from Mexico for ritual purpose by Native Americans or the unmonitored crossing of the international boundary by Indigenous nations like the Tohono O'odham, may in fact enjoy widespread sanction among the affected communities. Conversely, what can appear to the state like commonsense policing measures, such as the creation of "home guards" in Texas during the 1910s, may seem to Tejanos like little more than an open invitation for Anglos to engage in vigilante violence against them. Lawbreaking can reflect an ethical vision of the world; law enforcement can be difficult to differentiate from criminal behavior.

To study regimes of law enforcement along the border is therefore to enter into the vast, largely unmapped territory that exists between formal law and informal popular morality. As they search out landmarks to guide them across this terrain, scholars need to be cautious of uncritically replicating the ethical categories embedded in the documents preserved in the archive. Because borders are so problematic for modern nation-states, they generate a constant flow of written reports, studies, and the like. Once archived and made available to historians, these materials can mislead as much as illuminate, for they inevitably bear the traces of their origins in agencies charged with enforcing a particular vision of the border. The challenge for historians is to avoid simply seeing the border like a state, to paraphrase the scholar James Scott, neglecting the perspectives that have been marginalized, if not erased altogether, from the documentary record.[3]

It should not prove surprising that the subjective nature of law and lawlessness—as well as the limitations of the archive—are central features of one of the foundational works of borderlands history: Américo Paredes's *With His Pistol in His Hand*. First published in 1958, *With His Pistol in His Hand* relates the tale of Gregorio Cortez Lira, a ranch hand in South Texas who in 1901 killed a local sheriff after a misunderstanding about a horse trade (the interpreter asked about a *caballo*, when Cortez had in fact traded a *yegua*, or mare). Pursued by a posse of vengeful Anglos, Cortez attempted to flee to safety across the border into Mexico, only to be captured a few miles from the Rio Grande when a local Tejano, tempted by the promise of a reward, revealed his whereabouts to two Texas Rangers.[4]

What makes *With His Pistol in His Hand* such an important milestone in borderlands history is the manner in which Paredes incorporates not only conventional archive—sources like newspaper accounts and court records—but also the rich oral tradition of South Texas. This folklore, much of it preserved in *corridos* (ballads), enables Paredes to open a window onto a subaltern vision of history. If official records paint Cortez as the quintessential "bad hombre," the *corridos* of the Rio Grande Valley, in contrast, transform Cortez into a heroic figure: an ethnic Mexican with the fortitude to stand up to the injustices that he and so many other Tejanos suffered at the hands of oppressive Anglo lawmen.

> Decía Gregorio Cortez
> Con su pistol en la mano:
> —No corran, rinches cobardes,
> con un solo mexicano.
> (Then said Gregorio Cortez,
> With his pistol in his hand,
> "Don't run, you cowardly rangers,
> From just one Mexican.")[5]

Any attempt to study law and lawlessness along the border also engages the surprisingly slippery question of where "the border" itself begins and ends. At the turn of the twentieth century, US law enforcement agencies began to recast the border as a wide zone rather than just a thin line running along the international boundary. Interviewed in 1921 by the House Committee on Immigration and Naturalization, George J. Harris, the assistant supervising inspector of the Mexican Border District for the Immigration Service, explained: "There is no use of considering a patrol which simply marches up and down the border between certain fixed limits."[6] Instead, according to Harris, agents of the Immigration Service focused their efforts on locations many miles removed from the actual boundary line: "We have in the past had several men engaged in inspecting trains at what we call strategic points in the interior, junction points. That is what we call our second line of defense."[7]

Over time, this reconfiguring of the border into a broad zone in which law enforcement had considerable freedom to act became woven into American law and regulation. In the 1925 case *Carroll v. United States*, federal agents stopped a suspected smuggler named George Carroll in Grand Rapids, Michigan, some 152 miles from the US-Canada boundary, and found sixty-eight bottles of whiskey and gin hidden in the seats of his car. Carroll contested his arrest on the grounds that the officers' actions violated his Fourth Amendment right against unreasonable searches and seizures. The United States Supreme Court issued a ruling that permitted the officers' actions yet drew a sharp distinction between the border region and the interior. Citing the necessity of "national self protection," the court recognized few limits on searches of travelers crossing "an international boundary." Once the traveler had crossed the border into the interior of the country, however, they possessed "a right to free passage" unless law enforcement officials, in the justices' words, had "probable cause" that the individual was breaking the law.[8]

Even as this decision set an important precedent in defining probable cause, it did little to clarify the exact contours of the border. By declaring that federal agents needed probable cause to search Carroll, the justices implied that his arrest more than 150 miles from the US-Canada boundary fell outside of a reasonable definition of the border. Yet at the same time, they pointed to the proximity of this very same border as the preeminent reason why police had probable cause for stopping Carroll in the first place: "We know . . . that Grand Rapids is about 152 miles from Detroit, and that Detroit and its neighborhood along the Detroit River, which is the International Boundary, is one of the most active centers for introducing illegally into this country spirituous liquors for distribution into the interior."[9]

In the ensuing years, the United States has never quite resolved the uncertainties the Carroll case raises over where the border ends and the interior begins. Part of the reason for the ongoing confusion is that the United States maintains a distinction between customs searches (for illegal goods) and immigration searches (for undocumented migrants). To be valid, a customs search needs only to show that there has been no material "change in condition" since an individual crossed the border, so that whatever contraband the person possessed had been with them from the moment they entered the United States. In practice, this doctrine means that, as far as customs searches are concerned, the border is spatially elastic, limited only by the ability of law enforcement to demonstrate a continuity between border crossing and arrest.[10]

Immigration searches, however, follow a distinct logic. While the United States has allowed customs searches since 1789, immigration searches are more recent, emerging only as the United States attempted to limit the arrival of certain ethnic groups in the late nineteenth and early twentieth centuries. Not until 1946, in fact, in the face of bitter strikes by participants in the Bracero Program, did the attorney general officially grant the Border Patrol the power to conduct searches a "reasonable distance" away from the international boundary (although, as Assistant Inspector Harris's comments above highlight, immigration authorities had unofficially adopted such a policy long before).[11] In 1953, without any public debate or discussion, the US Department of Justice set the parameters of this "reasonable distance": one hundred miles from the international boundary. This decision, unnoticed at the time by most observers, remains in place to this day. The potential repercussions of this hundred-mile-wide border have turned out to be profound: between the Mexican, Canadian, and maritime boundaries, some 200 million Americans today live within the border zone, meaning that a majority of US citizens inhabit a zone of diminished constitutional protections.[12]

If we want to understand how this extraordinary state of affairs arose, the only way to do so is through careful historical scholarship of the sort showcased in *Border Policing*. Together, the case studies in this volume offer a collective portrait of the multiple interconnected pathways that brought us to our current condition. But they also provide glimpses of the paths not taken—of other forms of interaction along the United States' international boundaries that, if followed, might have led to a far different border regime. The border today may function as a space of exception, a set of practices that are increasingly untethered to the physical boundary line at the outer edge of the nation-state. But it remains up to each generation to decide how to address the tensions that the border raises: the boundary between law and lawlessness, between citizen and foreigner, between here and there, between us and them. These questions reside not at the periphery of North American life but rather at its very center.

Notes

1. The concept of the "space of exception" is a spatial reworking of Giorgio Agamben's notion of the "state of exception." See Derek Gregory, "The Black Flag: Guantánamo Bay and the Space of Exception," *Geografiska Annaler. Series B, Human Geography* 88, no. 4 (2006): 405–427; and Nick Vaughan-Williams, "The Generalised Bio-Political Border? Re-Conceptualising the Limits of Sovereign Power," *Review of International Studies* 35, no. 4 (2009): 729–749.

2. For more on territoriality, see Charles S. Maier, *Once Within Borders: Territories*

of Power, Wealth, and Belonging Since 1500 (Cambridge, MA: Harvard University Press, 2016).

3. For more on the political nature of archives, see Joan M. Schwartz and Terry Cook, "Archives, Records, and Power: The Making of Modern Memory," *Archival Science* 2 (2002): 12; Saidiya Hartman, "Venus in Two Acts," *Small Axe* 12, no. 2 (June 2008): 1–14; and Yale A. Sternhell, "The Afterlives of a Confederate Archive: Civil War Documents and the Making of Sectional Reconciliation," *Journal of American History* 102, no. 4 (March 2016): 1025–1050. The phrase "seeing like a state" comes from James Scott, *Seeing Like a State: How Certain Schemes to Improve the Human Condition Have Failed* (New Haven, CT: Yale University Press, 1998).

4. Américo Paredes, *With His Pistol in His Hand: A Border Ballad and Its Hero* (Austin: University of Texas Press, 1958).

5. Paredes, 160.

6. "Immigration on the Mexican Border," Hearings before the Committee on Immigration and Naturalization, House of Representatives, 67th Congress, 1st Session, Serial 5, 7.

7. "Immigration on the Mexican Border," 22.

8. *Carroll v. United States*, 267 U.S. 132 (1925).

9. *Carroll v. United States*, 267 U.S. 132 (1925).

10. "In Search of the Border: Searches Conducted by Federal Customs and Immigration Officers," *N.Y.U. Journal of International Law and Politics* 93 (1972): 100–104.

11. "In Search of the Border," 104–105; Hannah Gurman, "A Collapsing Division: Border and Interior Enforcement in the US Deportation System," *American Quarterly* 69, no. 2 (June 2017): 380.

12. ACLU, "The Constitution in the 100-Mile Border Zone," aclu.org/other/con stitution-100-mile-border-zone.

Acknowledgments

This project began as an informal conversation in 2016, when we met to discuss the recent launch of our first books. While we had both focused on the history of smuggling across modern North American borders, each focused on a different locale—one on the Rio Grande borderlands, the other the Detroit-Windsor region. As we discussed the findings and challenges we uncovered over the process of research and writing on two far-apart borderlands—both literally and metaphorically—it sparked points of both conversion and contrast that begged further exploration. This volume is a continuation of that conversation, one that brings in the voices of a diverse group of accomplished scholars working in the growing field of borderlands studies. We are thrilled to see *Border Policing* come to fruition and want to begin by thanking the many people who made this possible.

Edited volumes require their own unique process of collaborative writing, something historians are not often trained to embrace. Thanks largely to the hard work and dedication of our contributors, this was an engaging and rewarding process. They not only adhered to multiple, often short, deadlines and turnarounds (a feat of its own), but they worked hard to draw connections between each of their chapters. Their efforts have contributed much to a cross-border, interdisciplinary approach that we see as central to understanding spaces "in-between."

We would also like to thank the University of Texas Press. In particular, we appreciate the vision that our editor, Robert Devens, brought to the volume from the start. Sarah McGavick answered many questions in the final stages of preparing this book manuscript, and we are grateful for her guidance and clarity. Our anonymous reviewers provided detailed and important insight that ultimately enabled us to make this a stronger, more cohesive volume. Benjamin Johnson read an early draft of our introduction, and he posed excellent questions that helped us draw out some of our larger arguments. Houston Mount's maps illustrate the span of contemporary border policing across North America, and we thank his effort to visualize what we put into words. We would also like to thank our respective programs—the history departments at Oklahoma State University and University of Texas Rio Grande Valley—for their generous financial support in the final stages of the publication process.

Finally, we would like to thank our families and loved ones for their endless support. Their insight, company, patience, and love helped us complete the book before you.

Holly M. Karibo, Stillwater, Oklahoma

George T. Díaz, McAllen, Texas

Contributors

Lisa D. Barnett is an assistant professor of the history of Christianity at Phillips Theological Seminary (Tulsa, Oklahoma). She previously served as a lecturer in the history department at Texas Christian University (TCU). She earned her PhD from TCU in 2017, and her research interests are in Native American history and American religious history. Her article "Peyote and the Racialized War on Drugs" appeared on the *Christian Century Then & Now* blog in 2016. She continues to work on revisions to her dissertation, which focuses on the intersections of race and religion around peyote and the creation of the Native American Church.

Jensen Branscombe is assistant professor of history at Tarleton State University (Stephenville, Texas). She teaches courses on immigration, women and gender, and modern US history. Her research interests include immigrants' rights activism and immigration policy making and enforcement in the US-Mexico borderlands. Her current research explores the consequences of the 1965 (Hart-Celler) Immigration and Nationality Act for states, communities, and immigrants along the Texas-Mexico border.

Elaine Carey is professor of history and dean of the College of Humanities, Education, and Social Science at Purdue University Northwest. She is the author of *Plaza of Sacrifices: Gender, Power, and Terror in 1968 Mexico* (2005) and the award-winning *Women Drug Traffickers: Mules, Bosses, and Organized Crime* (2014). She is also coeditor with Andrae Marak of *Smugglers, Brothels, and Twine: Transnational Flows of Contraband and Vice in North America* (2011) and the editor/author of the textbook *Protests in the Streets: 1968 across the Globe* (2016). As a historian who researches crime and human rights, she has served as an expert witness in courts across the United States, and she has consulted for radio, film, television, archives, libraries, and museums.

Tyler Chartrand is a PhD candidate at York University, researching borders, migration, and colonialism. He resides on the lands of the Haudenosaunee, Anishinaabe, Huron-Wendat, Métis, and New Credit First Nation.

Devin Clancy is a PhD candidate at York University and an educator in Toronto — Haudenosaunee, Anishinaabe, and Huron-Wendat territories. He is an editor of *Upping the Anti: A Journal of Theory and Action* and researches radical activist media projects at York University.

George T. Díaz is an associate professor of history at the University of Texas Rio Grande Valley, where he teaches US history, borderlands, and Mexican American history. He earned his PhD at Southern Methodist University in 2010. Díaz received a postdoctoral fellowship and served as the visiting scholar at the Center for Mexican American Studies at the University of Houston (2011–2012). His book *Border Contraband: A History of Smuggling across the Rio Grande* (University of Texas Press, 2015) won the 2016 National Association of Chicana and Chicano (NACCS) Tejas Foco Non-Fiction Book Award as well as the 2015 Jim Parish Award for Documentation and Publication of Local and Regional History from the Webb County Heritage Foundation.

María de Jesús Duarte is an assistant professor of history at Eastern New Mexico University, where she teaches classes on the history of the United States, Latin America, New Mexico, and the American West. She earned her PhD at Indiana University. She is the author of *Frontera y diplomacia: Las relaciones México–Estados Unidos durante el porfiriato* (2001).

James Dupree is currently a visiting assistant professor at Eastern Oregon University. He received his PhD from the University of Oklahoma. His research focuses on border enforcement along the Mexican border before the Border Patrol was created, particularly how the federal government increasingly bureaucratized the border by instituting regulations, systems, and procedures among the immigrant inspectors who worked for the Bureau of Immigration. He is currently investigating the use of digital history in the classroom as well as sharing the histories of the West and the borderlands with the public through public history presentations.

Luis Alberto García was born in Monterrey, Mexico, in 1981. He has an MA and a PhD from Southern Methodist University and a BA in history from Universidad Autónoma de Nuevo León. He is currently a history professor at Universidad de Monterrey. He specializes in borderlands, particularly in northeastern Mexico and Texas, which is a topic he explores in his book *Guerra y frontera: El ejército del norte entre 1855 y 1858* (2006) and in several publications on warfare culture. In 2018 he won the 17th Atanasio G. Saravia Prize in the professional research category.

Santiago Ivan Guerra is associate professor of Southwest studies at Colorado College. He is an interdisciplinary scholar working at the intersection of anthropology, history, and Chicana/o/x studies. The majority of his scholarly work has focused on understanding the history and contemporary impact of drug trafficking and border policing along the South Texas–Mexico border. His research has appeared in *Text, Practice, and Performance*, *Latino Studies*, and *Uncharted Terrains: New Directions in Border Research Methods and Ethics*. He is currently completing a book manuscript tentatively titled *Narcos and Nobodies: Untold Stories of the Border Drug War*.

Benjamin Hoy is an assistant professor of history at the University of Saskatchewan. His research focuses on how Canada and the United States conceived of and enforced their shared border during the nineteenth and early twentieth centuries. He studies the relationship between racial perceptions and the border closure process and the variable impacts that the border had on Europeans, African Americans, Chinese, Lakota, Dakota, Nez Perce, Cree, Iroquois, Coast Salish, and Ojibwa. Finally, he writes about how board and card games have been used to teach history in contemporary and historic environments.

Anita Huizar-Hernández is an assistant professor of border studies in the Department of Spanish and Portuguese at the University of Arizona. Her research examines how narratives, both real and imagined, have shaped the political, economic, and cultural landscape of the Southwest borderlands in general and Arizona in particular. Her first book, *Forging Arizona: A History of the Peralta Land Grant and Racial Identity in the West* (Latinidad series, Rutgers University Press, 2019), looks back at a bizarre nineteenth-century land grant scheme that tests the limits of how ideas about race, citizenship, and national expansion are forged.

Karl Jacoby, the Allan Nevins Professor of American History at Columbia University, is the author of *Crimes Against Nature: Squatters, Poachers, Thieves, and the Hidden History of American Conservation* (2001), *Shadows at Dawn: A Borderlands Massacre and the Violence of History* (2008), and *The*

Strange Career of William Ellis: The Texas Slave Who Became a Mexican Millionaire (2016).

Holly M. Karibo is an assistant professor of comparative borderlands history at Oklahoma State University. Her research focuses on the history of vice, drug economies, and gender in the North American borderlands. She received her PhD from the University of Toronto. Her first book, *Sin City North: Sex, Drugs, and Citizenship in the Detroit-Windsor Borderland* (David J. Weber Series in New Borderlands History, University of North Carolina Press, 2015), won the 2016 Best Book Award from the Michigan Historical Society.

Thomas A. Klug is emeritus professor of history at Marygrove College in Detroit, Michigan. He earned his PhD in history at Wayne State University. A labor and social historian by training, he studies the politics of late nineteenth and early twentieth-century American labor markets, focusing on the complex interactions of employers, trade unions, and federal immigration authorities along the United States–Canada border. He is editor of the Great Lakes Series of Wayne State University Press and serves on the editorial board of the *Michigan Historical Review*.

Miguel A. Levario is an associate professor of US and borderlands history at Texas Tech University. He is the author of *Militarizing the Border: When Mexicans Became the Enemy* (Texas A&M University Press, 2012) and of several articles and chapters in other edited volumes. He is currently the chair of the Mexican American & Latina/o Studies Working Group at Texas Tech and a member of the university's Hispanic Serving Institute Committee. He is an active and contributing community member of Lubbock and the South Plains.

Andrae Marak is the dean of the College of Arts and Sciences & Graduate Studies and a professor of history and political science at Governors State University. He is the coeditor (with Elaine Carey) of *Smugglers, Brothels, and Twine: Historical Perspectives on Contraband and Vice in North America's Borderlands* (2011).

Edward J. Martin earned his doctorate in 2014 from the University of Maine, where he wrote a dissertation titled "The Prize Game in the Borderlands: Privateering in New England and the Maritime Provinces, 1775–1815." While completing his graduate work, he held the New England Atlantic Provinces Quebec Fellowship, the Chase Distinguished Research Assistantship, and the John J. Nolde Distinguished Lectureship. Dr. Martin's work appears in the *Historical Atlas of Maine*, the *Northern Mariner*, and *Maine History*. He currently teaches at Endicott College, Quincy College, and Saint Anselm's College. Dr. Martin has also worked as an interpreter at the Essex Shipbuilding Museum and Salem Maritime National Historic Site.

Carolina Monsiváis earned her doctorate in borderlands history at the University of Texas at El Paso. She holds an MFA from New Mexico State University and is the award-winning author of *Somewhere Between Houston and El Paso: Testimonies of a Poet*, *Elisa's Hunger*, and *Descent*.

Index

McNally, John, 109
Merritt, Nehemiah, 34, 42
mescal, 161, 165, 167–169, 172–173, 175
Métis, 63–64, 72, 278
Mexican-American War, 46–47
Mexican Border District, 116, 121, 125, 271
Mexicanization, 19, 22, 85, 93, 131, 134, 266
Mier, Mexico, 48, 53
Mirando City, Texas, 149
Misonks, 65
Missouri Pacific Railroad, 163
Montanan, 79, 94
Montejano, David, 8, 20, 57
Monterrey, Mexico, 51, 55–58
Mountie, 11, 22–23, 71, 93, 184
Mowry, Jabez, 33, 42

Nadelmann, Ethan, 13, 24
Narcotic Control Act, 197
National Coalition Against Contraband Tobacco, 227, 236
National Council of La Raza, 206, 216
National Origins Act, 9, 70
Nationality and Citizenship Law: the citizenship law, 80, 88–90
nation-state, 2, 10, 13–14, 27–28, 44–46, 54–55, 71, 222, 224–225, 227, 229, 269–270, 273
Native (Native American), 11, 15–17, 20, 51, 60–63, 65–71, 73–74, 82, 94, 105, 108, 113, 132, 147–149, 158–159, 162, 188, 211, 221–222, 224–227, 229–231, 233–235, 241, 270
Navarro, José Angel, 48
Ne-u-lub-vig, 65
new borderlands historians, 9
New Spain, 45
Ngai, Mae M., 216
9/11, 2, 10, 19, 22, 253–254
Noot-hum-mic, 65
norteño, 44–47, 52–53
North Fork (Red River), 152
northeastern borderlands, 15, 27–31, 33–34, 38, 40–41, 47, 49
North-West Mounted Police, 11, 22, 60

Nuevo León, Mexico, 44, 47, 51, 54–57, 278

Office of Indian Affairs, 16, 66–67, 73–74, 149, 164
Office of National Drug Control Policy, 239, 250
Ojibwa, 64
Ojinaga, 133–134
Operation Cassanova, 238
Operation Cleansweep, 210, 217
Operation Mygale, 219–221
Operation Secure Texas, 244–246, 248–249, 251
Operation Strong Safety, 240, 244
Operation Wetback, 10, 183, 199
order-in-council, 35–36, 39
Ornelas, Plutarco, 87

Paredes, Américo, 8, 20, 270–271, 274
Parker, A. Warner, 96
Parliament of Canada (Parliament), 229
Parnaby, Andrew, 11, 23
Passamaquoddy District, 31
Peavey, John, 165
Pelee Island/Pelee Islander, 106
peyotero, 150
peyotism/peyotist, 147–148, 150, 153, 155–159
Piedras Negras, Mexico, 48, 51
Plains Indians, 62
Porfirian, 84, 94–95
Porfiriato, 6
Portillo, Fernando, 80–81, 90, 92
Post, Louis F., 96–97
Powhatan Confederacy, 223
Prentis, Percy, 103–106, 113
presidio, 46
Presidio, Texas, 131, 134–135, 142
pro-immigrant, 208
Progressive Era, 21, 23, 148, 156, 159
Pullin, D. L., 166–169, 172
Pure Food and Drug Act, 148

Québec, 70, 188, 195, 219–221, 227, 230, 233–234
Quiroga, Julian, 54, 59